Insurance Law in Czech Republic

Insurance Law in Czech Republic

David Elischer
Roman Velich

This book was originally published as a monograph in the International Encyclopaedia of Laws/Insurance Law.

Founding Editor: Roger Blanpain
General Editor: Frank Hendrickx
Volume Editor: Herman Cousy

Wolters Kluwer

Published by:
Kluwer Law International B.V.
PO Box 316
2400 AH Alphen aan den Rijn
The Netherlands
E-mail: international-sales@wolterskluwer.com
Website: lrus.wolterskluwer.com

Sold and distributed by:
Wolters Kluwer Legal & Regulatory U.S.
7201 McKinney Circle
Frederick, MD 21704
United States of America
E-mail: customer.service@wolterskluwer.com

ISBN 978-94-035-3972-0

e-Book: ISBN 978-94-035-3973-7
web-PDF: ISBN 978-94-035-3974-4

About the Authors

Doc. JUDr. PhDr. David Elischer, PhD graduated from the Faculty of Law at Charles University in Prague in 2005 and received the degrees of JUDr. in 2006 and PhD in 2009. His dissertation is titled *'Liability for Damage: Unlawfulness and Damage in Light of Modern Trends in Torts'*. In 2015, he was appointed associate professor in the field of civil law. Since 2005, he has worked at the Department of Civil Law of the Faculty of Law, Charles University, where he teaches Substantive Civil Law, Contracts and Torts. In the past, he has participated in working groups of the Legislative Council of the Czech Government on drafting the Civil Code in the areas of rights in rem and tort law. He has co-authored commentaries to the Civil Code, textbooks of civil law and a several monographs. He is also a member of editorial boards of a number of scholarly journals (Jurisprudence, AUC Iuridica).

JUDr. Roman Velich graduated from the Faculty of Law of Charles University in Prague, where he obtained the title of JUDr. Since 2011 he has been working in various positions in Czech insurance companies, currently as the legal manager of UNIQA pojišt'ovna, a.s.

About the Authors

Table of Contents

Table of Contents

List of Abbreviations

ADR	Alternative dispute resolution for consumer disputes
AIC	Act No. 37/2004 Sb., on Insurance Contract
AoCJ	Act No. 6/2002 Sb., on Courts, Judges, Lay Judges and the State Administration of Courts and on the Amendment to some other Acts (Act on Court and Judges)
AoCP	Act No. 634/1992 Sb., on Consumer Protection
AoDIR	Act No. 170/2018 Sb., on the Distribution of Insurance and Reinsurance
AoPIL	Act No. 91/2012 Sb., on Private International Law (in English available at http://obcanskyzakonik.justice.cz/images/pdf/Act-Governing-Private-International-Law.pdf)
Brussels I *bis*	Regulation (EU) No. 1215/2012 of the European Parliament and of the Council of 12 December 2012 on jurisdiction and the recognition and enforcement of judgments in civil and commercial matters (recast)
Civil Code / CC	Act No. 89/2012 Sb., Civil Code (in English available at http://obcanskyzakonik.justice.cz/images/pdf/Civil-Code.pdf)
Charter	Charter of Fundamental Rights and Freedoms (in Czech 'Listina základních práv a svobod'), resolution of the presidium of the Czech National Council of 16 December 1992 on the declaration of the Charter of Fundamental Rights and Freedoms as a part of the constitutional order of the Czech Republic (in English available at https://www.usoud.cz/fileadmin/user_upload/ustavni_soud_www/Pravni_uprava/AJ/Listina_English_version.pdf)
CIA	Czech Insurance Association (in Czech 'Česká asociace pojišťoven')

List of Abbreviations

CIB	Czech Insurers' Bureau (in Czech 'Česká kancelář pojistitelů')
CJEU	Court of Justice of the European Union
CMR	Convention on the Contract for the International Carriage of Goods by Road
CNB	Czech National Bank (in Czech 'Česká národní banka')
Constitution	The Constitution of the Czech Republic; Constitutional Act No. 1/1993 Sb. adopted on 16 December 1992 (in English available at https://www.usoud.cz/fileadmin/user_upload/ustavni_soud_www/Pravni_uprava/AJ/Ustava_EN_ve_zneni_zak_c._98-2013.pdf)
CPC	Act No. 99/1963 Sb., Civil Procedure Code
CTIA	Czech Trade Inspection Authority (in Czech 'Česká obchodní inspekce')
CZK	Czech koruna (currency of the Czech Republic)
EBA	European Banking Authority
EGAP	Export Guarantee and Insurance Corporation (In Czech 'Exportní garanční a pojišťovací společnost, a. s.')
EIOPA	European Insurance and Occupational Pensions Authority
ESMA	European Securities and Markets Authority
ESRB	European Systemic Risk Board
EU	European Union
IDD	Directive (EU) 2016/97 of the European Parliament and of the Council of 20 January 2016 on insurance distribution (recast)
Insurance Act / IA	Act No. 277/2009 Sb., Insurance Act
Labour Code	Act No. 262/2006 Sb., Labour Code
MCR	Minimum Capital Requirement
MFI	Monetary Financial Institutions
MTPL	Motor third party liability insurance
MTPLIA	Act No. 168/1999 Sb., on Motor Third Party Liability Insurance and on the Amendment to some other related Acts (Motor Third Party Liability Insurance Act)
PEPP	Pan-European Personal Pension Product under the Regulation (EU) 2019/1238 of the European Parliament and of the Council of 20 June 2019 on a pan-European Personal Pension Product
Rome I	Regulation (EC) No. 593/2008 of the European Parliament and of the Council of 17 June 2008 on the law applicable to contractual obligations (Rome I)

Rome II	Regulation (EC) No. 864/2007 of the European Parliament and of the Council of 11 July 2007 on the law applicable to non-contractual obligations (Rome II)
SCR	Solvency Capital Requirement
SDR	Special Drawing Right as defined by the International Monetary Fund
Solvency II	Directive 2009/138/EC of the European Parliament and of the Council of 25 November 2009 on the taking-up and pursuit of the business of Insurance and Reinsurance (Solvency II)
SPS	Act No. 427/2011 Sb., on Supplementary Pension Savings

List of Abbreviations

Preface

The present publication presents a current synthesis of insurance law in the Czech Republic. It deals with both private law aspects and relevant public law contexts. It provides an overview – not exhaustive – of insurance modalities in their recent development in terms of the Czech legal system in the light of relevant European Union (EU) legislation. The insurance issue has undergone a very dynamic development, the insurance contract has been integrated into the Civil Code and submitted to the new private law dominated by the Civil Code of 2012. The publication also provides insights into current and previous case law on insurance issues. We believe that it will provide foreign readers with the necessary basis for easier orientation in all regulations and rules of insurance law in the Czech Republic.

General Introduction

§1. General Background Information

I. Political System

Key information about the Czech Republic
Area: 78,870 km^2
Population: 10.6 million
Workforce: 5.4 million
Capital: Prague
Language: Czech
Currency: Czech koruna (CZK)
Time zone: GMT +1, daylight saving time GMT +2
Source: Czech Statistical Office, 2020

1. The Czech Republic is a parliamentary democracy. Its highest legal document is the Constitution of the Czech Republic together with the Charter of Fundamental Rights and Freedoms. The Constitution in its current form has been in force since 1 January 1993, i.e., since the establishment of an independent Czech state, which was created by the division of Czechoslovakia. The power is divided into three branches; the legislative (bicameral Parliament of the Czech Republic), executive (government of the Czech Republic and President of the Republic) and judicial.[1]

1. For more details, *see* Gerloch, Aleš; Hřebejk, Jiří; Zoubek, Vladimír. *Ústavní systém České republiky.* 2nd revised and supplemented ed. Praha: Prospektrum, 1996; Kysela, Jan. *Deset let Ústavy České republiky: východiska, stav, perspektivy.* 1st ed. Praha: Eurolex Bohemia, 2003; Bahýľová, Lenka; Filip, Jan; Molek, Pavel; Podhrázký, Milan; Suchánek, Radovan; Šimíček, Vojtěch; Vyhnálek, Ladislav. *Ústava České republiky.* 1st ed. Praha: Linde, 2010; Filip, Jan. *Ústavní právo České republiky: 1 Základní pojmy a instituty. Ústavní základy ČR.* 4th revised and supplemented ed. Brno: Masarykova univerzita, Doplněk, 2003; Sládeček, Vladimír; Mikule, Vladimír; Suchánek, Radovan; Syllová, Jindřiška. *Ústava České republiky. Komentář.* 2nd ed. Praha: C. H. Beck. 2016; Holländer, Pavel. *Filosofie práva.* 1st ed. Plzeň: Aleš Čeněk, 2006; Klíma, Karel, et al. *Komentář k Ústavě a Listině.* 2nd extended ed. Plzeň: Aleš Čeněk, 2009; Schelleová, Ilona; Schelle, Karel, et al. *Soudnictví: historie, současnost a perspektivy.* 1st ed. Praha: Eurolex Bohemia, 2004; Cabada, Ladislav; Šanc, David. *Český stranický systém ve 20. Století.* 1st ed. Plzeň: Aleš Čeněk, 2005; Cabada,

2. The constitutional order of the Czech Republic also includes the Charter of Fundamental Rights and Freedoms (Act No. 2/1993 Sb.),[2] which was introduced as a part of the constitutional order by Article 3 of the Constitution.

3. The Constitution of the Czech Republic is a written constitution, which contains a preamble and eight chapters (a total of 113 articles). The preamble mentions the tradition of statehood and the determination to build a free and democratic country (most of the preamble was written by Václav Havel[3]). Title One contains the basic provisions dividing power into three independent branches that prevent the abuse and concentration of power (legislative power, executive and judicial defined by Titles Two, Three and Four). The content of Title Five is the Supreme Supervisory Authority, Title Six regulates Czech National Bank (CNB). Title Seven then lays down rules for territorial self-government. Title Eight contains transitional and final provisions.

4. The Constitution does not allow any change in the essentials democratic rule of law (Article 9 of the Constitution of the Czech Republic).[4] These fundamental principles are sovereignty of the people, democracy, majority principle and its limitations, rule of law, human rights, separation of powers, and the parliamentary system of government.

5. Within these constitutional limitations, two major amendments to the Constitution have taken place up to now. The first amendment was the so-called Euronovela connected directly with the accession of the Czech Republic to the European Union (EU). The amendment was necessary to allow for a transfer – within the framework of constitutionality – certain powers to EU supranational bodies. At the same time, the Article 10 provides the application primacy of international treaties over the statutes. The second amendment was the introduction of direct election of the president. Article 54(2) now provides that the President of the Republic shall be elected by direct universal suffrage elections.

Ladislav; Kubát, Michal et al. *Úvod do studia politické vědy.* 1st ed. Plzeň: Aleš Čeněk, 2007; Novák, Miroslav; Lebeda, Tomáš et al. *Volební a stranické systémy. ČR v mezinárodním srovnání.* 1st ed. Dobrá Voda: Aleš Čeněk, 2004.

2. The Charter of Fundamental Rights and Freedoms (in Czech 'Listina základních práv a svobod') is a document enacted in 1991 by the Czechoslovak Federative Republic, and continued as part of the constitutional systems of both the Czech Republic and Slovak Republic. In the Czech Republic, the document was kept in its entirety in its 1991 form as a separate document from the constitution, but imbued with the same legal standing as the constitution. For more *see* https://en.wikipedia.org/wiki/Charter_of_Fundamental_Rights_and_Freedoms.
3. Václav Havel was a Czech statesman, writer and former dissident, who served as the last President of Czechoslovakia from 1989 until the dissolution of Czechoslovakia in 1992 and then as the first President of the Czech Republic from 1993 to 2003.
4. There are three basic rules laid out in Art. 9, stating that the Constitution can only be changed by a Constitutional Act (para. 1), that not even such a change can remove or disrupt the substantive core of the Constitution (para. 3), and that not even construction or interpretation of legal regulations can remove or disrupt this core (para. 3). The second paragraph, stating that changing substantial features of a democratic state is not admissible, is what is known as entrenched substantive core of the Constitution. For more *see* https://en.wikipedia.org/wiki/Constitution_of_the_Czech_Republic#The_fundamental_principles.

6. The legislative power belongs to the Parliament made up of the Chamber of Deputies and the Senate (Article 15 of the Constitution). The Czech Republic is therefore a parliamentary republic with an asymmetric system of bicameralism, which means that the Chamber of Deputies dominates the Senate in its breadth of powers.

7. The Chamber of Deputies[5] has 200 members elected for four-year terms. A citizen can become a deputy if they have reached the age of 21 and has the right to vote. The electoral system is based on the principles of proportional representation. Based on the results of these elections, a new Government of the Czech Republic is established. Deputies are elected as representatives of individual political parties; after their election, the parties in the Chamber of Deputies form parliamentary clubs. Members of parliament are also divided into eighteen committees. The committees are to act as expert guarantors for any area of social and political life in the country. For example, the Budget Committee deals with state budget issues, the Agriculture Committee comments on legislation concerning the country's agricultural policy, and the foreign policy is dealt with by the Foreign Affairs Committee. Among the most important competencies of the Chamber of Deputies particularly include the right to discuss and approve laws, decisions on the form of the state budget, and the right to distrust the government. The Constitution does not allow membership in both chambers at the same time.

8. The Senate[6] was not established until 1996. Eighty-one senators are elected for six-year terms according to the principles of the majority electoral system. Every citizen of the Czech Republic who has the right to vote and has reached the age of 40 can be elected to the Senate. Elections are held every two years, when a third of new senators are elected.[7] The Senate is constructed as a counterweight to the Chamber of Deputies, as an element helping to improve the legislative process and also as an element of Parliament's continuity in the event that the Chamber of Deputies is dissolved. The Senate discusses and approves bills that it receives from the Chamber of Deputies, makes laws, expresses (dis)agreement with international agreements, expresses (dis)agreement to the declaration of a state of war, the stay of foreign troops in the Czech Republic or the deployment of armed forces outside the Czech Republic, (dis)agrees with the appointment of judges of the Constitutional Court, and submits to the President of the Republic proposals for the granting or awarding of state decorations. Only the Senate can file a lawsuit against the President of the Republic to the Constitutional Court for high treason.

9. The government[8] is the supreme body of executive power that must have the support of Parliament for its action. Government control is reserved for the Chamber of Deputies. Every newly appointed government must ask the Chamber of

5. https://public.psp.cz/en/sqw/hp.sqw.
6. https://www.senat.cz/index-eng.php?ke_dni=13.07.2020&O=12.
7. In the first elections to the Senate, a third of senators were elected for only two years, a third for four years and a third for six years.
8. https://www.vlada.cz/en/.

Deputies to express a vote of confidence. If the government does not gain confidence, the president shall appoint a new government, which must again ask for a vote of confidence in the Chamber of Deputies. If even this newly appointed government fails, the President of the Republic appoints the Prime Minister on the proposal of the chairman of the Chamber of Deputies. The proposed Prime Minister will form a new government which is appointed by the president. If the third appointed government is not trusted either, the President of the Republic may dissolve the Chamber of Deputies. However, the Chamber of Deputies may overrule the government even during the election period by means of expressing the distrust which requires the consent of an absolute majority of all deputies. In addition to the government, ministries and other administrative bodies are part of the executive branch. They can be established, and their scope defined only by law. The activities of the government are mainly based on the program statement of the government, with which the Prime Minister appears before the Chamber of Deputies. If the program is approved and the deputies gave a confidence to the government, the government can begin to exercise its powers.

10. The President of the Republic[9] is the head of state and the commander in chief of the armed forces. The President is elected by the citizens of the Czech Republic who have reached the age of 18 in direct universal suffrage (*see* amendment to Constitution No. 71/2012). The election of the President is held every five years. The term of office of the President begins on the day of taking the oath. The President of the Republic represents the state externally and is a symbol of the internal and external sovereignty of the state. The powers of the President are, on the one hand, the powers exercised by the President independently (i.e., a countersignature by a member of the government is not required), and on the other, the powers exercised by the President in cooperation with the Prime Minister (countersignature powers). The President of the Republic appoints and dismisses the Prime Minister and other members of the Government and accepts their resignation, removes the Government as a whole and accepts its resignation. They have the right to send an adopted law back to Parliament with the exception of a constitutional law. They sign laws and appoints judges to the Constitutional Court, its president and vice-presidents. The President may not be prosecuted during their term of office function.

11. In the Czech Republic, judicial power is exercised on behalf of the republic by independent courts. Judicial power is internally divided into a system of ordinary courts (civil agendas, criminal, and administrative), and one special court (Constitutional Court). The main principles of general justice are defined by the Constitution of the Czech Republic. The Czech Republic has a four-tier system of courts and two-instance proceedings. Judicial system consists of the Supreme Court, the Supreme Administrative Court, the superior courts (two), the regional courts (eight) and the district courts (eighty-six). A special law stipulates their competence and organization (Article 91 of the Constitution). At the lowest level, the district courts decide most disputes as first instance. Appellate instances for district courts

9. https://www.hrad.cz/en.

are regional courts, at the next level there are two superior courts to which it can be filed appeals against regional courts. The superior courts are located in Prague and Olomouc. The supreme judicial bodies are the Supreme Court and the Supreme Administrative Court, both based in Brno. The Supreme Court is an appeal authority ruling on extraordinary remedies relating to civil and criminal law. The Supreme Administrative Court decides on administrative matters. A judge is appointed by the President of the Republic and must be an innocent citizen with a university degree in law (Article 93 of the Constitution). When performing its function judge must be independent and impartial.

12. The Constitutional Court[10] of the Czech Republic stands outside the general courts structure. Its status and powers are enshrined directly in the Constitution of the Czech Republic. It is the judicial body responsible for constitutionality and the protection of fundamental human rights and freedoms that arise from constitutional order and to guarantee the constitutional character of the exercise of state power. This it achieves mainly through its power to annul statutes (or parts of them) if they are in conflict with the constitutional order (most important of them, the Constitution and the Charter of Fundamental Rights and Freedoms). This is because laws that are part of the constitutional order are legislative acts of the highest force, their enactment also requires a special majority in the parliament. Any other legislation is subordinate. This process is called the judicial review. Related to this is the power of the court to decide about the conformity with the constitutional order of an international treaty prior to its ratification. The seat of the court is in Brno.[11]

13. As for the territorial self-governance, immediately after the change in the political situation in 1989, the regional national committees were abolished, but the regions, as territorial units, remained the same. The new fourteen regions started existing on 1 January 2001. The establishment of higher territorial administrative units (regions) was the so-called first stage of public administration reform. In 2002 started the preparations for the so-called second stage, the essence of which is the abolition of district offices and their replacement by new administrative districts of municipalities with extended powers (sometimes called small districts; there are a total of 206, including Prague), all with effect from 1 January 2003.[12]

II. Commerce and Industry

14. The Czech Republic has a long-standing tradition in industrial production. The composition of its industries is being restructured to typically correspond to a small but mature market economy. In recent years, the share of food production has increased, while there has been a decline in the engineering segment, which, however, continues to be the most important industrial sector in the Czech Republic. The most developed areas in consumer goods production are the traditional sectors

10. https://www.usoud.cz/en/.
11. https://en.wikipedia.org/wiki/Constitutional_Court_of_the_Czech_Republic.
12. https://en.wikipedia.org/wiki/Regions_of_the_Czech_Republic.

manufacturing textiles and clothing, shoes, porcelain, ceramics, and costume jewellery. The most significant areas in food production are industries processing flour, sugar, meat, and brewing beer.[13] Agricultural production almost satisfies domestic demand. Mainly grain (wheat, barley, corn), potatoes, sugar beets, vegetables, flax, and rape are grown. Hop growing, arboriculture, and viticulture are also important. The basis of animal production is the breeding of cattle, pigs, and poultry, as well as beekeeping or breeding of freshwater fish (especially carp).[14]

CHARACTERISTICS AND STRUCTURE OF THE CZECH ECONOMY
- Small, open, export-oriented economy
- Main business partner is Germany
- Balanced trade balance with slight surplus in export
- Stable inflation and currency
- Low unemployment rate
- Strong business and ownership relations to the EU
- Long-term real convergence to the developed countries, in 2018 GDP per capita in PPS was 91% of the EU average
Source: Czech Statistical Office, Eurostat, January 2020

13. https://www.hrad.cz/en/czech-republic/about-the-czech-republic.
14. https://www.czregion.cz/vseobecne-info.

Source: CzechInvest 2020.[15]

Main Economic Indicators	2014	2015	2016	2017	2018	2019	2020
GDP growth (constant prices, %)	2.7	5.3	2.5	4.4	2.8	2.5	2.0
General government debt (% GDP)	42.2	40.0	36.8	34.7	32.6	31.2	30.5
Long-term interest rates (YTM of 10Y government bonds)	1.58	0.58	0.43	0.98	1.98	1.55	1.40
Average inflation rate (%)	0.4	0.3	0.7	2.5	2.1	2.8	2.8
Labour productivity (increase in %)	2.2	3.8	0.8	2.8	1.5	1.7	1.9
Unemployment rate (avg., %)	6.1	5.1	4.0	2.9	2.2	2.0	2.2
Average nominal gross wage (increase in %)	2.9	3.2	4.4	6.7	7.5	7.0	6.0
Average nominal monthly gross wage (CZK)	25k	26,5k	27,7k	29,6k	31,8k	34k	36k

15. https://www.czechinvest.org/en/Key-sectors/Business-Services.

Main Economic Indicators	2014	2015	2016	2017	2018	2019	2020
Exchange rate – CZK/USD (avg.)	20.7	24.60	24.43	23.39	21.74	22.94	22.80
Exchange rate – CZK/EUR (avg.)	27.5	27.28	27.03	26.33	25.65	25.67	25.40

Source: Macroeconomic Forecast of Ministry of Finance, 2020.

III. Financial Institutions

15. Financial institutions, generally speaking, are all organizations whose main activity is the management of financial resources or securities. That is, the intermediation, provision or storage of financial resources, securities, or various financial derivatives. Financial institutions in the Czech Republic include in particular: banks and branches of foreign banks, savings and credit unions (credit unions) providing deposits and loans only to their members, investment companies and investment funds operating on the principle of collective investment (represent a higher risk, bring higher returns), pension funds managing supplementary pension insurance, insurance companies, persons or entities authorized to trade in securities, capital market organizers (Securities Markets) and also persons or entities operating casinos, betting offices, out-of-court auctions, real estate transactions, financial leasing, financial activities, foreign exchange trading, intermediation of cash and non-cash transfers of funds, and savings intermediation or intermediary activities aimed at concluding insurance or reinsurance contracts. Financial institutions are subject to supervision and regulation at the national and international levels.[16]

16. Monetary financial institutions (MFIs) mean the central bank, resident banks, and all other resident financial institutions whose business is to receive deposits and/or close substitutes for deposits from entities other than MFIs and, for their own account (at least in economic terms), to grant loans and/or make investments in securities. The MFI sector in the Czech Republic is made up of the central bank,[17] commercial banks,[18] credit unions, and money market funds. The banks and foreign bank branches included in this list are subject to the duty to report to the CNB pursuant to Decree No. 346/2013 Sb., on Reporting of Banks and Foreign Bank Branches to the CNB, and Decree No. 314/2013 Sb., on the Submitting of Statements to the CNB by Entities that Belong to the Financial Institutions Sector. The European System of Central Banks (ESCB) has established procedures for continuously monitoring, checking, and updating the list of the institutions which form the MFI sector. The aim is to ensure that the list of MFIs is up-to-date, accurate, as

16. https://managementmania.com/en/financial-institutions.
17. https://www.cnb.cz/en/.
18. For the list of commercial banks operating in the Czech Republic, *see* https://cbaonline.cz/clenove.

homogeneous as possible and sufficiently stable for the purposes of compiling statistics, satisfying the regular and ad hoc analytical needs of the ESCB in safeguarding financial stability, and pursuing the ECB's monetary and financial policy.[19]

17. Concerning the banking sector in the Czech Republic, at the end of 2018, there were forty-nine entities in the Czech Republic with banking licenses. A total of forty entities (fourteen banks and twenty-six branches) under the control of foreign owners. Domestic owners control nine banks, two of which are state-owned banks. Actual banking sector structure is composed of four large banks, five medium-sized banks, nine small banks, twenty-six branches of foreign banks, and five building credit societies. The total value of the banking sector's assets was at the same time CZK 7,332 billion. The total volume of bank loans was CZK 3,306.5 billion. Banks provided loans to households in the total amount of CZK 1,550.5 billion and corporate loans reached the level of CZK 1,080.3 billion. The volume of client deposits reached CZK 4,445.6 billion at the end of 2018 and exceeded the volume of client loans by almost 34%. The excess of deposits over loans is traditionally generated by the household sector, where households had 61% more funds on deposits with domestic banks than they drew on loans. At the end of 2018, households had CZK 2,558.5 billion deposited with banks, while more than three quarters of their savings were deposited in demand deposits. In the corporate sector, the volume of deposits and loans is approximately balanced.[20]

IV. Currency Legislation and Monetary Regulations

18. According to Bakeš, monetary law in the Czech Republic is a set of legal norms governing currency (currency unit, currency issue, currency system, and their protection), treasury operations, money circulation, and payment system where Act No. 6/1993 Sb., on the CNB, has a key position and is also an implementing legislation adopted on the basis of Article 98(2) of the Constitution of the Czech Republic.[21]

19. The actual Czech legal money system consists of valid banknotes and coins issued by the CNB.[22] Among the coins, we make a distinction between coins in circulation, on one hand, and precious metal coins, commemorative coins and special coins intended for collectors, on the other. While circulation coins (and banknotes)

---

19. https://www.cnb.cz/en/statistics/money_and_banking_stat/lists-of-institutions-for-purposes-of-monetary-and-financial-statistics/list-of-monetary-financial-institutions/.
20. https://cbaonline.cz/o-bankovnim-sektoru.
21. Bakeš, Milan; Karfíková, Marie; Kotáb, Petr; Marková, Hana et al. *Finanční právo*. 6th revised ed. Praha: C. H. Beck, 2012, pp. 14 et seq.
22. The CNB has the exclusive right to issue banknotes and coins, as well as commemorative banknotes and coins (*see* § 12 of Act No. 6/1993 Sb., on the CNB). The CNB arranges banknote printing and coinage and oversees the protection and security of the circulation of unissued banknotes and coins and the safekeeping and destruction of printing plates, stamps and invalid and discarded banknotes and coins (*see* § 15 of Act No. 6/1993 Sb., on the CNB).

are exchanged at nominal value,[23] coins metals, commemorative coins,[24] and coins intended for collectors' purposes may be sold at prices other than their face value (*see* § 16(2) of the Act No. 6/1993 Sb., on the CNB).

20. The CNB shall determine by decree a) the denominations, dimensions, weight, material, appearance and other requisites of banknotes and coins and their issue into circulation and b) termination of banknotes and coins and the manner and time of their exchange for other banknotes and coins (§ 22 of the Act No. 6/1993 Sb., on the CNB).

21. Relevant legislation distinguishes between cash and non-cash circulation. The determining criterion for this distinction is the position and role of the payment service provider. Whereas in cash circulation the payment is made by handing over banknotes and coins between the payer and the payee (the only two entities whose participation is necessary), in cashless circulation the payment takes place between the payer's and the payee's payment accounts, with the payment always being mediated by the payment service provider. Therefore, three entities are obliged to participate in such payment.[25]

22. The obligation to accept Czech legal money is regulated in Act No. 136/2011 Sb., On the Circulation of Banknotes and Coins,[26] according to the mentioned Act everyone is obliged to accept domestic banknotes and coins without restriction, unless they are entitled to refuse their receipt. A credit institution[27] performing treasury operations may refuse to accept domestic banknotes or coins only if the banknotes or coins denominated in CZK have been declared invalid by the CNB and if the period stipulated by law during which it is obliged to exchange them has expired. Everyone (with the exception of the CNB and credit institutions performing treasury operations) may refuse to accept commemorative banknotes or commemorative coins and everyone may refuse to accept domestic banknotes or coins if there are more than fifty domestic coins in one payment.

23. Another restriction regulated by current monetary legislation[28] is the limitation of the total amount of payment made in cash. The payment provider, the

---

23. The legal money system in the Czech Republic now consists of banknotes of six denominations: CZK 5,000, CZK 2,000, CZK 1,000, CZK 500, CZK 200 and CZK 100 and current coins of six denominations: CZK 50, CZK 20, CZK 10, CZK 5, CZK 2 and CZK 1.
24. Commemorative coins in nominal values of CZK 10,000, CZK 5,000, CZK 2,500, CZK 2,000, CZK 1,000, CZK 500 and CZK 200.
25. Schlossberger, Otakar. *Platební služby*. 1st ed. Praha: Management Press, 2012. p. 12 ff.
26. To consult the text (in Czech) *see* https://www.zakonyprolidi.cz/cs/2011-136.
27. A credit institution carrying out cash operations within the meaning of § 3 of the Act on the Circulation of Banknotes and Coins means a bank (a branch of a foreign bank in the Czech Republic, a savings or loan association) performing acceptance of a deposit of domestic banknotes (coins) to an account held with a credit institution or their payment from this account at a place designated for that purpose by employees (authorized persons) of the credit institution.
28. Act No. 254/2004 Sb., on Restriction of Cash Payments. To consult the text (in Czech) *see* https://www.zakonyprolidi.cz/cs/2004-254.

amount of which exceeds CZK 270,000, is obliged to make the payment non-cash.[29] The recipient of a payment, the amount of which exceeds the limit, may not accept this payment if it has not been made non-cash. A payment in a foreign currency – for the purpose of this limitation – shall be converted into CZK at the exchange rate of the foreign exchange market announced by the CNB and valid on the day of the payment. The limit includes all payments in CZK and foreign currency made by the same payment provider to the same payee during one calendar day (*see* § 4 of the Act No. 254/2004 Sb., on Restriction of Cash Payments.). One of the main and declared reasons for adopting a legal limit for payments in cash is the fight against crime as well as an effort to eliminate the grey economy.

24. The protection of legal money and money circulation is, in the Czech Republic, ensured by a number of legal regulations. In addition to all the provisions already mentioned (the Act on the CNB, the Act on the Circulation of Banknotes and Coins and the Act on Restrictions of Cash Payments), it is necessary to mention the criminal law, particularly the Act No. 40/2009 Sb., Criminal Code.[30] Among the crimes against currency and means of payment we include counterfeiting and alteration of money (§ 233 of Criminal Code), unauthorized action, counterfeiting and alteration of a means of payment (§ 234 of Criminal Code), use of counterfeit and altered money (§ 235 of Criminal Code), manufacture and possession of counterfeit tools (§ 236 of Criminal Code), unauthorized production of money (§ 237 of Criminal Code), and threatening the circulation of domestic money (§ 239 of Criminal Code).

25. Needless to say, that, in addition to domestic and foreign banknotes and coins all banknotes and coins of the common European currency (the Euro), are also subject to protection in the Czech legal system.

V. Insurance Business, General Organization, and Special Features

26. The insurance business as such has no legal definition, but as insurance is a tool for economic elimination of the negative consequences of accidents and bad

29. The obligation shall not apply to:

- payments of taxes, fees and other similar pecuniary performances made in accordance with the Tax Code or the Customs Act, unless those laws provide otherwise;
- compulsory payments arising from employment relationships;
- payments of pensions from pension insurance, including one-off supplements and payments of benefits from pension funds and participating funds managed by a pension company;
- payments made in times of crisis declared in accordance with a special legal regulation;
- payments of insurance premiums and payments of insurance benefits from private insurance;
- payments made by the CNB for the sale of commemorative coins; or
- payments made by a bailiff, court or administrative authority in the execution or enforcement of a decision.

30. To consult the text (in Czech) *see* https://www.zakonyprolidi.cz/cs/2009-40.

chance, it can be defined as a specific sector of the economy that ensures the financial elimination of risks affecting various people's activities. The basic task and purpose are to create and distribute special cash reserves and funds through insurance activities and, within the set rules, to use them to cover insurance needs arising from accidental events depending on the effect of insurance risk. Thus, the operation of insurance is associated with the creation and distribution of the so-called collective reserve, in the creation of which all members of the risk group participate. Insurance is one of the financial services, the object of which is insurance protection provided for a fee. It is a service of an abstract nature with a close connection to random events, where it is often not clear whether the fact will or will not occur, because there is no clear time point of the situation (insured events), it is not clear which subject will be affected and often the extent of the impact is not known. Usually (but not necessarily) the insurance is of a long-term nature.[31]

27. Insurance might be also understood as a financial service contract in terms of Civil Code.[32] Insurance business then includes all insurance and reinsurance institutions with a public law authorization if they fulfil the conditions under the Insurance Act.

28. Insurance itself might be divided from various perspectives. In terms of time, we make the distinction between short-term and long-term insurance, in terms of price (premium) we refer to deserved and undeserved fulfilment, from a legal point of view we recognize voluntary and compulsory insurance, according to the method of financing we distinguish social, commercial, and health insurance, according to the type of covered risks we recognize life and non-life insurance and according to the method of creation insurance reserves we have risk and reserve-making insurance.

29. Another useful division is the division into contractual and statutory insurance. Statutory insurance falls under compulsory insurance, as the obligation of insurance for the relevant entity is given by law (ex lege), i.e., no insurance contract is concluded. In current legislation, there is only one statutory insurance in the

---

31. For more definitions and detailed explanatory notes *see* particularly: Janasová, Marie. *Účetnictví pojišťoven v ČR.* 1st ed. Ostrava: VŠB – Technická univerzita Ostrava, 2006; Ducháčková, Eva. *Principy pojištění a pojišťovnictví.* 3rd updated ed. Praha: Ekopress, 2009; Karfíková, Marie; Přikryl, Vladimír, Čechová, Jana. *Základy pojišťovacího práva.* 1st ed. Praha: Orac, 2001; Karfíková, Marie; Přikryl, Vladimír; Vybíral, Roman et al. *Pojišťovací právo.* 2nd revised ed. Praha: Leges, 2018; Jandová, Lucie; Šlauf, Petr; Svejkovský, Jaroslav. *Pojištění v novém občanském zákoníku. Komentář: [§ 2756-2872].* 1st ed. Praha: C. H. Beck, 2014; Smržová, Petra; Mrkývka, Petr. *Finanční a daňové právo.* 2nd updated and supplemented ed. Plzeň: Aleš Čeněk, 2016; Bakeš, Milan; Karfíková, Marie; Kotáb, Petr; Marková, Hana et al. *Finanční právo.* 6th revised ed. Praha: C. H. Beck, 2012; Spirit, Michal. *Pojistné právo.* 1st ed. Praha: Vysoká škola ekonomická, 2000.
32. For the purpose of regulating consumer contracts, a financial service contract shall mean any consumer contract concerning banking, credit, payment or insurance service, any contract concerning supplementary pension insurance, currency exchange, the issuing of electronic money and any contract concerning the provision of investment services or trading in the investment instruments market (*see* § 1841 CC). If such contract is concluded through a means of distance communication, the more protective regulation applies (*see* § 1842 CC).

Czech Republic, namely the employer's liability insurance for damage in the event of a work accident or an occupational disease.

30. Contractual insurance may also be compulsory if the obligation to conclude insurance contract for the given entities is stipulated by law. Nevertheless, if another statute obliges a particular person to conclude an insurance contract, the contract may derogate from the provisions of Civil Code only if permitted by a statute and if the scope of insurance provided by another statute is not thereby reduced (§ 2779(1) CC). In cases of compulsory-contractual insurance, the insurer has to conclude an insurance contract so that they incur the duty to provide insurance indemnity even where the damage has been caused by a deliberate (intentional) act of the policyholder, the insured person or any other person (§ 2779(2) CC). The insurer may refuse to provide indemnity from compulsory insurance only in situations where false information, incompletely answered questions (in written form) or knowingly false or grossly distorted information was provided exclusively by injured party, or another person with the injured party's knowledge (§ 2780 CC). The insurer has the right to withdraw from the contract or terminate the compulsory insurance only if permitted under another statute. This does not preclude other stipulations whereby the insurer acquires another right to penalize the policyholder or the insured person in the event of a breach of their duties (§ 2781 CC).

31. The Czech Civil Code divides insurance according to the method of payment of insurance indemnity, into insurance against loss and damage[33] and fixed-amount (lump sum) insurance.[34] Insurance against loss and damage compensates for the real loss of property caused by an insured event, while within the fixed-amount (lump sum) insurance the insurer has to provide a one-off or repeated insurance indemnity (pension) to the agreed extent regardless of any damage (or regardless of its extent).

32. Insurance law contains both substantive and procedural rules. In our country, insurance law is considered as a relatively independent legal field with an interdisciplinary character. It unites, in itself both, elements of public law (financial law) and elements of private law (i.e., commercial and civil law), the latter prevails.

33. The Czech Insurance Association (CIA)[35] is a professional association established on 1 January 1994 to organize and support mutual aid and cooperation as well as to secure the interests of insurance and reinsurance companies. The Association is a legal entity with its headquarters in Prague. The aims of the Association include representing, protecting, and enforcing common interests of member insurance companies and their clients with regard to state administration bodies, legislative authorities, and other entities. The CIA members' premiums constitute 98% of all

33. In Czech 'škodové pojištění'.
34. In Czech 'obnosové pojištění'.
35. http://www.cap.cz/en/.

premiums in the Czech Republic.[36] The CIA has actually (in 2020) twenty-five full members[37] and three members with special status.[38]

34. The main objectives of the CIA is to process comments on legislation relevant to the insurance industry, insurance and to other interests of insurance companies, and to accomplish necessary amendments to the Czech and European legislation, to develop instruments of loss prevention and insurance fraud prevention, to unify rules and procedures of the members regarding cooperation in the technical, information, and statistics area; to create information instruments for the public and to provide clear and unbiased information about the insurance market and insurance products development, to contribute to professional awareness of members and to provide educational opportunities, to create ethical principles in insurance; and to assist in dispute settlements among the members.

35. Insurance companies are not the only ones associated, but also the insurance intermediaries, loss adjusters, or actuaries are grouped into various associations, through which they coordinate and promote professional interests and by issuing the codes of ethics they give a certain guarantee of professional access. Currently, the following associations are on the market: The Association of Czech Insurance Brokers,[39] the European Federation of Insurance Intermediaries (BIPAR),[40] the Association of Financial Intermediaries and Financial Advisers of the Czech Republic,[41] the European Financial Planning Association – Czech Republic,[42] the Union of Financial Intermediation and Advisory Companies,[43] the Czech Chamber of Independent Loss Adjusters,[44] and the Czech Society of Actuaries.[45]

36. *Ibid.*
37. https://www.cap.cz/en/radni-clenove.
38. https://www.cap.cz/en/clenove-se-zvlastnim-statutem.
39. http://acpm.cz/index.php?lang=en.
40. https://www.bipar.eu/en/home.
41. https://afpcr.cz/.
42. https://efpa.cz/.
43. https://casfpz.cz.
44. http://www.ckslpu.com/.
45. https://www.actuaria.cz/.

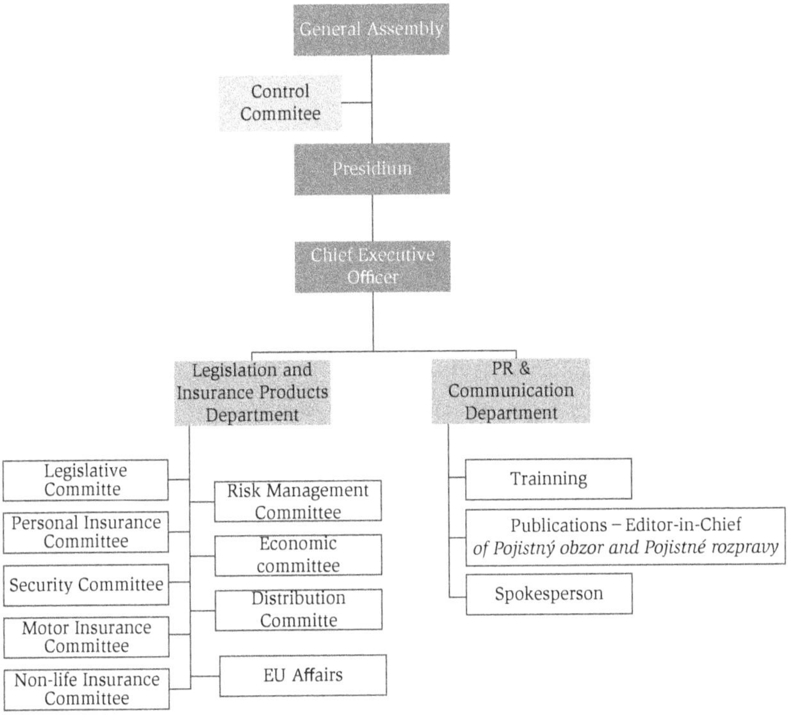

Source: CIA.

§2. Historical Background of Insurance and Insurance Legislation

36. The history of insurance in the territory of today's Czech Republic is documented from the end of the seventeenth century.[46] In 1699, Jan Kryštof Bořek[47] submitted a proposal for the introduction of compulsory fire insurance for buildings in Bohemia. A fire fund was to be set up in each city, created from contributions of

46. For more details, *see* particularly: Svoboda, Karel. *Historický vývoj pojišťovnictví.* Praha: Sdružení československého úřednictva ústavů peněžních, 1910; Karfíková, Marie; Přikryl, Vladimír, Čechová, Jana. *Základy pojišťovacího práva.* 1st ed. Praha: Orac, 2001; Marvan, Miroslav; Patoprstý, Ján et al. *Dějiny pojišťovnictví v Československu, 1. díl, Dějiny pojišťovnictví v Československu do roku 1918.* Praha: Novinář, 1989; Marvan, Miroslav; Chaloupecký, Josef. *Dějiny pojišťovnictví v Československu. 2. díl, Dějiny pojišťovnictví v Československu (1918-1945).* 1st ed. Bratislava: Alfa Konti, 1993. Marvan, Miroslav; Chaloupecký, Josef. *Dějiny pojišťovnictví v Československu. 3. díl, Dějiny pojišťovnictví v Československu (1945-1992).* 1st ed. Praha: Česká pojišťovna, 1997; Karfíková, Marie; Přikryl, Vladimír; Vybíral, Roman et al. *Pojišťovací právo.* 2nd revised ed. Praha: Leges, 2018; Hradec, Milan; Zárybnická, Jana; Křivohlávek, Václav. *Pojištění a pojišťovnictví.* 1st ed. Praha: Vysoká škola finanční a správní, 2005.
47. Jan Kryštof Bořek (1665 Švamberk or Bezdružice – 1730 Vienna) was a Czech nobleman, economist, and art collector. https://cs.wikipedia.org/wiki/Jan_Kry%C5%A1tof_Bo%C5%99ek.

citizens. During the reign of Maria Theresa (1740–1780), a fund was established to compensate for damage caused by fires, floods, and adverse weather. An insurance company in Brandýs nad Labem was established in 1776 against fire damage to field supplies, furniture, tools, and cattle. After 1822, two 'foreign' insurance companies based in Vienna and Trieste began operations in the Czech lands. In the nineteenth century, the foundations of the tradition of Czech insurance and the insurance industry as whole were laid, and the position of strong, financially stable Czech insurance companies on the insurance market flourished.

37. In the Habsburg monarchy, the first legal regulation of insurance and insurance operations appeared by a patent of Emperor Francis I, of 4 September 1819, which allowed insurance as a private business. However, the state retained the concession privileges for the establishment of insurance companies and their activities. The first Czech mutual insurance company in Prague was founded in 1827 by Josef Matyáš, Count of Thun and Hohenstein, and František Josef, Count of Vrba. This insurance company began operating real estate fire insurance, from 1864 property insurance and hail insurance, and from 1909 also life insurance and other products. In 1881, the company paid almost 300,000 gold coins for the damage caused by the fire of the National Theatre. A similar institute called the Moravian – Silesian Mutual Insurance Company was established almost simultaneously in Brno, in 1830. The wave of founding Czech insurance companies and insurance associations arose in the second half of the nineteenth century when many municipal, peasant, and mutual insurance companies were established. In 1869, for example, Slavia insurance company was founded.[48] Furthermore, in 1872, an important institution in reinsurance was established, namely the First Czech Reinsurance Bank in Prague. At the turn of the century, other companies were established, including the Fire Mutual Insurance Company in Brno.

38. Thanks to the expertise and political foresight of the representatives of the insurance industry, it was possible to save clients' funds during the war period 1914–1918 and to start a new stage of Czechoslovak insurance after the establishment of an independent Czechoslovak Republic. Since October 1922, Government Regulation No. 307/1922 Sb.,[49] which – among other things – introduced state supervision in the insurance industry. Despite this regulation, the position of policyholders is deteriorating, and the insurance industry is developing outside the state, due to speculation and increasing competition. As a result, the regulation was tightened by the new Act No. 145/1934 Sb., on the Insurance Contract[50] and by the Act

48. https://www.slavia-pojistovna.cz/en/history/.
49. Regulation of the Government of the Czechoslovak Republic of 19 Oct. 1922 on the Establishment and Management of Private Insurance Companies in Slovakia and Subcarpathian Russia (Insurance Regulations). To consult the text (in Czech) *see* https://www.noveaspi.cz/products/lawText/1/3101/1/2.
50. To consult the text (in Czech) *see* https://www.beck-online.cz/bo/chapterview-document.seam?documentId=onrf6mjzgm2f6mjugu.

of the National Assembly No. 147/1934 Sb., on Securing the Claims of Policyholders in Private Insurance and on State Supervision of Private Insurance Companies.[51] This legislation established the principles for the activities of domestic insurance companies as well as the rules for the business of foreign insurance companies in our territory. The legislation was substantially supplemented and changed by Government Decree No. 331/1942 Sb., which, among other things, changed the supervisory body from the Ministry of the Interior to the Ministry of Economy and Labour.[52]

39. Despite the decline of the insurance industry during the Protectorate in World War II, the pre-war period resulted in 733 insurance companies and insurance associations, of which 158 foreign representations in 1945.

40. These insurance companies were nationalized by Presidential Decree No. 103/1945 Sb. of 24 October 1945.[53] The nationalization of banks and insurance companies had a great economic impact. All joint-stock banks and private insurance companies became nationals, so that only cooperative and public institutions of the people's finance remained so far un-nationalized. An Insurance Board (in Czech 'Pojišťovací rada') with its seat in Prague was established to provide a unified management of the insurance industry within the existence of several insurance institutions; the Board was subjected to the Ministry of Finance.

41. On the basis of the presidential decree cited above and a government resolution, the Minister of Finance determined by ministerial decrees of 20 November 1946 that, with effect from 1 January 1947, only five insurance companies would be established as national enterprises, namely: Pojišťovna Slavia – national enterprise, Pražská pojišťovna – national enterprise, První československá pojišťovna – national enterprise, Pojišťovna Slovan – national enterprise, and Nemocenská pojišťovna – national enterprise. These five insurance companies (national enterprises) took over the rights and obligations of all insurance companies that had to come to an end.

42. However, even this situation changed rapidly and by a decree of the Ministry of Finance of 25 May 1948, the five insurance companies were merged into one 'Československá pojišťovna, n.p.' (Czechoslovak Insurance Company – national enterprise) The newly established insurance company became a monopoly

51. To consult the text (in Czech) *see* https://www.noveaspi.cz/products/lawText/1/5994/1/2/zakon-c-147-1934-sb-o-zabezpeceni-naroku-pojistniku-v-pojisteni-soukromem-a-o-statnim-dozoru-na-soukrome-pojistovny.
52. To consult the text (in Czech) *see* https://www.noveaspi.cz/products/lawText/1/10442/1/2/vladni-narizeni-c-331-1942-sb-o-doplneni-a-zmene-nekterych-ustanoveni-o-pojistovnach/vladni-narizeni-c-331-1942-sb-o-doplneni-a-zmene-nekterych-ustanoveni-o-pojistovnach.
53. Decree of the President of the Republic No. 103/1945 Sb., on the Nationalization of Private Insurance Companies. To consult the text (in Czech) *see* https://www.zakonyprolidi.cz/cs/1945-103.

on insuring domestic and foreign risks. From 1 January 1953, this insurance company was transformed into the 'Státní pojišt'ovna' (State Insurance Company) and thus the natural market development of the insurance industry was interrupted for several decades.[54]

43. In connection with the new federal organization of the Czechoslovak state in 1968, by Constitutional Act No. 143/1968 Sb., on the Czechoslovak Federation, two separate entities were created from single State Insurance Company, namely the Czech State Insurance Company with its registered office in Prague and the Slovak State Insurance Company with its registered office in Bratislava, both with nationwide scope, with effect from 1 January 1969. Each entity was subordinated to its national Ministry of Finance. The monopoly period of the Czech insurance industry lasted until the early 1990s.

44. On 28 May 1991, Act of the Czech National Council No. 185/1991 Sb., on Insurance Business was adopted,[55] which enabled the operation of insurance activities in the territory of the Czech Republic by entities that met the conditions for this activity stipulated by the new legal regulation. The purpose of this Act was to regulate the conditions of business in the insurance industry and state supervision over it. An insurance or reinsurance company established as a state-owned enterprise, a joint-stock company, or as a cooperative or a cooperative enterprise may conduct business in the insurance industry in the Czech Republic under the conditions stipulated by this Act. The insurance company may carry out activities other than those specified in this Act only within the scope of the permit granted by the supervisory authority. By that, the monopoly of the Czech State Insurance Company was abolished and a period of so-called de-monopolization of the insurance industry started.

45. This legal regulation introduces a concession system, defines a supervisory body, aims to regulate and define organizational and legal forms of companies operating activities focused on insurance, sets rules for the creation and use of special-purpose insurance funds, reserves and insurance companies, and determines rules for foreign insurance entities operating in the Czech Republic. Based on this law, about twenty insurance companies began operating insurance activities in our territory in 1991–1992. This number increased until 1997 when the insurance market began to gradually stabilize. The Act on Insurance Business was amended by Act No. 320/1993 Sb., which focused primarily on the issue of the financial management of insurance companies.

46. Among other milestones in the development of insurance in our territory after the 'Velvet revolution in 1989', we can mention 1999 when two important legal enactments were adopted. The first one – Act No. 168/1999 Sb., on Motor Third Party Liability Insurance (Motor Third Party Liability Insurance Act)[56] –

54. To *see* more Marvan, Miroslav; Chaloupecký, Josef. *Dějiny pojišt'ovnictví v Československu. 3. díl, Dějiny pojišt'ovnictví v Československu (1945-1992).* 1st ed. Praha: Česká pojišt'ovna, 1997.
55. To consult the text (in Czech) *see* https://www.zakonyprolidi.cz/cs/1991-185.
56. To consult the text (in Czech) *see* https://www.zakonyprolidi.cz/cs/1999-168.

removed the monopoly of 'Česká pojišťovna' (Czech Insurance Company) as the only operator of statutory liability insurance for damage caused by the operation of a motor vehicle, and allowed other insurance companies that applied for a license to operate this insurance product.

47. The second one – Act No. 363/1999 Sb., Insurance Act (entered into force on 1 April 2000), replacing the previous legislation (Act No. 185/1991 Sb. on Insurance Business), is trying to solve the practical problems that the previous legislation did not regulate as well as with regard to the new special obligations arising from European legislation. According to that Act, the insurance or reinsurance activities in the Czech Republic may be performed only by a legal entity with its registered office in the Czech Republic which is granted a permit issued by the Ministry of Finance. The insurance activity traditionally englobes concluding insurance contracts, managing insurance, and providing benefits from insurance contracts. Newly added activities allows the provision of assistance services and processing of personal data. The insurance activity also includes the management of assets, the source of which were technical reserves, the conclusion of contracts with reinsurance companies and the securing of liabilities, duties, and activities aimed at preventing the occurrence of damage and mitigating its consequences.

48. According to that legislation the insurance company had to take the form of a cooperative or a joint-stock company, while the reinsurance company could only be a joint-stock company. There has been a fundamental change, when the approving of general insurance conditions is not part of the permitting procedure anymore. Furthermore, it was newly stipulated that an insurance or reinsurance company must start its activities within one year after the permit was issued, otherwise the Ministry of Finance is entitled to withdraw the permit. In accordance with the EU law classification, the Czech law stipulated a minimum contribution of registered (basic) capital, depending on the sector – life and non-life insurance.[57] In addition, the law exhaustively established technical reserves for life and non-life insurance and then allowed the creation of other reserves, if approved by the Ministry of Finance. The function of the responsible actuary[58] has been introduced and minimum solvency

57. The minimum amount of the registered capital of an insurance company was for the operation of insurance activities according to one or more life insurance branches CZK 60,000,000 and for non-life insurance sectors from CZK 34,000,000 to CZK 200,000,000. The registered capital of a reinsurance company domiciled in the Czech Republic was at least CZK 1,000,000,000. For more details, *see* § 9) of Act No. 363/1999 Sb., Insurance Act.
58. The insurance company was obliged to have the responsible actuary confirm the correctness of distribution of income from financial placement in life insurance between the insured and the insurance company, calculation of premium rates, the amount of technical provisions, calculation of the minimum solvency margin and actuarial methods used in the insurance business. The reinsurance company was obliged to have the responsible actuary confirm the correctness of the amount of technical provisions, calculation of the minimum solvency margin, and actuarial methods used in reinsurance business. The responsible actuary confirms the correctness of the submitted data by their signature on the report. For more details, *see* § 23 of Act No. 363/1999 Sb., Insurance Act.

margin have been adjusted. The law stipulated that one-third of the minimum solvency margin constitute a guarantee fund. Insurance intermediation activities were newly regulated.[59]

49. One of the more significant amendments is the amendment under Act No. 39/2004 Sb., the aim of which was to harmonize the Czech legal regulation of insurance with the third generation of EU insurance directives. A significant change is the so-called single European passport. Based on it, Czech insurance companies are able to carry out cross-border activities or establish branches on the European market. The EU regulations are increasingly interfering in the domestic insurance sector, most notably, this can be seen in adopting new insurance legislation via Insurance Act,[60] which is largely just reflection and synthesis of different actual EU regulations. Among other trends we are now witnessing belong the tightening of the weaker party protection, i.e., more consistent protection of the policyholder or the increase in digitization and electronification.

§3. SOURCES OF INSURANCE LAW

I. Legislation

50. In the legal order of the Czech Republic, which is built on the tradition of continental legal culture, legislation is of fundamental importance as generally binding normative legislative acts, i.e., laws (acts of Parliament) and delegated legislative acts, which are together with ratified and promulgated international treaties[61] published in the Collection of Laws and International Treaties.[62]

59. The operation of intermediary activities by an insurance agent or an insurance or reinsurance broker was conditioned by its integrity and the fulfilment of the conditions laid down by Insurance Act. If this activity was carried out by a legal entity, the conditions had to be met by all natural persons who were authorized to act on behalf of this legal entity. The insurance or reinsurance broker and the insurance agent were obliged to carry out intermediary activities with professional care and were obliged to be insured in the event of liability for damage caused during the performance of this activity, for a minimum sum insured of CZK 5,000,000. Another condition for the operation of intermediary activities by an insurance or reinsurance broker was their registration with the Ministry. For more details, *see* § 25 of Act No. 363/1999 Sb., Insurance Act.
60. To consult the text (in Czech) *see* https://www.zakonyprolidi.cz/cs/2009-277.
61. Cf. Art. 10 of the Constitution.
62. *See* § 1 of Act No. 309/1999 Sb., on the Collection of Laws and International Treaties, according to which in the Collection of Laws and International Treaties are promulgated constitutional laws, laws, legislative measures of the Senate, Government orders and other delegated legislative acts issued by the ministry or another central administrative authority, referred to as 'decrees'. In addition, pursuant to Art. 79(3) of the Constitution, bodies of territorial self-government units (municipalities) may also issue generally binding legal regulations (on the basis of and within the bounds of the statute), and further pursuant to Art. 104(3) of the Constitution, within the limits of its competence, also a generally binding ordinances; however these regulations are not published in the Collection of Laws.

51. The legal regulation of private insurance and business of insurance in the Czech legal system has its basis primarily at the level of national primary legislation (laws), in accordance with the traditional continental division into public law and private law divided in two main areas.

52. The first area is the public law framework regulated at the level of national law primarily by Act No. 277/2009 Sb., Insurance Act (IA). The Insurance Act incorporates the relevant legislation of the EU and regulates the conditions for conducting insurance and reinsurance business and the performance of supervision of the insurance industry. In the introduction, the IA sets out the scope of its competence and defines basic terms. In Part Two, it lays down in detail the conditions for conducting insurance business, in particular for domestic insurance companies, insurance companies from another Member State and third-country insurance companies. A similar division is used by law to regulate the operation of reinsurance activities. Furthermore, the valuation of assets and liabilities, the creation of technical reserves, investments, and solvency of insurance and reinsurance companies, as well as accounting, audit, and information duties of insurance and reinsurance companies are regulated in the same part. Part Three of the IA regulates the supervision of the insurance industry, which is performed by the CNB in cooperation with the European Supervisory Authorities and the supervisory authorities of other Member States. According to the IA, insurance and reinsurance companies that conduct insurance or reinsurance activities in the Czech Republic, providers of externally provided (outsourced) services and other natural and legal persons are subject to supervision, if so stipulated by law. In this part of the IA, it also regulates the offences of natural and legal persons in the insurance sector and stipulates penalties for breach of duties imposed by this Act. Part Four regulates the obligation of confidentiality, both for the supervisory authorities (in regard to the facts which they get known in the course of supervision) and for the insurance and reinsurance undertakings themselves and for the persons acting for them (in regard to the facts concerning insurance of natural and legal persons). The final parts are devoted to common provisions (Part Five), empowering, final, transitional, and repealing provisions (Part Six), and the effectiveness of the Act (Part Seven), which occurred on 1 January 2010.[63]

53. Another key public law regulation in the field of insurance is Act No. 170/2018 Sb., on the Distribution of Insurance and Reinsurance (AoDIR), which regulates the distribution of private insurance and reinsurance. The AoDIR incorporates the relevant regulations of the EU and regulates the activities of persons authorized to mediate insurance or reinsurance, including the activities of such persons abroad, the rights and duties in the distribution of insurance or reinsurance and the powers of administrative authorities in the field of insurance or reinsurance distribution. In

63. On that date, IA replaced the previous Act No. 363/1999 Sb., Insurance Act.

the introductory part of the AoDIR, it defines the basic terms, the scope of its competence, and further regulates the conditions of the so-called fleet insurance.[64] In Part Two, it introduces four categories of insurance intermediaries, namely independent intermediaries, tied agents, supplementary insurance intermediaries, and insurance intermediaries with a home Member State other than the Czech Republic, and lays down the conditions for granting authorization to engage in intermediary activities. Part Three regulates the register of insurance intermediaries and accredited persons, which is administered and operated in electronic form by the CNB. Part Four lays down general rules to ensure the proper conduct of intermediation activities and other distribution rules, including rules for the prevention, detection, and management of conflicts of interest, regulation of distributors' remuneration or product oversight and governance. In Part Five of the AoDIR, it regulates the personnel prerequisites for the operation of the intermediation activity, including the expertise and trustworthiness of distributors. In Part Six, the law sets out detailed rules for dealing with the client, including the obligation of confidentiality, information obligations, the obligation to provide recommendations or advice to the client, and the obligation to make a record of the meeting or to keep documents and records. In Part Seven, the supervision, which is also performed by the CNB in the area of insurance distribution, is regulated. In Part Eight, the Act provides for penalties for natural and legal offences in the area of insurance and reinsurance distribution. The final parts, Nine and Ten, are devoted to transitional and the final provisions. The effectiveness of the AoDIR was determined on the first day of the fourth calendar month following the day of its promulgation, which in turn fell on 1 December 2018.[65]

54. The second main area is the private law regulation of insurance contracts and insurance as a legal relationship between the insurer and the policyholder in Act No. 89/2012 Sb., Civil Code (CC). The Civil Code is a basic general regulation of private law, which is a subsidiary source of private law rules for all other areas of law. In this context, the insurance contract is only one of many types of contracts regulated within the framework of the Civil Code and it is governed (unless otherwise stipulated by law or agreed by the parties) by the general provisions on obligations (§§ 1721–2054 CC), including the rules of creation (this includes, among other things, general issues of contracting, i.e., negotiating and concluding an insurance contract), changes, or termination of obligations. In the same way, of course, the general regulation of juridical acts, or, for example, the regulation of consumer contracts (especially, special rules for contracts on financial services in the provisions of §§ 1841–1851 CC) shall apply to insurance. The main part of the insurance regulation is concentrated within the regulation of the so-called aleatory contracts in the

64. Which is not necessarily a fleet insurance of vehicles, as the name might suggest, but a policyholder's activity consisting in offering the possibility to become insured if it is operated in a business manner according to § 4 AoDIR.

65. On that date, AoDIR replaced the previous Act No. 38/2004 Sb., on Insurance Intermediaries and Independent Loss Adjusters and on the amendment of the Trade Licensing Act (Act on Insurance Intermediaries and Loss Adjusters).

provisions of §§ 2758–2782 CC, which regulate general issues of creation and termination of insurance, essential requisites and form of insurance contract, an insurable interest (§§ 2761–2774), insurance premium (§§ 2782–2789), general rules for compulsory insurance (§§ 2779–2781), or investigation of an insured event (§§ 2796–2801), as well as general issues of insurance against loss and damage (§§ 2811–2820) and fixed-amount insurance (§§ 2821–2823), general rules for personal insurance (§§ 2824–2832), as well as special rules for individual insurance branches, namely, life insurance (§§ 2833–2843), accident insurance (§§ 2844–2846), sickness insurance (§§ 2847–2848), property insurance (§§ 2849–2855), legal expenses insurance (§§ 2856–2860), third-party liability insurance (§§ 2861–2867), credit or guaranty insurance (§§ 2868–2870), and insurance of financial losses (§ 2871).

55. In addition to the above-mentioned laws, a number of other legislative acts apply in the field of insurance and insurance business. At the level of primary legislation (laws), it is mainly Act No. 168/1999 Sb., on Motor Third Party Liability Insurance (MTPLIA), which regulates public and private aspects of the compulsory MTPL. Furthermore, all special laws governing compulsory insurance; it is possible to mention above all Act No. 372/2011 Sb., on Health Services and on Conditions of their Provision (Health Services Act); Act No. 373/2011 Sb., on Specific Health Services; Act No. 266/1994 Sb., on Railways; Act No. 114/1995 Sb., on Inland Navigation (in connection with the implementing Decree of the Ministry of Transport No. 223/1995 Sb., on the Suitability of Vessels for Operation on Inland Waterways); Act No. 49/1997 Sb., on Civil Aviation (in conjunction with Regulation (EC) No. 785/2004 of the European Parliament and of the Council of 21 April 2004 on insurance requirements for air carriers and aircraft operators); Act No. 85/1996 Sb., on the Legal Profession; Act No. 358/1992 Sb., on Notaries and Their Activities (Notarial Procedure Act); Act No. 120/2001 Sb., on Licensed Executors and Execution (Execution Procedure Act); Act No. 182/2006 Sb., on Insolvency and Methods of Resolving It (Insolvency Act); Act No. 523/1992 Sb., on Tax Counselling and the Chamber of Tax Advisors of the Czech Republic; Act No. 93/2009 Sb., On Auditors (Act on Auditors); Act No. 360/1992 Sb., on the Profession of Authorised Architects and the Profession of Authorised Engineers and Technicians Active in Construction; Act No. 18/1997 Sb., on Peaceful Utilisation of Nuclear Energy and Ionising Radiation (Atomic Act); Act No. 406/2000 Sb., on Energy Management; Act No. 449/2001 Sb., on Game Management; Act No. 159/1999 Sb., on Certain Conditions of Business and on the Performance of Certain Activities in the Area of Tourism (compulsory guaranty insurance in the event of bankruptcy of a travel agency); and Act No. 326/1999 Sb., on the Residence of Foreign Nationals in the Czech Republic (compulsory travel health insurance for foreigners), which, however, does not end the list of special regulations governing compulsory insurance.

56. From the area of social security, i.e., outside the scope of Insurance Act, it is also possible to mention Act No. 48/1997 Sb., on Public Health Insurance; Act No. 187/2006 Sb., on Sickness Insurance; Act No. 155/1995 Sb., on Pension Insurance; Act No. 42/1994 Sb., on State-Contributory Supplementary Pension Insurance; Act No. 426/2011 Sb., on Retirement Savings; Act No. 427/2011 Sb., on

Supplementary Pension Savings (SPS); and Act No. 340/2006 Sb., on Activities of Institutions for Occupational Retirement Provision. In the field of non-private insurance, it is necessary to also mention Act No. 58/1995 Sb., on Insuring and Financing Export with State Support, which regulates the activities of the fully state-owned Export Guarantee and Insurance Corporation (in Czech 'Exportní a garanční pojišťovna, a. s.', EGAP).[66]

57. In addition to national legislation, the European law has fundamental importance to the insurance sector. First and foremost, these are the sources of primary law – international treaties, which create the system of institutions of the EU itself and the framework for the creation of secondary European legislation.[67]

58. The basic source of primary law in the field of insurance is the Treaty on the Functioning of the European Union, which enshrines the fundamental principles of the common European market, including free movement of goods (removal of tariff barriers, prohibition of quantitative restrictions between states) and services (prohibition of restrictions on the free movement of services within the Union), free movement of persons (free movement of workers, freedom of establishment), and free movement of capital (prohibition of restrictions on the movement of capital and prohibition of restrictions on payments between Member States and between Member States and third countries). The concept of the free market allows insurance companies, among other things, to do business without special restrictions in other Member States on the basis of the so-called single European passport, where an authorization granted in the home state is valid for all other Member States, and entitles the insurance company to conduct the insurance or reinsurance business in the territory of another Member State, either through a branch or under the freedom to provide services on a temporary basis.

59. An equally important role in the area of insurance is played by the sources of European secondary law, which can be generally defined as law created by the institutions of the EU on the basis of and in the boundaries of primary law; these include, in particular, directly applicable regulations, directives which have a harmonizing purpose and are binding on Member States only as to the result to be achieved, decisions and non-legally binding recommendations, and opinions of the relevant EU institutions. The importance of the European law is mainly reflected on two levels. On the one hand, the national legislation discussed above largely incorporates (transposes) the relevant directives, or complements and expands on some directly applicable European acts, on the other hand, in addition to the national legislation, directly applicable European regulations also apply (a national authority must not apply a national rule incompatible with directly effective EU regulation). The current wording of the IA[68] takes into account changes in EU legislation

66. https://www.egap.cz/en/profile.
67. For more details, *see* e.g., Tomášek, Michal; Týč, Vladimír et al. *Právo Evropské unie.* 1st ed. Praha: Leges, 2013. pp. 55 et seq.
68. After the amendment transposing the Solvency II, implemented by Act No. 304/2016 Sb.

related, in particular, to the adoption of the Treaty of Lisbon and the so-called Lamfalussy process, which consists in modifying the current hierarchical arrangement of EU legislation in the financial market area and the creation of European Supervisory Authorities (ESAs) and their powers. EU legislation in the field of insurance is thus divided into three levels. On the first level, the directives regulates the basic principles, which are further elaborated on the second level by delegated and implementing acts, in the form of directly applicable European Commission regulations, and on the third level by technical standards proposed by the European Insurance and Occupational Pensions Authority (EIOPA) and adopted by the European Commission.[69] The fourth level of regulation is often referred to as non-legally binding soft law in the form of guidelines and recommendations issued by EOIPA pursuant to Article 16 of Regulation (EU) No. 1094/2010 of the European Parliament and of the Council.

II. Governmental Regulations, Regulation by Governmental Agencies

60. The above-discussed level of national primary legislation is followed by the level of secondary implementing legislation, which is issued *secundum et intra legem*, thus on the basis and within the bounds of the statute. These are mainly the Government orders (in Czech 'nařízení vlády') and legislative acts of ministries, other administrative authorities and local self-government bodies, referred to as 'decrees' (in Czech 'vyhlášky').[70] While the Government is at the constitutional level and generally empowered to implement any law by an order,[71] ministries, other administrative authorities, and local self-government bodies may issue legislative acts only if they are expressly empowered to do so by law.[72] In the area of insurance, the most important secondary legislation are undoubtedly the decrees issued by the CNB and the Ministry of Finance. At present, these are mainly the following decrees:

- Decrees of the CNB implementing certain provisions of the Insurance Act, specifically Decree No. 305/2016 Sb., on Reporting by Insurance Undertakings and Reinsurance Undertakings to the Czech National Bank; Decree No. 306/2016 Sb., Implementing Certain Provisions of the Insurance Act; and Decree No. 307/2016 Sb., on Applications under the Insurance Act.
- Decrees of the CNB implementing certain provisions of Act No. 170/2018 Sb., on the Distribution of Insurance and Reinsurance, namely Decree No. 195/2018 Sb., on Professional Qualifications for the Distribution of Insurance; and Decree No. 196/2018 Sb., on Applications under the Act on the Distribution of Insurance and Reinsurance.

69. Přikryl, Vladimír; Čechová, Jana. *Zákon o pojišťovnictví. Komentář. § 1* [ASPI System]. Wolters Kluwer [cit. 2020-4-25]. ASPI_ID KO277_2009CZ. Available in the ASPI System. ISSN: 2336-517X.].
70. Cf. § 1(2) of Act No. 309/1999 Sb., on the Collection of Laws and International Treaties.
71. *See* Art. 78 of the Constitution.
72. *See* Art. 79(3) of the Constitution.

- Decree of the Ministry of Finance No. 205/1999 Sb., on Implementing Certain Provisions of the Motor Third Party Liability Insurance Act;.
- Decree of the Ministry of Finance No. 125/1993 Sb., Stipulating the Conditions and Premium Rates of the Statutory Employer's Liability Insurance for Damage in relation to Work Accident or Occupational Diseases.

61. Furthermore, the CNB pursuant to § 49a of Act No. 6/1993 Sb., on the Czech National Bank, issues Official information (in Czech 'úřední sdělení'), which are published in the Bulletin of the Czech National Bank and provide information, in particular, on the Bank Board's interest rate decisions, interpretative opinions of the CNB, the conditions for the transactions of the CNB, and facts important to persons operating in the financial market. The supervisory official information and benchmarks published on the CNB's website are particularly important for the insurance sector.[73] The CNB's official information and benchmarks are soft law in nature. Although they are not legally binding and enforceable, the CNB communicates to the supervised persons its expectations in relation to the fulfilment of obligations imposed by the relevant legislation, thus enabling regulated persons to obtain information on supervisory procedures and assessments.

III. Court Decisions

62. Although court decisions are not a formal source of law in the Czech Republic, case law is essential for the application of law and there is no difference in the area of insurance, where courts, as in other branches, substantially refine, supplement, and complete formal sources of law. Decisions of higher courts are of fundamental importance for practice, among them, the decisions of the Constitutional Court of the Czech Republic in its proceedings on constitutional complaints[74] and decisions and opinions of the Supreme Court of the Czech Republic, whose task is to ensure unity and legality of general courts by deciding on extraordinary remedies filed against decisions of lower courts and further by monitoring and evaluating final court decisions in civil and criminal proceedings and, on the basis of them, takes opinions on the decision-making activity of courts in certain types of matters. For this purpose, the Supreme Court issues a Collection of Judicial Decisions and Opinions,[75] in which the opinions of the Supreme Court taken by its Divisions[76] or the Plenum, and selected decisions of the Supreme Court and other courts are published in the interest of uniform court decisions. In selected areas (e.g., compulsory MTPL, equal treatment, or private international law), the judgements of the Court of Justice of the European Union (CJEU) are also of considerable importance in the

---

73. Available at https://www.cnb.cz/cs/dohled-financni-trh/vykon-dohledu/dohledova-uredni-sdeleni-a-benchmarky/.
74. *See* §§ 72 et seq. of Act No. 182/1993 Sb., on the Constitutional Court.
75. Available at https://sbirka.nsoud.cz/.
76. At present, the Supreme Court has two Divisions, namely the Civil Law and Commercial Division and the Criminal Division.

insurance industry. Some of the important individual court decisions will be mentioned below in the interpretation of the relevant issues.[77]

IV. Private International Law

63. Given that there is currently no international treaty or other directly applicable regulation that would contain a unified direct regulation of insurance and reinsurance contracts with an international element, it is necessary to determine the applicable law for these contracts on the basis of conflict-of-law rules. The source of these rules in the Czech legal system is, on the one hand, the national regulation of Act No. 91/2012 Sb., on Private International Law (AoPIL), as well as mutual legal assistance treaties concluded between the Czech Republic and a third country and, within the European area, Regulation (EC) No. 593/2008 of the European Parliament and of the Council of 17 June 2008 on the law applicable to contractual obligations (Rome I).[78] In regard to the interrelationship between those conflict-of-law rules, in accordance with § 2 of the AoPIL and the general principles of the application of European law, the Rome I Regulation is directly binding in the scope of the matters it governs and has application priority over national regulation.[79] In accordance with Article 25 of Rome I, this Regulation shall not prejudice the application of international conventions between a Member State and a third country and those international conventions therefore shall be used preferentially. Due to the fact that mutual legal assistance treaties between the Czech Republic and third countries either do not contain conflict-of-law rules for contractual obligations, or contain conflict-of-law rules for contractual obligations, which do not reflect the specifics of insurance,[80] remains a key source of conflict-of-law rules for the area of insurance and reinsurance the Rome I Regulation, which, as has been said, shall take precedence over the AoPIL. The application of the AoPIL conflict-of-law rules is thus, in principle, limited to matters which do not fall within the scope of the Rome I Regulation or of the international treaties concluded between the Czech Republic and a third country.[81]

---

77. All decisions of the Supreme Court are searchable at https://www.nsoud.cz/Judikatura/ns_web.nsf/WebSpreadSearch; decisions of the Constitutional Court are available at https://nalus.usoud.cz/Search/Search.aspx.
78. The Rome I Regulation entered into force on the twentieth day following that of its publication in the Official Journal of the European Union and, in accordance with Art. 28 thereof, will apply to contracts concluded after 17 Dec. 2009; the Rome I Regulation substantively follows the so-called Rome Convention on the Law Applicable to Contractual Obligations, signed in Rome on 19 Jul. 1980, which entered into force on 1 Apr. 1991, with the Czech Republic becoming a signatory on 14 Apr. 2005 and ratifying it on 6 Apr. 2006 with effectiveness from 1 Jun. 2006; the Rome Convention was promulgated by the Communication of the Ministry of Foreign Affairs No. 64/2006 Sb. m. s.
79. *See* § 2 of the AoPIL: 'The Act shall be applied within the limits of the provisions of promulgated international treaties by which the Czech Republic is bound … and directly applicable provisions of European law.'
80. Dobiáš, Petr. *Autonomie vůle stran při uzavírání mezinárodních pojišťovacích a zajišťovacích smluv.* Sborník Dny práva 2016. Masarykova univerzita. Brno. 2017, p. 8.
81. Closer to the relationship between national regulation, European law and international conventions in the area of private international law, *see* e.g., Kučera, Zdeněk; Pauknerová, Monika; Růžička,

64. Specifically, in the area of insurance contracts, the modification of the Rome I Regulation represents a significant shift compared to the previous Rome Convention. While the Rome Convention explicitly excluded insurance contracts covering risks located in the territories of the Member States of the European Economic Community from its scope,[82] and was only applied to insurance contracts covering risks outside the Community (whereas pursuant to Article 1(4) in its scope also reinsurance contracts included), however, the Rome I Regulation contains a very detailed or even casuistic regulation of insurance contracts (*see* especially Article 7 of Rome I). From the point of view of the scope of the Regulation, it is no longer decisive whether the risk covered by the insurance contract is inside or outside the EU.[83] At the same time, the rules on insurance contracts are one of the most complex areas covered by Rome I in terms of practical application, as they contain numerous exceptions and are largely linked to the relevant insurance directive law.[84]

65. The conflict-of-law rules for insurance contracts can be found in Article 7 of the Rome I Regulation. From the point of view of the interpretation of that provision, it is also necessary to mention points 32 and 33 of the recital to the regulation. Point 32 justifies a high level of protection for the weaker party under Article 7, stating that, owing to the particular nature of insurance contracts, specific provisions should ensure an adequate level of protection for policyholders. The provisions of Article 6, which contains conflict-of-law rules for consumer contracts, should not apply in the context of insurance contracts. Point 33 of the recital states, that where an insurance contract not covering a large risk covers more than one risk, at least one of which is situated in a Member State and at least one of which is situated in a third country, the special rules on insurance contracts in this Regulation should only apply to the risk or risks situated in the relevant Member State or Member States. This provision eliminates the shortcomings of the application of the previous Rome Convention, which excluded from its scope insurance contracts covering risks situated in the territory of the Member States and, conversely, covered insurance contracts covering risks outside the Community, but did not respond to a situation, where one insurance contract covered risks both inside and outside the Community. According to point 33 of the recital, the obligation statute of insurance contracts not covering large insurance risks is split, if the contract covers risks both inside and outside the EU. Article 7 shall apply to risks situated within the territory of the EU and the general conflict-of-law rules laid down in Articles 3 and 4 of the

---

Květoslav et al. *Mezinárodní právo soukromé.* 8th ed. Plzeň – Brno: Aleš Čeněk – Doplněk. 2015, pp. 59 et seq.

82. *See* Art. 1(3) of the Rome Convention on the Law Applicable to Contractual Obligations.
83. Reinsurance contracts are expressly excluded from the application of special rules in Art. 7, for which the general provisions of Arts 3 and 4 of the Rome I Regulation apply.
84. Cf. also Rozehnalová, Naděžda. In: Rozehnalová, Naděžda; Valdhans, Jiří; Drličková, Klára; Kyselovská, Tereza. *Mezinárodní právo soukromé Evropské unie (Nařízení Řím I, Nařízení Řím II, Nařízení Brusel I).* 1st ed. Praha: Wolters Kluwer. 2013, p. 64: 'The Rome I Regulation sought to take another step towards unifying the regulation of insurance contracts. Exclusion of the scope of the Rome Regulation in respect of certain insurance contracts referred to in Art. 1(2)(h), application of Arts 3 and 4 for some of the types of insurance contracts and at the same time the special regulation of insurance contracts in Art. 7 thus create a real application delicacy in this area.'

Rome I Regulation shall apply to risks located outside the EU. This bifurcation can be problematic, for example, from the point of view of assessing the validity of an insurance contract, in such a case it would be assessed under the law of two (or more) states and the consequences of possible invalidity would be assessed under different legal systems.[85]

66. The Rome I Regulation excludes in Article 1(2)(j) specific insurance contracts arising out of operations carried out by organizations other than undertakings referred to in Article 2 of Directive 2002/83/EC of the European Parliament and of the Council of 5 November 2002 concerning life insurance, the object of which is to provide benefits for employed or self-employed persons belonging to an undertaking or group of undertakings, or to a trade or group of trades, in the event of death or survival or of discontinuance or curtailment of activity, or of sickness related to work or accidents at work.[86] The specific nature of these insurances and their similarity to public social security schemes are cited as grounds for exclusion from the Rome I Regulation.[87] The conflict-of-law rules contained in the private international law of the EU Member States will thus apply to these insurances with an international element.[88]

67. The key Article 7 of the Rome I Regulation applies to insurance contracts with an international element which cover large insurance risks,[89] regardless of where the risk covered by this contract is located (whether in a Member State or outside the EU). Article 7 applies also to other insurance contracts (i.e., contracts covering non-large insurance risks) where the risk covered by this contract is situated in the territory of the Member States. If the risk is situated outside the EU, the general conflict-of-law rules set out in Articles 3 and 4 of the Regulation apply.

68. Under Article 7(2) of the Rome I Regulation, insurance contracts covering large insurance risks shall be governed by the law chosen by the parties in accordance with Article 3. To the extent that the applicable law has not been chosen by the parties, the insurance contract shall be governed by the law of the country where the insurer has their habitual residence. Where it is clear from all the circumstances of the case that the contract is manifestly more closely connected with another country, the law of that other country shall apply (Article 7(2) second subparagraph). The substitute determinant is specially set here for insurance contracts covering large insurance risks in relation to the general regulation of Article 4 of the Regulation.

---

85. Dobiáš, Petr. *Evropské právo: Aplikace nařízení Řím I, Řím II a Brusel Ibis*. Pojistný obzor. 2016, No. 1, p. 38.
86. These are insurance excluded from the scope of the Directive of the European Parliament and of the Council 2002/83/ES of 5 Nov. 2002 concerning life assurance (cf. Art. 3(3) of the said Directive), more precisely from the scope of Solvency II (cf. Art. 9(2) of the Solvency II); for more details, *see* e.g., Richard Plender & Michael Wilderspin, *The European Private International Law of Obligations* 128–129 (Thomson Reuters 3rd ed. 2009).
87. Dobiáš, Petr. *Evropské právo: Aplikace nařízení Řím I, Řím II a Brusel Ibis*. Pojistný obzor. 2016, No. 1, p. 38.
88. *Ibid.*
89. As defined in § 131 of the Insurance Act in connection with the definition of large risks in Art. 13(27) of the Solvency II Directive.

69. For insurance contracts covering other than insurance risks not deemed to be large (situated within the EU), the rules of Article 7(3) of the Rome I Regulation, which restricts the choice of applicable law, apply. In such a case, the parties may only choose the following rights: (a) the law of any Member State where the risk is situated at the time of conclusion of the contract; (b) the law of the country where the policyholder has their habitual residence; (c) in the case of life assurance, the law of the Member State of which the policyholder is a national; (d) for insurance contracts covering risks limited to events occurring in one Member State other than the Member State where the risk is situated, the law of that Member State; (e) where the policyholder of a contract falling under this paragraph pursues a commercial or industrial activity or a liberal profession and the insurance contract covers two or more risks which relate to those activities and are situated in different Member States, the law of any of the Member States concerned or the law of the country of habitual residence of the policyholder. In the cases referred to under letter a), b), and e) the Rome I Regulation allows Member States to give the parties a greater degree of freedom in choosing the applicable law. This option has been used in Czech law in § 87(3) of the AoPIL,[90] which stipulates that the contractual parties may choose the applicable law for the insurance policy; if this involves an insurance policy which is subject to a directly applicable EU regulation, the contractual parties may, to the extent permitted by this regulation, choose any applicable law. According to the last subparagraph of Article 7(3), to the extent that the applicable law has not been chosen by the parties, such a contract shall be governed by the law of the Member State in which the risk is situated at the time of conclusion of the contract. Paragraph 6 then, in regard to the concept of 'state in which the risk is situated', refers to the relevant insurance directive, which implies that in non-life insurance the Member State where the risk is situated will be: (a) the Member State in which the property is situated, where the insurance relates either to buildings or to buildings and their contents, in so far as the contents are covered by the same insurance policy; (b) the Member State of registration, where the insurance relates to vehicles of any type; (c) the Member State where the policyholder took out the policy in the case of policies of a duration of four months or less covering travel or holiday risks, whatever the class concerned; (d) in all cases not explicitly covered by points (a), (b), or (c), the Member State in which either of the following is situated the habitual residence of the policyholder; or if the policyholder is a legal person, that policyholder's establishment to which the contract relates.[91] In life insurance, the State in which the risk is situated, shall be the 'Member State of the commitment', which means the Member State in which the habitual residence of the policyholder is situated; or if the policyholder is a legal person, the policyholder's establishment, to which the contract relates, is situated.[92]

90. An overview of individual national regulations in relation to whether and how they have used this discretion *see* e.g., Dobiáš, Petr. *Autonomie vůle stran při uzavírání mezinárodních pojišťovacích a zajišťovacích smluv.* Sborník Dny práva 2016. Masarykova univerzita. Brno. 2017, pp. 12–15.
91. *See* Art. 13(13) Solvency II.
92. *See* Art. 13(14) Solvency II.

70. The above-mentioned rules can be illustrated by the example of a life insurance contract concluded between a Czech insurer and a German citizen living in the Czech Republic. According to the last subparagraph of Article 7(3), to the extent that the law applicable has not been chosen by the parties, such a contract shall be governed by the law of the Member State in which the risk is situated at the time of conclusion of the contract. According to Article 7(6) regarding life insurance, the Member State in which the risk is situated means the Member State of the commitment, which is (according to Article 13(14) of the Solvency II Directive) the Member State, in which the habitual residence of the policyholder is situated, i.e., the Czech Republic. Thus, in such a case, the insurance contract will be governed by Czech law in a situation where the contractual parties do not choose another applicable law. In this choice, the parties are limited by Article 7(3)(c), as in the case of life insurance they can only choose the law of the Member State of which the policyholder is a national, i.e., German law. In other words, instead of Czech law (which governs the contract if no choice is made), the parties may not choose a law other than German law.

71. The special regime applies to compulsory insurance to which the following additional rules apply. In accordance with Article 7(4) of the Rome I Regulation: (a) the insurance contract shall not satisfy the obligation to take out insurance unless it complies with the specific provisions relating to that insurance laid down by the Member State that imposes the obligation; where the law of the Member State in which the risk is situated and the law of the Member State imposing the obligation to have insurance contradict each other, the latter shall prevail; (b) by way of derogation from Article 7(2) and (3), a Member State may lay down that a insurance contract shall be governed by the law of the Member State that imposes the obligation to take out insurance.

72. Article 7(5) of the Rome I Regulation provides for a common rule for insurance contracts under paragraph (3) (i.e., covering non-large insurance risks within the EU) and paragraph (4) (compulsory insurance) in regard to the determination of the country in which the risk is situated in situations where risks located in different Member States are covered in one contract. In such a case, the obligation statute is split, and the insurance contract shall be considered as constituting several contracts each relating to only one Member State.

73. The reinsurance contracts are expressly excluded from the application of the special provisions of Article 7 (*see* Article 7(1) of the Rome I Regulation). The applicable law for reinsurance contracts (as well as for insurance contracts covering non-large insurance risks outside the EU) is thus determined according to the general conflict-of-law rules in Articles 3 and 4 of the Regulation, i.e., in the first place according to the choice of law made by the parties under Article 3; if the law is not chosen by the parties, the contract will be governed in accordance with Article 4(2) by the law of the country, where the party was required to effect the characteristic performance of the contract has their habitual residence; or eventually, in accordance with Article 4(3), by the law of the country with which is the contract most closely connected.

74. At this point, it is necessary to mention, at least briefly, the issue of determining the applicable law in related non-contractual obligations. This area is primarily the subject of Regulation (EC) No. 864/2007 of the European Parliament and of the Council of 11 July 2007 on the law applicable to non-contractual obligations (Rome II). In this context, Article 18 of Rome II is particularly noteworthy, which deals with direct claims against a liability insurer, and which – in order to strengthen the injured party's legal position – provides that the person having suffered damage may bring their claim directly against the insurer of the person liable to provide compensation if the law applicable to the non-contractual obligation or the law applicable to the insurance contract so provides. The law applicable to a given non-contractual obligation (to the tortious relationship between the tortfeasor and the injured party) is usually determined by Rome II, while the law applicable to the insurance contract is usually determined by Rome I. According to the applicable law thus determined, it is necessary to assess the existence of the injured party's direct right against the liability insurer, i.e., the actual possibility and conditions of making a direct claim against the tortfeasor's insurer. However, in order to determine the scope of indemnity from liability insurance, it is necessary to apply the law governing the insurance contract from which the indemnity is to be provided.

75. In accordance with Article 28 of the Rome II Regulation, this Regulation shall not prejudice the application of international conventions to which one or more Member States are parties at the time when this Regulation is adopted and which lay down conflict-of-law rules relating to non-contractual obligations. Such is the nature of the Hague Convention on the Law Applicable to Traffic Accidents,[93] to which the Czech Republic is a ratified member, and which must be applied in the Czech Republic within the scope of its competence in the case of traffic accidents with an international element in preference to the AoPIL and the Rome II Regulation. The Hague Convention provides for the regulation of direct claims of injured parties in Article 9, according to which persons who have suffered injury or damage shall have a right of direct action against the insurer of the person liable if they have such a right under the law applicable according to Articles 3, 4, or 5 of the Convention. If the law of the State of registration is applicable under Article 4 or 5 and that law provides no right of direct action, such a right shall nevertheless exist if it is provided by the internal law of the State where the accident occurred. If this right does not belong under any of these legal orders, it arises, however, if the legal system governing the insurance contract so provides.

V. Jurisdiction

76. Closely related to the previous interpretation is the issue of determining jurisdiction in relation to the international element. The jurisdiction of Czech courts in relation to abroad is generally defined in the provision of § 6 AoPIL, according to which the jurisdiction of the Czech courts is given, if a court located within the

93. Concluded in Hague on 4 May 1971 and promulgated in the Czech Republic by Decree of the Ministry of Foreign Affairs No. 130/1976 Sb.

territory of the Czech Republic has the territorial jurisdiction over the proceedings according to the procedural regulations, unless stated otherwise in the provisions of this Act or any other legal regulation. The territorial jurisdiction of the Czech courts is regulated in §§ 84–89a Act No. 99/1963 Sb., Civil Procedure Code (CPC). If in a case with an international element it is possible to determine the territorial jurisdiction on the basis of one of the criteria specified in these provisions, the jurisdiction of the Czech courts to hear such a case is given.[94] If the Czech courts have jurisdiction with regard to a given matter, said jurisdiction will also apply to any mutual motions arising from the legal relations in question or from the same factual circumstances (§ 6(2) AoPIL). In § 85 AoPIL a prorogation agreement is generally permitted, where the parties may establish the jurisdiction of the Czech courts in matters of the law of obligations and other property rights by agreement in writing. Pursuant to the provisions of § 86 the parties may also derogate from the jurisdiction of Czech courts and establish the jurisdiction of a foreign court by an agreement in writing in matters of the law of obligations and other property rights. However, in matters of insurance and consumer contracts, such an agreement is permissible only after the dispute has arisen or if it only enables the policyholder, the insured, another beneficiary, the injured party, or the consumer to commence proceedings at a court in another state. In § 86(2) the exceptions are stipulated, where – despite the derogation agreement – the case is heard by a Czech court, namely if: (a) if the participants identically declare that they do not insist upon their initial agreement; (b) a judgement issued abroad could not be recognized in the Czech Republic; (c) the foreign court has refused to concern itself with the matter; or (d) the agreement on the jurisdiction of the foreign court is at odds with public order.

77. As in the previous interpretation of the issue of determining the applicable law in substantive insurance relationships, it is necessary to emphasize in international procedural law, that the above provisions of national law only have a limited scope of application, due to the application priority of European law or of international conventions by which the Czech Republic is bound.[95] The key document for practical application is again the directly applicable EU regulation, which is Regulation (EU) No. 1215/2012 of the European Parliament and of the Council of 12 December 2012 on jurisdiction and the recognition and enforcement of judgements in civil and commercial matters, as recast (Brussels I *bis*),[96] and the related so-called new Lugano Convention (or also the Lugano Convention II), which extends the regime of the Brussels I *bis* Regulation to the Member States of the European Free

94. Cf. e.g., § 86(3) of the CPC: 'An action (petition for commencement of proceedings) against a foreign person may be filed also before the court in whose district in the Czech Republic its enterprise or an organizational component of the enterprise are situated.'

95. On the relationship between the Brussels I *bis* Regulation and bilateral conventions and agreements *see* Art. 73(3) of the Brussels I *bis* Regulation.

96. The Brussels I *bis* shall apply to legal proceedings instituted, to authentic instruments formally drawn up or registered and to court settlements approved or concluded on or after 10 Jan. 2015 (*see* Arts 66 and 81 of the Regulation); Brussels I *bis* replaced the previous Council Regulation (EC) No. 44/2001 of 22 Dec. 2000 on jurisdiction and the recognition and enforcement of judgements in civil and commercial matters (the so-called Brussels I), which in turn replaced the former Brussels Convention on jurisdiction and the enforcement of judgements in civil and commercial matters with effect from 1 Mar. 2002 (concluded in Brussels on 27 Sep. 1968).

Trade Association.[97] The Brussels I *bis* Regulation represents a regional unification of selected issues of international procedural law. Within its scope it addresses, *inter alia*, issues of determining the jurisdiction of the courts of the EU Member States, issues of *lis pendens*, interim and precautionary measures or mutual recognition and enforcement of decisions.

78. It is stated in points 18 and 19 of the recital of Brussels I *bis* that, in the case of insurance contracts, the weaker party should be protected by rules of jurisdiction more favourable to their interests than the general rules. In regard to the choice of jurisdiction, the contractual freedom of the parties should be respected, but in the case of insurance contracts the choice is limited.

79. Specific rules for determining jurisdiction in matters relating to insurance[98] are set out in Section 3, Articles 10 to 16 of the Brussels I *bis* Regulation. According to Article 10, in matters relating to insurance, jurisdiction shall be determined by this Section, without prejudice to the general rules of Article 6, and the rules of the so-called alternative jurisdiction in Article 7(5) for disputes arising out of the operations of a branch, agency, or other establishment.

80. In accordance with Article 11, an insurer domiciled in a Member State may be sued: (a) in the courts of the Member State in which he is domiciled;[99] (b) in another Member State, in the case of actions brought by the policyholder, the insured or a beneficiary, in the courts for the place where the claimant is domiciled; or (c) if he is a co-insurer, in the courts of a Member State in which proceedings are brought against the leading insurer. If the insurer is not domiciled in a Member State but has a branch, agency, or other establishment in one of the Member States shall, in disputes arising out of the operations of the branch, agency, or establishment, be deemed to be domiciled in that Member State.

81. In addition, in matters of liability insurance and insurance of immovable property (as well as movable property situated in the affected immovable property), the insurer may be sued in the courts for the place where the harmful event occurred (*see* Article 12). This place means both the place of the event which gave rise to the damage, that is to say, the place of the infringement (*locus delicti commissi*) and the place where the damage occurred (*locus damni infecti*); the choice is up to the plaintiff.[100]

---

97. For more details, *see* e.g., Bříza, Petr. *Volba práva a volba soudu v mezinárodním obchodě.* 1st ed. Praha: C. H. Beck, 2012. pp. 191–192.
98. The term 'matters relating to insurance' is not defined by the Brussels I *bis* Regulation, but its substantive definition does not cause problems in practice; the rules apply on the rights and obligations of participants in private insurance, including issues of creation, change, termination, breach of insurance contracts or issues of direct claims to indemnity.
99. Cf. Art. 63 Brussels I *bis*.
100. Valdhans, Jiří. In: Rozehnalová, Naděžda; Valdhans, Jiří; Drličková, Klára; Kyselovská, Tereza. *Mezinárodní právo soukromé Evropské unie (Nařízení Řím I, Nařízení Řím II, Nařízení Brusel I).* 1st ed. Praha: Wolters Kluwer. 2013, p. 271.

82. In respect to liability insurance, the insurer may also, if the law of the court permits, be joined in proceedings which the injured party has brought against the insured (*see* Article 13). Articles 10, 11, and 12 shall apply to actions brought by the injured party directly against the insurer, where such direct actions are permitted (*see* Article 13(2)).[101] If the law applicable to such a direct action provides that the policyholder or the insured may join the action, the same court shall have jurisdiction over those persons (Article 13(3)).

83. The protection of the weaker party is also reflected in the definition of jurisdiction where the proceedings were brought by an insurer, where under Article 14 of Brussels I *bis* the insurer may bring proceedings only in the courts of the Member State in which the defendant is domiciled, irrespective of whether they are the policyholder, the insured or a beneficiary, without, however, excluding the insurer's right to bring a counterclaim in the court in which, in accordance with this Section, the original claim is pending.

84. Prorogation agreements in insurance matters are limited in the interest of the protection of weaker party in Article 15 of Brussels I *bis*, which allows the agreement to derogate from the provisions of Section 3 only in exhaustively defined cases: (i) if the agreement is entered into after the dispute has arisen; (ii) if the agreement allows the policyholder, the insured, or a beneficiary to bring proceedings in courts other than those indicated in Section 3; (iii) if the agreement is concluded between a policyholder and an insurer, both of whom are at the time of conclusion of the contract domiciled or habitually resident in the same Member State, and has the effect of conferring jurisdiction on the courts of that Member State even if the harmful event were to occur abroad, provided that such an agreement is not contrary to the law of that Member State;[102] (iv) where the agreement is concluded with a policyholder domiciled outside the EU (except in so far as the insurance is compulsory or relates to immovable property in a Member State); or (v) where the prorogation relates to a contract of insurance in so far as it covers one or more of the risks set out in Article 16 of the Regulation. These are, in particular, the specific risks of damage to sea-going ships, installations situated offshore or on the high seas (e.g., oil rigs), or aircraft, arising from perils which relate to their use for commercial purposes; all liability risks (excluding liability for bodily injury to passengers or loss of or damage to their baggage), financial loss connected with the use or operation of these ships, installations or aircraft, and in particular all large insurance risks as defined in Article 13(27) of Solvency II.

---

101. In judgement of the CJEU C-463/06 of 13 Dec. 2007, *FBTO Schadeverzekeringen NV v. Jack Odenbreit*, ECLI:EU:C:2007:792, the court found that it is not decisive for the application of this rule how the action is qualified in national law and whether the injured party's direct claim under national law is in the nature of the tortious or contractual obligation.

102. Under the judgement of the CJEU C-112/03 of 12 May 2005, *Société financière et industrielle du Peloux v. Axa Belgium and Others*, ECLI:EU:C:2005:280, the insurer cannot invoke this prorogation agreement with the policyholder towards the insured person or the beneficiary (if they are persons other than the policyholder) as against the weaker participants in the insurance who, moreover, are not a party to the prorogation agreement.

85. From the application of the special rules in Section 3 of Brussels I *bis* Regulation according to case law of CJEU disputes between insurers with each other,[103] disputes between insurers and reinsurers,[104] or subrogation claims against liability insurers are excluded,[105] because in these cases there will usually be economically and legally balanced entities on both sides of the dispute and the protective function of the special rules in Articles 10–16 of the Brussels I *bis* will not apply.

86. Article 26 of the Brussels I *bis* Regulation provides for the so-called implied choice of jurisdiction, where either the rules on choice of jurisdiction are missing or violated, and the jurisdiction is established if the defendant actively participates in the proceedings before that court (so-called submission to jurisdiction). However, the above does not apply if the defendant in the proceedings expressly objects to the lack of jurisdiction of the court, and further in cases where the exclusive jurisdiction of another court is given under Article 24 of the Regulation. In this context, it is worth noting the new duty of instruction of the court provided for in Article 26(2) of the Brussels I *bis*, according to which in the case of insurance where the policyholder, the insured, a beneficiary of the insurance contract, the injured party, the consumer, or the employee is the defendant, the court shall, before assuming jurisdiction under Article 26(1), ensure that the defendant is informed of their right to contest the jurisdiction of the court and of the consequences of entering or not entering an appearance.[106]

§4. Dispute Settlement and Arbitration

87. The power to decide civil law disputes, including insurance disputes, is entrusted to the judiciary in the Czech Republic at the constitutional level. Pursuant to Article 90 of the Constitution, courts are primarily called upon to provide protection of rights in the manner prescribed by law. Pursuant to Article 36(1) of the Charter, anyone may, in accordance with the prescribed procedure, claim their right before an independent and impartial court and, in specified cases, before another body.[107] According to Article 38 of the Charter, the jurisdiction of the court and the

103. Judgement of the CJEU C-77/04 of 26 May 2005, *Groupement d'intérêt économique (GIE) Réunion européenne and Others v. Zurich España*, Société pyrénéenne de transit d'automobiles (Soptrans), ECLI:EU:C:2005:327.
104. Judgement of the CJEU C-412/98 of 13 Jul. 2000, *Group Josi Reinsurance Company SA v. Universal General Insurance Company (UGIC)*, ECLI:EU:C:2000:399.
105. Judgement of the CJEU C-347/08 of 17 Sep. 2009, *Vorarlberger Gebietskrankenkasse v. WGV-Schwäbische Allgemeine Versicherungs AG*, ECLI:EU:C:2009:561.
106. This duty of instruction was introduced into the Regulation in response to the judgement of the CJEU C-111/09 of 20 May 2010, Česká podnikatelská pojišťovna, a.s., *Vienna Insurance Group v. Michal Bilas*, ECLI:EU:C:2010:290; *see also* Dobiáš, Petr. *Evropské právo: Aplikace nařízení Řím I, Řím II a Brusel Ibis*. Pojistný obzor. 2016, No. 1, pp. 40–41.
107. Further cf. also Art. 6 of the Convention for the Protection of Human Rights and Fundamental Freedoms (promulgated in the Czech Republic by Communication of the Federal Ministry of Foreign Affairs No. 209/1992 Sb.

competence of the judge are set by law. This law is Act No. 99/1963 Sb., Civil Procedure Code (CPC), which defines the jurisdiction of general courts in the provisions of § 7(1) so that in civil court proceedings the courts hear and decide disputes and other legal matters arising from the ratio of private law, unless they are discussed and decided by other bodies in accordance with the law. Such a body in the field of insurance is the Financial Arbitrator established under Act No. 229/2002 Sb., on the Financial Arbitrator, which will be discussed in more detail in §5. Consumer protection. If the hearing and decision of the case is handled by a special law to another body, even in such a case the party to the proceedings is provided with a guarantee of judicial review in accordance with Part Five of the CPC (*see* § 7(2) CPC).

88. According to Article 91(1) of the Constitution, the system of general courts (in the organizational sense) consists of the Supreme Court, the Supreme Administrative Court, and superior, regional, and district courts. Pursuant to Article 91(2), jurisdiction and the organization of courts shall be defined by law, which is Act No. 6/2002 Sb., on Courts and Judges (AoCJ). The basic element of the judicial system consists of district courts, which decide as courts of first instance, unless the procedural law stipulates otherwise and further decide in other cases prescribed by law (§§ 33–36 AoCJ). Regional courts decide as courts of second instance in cases in which district courts belonging to their district have ruled in the first instance; as courts of first instance, they decide in cases stipulated by the procedural law, and they also decide in matters of administrative justice and in other cases prescribed by law (§§ 29–32 AoCJ). Superior courts decide as courts of second instance in cases in which regional courts belonging to their district decide in the first instance and further decide in other cases stipulated by law (§§ 25–28 AoCJ). Currently, the superior courts are located in Prague and Olomouc. The Supreme Court[108] is the supreme judicial body in matters falling within the jurisdiction of courts, with the exception of matters decided by the Constitutional Court or the Supreme Administrative Court (*see* Article 92 of the Constitution). The Supreme Court is thus the supreme judicial body in matters falling within the jurisdiction of courts in civil and criminal proceedings. It ensures the unity and legality of decision-making, in particular by deciding on extraordinary remedies in cases provided by procedural law, and further monitors and evaluates final court decisions in civil and criminal proceedings and, on the basis of them, takes opinions on court decision-making in matters of a certain type, which together with selected decisions is published in the Collection of Judicial Decisions and Opinions[109] (§§ 14–24 AoCJ). The Supreme Court is located in Brno (§ 10 AoCJ).

89. In the perspective of substantive jurisdiction, the district courts have jurisdiction to proceed in the first instance, unless otherwise provided by law (§ 9(1) CPC). The vast majority of disputes arising from private insurance (typically disputes over the validity of the insurance contract, right to indemnity, outstanding premiums, over the exercise of insurer's penal rights, etc.) are decided in the first

108. http://www.nsoud.cz/Judikatura/ns_web.nsf?openDatabase&lng=EN.
109. *See* fn. 76.

instance by district courts. Regional courts in the first instance decide only in cases defined exhaustively in the provisions of § 9(2) CPC.[110]

90. In the perspective of functional jurisdiction, regional courts decide on appeals[111] against decisions of district courts. Appeals against decisions of regional courts as courts of first instance are decided by superior courts (§ 10 CPC). The Supreme Court decides on appellate reviews[112] against decisions of regional or superior courts as courts of appeal.

91. The territorial jurisdiction is defined in the provisions of §§ 84 et seq. CPC. Unless otherwise provided, the so-called general court of the participant against whom the petition is directed (i.e., the defendant), has jurisdiction over the proceedings (§ 84 CPC). The general court in the case of a natural person is the district court in whose district the participant has their residence; unless the participant has any residence, the district court in whose district the participant stays. If a natural person resides in more than one place, its general court is all district courts in whose district they reside with the intention of staying there permanently (§ 85(1) CPC). The general court of a natural person who is an entrepreneur, in matters resulting from their business activities, is the district court in whose district they have their seat (§ 85(2) CPC). The general court of a legal entity is the district court in whose district it has its registered office (§ 85(3) CPC). Provision of § 87 CPC regulates the so-called jurisdiction given to choose, which allows the plaintiff to choose (in addition to the general court of the defendant) another court, which may be, for example, the court in whose district the defendant has its permanent workplace, in whose district the event giving rise to the right to damages has occurred,[113] or the court in whose district the branch of a natural or legal person who is the defendant is located, if the dispute concerns the branch. The parties to proceedings in matters concerning the relations between entrepreneurs arising from business activities may agree in writing on the territorial jurisdiction of another court of first instance unless the law provides for exclusive jurisdiction.

110. These are, e.g., disputes in the field of public insurance; decisions in matters arising from legal relations associated with the establishment of business corporations, institutes, foundations and endowment funds; disputes between business corporations, their partners or members, as well as between partners or members of each other, if they result from participation in a business corporation; disputes between commercial corporations, their partners and members of their bodies or liquidators, in relation to the performance of their function; decisions on matters relating to the protection of the name and reputation of a legal person, etc.
111. A proper remedy against invalid decisions of first instance courts (for more details, *see* the §§ 201 et seq. CPC).
112. An extraordinary remedy against final decisions of the courts of appeal (for more details, *see* the §§ 236 et seq. CPC).
113. However, it should be noted that according to the case law the injured party is not allowed to choose this option if he assert a direct claim for insurance indemnity against the liability insurer, as this claim does not have the nature of a right to damages (cf. the resolution of the Municipal Court in Prague of 24 Apr. 2009, file No. 21 Co 139/2009, published in the Collection of Judicial Decisions and Opinions under No. 81/2011; the resolution of the Supreme Court of the Czech Republic of 26 Nov. 2014, file No. 25 Cdo 2904/2014), likewise, this option cannot be selected by the regressing health insurance company (cf. the resolution of the Supreme Court of the Czech Republic of 18 Aug. 2015, file No. 25 Cdo 2773/2015).

92. The proceedings take place in the court that has substantive and territorial jurisdiction. The determination of substantive and territorial jurisdiction is at the end of the proceedings governing the circumstances existing at the time of its initiation. If several courts have territorial jurisdiction, the proceedings may take place in any of them (§ 11 CPC).

93. In addition to decisions of general courts, decisions of the Constitutional Court of the Czech Republic[114] are also of fundamental importance, especially decisions in proceedings on constitutional complaints pursuant to §§ 72–84 of Act No. 182/1993 Sb., on the Constitutional Court. These types of proceedings is by far the most frequent legal process taking place before the Constitutional Court. The Constitutional Court decides on constitutional complaints of natural and legal persons against final decisions or other encroachments by public authorities infringing constitutionally guaranteed fundamental rights and basic freedoms. Very often also against decisions of general courts, which the Constitutional Court indirectly (because, as it repeatedly emphasizes, is not another instance in the system of general courts, but is a judicial body for the protection of constitutionality, whose task is 'only' to review the constitutionality of judicial decisions and proceedings, which preceded their issuance) corrects the decision-making practice of general courts, including decisions of the Supreme Court of the Czech Republic.

94. An alternative to civil proceedings is arbitration regulated by Act No. 216/1994 Sb., on Arbitration Proceedings and Enforcement of Arbitral Awards. Arbitration proceedings are based on voluntariness, where the decision in the dispute is entrusted to an impartial third party – the arbitrator – on the basis of an agreement of the participants under the conditions defined by law. The parties may agree that property disputes between them (with the exception of disputes arising from consumer contracts,[115] disputes arising in connection with the enforcement of decisions and incidental disputes), which are otherwise decided by a court, to be decided by one or more arbitrators, or by a permanent arbitral tribunal (arbitration agreement). An arbitration agreement may be validly concluded if the court settlement on the subject matter of the dispute is permissible.[116] An arbitration agreement may cover an individual dispute that has already arisen (an arbitration agreement), or all disputes that would arise in the future from a certain legal relationship or from a defined range of legal relationships (arbitration clause). There is currently no common practice of the insurers in the Czech Republic to use this type of proceeding and arbitration finds its place in specific areas, especially in disputes with an international element, especially between economically and legally comparatively strong partners, i.e., especially in mutual disputes between insurers, reinsurers, assistance

114. https://www.usoud.cz/en/.
115. The explicit impossibility of negotiating an arbitration clause in consumer contracts was incorporated into the act with effect from 1 Dec. 2016 for contracts concluded after this date. Until then, the arbitration clause in consumer relations was generally permissible, but under stricter conditions defined by law (e.g., the arbitration clause had to be negotiated separately and not as part of the terms governing the main contract, it had to contain true, accurate and complete information about the arbitrator and arbitration, etc.).
116. Cf. § 99 CPC.

companies, etc. Special rules for arbitration proceedings with an international element and matters of recognition and enforcement of foreign arbitral awards are set out in the provisions of §§ 117 et seq. of the AoPIL.

§5. CONSUMER PROTECTION

95. As in other segments of the financial market, considerable attention is paid to consumer protection issues in the insurance industry. Consumer law is largely harmonized by European law.[117] In the Czech Republic, consumer protection legislation is fragmented, not codified, and consumer law is a cross-cutting branch of law.

96. At the level of private law, the basic principles of consumer protection are regulated by the Civil Code. According to § 419 CC, a consumer is any individual who, outside their trade, business, or profession, enters into a contract or has other dealings with an entrepreneur.[118] The basic purpose of civil law regulation of consumer protection is to compensate for the factual inequality of contracting or otherwise acting parties, where the consumer is usually a weaker party,[119] which must be provided with the necessary information and rights so as not to be disadvantaged when dealing with professionals. From a broader perspective, consumer protection also includes requirements for the quality of goods, whether it is food safety or

117. These include, e.g., Council Directive 93/13/EEC of 5 Apr. 1993 on unfair terms in consumer contracts; Directive 2002/65/EC of the European Parliament and of the Council of 23 Sep. 2002 concerning the distance marketing of consumer financial services and amending Council Directive 90/619/EEC and Directives 97/7/EC and 98/27/EC; Directive 2011/83/EU of the European Parliament and of the Council of 25 Oct. 2011 on consumer rights, amending Council Directive 93/13/EEC and Directive 1999/44/EC of the European Parliament and of the Council and repealing Council Directive 85/577/EEC and Directive 97/7/EC of the European Parliament and of the Council; Directive (EU) 2019/2161 of the European Parliament and of the Council of 27 Nov. 2019 amending Council Directive 93/13/EEC and Directives 98/6/EC, 2005/29/EC and 2011/83/EU of the European Parliament and of the Council in regard to the better enforcement and modernization of Union consumer protection rules; In addition, for an indicative (but not exhaustive) overview of EU consumer protection rules, reference may be made to Annex 1 to Regulation (EU) 2017/2394 of the European Parliament and of the Council of 12 Dec. 2017 on cooperation between national authorities responsible for the enforcement of consumer protection laws and repealing Regulation (EC) No. 2006/2004.

118. According to § 420 CC, an entrepreneur is a person who, on their own account and responsibility, independently carries out a gainful activity in the form of a trade or in a similar manner with the intention to do so consistently for profit is considered. For the purposes of consumer protection, any person who enters into contracts related to their own commercial, production or similar activities, or within their trade, business or profession, or a person acting in the name or on the account of an entrepreneur is considered to be an entrepreneur.

119. Cf. § 433 CC: A person who acts as an entrepreneur with respect to other persons in economic transactions may not abuse their expertise or economic position to create or take advantage of the dependence of the weaker party and to achieve a clear and unjustified imbalance in the mutual rights and duties of the parties. It is presumed that the person who, in economic transactions, acts with respect to the entrepreneur in a manner unrelated to their own business activities is always the weaker party. The concept of the weaker party is therefore broader than the concept of the consumer. In a specific case, the weaker party may be the entrepreneur, if, e.g., deals with a professional in an area in which they are not equipped with the appropriate expertise.

product safety. Consumer protection is therefore not limited to consumer protection in contractual relations but covers broader aspects such as protection of persons and their health. The basis of private consumer protection is the regulation of consumer contracts in §§ 1810 et seq. CC. Rules regulated in §§ 1810 et seq. CC are applied to contracts concluded with a consumer by an entrepreneur. Consumer contracts are therefore not a special type of contract, and may be purchase contracts, contracts for work, loans, credits, custody, intermediation, travel contracts, insurance contracts, etc., including innominate contracts. In essence, it is a set of restrictions and deviations from the general regulation of obligations, the purpose of which is to balance the 'rules of the game', very often by prohibiting certain types of contractual arrangements, respectively banning certain behaviour of the entrepreneur as a stronger party that would unfairly and disproportionately disadvantage consumers.[120] In §§ 1820 et seq. the law regulates specific rules for concluding distance contracts and obligations arising from contracts negotiated away from business premises, where the law imposes broad pre-contractual information obligations on entrepreneurs and expands the consumer's options to withdraw from a concluded contract without giving any reason. Subdivision 2 regulates the special rules applicable to financial services, which thus affect, *inter alia*, insurance contracts. Private law regulation of consumer relations is also contained in a number of other regulations, such as Act No. 257/2016 Sb., on Consumer Credit, Act No. 170/2018 Sb., on the Distribution of Insurance and Reinsurance, Act No. 458/2020 Sb., on Business Conditions and Public Administration in the Energy Sectors (Energy Act), etc.

97. Public consumer protection is concentrated primarily in Act. No. 634/1992 Sb., on Consumer Protection (AoCP), which incorporates the relevant European law and regulates certain business conditions important for consumer protection, alternative dispute resolution for consumer disputes, the competence of public authorities in the field of consumer protection or consumer rights and consumers' associations (§ 1(1) of AoCP). The AoCP prohibits the use of unfair commercial practices (§ 4 AoCP), especially misleading commercial practices[121] and aggressive commercial practices.[122] It also prohibits discrimination against consumers in the provision of goods and services (§ 6 AoCP), imposes basic information obligations (§§ 9 et seq. AoCP) and regulates a number of other obligations which sellers are obliged to comply with when selling products or providing services. Last but not least, it regulates the supervision of the fulfilment of obligations regulated by this Act, which is primarily entrusted to the Czech Trade Inspection Authority

120. Cf. § 1813 CC: Stipulations which establish, contrary to the requirement of proportionality, a significant imbalance in the rights or duties of the parties to the detriment of the consumer are presumed to be prohibited. This does not apply to stipulations on a subject of performance or price if they are provided to the consumer clearly and understandably. Further cf. § 1814 CC, which contains an illustrative list of prohibited stipulations, including arrangements that exclude or limit the rights of the consumer arising from a defective performance or to compensation for harm, entitle the entrepreneur to terminate an obligation for no reason deserving special consideration without an appropriate notice period, or that allow the entrepreneur to change the rights or duties of the parties at their discretion. Disproportionate stipulations are disregarded unless invoked by the consumer (§ 1815 CC).
121. *See* §§ 5, 5a and Annex 1 to the AoCP.
122. *See* § 5b and Annex 2 to the AoCP.

(CTIA)[123] and in partial aspects to specialized public authorities such as the CNB, the Czech Agricultural and Food Inspection Authority,[124] the State Institute for Drug Control,[125] and the Czech Telecommunications Office[126] (for more details *see* § 23 AoCP). The CNB plays an important role in this area in relation to the supervised entities, as the law entrusts it with supervising compliance with the obligations set out in the Civil Code for distance contracts for financial services, compliance with the prohibition on unfair commercial practices, compliance with the prohibition of discrimination against consumers, compliance with obligations and rules for informing about the price of services and the method of determining them, or compliance with information obligations on out-of-court settlement of consumer disputes.[127] In addition to Act No. 634/1992 Sb., public regulation of consumer protection is contained in a number of special legal regulations, among others, for example, in Act No. 22/1997 Sb., on Technical Requirements for Products; Act No. 372/2011 Sb., On Health Services and on Conditions of their Provision (Health Services Act); Act No. 29/2000 Sb., On Postal Services and on Amendments to Certain Acts (Postal Services Act); Act No. 526/1990 Sb., on Prices, etc. Harming the consumer is also a criminal offence (*see* § 253 of Act No. 40/2009 Sb., Criminal Code).

98. The area of alternative dispute resolution for consumer disputes (ADR) is gradually gaining in importance, the basic aspects of which are also regulated in Act No. 634/1992 Sb., on Consumer Protection, in the provisions of § 20d et seq. The competent authority for ADR within the meaning of this Act is:

- in the field of financial services, the Financial Arbitrator within the scope of competence stipulated by the legal regulation governing the Financial Arbitrator;[128]
- in the field of electronic communications and postal services, the Czech Telecommunication Office within the scope specified in the legal regulation governing electronic communications and postal services;[129]
- in the field of electricity, gas, and heating industry, the Energy Regulatory Office within the scope of competence stipulated by the regulation governing electricity, gas, and heating industry;[130]
- in cases where the competence of the above-mentioned bodies is not given, the CTIA or another body authorized by the Ministry of Industry and Trade.

123. https://www.coi.cz/en/.
124. https://www.szpi.gov.cz/en/default.aspx.
125. http://www.sukl.eu/.
126. https://www.ctu.eu/.
127. *See* § 44a of Act No. 6/1993 Sb., on Czech National Bank, and § 23(8) of the AoCP.
128. Act No. 229/2002 Sb., on the Financial Arbitrator.
129. Act No. 127/2005 Sb. on Electronic Communications and on Amendment to Certain Related Acts (Electronic Communications Act), and Act No. 29/2000 Sb., on Post Services and on Amendment to Certain Related Acts (Act on Post Service).
130. Act No. 458/2000, Sb. on Business Conditions and Public Administration in the Energy Sectors and on Amendment to Certain Laws (Energy Act).

99. The purpose of ADR is to offer a fast, easier, less formal, cheaper, and more flexible alternative to the often lengthy, costly, and formalized civil court proceedings. The primary objective is to reach an amicable settlement of the dispute and the agreement of the parties.

100. In relation to the insurance industry, it is necessary to highlight the activities of the Financial Arbitrator[131] regulated by Act No. 229/2002 Sb., on the Financial Arbitrator. Pursuant to the provisions of § 1, the Financial Arbitrator is competent, *inter alia*, to resolve disputes between a consumer and an insurer or insurance intermediary in the distribution of life insurance or in the exercise of rights and fulfilment of life insurance obligations. The competence of the financial arbitrator in matters of insurance is thus exclusively limited to the area of life insurance, namely life insurance in the sense of private law, regardless of the public law classification of the product.[132] It should be emphasized that the Financial Arbitrator, unlike other bodies operating in the field of ADR, is entitled to give a binding decision on the merits, constituting a writ of execution under the CPC.[133] The Financial Arbitrator decides in administrative proceedings, which are regulated in the provisions of §§ 8 et seq. of Act No. 229/2002 Sb., in the alternative, Act No. 500/2004 Sb., Administrative Procedure Code. The Financial Arbitrator is thus a body entrusted in accordance with the provisions of § 7 of the CPC with the power to hear and decide disputes arising from private law, which are otherwise entrusted exclusively to the courts. However, the participants in the proceedings retain the guarantee of judicial review in accordance with the procedure pursuant to Part Five of the CPC (§ 7(2) and the Part Five of the CPC). Proceedings before the Financial Arbitrator are initiated at the consumer's application, free of charge, and the parties bear their own costs without the possibility of awarding costs to the successful party. The proceedings are governed by the principle of investigation, where the Financial Arbitrator is not bound by the participant's proposal and actively provides evidence. The Arbitrator bases their decision on the facts of the case and freely evaluates the evidence. In the decision by which the Arbitrator satisfies the consumer, even if only partially, they shall at the same time impose on the unsuccessful institution an obligation to pay a penalty of 10% of the amount that the institution is required to pay to the claimant, but at least CZK 15,000. The payment of CZK 15,000 shall be imposed even in cases where the subject of the dispute is not a monetary amount. These sanctions are revenue of the state budget.[134]

---

131. https://finarbitr.cz/en/.
132. For more details, *see* fn. 228, as well as the introduction to Part V. Insurance of the Person; further cf. e.g., resolution of the Financial Arbitrator of 10 Jan. 2017, file No. FA/ZP/1922/2016; resolution of the Financial Arbitrator of 29 Dec. 2016, file No. FA/ ZP/1897/2016, and the subsequent decision of the Financial Arbitrator on the objections of 30 Jan. 2017, file No. FA/ZP/1897/2016; or the resolution of the Financial Arbitrator of 30 Aug. 2016, file No. FA/ZP/141/2016, and the subsequent decision of the Financial Arbitrator on the objections of 11 Oct. 2016, file No. FA/ZP/141/2016 (available at https://finarbitr.cz/cs/reseni-sporu/sbirka-rozhodnuti.html), which states that the Financial Arbitrator is not competent to decide disputes from accident insurance, as it is a non-life insurance.
133. *See* §§ 15 and 17 of Act No. 229/2002 Sb.
134. *See* § 17a of Act No. 229/2002 Sb.

101. Residual competence for ADR in matters of insurance not falling within the competence of the Financial Arbitrator, i.e., for the area of non-life insurance, is according to the provisions of § 20e(d) of the AoCP entrusted to the CTIA. Unlike a court or the Financial Arbitrator, the CTIA is not entitled to make a binding decision on the merits. The primary objective of the proceedings regulated in the provisions of §§ 20n et seq. AoCP is to reach an amicable settlement of the dispute and the agreement of the parties. If the parties fail to reach an agreement within the set time limit,[135] the proceedings shall be terminated without further ado.[136] If no agreement is found in the ADR, either party may bring a civil action before the court with substantive and territorial jurisdiction. ADR before the CTIA is free of charge and the costs of the proceedings are borne by the participants themselves. Based on the empowerment in the provisions of § 20(x) of the AoCP, the CTIA lays down more detailed rules for the proceedings.[137] The proceedings shall be conducted in accordance with the Administrative Procedure Code, unless otherwise stipulated by law.

102. The law empowers the Ministry of Industry and Trade to entrust another body with the ADR in addition to the CTIA. This may be in accordance with the provisions of § 20(f) of the AoCP. A person who has requested in writing and proved that the conditions set out in Parts Three and Four of the AoCP have been met. For the insurance industry, such a body is currently the Office of the Ombudsman, which operates under the auspices of the CIA.[138] The competence of the CIA Ombudsman is (similarly to the CTIA) defined for consumer disputes for which the competence of the Financial Arbitrator is not given, i.e., for the area of non-life insurance. ADR before the CIA Ombudsman is subject to similar rules as in proceedings before the CTIA.

103. In addition to the above-mentioned authorities, consumers may also benefit from The European Online Dispute Resolution (ODR) platform operated by the European Commission[139] under Regulation (EU) No. 524/2013 of the European Parliament and of the Council of 21 May 2013 on online dispute resolution for consumer disputes and amending Regulation (EC) No. 2006/2004 and Directive 2009/22/EC (Regulation on consumer ODR), in the case of online sales or service contracts.[140]

104. A subtle but welcome change in the area of insurance was brought by the amendment to the Civil Code implemented by Act No. 171/2018 Sb., which, with

135. Which is ninety days from the commencement of the proceedings, while in the case of particularly complex disputes, the time limit may be extended by a maximum of another ninety days (*see* § 20t AoCP).
136. *See* § 20u(1)(d) AoCP.
137. Available at https://www.coi.cz/wp-content/uploads/2017/08/2017-08-15-pravidla-adr.pdf.
138. https://www.ombudsmancap.cz/.
139. https://ec.europa.eu/consumers/odr/main/index.cfm?event=main.home2.show&lng=EN.
140. 'Online sales or service contract' means a sales or service contract where the trader, or the trader's intermediary, has offered goods or services on a website or by other electronic means and the consumer has ordered such goods or services on that website or by other electronic means (Art. 4(1)(e) Regulation (EU) No. 524/2013).

effect from 1 December 2018, made it clearer on the issue of applying the general regulation of consumer contracts to insurance policies. It should be noted that the insurance policy is a financial service contract within the meaning of the provisions of § 1841 CC.[141] The said amendment, among other things, added to the provisions § 1811(3) CC explicit exception to the general pre-contractual information obligations for financial service contracts, as they are specially regulated in the particular sectoral law, which also avoids unwanted duplication when applying general and special regulation.[142] The amendment also added a similar exception to the provisions of § 1840(1)(f) CC, from which it is submitted that the general provisions for distance contracts and contracts negotiated away from business do not apply to financial services contracts, i.e., the provisions of §§ 1820–1840 CC. It follows from the above that the general provisions on consumer contracts in §§ 1810–1819 CC (except for the pre-contractual information obligations set out in § 1811(2) CC) and the special rules for financial services contracts set out in §§ 1841 et seq. CC will apply to insurance contracts.

105. In accordance with § 1842 CC, the regulation of financial services shall apply to a contract for financial services and the rights and duties arising therefrom if the contract was concluded solely through a means of distance communication. In other provisions, the Act stipulates more detailed rules for contracts concluded in this way, including broad pre-contractual information obligations of the entrepreneur (§ 1843 CC) or the possibility for the consumer to withdraw from the contract without giving any reason (§§ 1846 et seq. CC). Pursuant to the § 1846(1) CC, the consumer may exercise the right of withdrawal within fourteen days from the conclusion of the contract; however, if the information were communicated to them in accordance with §§ 1843–1845 CC only after the conclusion of the contract, they may exercise the right of withdrawal within fourteen days from the date on which it was communicated. A consumer may withdraw from a life insurance contract or a supplementary pension insurance contract within thirty days from the date on which they were informed by the entrepreneur that a distance contract had been concluded. In this context, it is necessary to mention the right of withdrawal provided for in the regulation of the insurance contract, specifically in § 2808(3) CC, which stipulates that if the insurance contract was concluded in the form of a distance contract, the policyholder[143] has the right to withdraw from the contract without giving any reason within fourteen days from the day of its conclusion or from the date on which they were provided with the insurance conditions, if they were provided at their request after the conclusion of the contract. In the case of insurance falling

141. For the purpose of regulating consumer contracts, a financial service contract shall mean any consumer contract concerning banking, credit, payment or insurance service, any contract concerning supplementary pension insurance, currency exchange, the issuing of electronic money and any contract concerning the provision of investment services or trading in the investment instruments market.
142. This solution is fully complied with European law, as the provisions of § 1811 CC transposes into the Czech law Directive 2011/83/EU of the European Parliament and of the Council of 25 Oct. 2011 on consumer rights, which also excludes financial services contracts from its scope (*see* Art. 3(3)(d) of the mentioned Directive).
143. Regardless of whether they are a consumer or entrepreneur.

under the life insurance category, the policyholder is entitled to withdraw from the contract within thirty days from the date on which they were notified of having concluded a distance contract, or from the date on which they were provided with the insurance conditions, if they were provided at their request after the conclusion of the contract. In the case of life insurance, the policyholder may thus withdraw from the insurance contract even if the contract was concluded otherwise than in the form of distance contract (§ 2808(3) CC in fine). If the policyholder withdraws from the contract under the regime of the said provision, the insurer shall return to them the premiums paid without undue delay, but no later than thirty days after the date on which the withdrawal becomes effective; in doing so, the insurer has the right to deduct the amount of insurance indemnity already paid. However, if the insurance indemnity has been paid in excess of the amount of the premiums paid, the policyholder, the insured person, or the ultimate beneficiary shall return to the insurer the amount of the insurance indemnity paid which exceeds the insurance premiums paid (§ 2808(5) CC). The policyholder does not have the right to withdraw from the contract in the case of short-term travel insurance contracts concluded for a period of less than one month (§ 2808(4) CC). It needs to be said that partial aspects of private law regulation of consumer protection are also contained in the relevant sectoral regulations, for the insurance sector in particular in AoDIR, which generally strengthens the client's[144] position in negotiations with insurance distributors.

§6. Compulsory Insurance

106. Insurance is most often established by concluding an insurance contract between the policyholder and the insurer. Three basic situations can be distinguished: (i) the conclusion of the insurance contract is left purely to the discretion of the contractual parties (so-called voluntary contractual insurance, which will be discussed in particular in Part II. The insurance Contract – General); (ii) the law imposes an obligation of conclusion of the insurance contract on one or both participants (so-called compulsory insurance); and (iii) insurance is established ex lege when certain statutory conditions are met (so-called statutory insurance).

107. If a certain human activity is associated with an increased risk of harm, or if there is a more intense public interest in the protection of potential victims,[145] the lawmaker constructs insurance as so-called compulsory insurance. This means that the decision whether (and, if so, under what conditions) the participants will conclude an insurance contract is not left to their will alone. This construction can most often be found in liability insurance. In this way, the lawmaker generally interferes with the contractual autonomy of a potential tortfeasor by not relying on them to

144. A Client means a person interested in conclusion of insurance or reinsurance contract, policyholder (*see* § 2 let. l) AoDIR), i.e., not only the consumer, but every person in a given position.

145. A similar motivation of the lawmaker can be found in many foreign legislations, closely cf. Fenyves, Attila; Kissling, Christa; Perner, Stefan et al. *Compulsory Liability Insurance from a European Perspective.* Berlin: De Gruyter, 2016, p. 431.

adequately assess the risks arising from their activity, and therefore imposes a preventive obligation to conclude an insurance contract and maintain insurance for the duration of such activity. The obligation of the potential tortfeasor to conclude an insurance contract in the role of policyholder is referred to as a contracting obligation. A specific exception is MTPL, for which MTPLIA stipulates the obligation to conclude an insurance contract not only for a potential tortfeasor but also for the insurer.[146] The obligation to conclude an insurance contract may also be imposed by a contract,[147] or decision of a court, or other public authority.[148]

108. The general legal regulation of compulsory insurance is concentrated in the Civil Code in the provisions of §§ 2779–2781. The obligation to conclude an insurance contract and any special rules for compulsory insurance is contained in specific sectoral legislation governing the activities to which the contracting obligation is associated. The contractual autonomy of the participants is not only limited in deciding whether to conclude an insurance contract, but also in the possibility of derogation from the general insurance regulation in the Civil Code, because in compulsory insurance, if the statute obliges a particular person to conclude an insurance contract, the contract may derogate from the provisions governing insurance (§§ 2758–2872 CC) only if permitted by a statute and if the scope of insurance provided by another statute is not thereby reduced (§ 2779(1) CC). In the case of cross-border compulsory insurance, it is also necessary to draw attention to the additional rules set out in § 132a(1) of the Insurance Act, according to which, if the legislation of a Member State stipulates the obligation to conclude insurance, this obligation is fulfilled only if the insurance contract is concluded in accordance with the legislation of a Member State relating to such private insurance.[149]

109. With regard to the public interest in the duration of compulsory insurance and the principle of the protection of victims, the insurer is also limited in the possibilities of terminating the compulsory insurance contract, as they have the right to withdraw from the contract or terminate compulsory insurance only if so permitted under another statute (*see* § 2781 CC). At this point, it is necessary to note that the sectoral legislation does not use this discretion – with a few exceptions[150] – and the

146. Cf. § 3(1) second sentence of the MTPLIA: 'The insurer is always obliged to conclude an insurance contract if the proposal for its conclusion does not contradict this Act, the law governing the insurance contract or the insurance conditions.'
147. Cf. § 1251(2) CC.
148. Cf. § 465(2) CC.
149. Cf. also Art. 179(2) of Solvency II. If the insurance risk is situated in the territory of more than one Member State, the insurance contract is governed by the law of the Member State which imposes the obligation to conclude such insurance.
150. An example of such an exception is the provision of § 12(1)(f) MTPLIA, which refers back to the Civil Code in the possibilities of termination of compulsory MTPL contract. A similar conception appears in response to the comments of the professional public in the latest legislation governing compulsory insurance – cf. e.g., § 22(5) of Act No. 254/2019 Sb., on Experts, Expert Offices and Expert Institutes; § 22(4) of Act. No. 354/2019 Sb., on Court Appointed Interpreters and Translators; or § 7(3) of Act No. 39/2020 Sb., on Real Estate Brokerage, which stipulate that the insurer may terminate the insurance only for the reasons stated in the provisions of the Civil Code governing the insurance contract. The explanatory memorandum to the latter provision explains that 'if

right of termination is often denied even where the insurer would have a legitimate reason to do so. To a certain extent, the lawmaker compensates for this restriction by explicitly allowing an arrangement establishing an insurer's other right to penalize the policyholder or the insured in the event of a breach of their obligation (§ 2781 second sentence CC). The principle of the protection of the injured party further precludes the insurer from deducting from the insurance indemnity from the compulsory insurance their premiums receivable or other insurance receivables, as otherwise generally permitted by law (§ 2787 second sentence CC). Compulsory insurance also cannot be interrupted (§ 2801(3) CC). Finally, the Civil Code also restricts the possibility of the insurer refusing the indemnity when it stipulates in § 2780 that in the case of compulsory insurance the insurer may refuse the indemnity only if false information, incompletely answered questions made in writing, or knowingly false or grossly distorted information were provided exclusively by the injured party or another person with the knowledge of the injured party. However, this provision is extremely problematic in its interpretation, as it is a relic of the former provision of § 5(3) of Act No. 37/2004 Sb., on Insurance Contract (AIC), and unfortunately does not reflect that the new Civil Code did not take over the possibility of refusing indemnity provided for in § 24(1)(b) AIC, according to which the insurer could refuse indemnity from the insurance contract if the beneficiary stated knowingly false or grossly distorted information concerning the scope of the insured event or concealed material information concerning this event.[151] However, the Civil Code in § 2809 only provides the right to refuse indemnity if the cause of the insured event was a fact which the insurer learned after the occurrence of the insured event, which they could not find out when negotiating insurance contract or its change due to culpable breach of duty in § 2788 and at the same time if, knowing this fact, they did not conclude such contract or would conclude it under other conditions (which corresponds to the former provision of § 24(1)(a) AIC). Thus, although the Civil Code has abandoned the possibility of refusing the indemnity previously regulated in § 24(1)b) AIC, the provision of § 2780 CC clearly refers to this provision – which does not exist in the current wording of the law. It is therefore not clear how the conditions for the application of § 2780 CC could be met, because this provision makes the possibility of refusing indemnity conditional on the provision of false information by the injured party (i.e., undoubtedly only in the event of a loss event, as the injured party is usually not known when concluding the insurance contract), while § 2809 CC allows the refusal of indemnity only in the case of providing false information when negotiating the insurance contract. It can therefore be agreed with Haas that the interpretation must be based on the clear

this option were not allowed, there could be a situation where insurers (insurance companies) may not be able to offer the insurance required by this Act. This would probably apply to smaller insurance companies, which would mean less competition in the market. At the same time, the assumption of increased risk by the insurer, if the legal regulation contained in this Act would not allow to respond to some specific and high-risk situations, which are also envisaged in the Civil Code, would undoubtedly have a negative impact on the premium.'

151. Cf. Explanatory Memorandum to the provisions of § 2809 CC: 'It is proposed not to take over into the new regulation the factual substance referred to in § 24(1)(b), which was incorporated into private law from the Criminal Code (§ 250a) and in which there is no factual reason to refuse indemnity; other legal institutes will suffice, in particular unjust enrichment and damages.'

intention of the lawmaker expressed in the explanatory memorandum to § 2809 CC and state that 'the statutory institute of sanctional refusal of indemnity on the grounds of "false claim" was by the lawmaker repealed completely for all, including compulsory insurance, and that § 2780 is a mere legislative error of the lawmaker and a so-called dead provision'.[152]

110. The already considerable legal uncertainty in the application of the general legal regulation of compulsory insurance is further exacerbated by the question of whether the insurer has, in addition to explicit legal restrictions (i.e., in particular restrictions on the possibility to refuse indemnity, terminate or withdraw from an insurance contract, or derogate from the general regulation of insurance at the expense of the scope of insurance stipulated by another law) the right to apply other sanction institutes, which are not regulated in any way by the general regulation of compulsory insurance, and thus not explicitly prohibited. In practice, it may include, for example, the right to a sanctional reduction of indemnity under the provisions of § 2800 CC or the refundation right under § 2866(1) CC. Here too, it is appropriate to agree with Haas' opinion that 'the insurer is entitled to use also in compulsory insurance all legal institutes, i.e., sanctions, which the whole Section 2 regulating the insurance offers them and which § 2780 and 2781 do not explicitly prohibit'.[153]

111. Mandatory regulation of compulsory insurance in the interest of the protection of victims in some respects fundamentally interferes with the basic principles of insurance, when (if so provided by another law) it obliges the insurer to pay even if the damage was caused by intentional conduct of the policyholder, insured, or other person (cf. § 2779(2) and § 2799 CC). This undoubtedly weakens the element of randomness, as the intentional conduct of the insured precludes randomness to a certain extent. However, the accidentality of the occurrence of an insured event is only relatively excluded, as it is preserved in relation to potential victims, for the protection of which compulsory insurance primarily serves. For obvious reasons, this rule is mainly used by MTPLIA, which at the same time establishes the insurer's right to get a refund from the insured in this case.[154]

112. Compulsory insurance is currently regulated in the Czech legal system by dozens of laws. These include, in particular, MTPLIA, which is undoubtedly the most important legislative act governing compulsory insurance and excels among others in very detailed regulation of insurance conditions, including the scope of insurance, conditions for entitlement to indemnity, indemnity limits, direct claim of the injured party against the insurer, comprehensive adjustment of exclusions, the sanction right of the insurer to get a refund from the insured, termination of insurance, and a number of other aspects of this compulsory insurance.[155] In comparison

152. Haas, Karel. In: Švestka, Jiří; Dvořák, Jan; Fiala, Josef et al. *Občanský zákoník: komentář. Svazek VI (§ 2521–3081).* § 2780 [ASPI System]. Wolters Kluwer [cit. 2020-9-3]. ASPI_ID KO89_f2012CZ. Available in the ASPI System. ISSN: 2336-517X.].
153. *Ibid.*
154. Cf. § 10(1) MTPLIA.
155. This is undoubtedly also due to the fact that this area is largely harmonized by the EU legislation (currently by the Directive 2009/103/EC of the European Parliament and of the Council of 16 Sep.

with the MTPLIA, the vast majority of regulations establishing compulsory insurance are limited to simply stipulating the obligation to conclude an insurance contract and maintain insurance for the entire period of activity, without the ambition to further regulate matters of the scope of insurance, temporal, material or territorial scope, indemnity limits, exclusion from insurance, possibilities of termination, or withdrawal from the insurance contract, etc.[156] Eventually, these regulations set the requirements for the scope of insurance only in a very general way, often even where a more detailed regulation would undoubtedly be desirable.[157] In addition to the above-mentioned MTPLIA, several other regulations can be found in which the lawmaker tries to define compulsory insurance more comprehensively, usually by setting at least minimum indemnity limits or closer defining the required scope of insurance.[158]

113. Other important compulsory insurances include compulsory insurance of healthcare providers according to Act No. 372/2011 Sb., on Health Services and on Conditions of their Provision (Health Services Act); and Act No. 373/2011 Sb., on Specific Health Services, compulsory insurance of authorized architects, engineers, and technicians active in construction according to Act No. 360/1992 Sb., on the Profession of Authorised Architects and the Profession of Authorised Engineers and Technicians Active in Construction, insurance of a carrier operating rail transport pursuant to Act No. 266/1994 Sb., on Railways, attorneys' insurance according to Act No. 85/1996 Sb., on the Legal Profession, and a number of others.

114. The vast majority of compulsory insurance in the Czech legal environment is conceived on the basis of liability insurance. However, it is also possible to come across other types of compulsory insurance, which can be constructed on the basis of property insurance,[159] guarantee insurance,[160] or, for example, accident insurance.[161] In addition, it is possible to encounter cases where the law does not strictly

2009 relating to insurance against civil liability in respect of the use of motor vehicles, and the enforcement of the obligation to insure against such liability).

156. Cf. e.g., the provisions of § 35(2)(d) of Act No. 266/1994 Sb., on Railways, provisions of § 16 of Act No. 360/1992 Sb., on the Profession of Authorised Architects and the Profession of Authorised Engineers and Technicians Active in Construction, or the provisions of § 146(2) of the Act No. 183/2006 Sb., on Urban Planning and the Building Code.

157. For example, § 45(2)(n) of Act No. 372/2011 Sb., on Health Services and on Conditions of their Provision (Health Services Act).

158. An example can be the provisions of §§ 24a–24c and § 35t of Act No. 85/1996 Sb., on the Legal Profession, or the provisions of § 48 of Act No. 449/2001 Sb., on Game Management.

159. For example, compulsory property insurance of agricultural public warehouses and stored goods pursuant to the provisions of § 23 of Act No. 307/2000 Sb.

160. Compulsory guarantee insurance in the event of bankruptcy of a travel agency pursuant to the provisions of §§ 6 et seq. of Act No. 159/1999 Sb., or compulsory guarantee insurance in the event of bankruptcy of an employment agency pursuant to the provisions of § 58a of Act No. 435/2004 Sb.

161. Compulsory accident insurance for members of a social cooperative pursuant to the provisions of § 764(2) of Act No. 90/2012 Sb., on Business Companies and Cooperatives (Act on Business Corporations).

oblige the participants to conclude an insurance contract, but regulates insurance as one of the possible alternatives for meeting legal conditions.[162]

115. The number of compulsory liability insurance in the Czech legal system is constantly increasing.[163] Examples include the recently adopted Act No. 254/2019 Sb., on Experts, Expert Offices and Expert Institutes;[164] Act No. 354/2019 Sb., on Court Appointed Interpreters and Translators;[165] or Act No. 39/2020 Sb., on Real Estate Brokerage.[166] All the mentioned regulations establish new compulsory liability insurance as one of the conditions for the performance of activities regulated by them. The new compulsory insurance is also included, for example, in the currently adopted Waste Act[167] or the forthcoming draft of the Act on Private Security Activities.[168]

I. Statutory Insurance

116. A specific case of the establishment of insurance is a situation where the insurance relationship arises without the conclusion of an insurance contract ex lege on the basis of a certain fact provided for by the relevant legislation. Characteristic of this type of insurance is the weakening of private law principles and, conversely, the strengthened public nature of the regulation. This is mainly due to the public interest in the existence of the relevant insurance, which is so urgent that in these cases the state does not rely on the free action of participants in private law relations or even setting an explicit obligation to conclude an insurance contract is not sufficient in these cases. The state enforces the certainty of the existence of the relevant insurance by the fact that the statutory insurance arises when the legal conditions are met without further ado, i.e., regardless of the will of its potential participants. A common element of all statutory insurance is the emphasis on the protection of the injured party.

117. At present, the only example of this approach in Czech law remains the statutory employer's liability insurance for damage in the event of an accident at work or an occupational disease. The legal regulation of this insurance was to be

162. An example may be the requirement of financial capacity of the carrier according to the provisions of § 8 of Act No. 111/1994 Sb.
163. *See also* e.g., Karfíková, Marie; Vybíral, Roman. *Povinné pojištění v moderní ekonomice.* Pojistné rozpravy. 2018, No. 35, pp. 72–75.
164. Published in the Collection of Laws on 9 Oct. 2019 with effect from 1 Jan. 2021.
165. Published in the Collection of Laws on 20 Dec. 2019 with effect from 1 Jan. 2021.
166. Published in the Collection of Laws on 17 Feb. 2020 with effect from 1 Jan. 2020; however, in accordance with the legal opinion of the Supreme Administrative Court of the Czech Republic contained in the judgement of 28 Nov. 2008, file No. 4 Ans 5/2007, in conjunction with Art. LXV of Act No. 277/2019 Sb., it is necessary to apply the provisions of § 3(3) of Act No. 309/1999 Sb., on the Collection of Laws and the Collection of International Treaties, as amended until 30 Dec. 2019, according to which the Act is effective on the fifteenth day after its promulgation, i.e., from 3 Mar. 2020.
167. Act No. 541/2020 Sb., Waste Act.
168. Available at https://www.psp.cz/sqw/historie.sqw?o=8&t=858.

repealed on 1 January 2013, when Act No. 266/2006 Sb., on Accident Insurance of Employees, which was supposed to bring, among other things, a change in the concept from liability insurance to accident insurance. The effectiveness of this Act was repeatedly postponed until the Act was finally repealed on 1 October 2015, without ever entering into force. Subsequently, the substantive legal regulation of compensation for occupational accidents and diseases, temporarily contained (until the entry into force of the new Act on Accident Insurance of Employees) in the transitional provisions of Act No. 262/2006 Sb., the Labour Code, was moved to the eleventh part of the Labour Code, in which the legal regulation of compensation for pecuniary and non-pecuniary damage in labour relations is concentrated. The statutory employer's liability insurance thus remains in a certain provisional regime, where the provisions of § 365 of the Labour Code refer to older legislation and stipulates that the statutory employer's liability insurance for damage in the event of an accident at work or occupational disease is governed by § 205d of the previous Labour Code[169] and the Decree of the Ministry of Finance No. 125/1993 Sb., Stipulating the Conditions and Premium Rates of the Statutory Employer's Liability Insurance for Damage in relation to Work Accident or Occupational Diseases. Insurance in accordance with § 1(3) of the mentioned Decree No. 125/1993 Sb. shall arise on the day of the first employment relationship with the employer and lasts for the duration of the employer's existence.

118. Another historical example of the legal regulation of statutory liability insurance is the system of MTPL before 2000, regulated by the Decree of the Ministry of Finance No. 492/1991 Sb. which was replaced with effect from 1 January 2000 by the system of compulsory-contractual insurance according to the currently still valid and effective Act No. 168/1999 Sb., on MTPL.

169. Act No. 65/1965 Sb., Labour Code.

Part I. The Insurance Company

Chapter 1. The Insurance Company: Its Form

119. The public law regulation of private insurance and the insurance industry in the Czech Republic is concentrated in IA, which, in connection with the relevant EU legislation,[170] regulates the sphere of private insurance and reinsurance and the conditions for the performance of insurance and reinsurance activities in the Czech Republic.

120. The IA defines who and under what conditions is entitled to perform insurance and reinsurance activities in the Czech Republic. According to the location of the registered office of the entity, it distinguishes between: (i) domestic insurance and reinsurance companies,[171] (ii) insurance and reinsurance companies from another Member State,[172] and (iii) insurance and reinsurance companies from third countries.[173]

121. Pursuant to the provisions of § 4(1) of the IA, a domestic insurance company that has been granted a permit by the CNB to conduct this activity may conduct insurance business in the Czech Republic. In addition to domestic insurance companies, the law allows insurance companies from another Member State to conduct insurance business in the Czech Republic in accordance with the principles of the single European market (single European passport), based on the right to establish branches, or, on the basis of freedom, to provide services temporarily.[174] As in the case of domestic insurance companies, the operation of insurance activities by insurance companies from third countries is subject to the approval of the CNB.

170. For more details, *see* General Introduction, §3. Sources of insurance law.
171. Domestic insurance (reinsurance) company means a legal person with its registered office in the territory of the Czech Republic, which has been granted a permit by the CNB to operate insurance (reinsurance) activities according to IA (*see* § 3(1)(b) and (h) IA).
172. An insurance (reinsurance) company from another Member State means a legal person with its registered office in the territory of another Member State, which has been authorized in that other Member State to conduct insurance (reinsurance) business (*see* § 3(1)(c) and (i) IA).
173. An insurance (reinsurance) company from a third country means a legal person with its registered office in the territory of a third country which, in accordance with the law of the country of its registered office, is authorized to conduct insurance (reinsurance) business (*see* § 3(1)(d) and (j) IA).
174. Reciprocally, an authorization granted by the CNB under the conditions set by IA to a domestic insurance company is valid for all Member States and entitles it to conduct insurance or reinsurance activities in the territory of another Member State, either through a branch or on the basis of freedom to provide services temporarily (*see* § 6(3) IA).

Analogous rules apply to the performance of reinsurance activities by reinsurance companies (§ 4(2) IA). In addition to reinsurance companies, insurance companies may also conduct reinsurance activities if the conditions are met (§ 4(3) IA).

122. Pursuant to the provisions of § 13(3) of the IA, a domestic insurance company is entitled to conduct insurance business as a joint-stock company or cooperative,[175] provided that its registered and factual office is located in the Czech Republic.[176] In addition to these explicitly regulated forms, insurance companies in the Czech Republic may also operate in legal forms arising from European law, specifically in the form of a European Company[177] or European Cooperative Society.[178] Other legal forms are not considered appropriate for insurance companies in terms of organization and liability.[179] In addition to IA, the general legal regulation of business corporations applies to the personal status and internal and external relations of insurance companies[180] or general regulations of legal persons in the Civil Code.[181]

123. The business name of an insurance company is protected. Provision of § 5(1) of the IA stipulates that a domestic insurance company shall use the word 'insurance company' (in Czech 'pojišt'ovna') in its business name and reserves the right to use this designation (and its translations or derivative forms) in the business name only to a legal entity that is authorized to conduct insurance business, with the exception of an insurance company whose business is regulated by another legal regulation and with the exception of an insurance intermediary and an independent claims adjuster.

124. In this context, it is necessary to draw attention to the need for terminological distinction between the term's insurance company and insurer. While in the Czech legal environment an insurance company is an entity operating in a business manner[182] the insurance activity, the term insurer is purely a private law term designating the contractual party concluding the insurance contract with the policyholder.[183] In accordance with the provisions of § 2758(1) CC, an insurer means a

175. In practice, in the vast majority of cases, domestic insurance companies are established as joint-stock companies.
176. *See* § 4(5) IA.
177. Council Regulation (EC) No. 2157/2001 of 8 Oct. 2001 on the Statute for a European company (SE) and Act No. 627/2004 Sb., on the European Company.
178. Council Regulation (EC) No. 1435/2003 of 22 Jul. 2003 on the Statute for a European Cooperative Society (SCE) and Act No. 307/2006 Sb., on the European Cooperative Society.
179. Přikryl, Vladimír; Čechová, Jana. *Zákon o pojišt'ovnictví. Komentář.* § 13 [System ASPI]. Wolters Kluwer [cit. 2020-2-29]. ASPI_ID KO277_2009CZ. Available in the ASPI System. ISSN: 2336-517X.]; identically the explanatory memorandum to the Insurance Act.
180. In particular, Act No. 90/2012 Sb., on Business Companies and Cooperatives (Act on Business Corporations).
181. *See* in particular the provision of §§ 118 et seq. CC.
182. However, the operation of insurance activities is also possible on a non-profit (non-commercial) principle, i.e., on the principle of reciprocity (in domestic practice in the form of a cooperative, abroad the form of a mutual insurance association is widely used).
183. However, even the lawmaker is not entirely consistent in distinguishing between these concepts, when, e.g., in the provision of § 1354(1) CC stipulates that 'if a pledged thing is insured and an

person who undertakes to provide the policyholder or a third person with insurance indemnity in the case of a random event covered by insurance (an insured event).

125. At the same time, it is necessary to realize that the ability to be an insurer (party to an insurance contract) does not depend on the existence or non-existence of a public permit to conduct insurance business. The lack of a public permit of the insurer does not result in the invalidity of the concluded insurance contract. This reflects the general principle that the application of private law is independent of the application of public law (§ 1(1) CC), while protecting the legitimate expectations and good faith of the other party, i.e., the policyholder, who in good faith expects the insurance contract to be valid.

126. In this respect, it is a departure from the previous regulation contained in the AIC, which in the provisions of § 3(f) defined the insurer as a legal person who is authorized to conduct insurance business under a special law.[184] At the same time, this does not change the fact that in practice the insurer will, in the vast majority of cases, be a legal person authorized by the CNB (or a supervisory authority in another Member State) to conduct insurance business.

§1. Business of Insurance and Operations Arising Directly Therefrom

127. Pursuant to the provisions of § 6(1) of the IA, an insurance company is only entitled to conduct insurance or reinsurance business within the scope of the permit granted to it by the supervisory authority. Insurance business is defined in the provisions of § 3(1)(f) IA and it means the activity consisting in assumption of insurance risks on the basis of concluded insurance contracts and provision of indemnity from them. The part of insurance business are operations arising directly therefrom, in particular activities related to the creation of insurance and its administration,[185]

---

insured event occurs, the insurance company shall provide a performance under the insurance contract to the pledgee ... ' It is clear that in this context it would be more appropriate to use the term 'insurer'.

184. For more details, *see* the explanatory memorandum to the provisions of § 2758 CC.

185. Insurance administration means activities ensuring the duration and updating of the status of insurance or reinsurance contracts (§ 3(2)(f) IA).

claims handling,[186] provision of assistance services,[187] investing,[188] concluding contracts by the insurance company with reinsurance companies on securing the insurance company's liabilities and activities aimed at preventing the occurrence of loss and mitigating its consequences.

128. Within the legal definition of business of insurance, it is therefore possible to distinguish: (i) the insurance business itself, consisting in assumption of insurance risks, which represents the immanent and core activity of insurance companies (and as such cannot be outsourced to another entity), and (ii) other operations that directly arise from the principal insurance business and are an integral part of it.

129. With regard to operations directly arising from the business of insurance, the law does not offer their legal definition and is limited to an exemplary list, according to which these activities include, in particular: (i) activities related to the creation of insurance and its administration; (ii) claims handling; (iii) the provision of assistance services; (iv) investments; (v) the conclusion of contracts with reinsurance companies; and (vi) activities aimed at preventing loss and mitigating its consequences. In addition to these explicitly regulated activities, insurance companies may perform other activities as part of the insurance business, but only provided that such activity directly results from the main insurance activity.

130. At this point, it should be noted that until September 2016 (when the implementing amendment to the IA adopted in connection with the Solvency II Directive came into force), the IA defined the main activities of insurance companies differently. It stipulated in § 6(1) that the insurance company is entitled to conduct 'only insurance or reinsurance business and related activities permitted by the competent supervisory authority'. The related activities were defined in the provisions of § 3(1)(n) as intermediary activities performed in connection with insurance or reinsurance business, consulting activities related to the insurance, claims handling, educational activities in the field of insurance and other financial services, intermediation of other financial services, and other activities related to the performance of authorized business of insurance.

131. An inconspicuous, yet a very significant material change consists in leaving the institute of the so-called related activities and replacing them with an integral business of insurance, of which operations arising directly therefrom are an

186. Claims handling means a set of activities, starting with an investigation aimed at determining the insurance company's obligation to perform from an event caused by an insured peril, determining the amount of such indemnity, and ending with its payment to the beneficiary or the injured party, or a statement that this obligation did not arise (§ 3(1)(n) IA).
187. Assistance services are provided for persons who fall into difficulties while travelling, while away from their home or their habitual residence, which consists in the obligation of an insurance company to provide, on the basis of prior payment of the premium, immediately available assistance to the beneficiary, if this person gets into difficulties as a result of the insured event (§ 3(2)(l) IA).
188. For the purposes of IA, investment means the management of all assets owned by an insurance or reinsurance company (§ 3(1)(m) IA).

immanent part. As the activities of domestic insurance companies before the amendment often included a number of related activities, including intermediation of insurance products or other financial services of third parties, the fundamental question arose in practice whether, after the amendment, did these companies lose the right to operate these related activities.

132. In seeking an answer to this question, it should first be noted that the IA amendment in question is literally based on Article 18(1) of the Solvency II Directive, which provides that the home Member State shall require each insurance company 'to limit their objects to the business of insurance and operations arising directly therefrom, to the exclusion of all other commercial business'.[189] Therefore, a change in domestic law cannot be justified by a mere reference to the requirements of the new directive. The explanatory memorandum to the relevant amendment to the IA states that:

> the law does not prevent an insurance or reinsurance company from carrying out any activity directly resulting from the authorized insurance or reinsurance business and it is only up to the insurance company or a reinsurance company to demonstrate to the supervisory authority that the activities which it pursues meet this condition. It is in the interest of consumer protection that the concentration of risks from insurance and reinsurance and other activities does not jeopardize the fulfilment of obligations arising from insurance and reinsurance contracts.

133. The obvious purpose of the legislation is therefore, on the one hand, to limit the activities of insurance companies to their core insurance business so that their other activities do not jeopardize the fulfilment of liabilities from the main insurance business,[190] on the other hand, the need to harmonize the scope of the authorized activity so that the single European passport system can function effectively in the Member States.

134. As part of the subsequent communication between the CIA and the CNB as the supervisory authority, the CNB postulated that:

> the relevant insurance company shall therefore prove that in each individual case the activity operated is either directly a business of insurance under an authorization granted by the CNB, or an operation directly arising from its insurance business. … an overview of the activities currently carried out by

189. Cf. also Art. 8(1)(b) First Council Directive 73/239/EHS of Jul. 24, 1973 on the coordination of laws, regulations and administrative provisions relating to the taking-up and pursuit of the business of direct insurance other than life assurance.
190. Cf. also Přikryl, Vladimír; Čechová, Jana. *Zákon o pojišťovnictví. Komentář.* § 6 [System ASPI]. Wolters Kluwer [cit. 2020-3-5]. ASPI_ID KO277_2009CZ. Available in the ASPI System. ISSN: 2336-517X.]: 'Neither the insurance nor the reinsurance company may perform other activities, as this would burden its activities with risks not directly arising from its insurance or reinsurance activities. (…).'

insurance companies … shows that it will probably not be possible to subsume some of the so-called related activities to the insurance company's permissible activities.[191] … the wording of the Insurance Act implies the criterion of product connection, i.e., taking into account the mutual relationship between the insurance company's 'own' insurance business and the arising operation, while the arising operation should have an accompanying, factually related character.[192]

135. The above question, whether insurance companies may continue to carry out activities corresponding to former 'related activities', must therefore be answered in part in the affirmative. The least problematic in this respect is education and consulting activities in the field of insurance, for which the direct link to the main insurance business is quite clear. As far as the intermediation of other insurance products is concerned, there is a consensus that it is also undoubtedly an activity directly arising from the business of insurance, which was later confirmed by the current distribution regulation.[193]

136. When it comes to intermediation of other financial services, the situation is more complicated. Even these activities are not generally excluded, and insurance companies can provide them, but only on condition that they are able to prove to the supervisory authority a factual (product) connection with the main insurance business. In this sense, the CNB later confirmed, for example, that 'insurance companies may, under certain conditions, provide or intermediate loans as an operation directly arising from an authorized insurance business', but 'the provision and intermediation of consumer loan which an insurance company would conduct as an arising operation must be authorized under the Consumer Credit Act'.[194]

137. At the same time, as confirmed by the case law of the CJEU,[195] it is not excluded that insurance companies can conduct the secondary activities indirectly through participation in other companies. If this is tolerated under certain conditions by the Court, it would be unreasonable to restrict insurance companies when only intermediating such related services, as it is clear that the risks of direct participation in such companies are higher than mere intermediation of such services.[196] However, according to the provisions of § 6(2) IA, a domestic insurance

191. Note of the CNB of Sep. 13, 2016, File No. 2016/099096/CNB/001, addressed to the Czech Insurance Association.
192. Note of the CNB of Oct. 24, 2016, File No. 2016/118136/CNB/001, addressed to the Czech Insurance Association.
193. Cf. § 5(2) AoDIR.
194. Note of the CNB of Apr. 27, 2017, File No. 2017/060589/CNB/560, addressed to the Czech Insurance Association.
195. Cf. e.g., judgements of the CJEU C-109/99 of Sep. 21, 2000 in the case *Association basco-béarnaise des opticiens indépendants v. Préfet des Pyrénées-Atlantiques*, ECLI:EU:C:2000:483; and C-241/97 of Apr. 20, 1999 in the case Försäkringsaktiebolaget Skandia, ECLI:EU:C:1999:179.
196. *See* Kunertová, Tereza. *Povolené činnosti pojišťoven v hledáčku bruselského regulátora.* Pojistný obzor. 2016, No. 2, pp. 47–50; also Přikryl, Vladimír; Čechová, Jana. *Zákon o pojišťovnictví. Komentář.* § 6 [System ASPI]. Wolters Kluwer [cit. 2020-3-5]. ASPI_ID KO277_2009CZ. Available in system ASPI. ISSN: 2336-517X.]: 'As is clear from the judgement of the ECJ (CJEU) of

company may not be an unlimited liability partner of a business corporation, including a corporation domiciled in a state other than the Czech Republic.

§2. MUTUAL INSURANCE, PREMIUM INSURANCE, OTHER

138. Although, historically, mutual insurance companies and mutual insurance associations have played an irreplaceable role in the Czech territory.[197] Their activities were violently interrupted as a result of the monopolization of the Czechoslovak insurance industry after February 1948.[198] Even after the de-monopolization of the market in the early 1990s, it was no longer possible to continue this tradition, and insurance companies based on the principles of reciprocity are currently of very marginal importance in the Czech Republic.[199]

139. In its classic form, where all owners of an insurance company are policyholders at the same time, and the risk assumed is distributed among the members of such insurance company, mutual insurance companies are not currently allowed in the Czech Republic because – after negative historical experience with the so-called campelics (in Czech 'kampeličky')[200] – fears of the abuse of this form still prevail.[201]

140. Nevertheless, in recent years, in connection with wider global trends, new forms of insurance businesses have appeared in the Czech Republic. As an example of this phenomenon, we can mention the developing concept of peer-to-peer insurance companies which build on the principles of shared economy.[202]

---

20. 4. 1999 – Case C-241/97 – Försäkringsaktiebolaget Skandia, EU law does not prevent insurance companies from managing their free assets and thus expanding their business activities through their participation in other legal entities.'

197. For more details, *see* General Introduction, §2. Historical Background of Insurance and Insurance Legislation.
198. Decree of the President of the Republic of 24 Oct. 1945, No. 103/1945 Sb., on the Nationalization of Private Insurance Companies.
199. As stated in the explanatory memorandum to Act No. 304/2016 Sb., amending the Insurance Act: 'In 1945, a total of 733 insurance companies and insurance associations operated on the territory of the Czech Republic, of which 158 were representations of foreign insurance companies and most of the domestic insurance companies had the legal form of a mutual insurance association. This development was interrupted by the centrally controlled economy, and even after the return to a market economy, there was no social need to return to insurance on the principle of reciprocity, although the legal form of a cooperative has been allowed in the insurance industry since 1991.' At present, only four registered entities operating as mutual insurance companies with the legal form of a cooperative can be traced in the Czech Republic.
200. Small credit unions, which were set up spontaneously in large numbers in the second half of the 1990s, and subsequently, as a result of insufficient regulation and supervision in combination with incompetent proceedings, often ended up in insolvency.
201. Přikryl, Vladimír; Čechová, Jana. *Zákon o pojišťovnictví. Komentář.* § 2 [System ASPI]. Wolters Kluwer [cit. 2020-3-4]. ASPI_ID KO277_2009CZ. Available in system ASPI. ISSN: 2336-517X.].
202. Although this trend follows the current dynamic development of digital technologies and services of the shared economy, significant reminiscences of traditional insurance solutions can be found at the core of the peer-to-peer insurance concept. In a way, it is a return to the roots, when peer-to-peer insurance builds on the principles of reciprocity and solidarity, where a certain group of people

141. In the domestic insurance sector, private business entities – insurance companies – continue to play a key role. The vast majority, operate as joint-stock companies.

142. However, not all insurance activities are subject to IA regulation. The IA excludes from its scope: (i) mutual insurance companies, the benefits of which vary according to the resources available and which require each of their members to pay the same contribution; (ii) institutions and insurance companies domiciled in another Member State excluded from the scope of an EU directive governing the taking-up and pursuit of the business of insurance and reinsurance; (iii) institutions other than insurance companies consisting in the provision of assistance in the event of a breakdown or accident of a road vehicle occurring in the territory of the Czech Republic; (iv) activities consisting in the insurance of export credits for the account of the state or with the guarantee of the state; (v) the activities of the Financial Market Guarantee System and the funds managed by it pursuant to the Act regulating the recovery procedures and resolution of the crisis on the financial market and the Act regulating the activities of banks; (vi) activities of the Securities Traders Guarantee Fund, etc.[203]

143. Pursuant to the provisions of § 2(4) of IA, this regulation does not apply to reinsurance activities performed or fully guaranteed by the Czech Republic and operated for reasons of public interest in the existence of insurance coverage, where the nature of the insurance risk or the market situation does not allow to obtain adequate private reinsurance. At present, there is no such entity in the Czech Republic.[204] In some aspects, the model is close to the activities of EGAP, which, however, is solely focused on the area of export risk insurance.

144. Also excluded from the scope of the Solvency II Directive are the 'very small insurance undertakings', i.e., those insurance companies whose annual gross premium income is less than EUR 5 million.[205] The IA has not taken over this Directive exemption and does not regulate this type of insurance company.[206] In

creates a financial fund from which it continuously satisfies the insurance needs of its members with an emphasis on simplicity and reduction of cost of the entire service. At the same time, it strongly recalls the beginnings of modern maritime insurance in European coastal states, when cargo ship owners created mutual funds to mitigate the financial consequences of maritime disasters. Mutual insurance associations in the Austrian Empire, e.g., worked in a similar way (*see* among others Dobiáš, Petr. *Vývoj právní úpravy pojistné smlouvy v rakouském Všeobecném zákoníku z roku 1811.* Sborník 200 let Všeobecného občanského zákoníku. Praha: Wolters Kluwer, 2011, pp. 615- 616).

203. *See* § 2(2) IA.

204. In the future, the creation of a similar entity may be practical especially in connection with the so-called uninsurable risks such as flood risk in flood areas or catastrophic drought risk in the agricultural insurance segment, which the actual commercial sector cannot satisfactorily cover.

205. Cf. Art. 4 of the Solvency II Directive; further cf. point (5) of the recital of the Solvency II Directive: 'Very small insurance undertakings fulfilling certain conditions, including gross premium income below EUR 5 million, are excluded from the scope of this Directive. … Undertakings that are excluded from the scope of this Directive should be able to make use of the basic freedoms granted by the Treaty. Those undertakings have the option to seek authorisation under this Directive in order to benefit from the single licence provided for in this Directive.'

206. *See also* the explanatory memorandum to Act No. 304/2016 Sb., amending the Insurance Act.

other words, the Czech regulation also affects the 'very small insurance undertakings' operating in the Czech Republic (with the exception of partial reliefs resulting from the principle of proportionality) in the entire scope of the regulation of the Insurance Act.

145. The social security systems and other related systems, which will be discussed below, are completely outside the system of private insurance and IA regulation (cf. in particular the provisions of § 2(1) IA).

§3. PUBLIC OR PRIVATE NATURE

146. There are a number of related insurance systems in the Czech Republic which are operated by the state, or other public, private, or mixed entities.

147. Although it is possible to find some common elements in comparison with commercial insurance activities, the IA excludes them from its scope due to their predominant differences (*see* § 2(1) IA).

148. These are, in particular, the following areas: public health insurance, sickness insurance, pension insurance, pension savings, state-contributory supplementary pension insurance, supplementary pension savings, employee pension insurance and employee accident insurance.

149. While private insurance is typically provided by commercial corporations and arises on the basis of an insurance contract concluded between the insurer and the policyholder (*see* §§ 2758 et seq. CC), the above-mentioned social security schemes[207] are characterized by the fact that they are operated and organized by the state (sickness and pension insurance), or other entities of a public or mixed nature (public health insurance provided by public health insurance companies).

150. As a rule, insurance in social security systems arises ex lege on the basis of the fact provided for by the relevant law, without requiring the conclusion of an insurance contract. Membership in social security systems is usually mandatory and the operation of the system is based on 'pay-as-you-go' financing.[208]

151. In addition to social security systems, other insurance systems operated with significant public interference can be found in the Czech Republic. These are, for example, activities consisting in the insurance of export credits on behalf of the state or with a state guarantee, i.e., the area regulated by Act No. 58/1995 Sb., on

207. *See also* for details Part V. Ch. 5. Pension Funds and Part VI. Private Insurance – Social Security.
208. 'In the social security system, liabilities payable in future years must be paid from premiums collected in the future, which is, however, uncertain. For this reason, social security liabilities are guaranteed by the state, while private insurance and reinsurance liabilities are guaranteed by insurance and reinsurance companies with all their assets.' (Přikryl, Vladimír; Čechová, Jana. *Zákon o pojišťovnictví. Komentář.* § 2 [System ASPI]. Wolters Kluwer [cit. 2020-3-4]. ASPI_ID KO277_2009CZ. Available in system ASPI. ISSN: 2336-517X.]).

Insuring and Financing Export with State Support. This Act regulates the activities of the EGAP, which has been operating on the Czech market since 1992 as a joint-stock company fully owned by the state. It is a credit insurance company focused on uninsurable political and commercial risks associated with financing the export of goods, services and investments from the Czech Republic. It is expressly stipulated that EGAP is not an insurance company under the IA and its activities are subject to the conditions of the Insurance Act only to the extent not regulated by Act No. 58/1995 Sb. For the purposes of supervision (performed by the CNB), EGAP is however considered an insurance company. The law governing the distribution of insurance and reinsurance shall not apply to the distribution of insurance and reinsurance operated by EGAP (§ 4(1) of Act No. 58/1995 Sb.).

§4. Factual Data[209]

152. In terms of basic macroeconomic indicators in the Czech Republic, the growth of the gross domestic product continued in 2019 for the sixth year in a row, but with a slight decrease in year-on-year growth to 2.6%, which was 1.1 pp above the EU average. The main pro-growth factors were final consumption expenditure as well as fixed-capital investments. The year-on-year growth rate of the average consumer prices reached 2.8%. The unemployment rate further decreased to 2.0%, which was the lowest level in the EU and well below the EU average of 6.3%.[210]

153. Gross premiums written continued to step up for the third year in a row, this time by 6.6% to CZK 165.9 billion. The overall growth of the sector was driven by the non-life insurance segment (by 13.2%), while life insurance decreased (by 5.0%). The total number of insurance contracts did not change significantly year-on-year (increased by 0.7%). However, the number of newly concluded contracts decreased (by 1.0%), which was mainly due to the drop in the new life insurance contracts (a decrease of 12.6%). The insurance sector had to cope with higher settlement costs due to the hurricane Eberhard and strong hailstorms. The insurance companies therefore resolved the second highest number of incidents in a decade.[211]

209. The data presented in this section were drawn mainly from the following sources, as of 31 Dec. 2019: CNB's Annual Reports (available at https://www.cnb.cz/en/about_cnb/performance/annual-reports/), CNB's Financial Market Supervision Reports (available at https://www.cnb.cz/en/supervision-financial-market/aggregate-information-financial-sector/financial-market-supervision-reports/), public statistical database ARAD operated by the CNB (available at https://www.cnb.cz/docs/ARADY/HTML/index_en.htm), Reports on Financial Market Developments of the Ministry of Finance (available at https://www.mfcr.cz/en/statistics/financial-market-analyses), CIA's Annual Reports (available at https://www.cap.cz/vyrocni-zpravy), CIA's regular reports on the development of the insurance market (available at https://www.cap.cz/statistiky-prognozy-analyzy/vyvoj-pojistneho-trhu).

210. Ministry of Finance of the Czech Republic. Report on Financial Market Developments in 2019, p. 3 (available at https://www.mfcr.cz/cs/soukromy-sektor/financni-stabilita-a-dohled/vyvoj-financniho-trhu/2019/zprava-o-vyvoji-financniho-trhu-v-roce-2-38890).

211. *Ibid.*, p. 4.

However, due to the continuing boom, a more pronounced acceleration in the growth rate of the insurance sector was not reflected in the insurance coverage ratio, which remained at 2.9%.[212]

154. The ratio of life and non-life insurance segments stabilized at 68:32% in favour of non-life insurance at the end of 2019, indicating a further deviation of both segments compared to developed Western European countries, where the ratio of both segments is roughly reversed.[213]

155. A positive pre-tax profit was achieved in all monitored financial market sectors. The insurance sector reported a significant increase in profit in 2019 (from CZK 17.4 billion in 2018 to a total of CZK 19.1 million in 2019), which, however, can be considered extraordinary as it was caused by transactions related to mergers of some insurance companies.[214]

156. At the end of 2019, according to CNB, a total of forty-eight entities operated on the Czech insurance market, of which forty-five were private insurance companies, one was a state-owned insurance company,[215] one reinsurance company,[216] and one interest association of insurers providing MTPL established by MTPLIA.[217] The private insurance segment consisted of twenty-five domestic insurance companies (thirteen of which are insurance companies with a decisive Czech participation and twelve are insurance companies with a decisive foreign participation) and twenty branches of foreign insurance companies (nineteen of which are from the EU and one is a branch of an insurance company from a third country).

157. At the end of 2019, out of the total number of forty-seven insurance companies,[218] seven were life insurance companies, twenty-six were non-life insurance companies and fourteen were mixed (composite) insurance companies operated in the Czech Republic.

158. While the total number of domiciled insurance companies and foreign branches is changing albeit very slowly,[219] the number of foreign insurance companies and branches of insurance companies providing cross-border services in the

---

212. *Ibid.*, p. 37.
213. *Ibid.*, for detailed statistics, *see* pp. 37 et seq.
214. *Ibid.*, p. 14.
215. Export Guarantee and Insurance Corporation (EGAP), mentioned in more detail above in §3. Public or Private Nature.
216. VIG RE reinsurance company (in Czech 'VIG RE zajišťovna, a.s.'), https://www.vig-re.com/.
217. Czech Insurers' Bureau, CIB (in Czech 'Česká kancelář pojistitelů', ČKP).
218. Including EGAP and CIB.
219. With a ten-year high as of 31 Dec. 2015, when a total of fifty-five entities were operating on the Czech market, a trend of gradual market homogenization can be observed, mainly due to mergers of large insurance companies – e.g., the merger of Czech market number two Česká pojišťovna a.s. with the the number six Generali Pojišťovna a.s. within the Italian group Generali under the new company Generali Česká pojišťovna a.s. at the end of 2019.

Czech Republic is constantly increasing. While in 2009 there were 621 subjects, by the end of 2019 a total of 976 subjects were registered, which represents an increase of more than 57% over 10 years.

159. The segment of insurance intermediaries underwent dynamic development, which was significantly affected by the new distribution regulation, which introduced three new basic categories of insurance intermediaries – independent intermediaries, tied agents, and supplementary insurance intermediaries. As a result of the transitional provisions of the AoDIR, some entities lost their activity and after the end of the transitional period the total number of insurance intermediaries decreased to 37,381 from the original number of 162,863[220] insurance intermediaries registered on the date of entry into force of the Act, i.e., to less than a quarter of the original number.[221] At the end of 2019, the CNB supervised a total of 38,481 insurance intermediaries, of which 1,164 were independent intermediaries, 35,049 were tied agents, and 2,268 were supplementary insurance intermediaries. In addition, another 6,612 insurance intermediaries operated in the Czech Republic with a home Member State other than the Czech Republic.

160. AoDIR has recently established a category of accredited persons who administratively ensure the professional examinations of insurance distributors in accordance with the new legislation. As of 31 December 2019, a total of eighteen of these accredited persons were registered.

161. Since 2011, the CNB has been conducting regular stress tests with selected domestic insurance companies. The results of the tests are published once a year in June in the Financial Stability Report or in a separate report at the second half of the year, depending on the timetable of the tests.[222] The results of the supervisory stress tests conducted in selected insurance companies in 2019 confirmed that the sector was sufficiently resilient to potential adverse shocks. The overall solvency ratio of the insurance companies tested was 157% after the application of shocks for market and insurance risks and was thus relatively high above the regulatory minimum of 100%.[223]

---

220. CNB. Annual Report 2019 (available at https://www.cnb.cz/export/sites/cnb/cs/o_cnb/.galleries/hospodareni/vyrocni_zpravy/download/vyrocni_zprava_2019.pdf); in absolute numbers and in terms of population, it was one of the highest figures in Europe, however, after deducting potentially inactive entities and duplicate entries, it was estimated that there are about 30,000 active intermediaries operating on the Czech market (as shown by the Evaluation of the Structure of Insurance Intermediaries Markets in Europe for 2017, published by EIOPA, available at https://www.eiopa.europa.eu/content/eiopa-evaluates-european-insurance-intermediaries-markets_en).
221. This confirmed, among other things, the above-mentioned assumption of a high proportion of inactive persons and duplicate entries in the original records; this negative factor should be eliminated in the future by the obligation of the insurance intermediary to actively pay the administrative fee every year if its authorization is to be extended for another twelve months.
222. *See* https://www.cnb.cz/en/financial-stability/stress-testing/insurance-sector/.
223. CNB's Supervisory stress tests of selected insurance companies 2019. p. 1. (available at https://www.cnb.cz/export/sites/cnb/en/financial-stability/.galleries/stress_testing/2019/zatezove_testy_pojistovny_2019_12_en.pdf).

162. The latest CNB's Financial Stability Report at the turn of 2019 and 2020 shows that the total assets of domestic insurance companies continued to decline in 2019 (by 4.1%, or CZK 19 billion, year-on-year to CZK 457 billion). The capital adequacy of domestic insurance companies remained sufficient in 2019, and the aggregate solvency ratio remained safely above the regulatory threshold.[224]

224. CNB's Financial Stability Report 2019/2020, p. 48. (available at https://www.cnb.cz/export/sites/cnb/en/financial-stability/.galleries/fs_reports/fsr_2019-2020/fsr_2019-2020.pdf).

Chapter 2. Access to Business: Authorization – Requirements and Procedures

163. As mentioned above in Chapter 1, an insurance company may operate as: (i) a domestic insurance company that has been granted a permit by the CNB to conduct insurance business; (ii) an insurance company from another EU Member State that may conduct insurance business in the Czech Republic on the basis of the right to establish branches or on the basis of the freedom to provide services temporarily; or (iii) an insurance company from a third country which has been granted a permit by the CNB to conduct insurance business (§ 4(1) IA). Similar rules apply to the conduct of reinsurance business by reinsurance companies (§ 4(2) IA).

164. Any application for the granting of a permit for insurance or reinsurance activity or for the acquisition of a participation pursuant to the IA may not be assessed with regard to the economic needs of the domestic market. The CNB will grant the permit without further notice if the conditions set by the IA are met (§ 4(4) IA).[225] The head office of the insurance company and the registered office in a public or similar register must be located in the same state as the state of its home supervisory authority (§ 4(5) IA) in order to fully guarantee the possibility of effective supervision of the entity.[226]

165. The conditions for granting a permit to conduct insurance business by a domestic insurance company are regulated in the provisions of §§ 13 et seq. IA. The CNB grants authorization to conduct insurance business pursuant to: (i) life insurance branches listed in Part A of Annex 1 to the IA, (ii) non-life insurance branches listed in Part B of Annex 1 to the IA, or according to (iii) non-life insurance groups listed in Part C of Annex 1 to the IA. The authorization shall cover the conduct of insurance business for all risks falling within those classes, unless an authorization to conduct insurance business is specifically required for certain risks falling within those classes.[227]

166. The CNB may limit the required scope of activity if the applicant's ability to financially or operationally ensure the operation of the activity to the required scope is not sufficiently proven (§ 13(1) IA). A domestic insurance company is entitled to conduct insurance business on the basis of, and, within the scope of, the

225. Cf. Art. 22 of the Solvency II Directive.
226. Cf. Art. 20 of the Solvency II Directive.
227. At this point, it is necessary to draw attention to the need for a consistent distinction between public and private definition of individual insurance classes (types) of insurance. While the IA defines individual insurance classes in Annex 1 for public law purposes, the Civil Code, as part of the regulation of an insurance contract, regulates individual types of insurance autonomously and independently of this public division. Therefore, e.g., accident or sickness insurance arranged as a supplement to life insurance falls within the scope of public law in the life insurance (*see* Part A, point I(c) of Annex 1 to the IA), although from private point of view it is non-life insurance. (cf. also systematic classification outside the scope of life insurance regulation in the provisions of §§ 2844–2846 CC, or Bohman, Ludvík. In: Hulmák, Milan a kol. *Občanský zákoník VI. Závazkové právo. Zvláštní část (§ 2055–3014). Komentář.* 1st ed. Praha: C. H. Beck, 2014, p. 1419).

permit granted by the CNB,[228] in the form of a joint-stock company or cooperative,[229] provided that its actual head office and registered office is in the Czech Republic (§ 13(2) and § 4(5) IA).

167. Provision of § 13(3) IA enshrines into national legislation the principle of the so-called single European passport, according to which the authorization granted by the CNB under the conditions set by the IA is valid for all other EU Member States and entitles the insurance company to operate insurance (or reinsurance) business in the territory of another EU Member State, either through a branch or under the freedom to provide services on a temporary basis.

168. The permit is granted by the CNB on the basis of an electronically submitted and paid[230] application, to which the applicant attaches documents proving the fulfilment of all conditions set by the IA, before the date of registration of the insurance company in the Commercial Register. The CNB shall decide on the application no later than six months from the date on which it was received. The authorization to conduct insurance business itself will be made available for a domestic insurance company on the day of its entry in the Commercial Register.

169. The formal requirements of the application, including the definition of the necessary annexes, are set out in an implementing legal regulation, which is currently the Decree of the CNB No. 307/2016 Sb., on Applications under the Insurance Act. The individual conditions for granting the authorization are set by the IA in the provisions of § 13(6).

170. In particular, it concerns: (i) the fulfilment of the condition for the existence of the head office and registered office in the territory of the Czech Republic; (ii) the fulfilment of all conditions for the conduct of insurance business laid down by the IA or directly applicable EU regulations, in particular as regards financial stability, adequacy of personnel, technical and organizational prerequisites; (iii) communication of the identification data of all persons who are to have a qualifying holding in the insurance company and who must at the same time meet the conditions for the due and prudent management of the insurance company; (iv) fulfilment of eligibility, credibility[231] and the absence of conflicts of interest in persons with key functions;[232] (v) the absence of obstacles to effective supervision; (vi) proof of

228. For more information on the scope of permitted activities, *see* §1. Business of insurance and operations arising directly therefrom.
229. Alternatively, in legal forms deriving from European law, i.e., in the form of a European Company or a European Cooperative Society; *see* closer Ch. 1. The Insurance Company: Its Form.
230. Currently, the acceptance of an application for a permit to conduct insurance business by a domestic insurance company or by a domestic reinsurance company is charged with the amount of CZK 200,000 (item 65 para. 1 let. c) of the tariff of fees in the Annex to Act No. 634/2004 Sb., on Administrative Fees).
231. *See also* Official information of the CNB of 5 Aug. 2020, on the Interpretation of the terms Credibility and Professional Competence (available at https://www.cnb.cz/export/sites/cnb/cs/legislativa/.galleries/Vestnik-CNB/2020/vestnik_2020_18_22320560.pdf).
232. A person with a key function means a person who effectively manages an insurance or reinsurance company or controls the activities of an insurance or reinsurance company or a person responsible

the corresponding amount of share capital;[233] (vii) proof of the origin of the insurance company's capital and other financial resources; (viii) meeting the prerequisites for the functionality and effectiveness of the proposed management and control system;[234] (ix) demonstration of the ability to hold eligible capital in the amount of the Solvency Capital Requirement (SCR)[235] and the Minimum Capital Requirement (MCR);[236] (x) submission of the insurance company's business plan based on realistic economic calculations;[237] (xi) designation of claims representatives in EU Member States in the case of vehicle liability insurance;[238] and (xii) an explicit statement by the applicant that the information provided in the application is true. All changes in the scope of the insurance activity performed are also subject to the authorization procedure,[239] if the IA does not stipulate that notifications will suffice[240] (§ 13(4) IA and further cf. §§ 19 et seq. IA).

171. In accordance with the requirements of European law,[241] the IA does not allow the authorization of a domestic insurance company to conduct insurance business simultaneously according to the life and non-life insurance branches (with the exception of concurrent life insurance and supplementary non-life accident or sickness insurance). However, this restriction does not apply in the case of mixed (composite) insurance companies, which were granted a permit in the Czech Republic prior to 1 April 2000 (i.e., before the entry into force of Act No. 363/1999 Sb.). They can thus operate insurance activities in the life and non-life insurance sectors in parallel, under the conditions of separate management of both activities.[242]

172. If an insurance company is established as a subsidiary of a foreign insurance company, reinsurance company, bank or securities trader, the CNB shall request the opinion of the supervisory authority of the Member State concerned

---

for risk management, compliance control, internal audit or actuarial activities, or a person responsible for other activities designated by the insurance company or reinsurance company as key; in the case of a monistic system of the internal structure of a domestic insurance or reinsurance company, the person who manages it is also a member of its board of directors (§ 3(6)(k) IA, further *see also* § 7(a) IA).

233. The minimum required amount of registered capital is graded according to the material scope of the performed activity; for more details, *see* the provisions of § 18 IA.
234. *See* the provisions of §§ 7 et seq. IA.
235. *See* the provisions of § 73 IA.
236. *See* the provisions of § 79 and § 79a IA, also *see* Ch. 3, §2. Solvency Control.
237. *See* the provisions of § 15 IA.
238. Cf. § 9a MTPLIA.
239. Acceptance of an application for a change in the scope of permitted activities of a domestic insurance company is charged with the amount of CZK 70,000 (item 65(5)(c) of the tariff of fees in the annex to Act No. 634/2004 Sb., on Administrative Fees).
240. In accordance with the principles of operation of the single European passport, a mere notification under the conditions is sufficient, especially in the case of establishing a branch of a domestic insurance company in another EU Member State (§ 20 IA) and starting insurance business in another EU Member State on the basis of freedom to provide services (§ 22 IA).
241. Cf. Arts 73 and 74 of the Solvency II Directive.
242. Cf. § 17 IA.

before granting authorization, in particular in relation to the credibility and competence of controlling entities or natural persons with key functions in legal entities subject to supervision (§ 16 IA).

173. Similar to the business of domestic insurance companies in other EU Member States, in principle, reciprocal rules apply in the case of insurance business in the Czech Republic operated by insurance companies from other Member States. In accordance with the single European passport, these entities are entitled to conduct insurance business in the Czech Republic on the basis of the right to establish branches or the freedom to provide services on a temporary basis, to the extent that they have been authorized to operate insurance activities in their home state without being subject to an authorization procedure in the Czech Republic (§§ 28 et seq. IA).

174. The situation is different in the case of insurance companies from third countries that cannot take advantage of the single European passport and their authorization to conduct insurance business in the Czech Republic is (similar to domestic insurance companies) subject to the CNB approval. In addition, they are entitled to operate their activities in the Czech Republic only through a branch as their subsidiary established in the Czech Republic and registered in the Commercial Register.

175. If the conditions pursuant to the provisions of § 49(3) IA are met, an insurance company from a third country may also conduct reinsurance business in the territory of the Czech Republic (§§ 32 et seq. of the IA).

176. A certain relief (transposing Article 167 of the Solvency II Directive) is provided by § 35 IA, which allows a third-country insurance company operating in more than one Member State to apply to the supervisory authorities in the Member States concerned for an advantage consisting in: (i) the SCR shall be calculated in relation to the full range of activities pursued within all Member States concerned; (ii) the minimum assets deposited will be located in only one Member State; and (iii) the MCR assets may be located in any Member State in which a third-country insurance company carries on its insurance business. The requirements will then be supervised by a single supervisory body chosen by the insurance company (for which the deposit referred to in point (ii) will also be located).[243]

177. According to § 1(3) of Act No. 6/1993 Sb., on the Czech National Bank, the CNB is entrusted with the competences of the administrative authority to the

243. These advantages may only be granted at the same time and only with the agreement of the supervisory authorities of all the Member States in which the application has been made. At the request of one or more of the authorities of the Member States concerned, the advantages shall be withdrawn.

extent stipulated by this Act and other legal regulations. The granting (or withdrawal) of a permit to operate insurance, or reinsurance business are thus decided by the CNB in administrative proceedings conducted pursuant to Act No. 500/2004 Sb., the Administrative Procedure Code.

178. A proper remedy against the CNB's first-instance decision is a remonstrance (in Czech 'rozklad').[244] The remonstrance is submitted to the CNB department that issued the decision and is decided by the CNB Bank Board.[245] The legality of administrative final decisions can be reviewed in review proceedings.[246]

179. After exhaustion of remedies in administrative proceedings, it is also possible to use judicial review of a final decision of the CNB, in particular by filing a complaint against a decision of an administrative authority pursuant to the provisions of §§ 65 et seq. Act No. 150/2002 Sb., Code of Administrative Justice, or subsequent cassation complaint pursuant to the provisions of §§ 102 et seq. of the said Act.

180. In justified cases, a constitutional complaint pursuant to the provisions of §§ 72 et seq. of the Act No. 182/1993 Sb., on the Constitutional Court, or submission to the European Court of Human Rights may occur.

244. Cf. § 152 of Act No. 500/2004 Sb., Administrative Procedure Code.
245. Cf. § 5(2)(h) Act No. 6/1993 Sb., on the Czech National Bank.
246. Cf. §§ 94 et seq. of Act No. 500/2004 Sb., Administrative Procedure Code.

Chapter 3. Supervision

181. The operation of insurance and reinsurance activities is subject to supervision.[247] The CNB is the body supervising the financial market in the Czech Republic.[248]

182. According to the provisions of § 44 of Act No. 6/1993 Sb., on the Czech National Bank, the CNB supervises, *inter alia*, banks, savings and credit unions, electronic money institutions, payment institutions, securities traders, securities issuers, the central depository, investment funds, market organizers with investment, non-bank consumer credit providers, consumer credit intermediaries, but for the purposes of this publication also above all insurance companies, reinsurance companies, insurance intermediaries, pension funds, pension companies and other persons operating in the field of insurance.

183. As part of its supervision, the CNB generally: (i) decides on applications for licenses, permits, registrations and consents pursuant to special legal regulations; (ii) monitors compliance with the conditions set out in granted licenses and permits; (iii) monitors compliance with laws and directly applicable regulations of the EU, if the CNB is authorized to do so by this Act or other legal regulations; (iv) monitors compliance with decrees issued by the CNB; (v) obtains information necessary for supervision under other legal regulations, enforces and verifies their truthfulness, completeness and uptodateness; (vi) imposes remedial measures and administrative penalties; and (vii) discusses and decides on proceedings on offences in supervised areas.

184. A supervision is performed by the CNB on an individual basis in relation to each individual supervised person, on a consolidated basis[249] or in a group,[250] or as supplementary supervision in financial conglomerates pursuant to Act No. 377/2005 Sb., on Financial Conglomerates.

247. A distinction can be found in national regulations as well as in domestic doctrine between the terms 'supervision' and 'surveillance'. The term 'supervision' (or 'state supervision') expresses the ultimate responsibility of the state for the situation in which in a certain state territory the supervision of financial activities carried out mostly by non-state entities takes place, while the performance of this supervision and its conditions is based on state authority and legal rules approved and enforced by the state. The performance of this supervision does not always have to be performed by the state and may be entrusted to entities other than the state, public and private corporations or self-governing institutions; the fact that the relevant supervisory activity is performed by an entity formally different from the state (especially the CNB) justifies a change in the designation of this activity for which the legislation uses the term 'surveillance'. Despite various terminological designations, however, the substantive content of state supervision and surveillance remains identical (Bakeš, Milan; Karfíková, Marie; Kotáb, Petr; Marková, Hana et al. *Finanční právo.* 6th revised ed. Prague: C.H. Beck, 2012, pp. 52–53).
248. https://www.cnb.cz/en/.
249. According to § 2(p) Act No. 377/2005 Sb.
250. Specific rules for group supervision in the insurance industry are regulated in the provisions of §§ 87 et seq. IA.

185. Last but not least, the CNB also performs important tasks in the area of consumer protection in financial markets, as the law also entrusts it with supervising compliance with the obligations set out in the Civil Code for distance contracts for financial services and compliance with the ban on unfair use of business practices, compliance with the prohibition of consumer discrimination, compliance with obligations and rules for informing about the price of services and the method of their determination, or compliance with information obligations on out-of-court settlement of consumer disputes.[251]

186. Specifically, for the area of insurance, the rules of supervision are regulated in the provisions of §§ 84 et seq. IA. The CNB supervises the insurance industry in the interest of protecting policyholders, insured persons, and beneficiaries[252] and with a view to maintaining the financial stability of insurance and reinsurance companies.[253]

187. In exercising its supervision, the CNB must carefully consider the potential effects of its decisions on the stability of the financial systems in the EU and take into account the potential pro-cyclical effects of its conduct, especially in times of exceptional movements in financial markets.[254]

188. In terms of scope, it is a comprehensive, legal, and financial supervision of the overall activities of the insurance company.[255]

189. The CNB specifies the purpose, objectives and means of supervision in a legally non-binding document entitled 'Long-term supervisory strategy of the Czech National Bank',[256] according to which 'The CNB's objective in the area of supervision, as defined by law, is to ensure financial stability and the safe and sound operation of the financial system in the Czech Republic, thereby contributing to achieving its primary objective, namely to maintain price stability.'[257]

251. Cf. provisions of § 44a of Act No. 6/1993 Sb., on the Czech National Bank, and provisions of § 23(8) of Act No. 634/1992 Sb., on Consumer Protection.
252. According to Art. 27 of the Solvency II Directive, the protection of policyholders and beneficiaries is the main objective of supervision.
253. The protection of the stability of insurance or reinsurance companies must not take precedence over the main objective of supervision, which is the protection of policyholders, insured and beneficiaries (both Přikryl, Vladimír; Čechová, Jana. *Zákon o pojišťovnictví. Komentář.* § 84 [System ASPI]. Wolters Kluwer [cit. 2020-5-17]. ASPI_ID KO277_2009CZ. Available in system ASPI. ISSN: 2336-517X.]; further cf. also Art. 28 and point 16 of the recital of the Solvency II Directive: 'Financial stability and fair and stable markets are other objectives of insurance and reinsurance regulation and supervision which should also be taken into account but should not undermine the main objective.'
254. Cf. Art. 28 of the Solvency II Directive.
255. Kubáň, Drahomír. *Účel dohledu v pojišťovnictví.* Pojistné rozpravy. 2019, No. 36, p. 26.
256. Long-term supervisory strategy of the CNB (available at https://www.cnb.cz/export/sites/cnb/en/supervision-financial-market/.galleries/long-term_supervisory_strategy/long-term_supervisory_strategy.pdf).
257. *Ibid.*, p. 4.

190. The CNB pursues these objectives in three main areas, namely in the area of supervision of: (i) compliance with prudential rules, (ii) compliance with the rules of conduct of business, and (iii) in the area of supervision of anti-money laundering and combating the financing of terrorism (AML/CFT).

191. The CNB perceives the insurance sector from the perspective of the entire financial market as a systemically important sector in which supervision should be based on continuous contact with insurance companies, must build on good knowledge of the actual functioning of individual insurance companies, should not rely solely on suggestions from the public, should be proactive, systematic, and requires a sufficient supervisory presence in selected entities.[258]

192. The CNB acts in supervision in cooperation with the EIOPA,[259] with other European Supervisory Authorities established by directly applicable EU rules, i.e., the European Banking Authority (EBA),[260] European Securities and Markets Authority (ESMA)[261] and the European Systemic Risk Board (ESRB),[262] with the supervisory authorities of other EU Member States, international organizations, central administrations and insurance organizations.

193. Insurance supervision is based on a prospective approach (i.e., taking into account possible future developments) appropriate to the nature, extent and complexity of the risks associated with the insurance or reinsurance activities. The supervision of insurance and reinsurance companies shall involve an appropriate combination of off-site activities and on-site inspections.[263] It should be carried out in a transparent manner taking into account the protection of confidential information,[264] the protection of policyholders, insured and beneficiaries and the stability of the sector and the financial system as a whole.

194. The subject of supervision are: (i) domestic and foreign insurance companies that conduct insurance or reinsurance activities in the Czech Republic, (ii)

---

258. *Ibid.*, pp. 36–38.
259. https://www.eiopa.europa.eu/; established by Regulation (EU) No. 1094/2010 of the European Parliament and of the Council of 24 Nov. 2010 establishing a European Supervisory Authority (European Insurance and Occupational Pensions Authority), amending Decision No. 716/2009/EC and repealing Commission Decision 2009/79/EC.
260. https://eba.europa.eu/; established by Regulation (EU) No. 1093/2010 of the European Parliament and of the Council of 24 Nov. 2010 establishing a European Supervisory Authority (European Banking Authority), amending Decision No. 716/2009/EC and repealing Commission Decision 200 9/78/EC.
261. https://www.esma.europa.eu/; established by Regulation (EU) No. 1095/2010 of the European Parliament and of the Council of 24 Nov. 2010 establishing a European Supervisory Authority (European Securities and Markets Authority), amending Decision No. 716/2009/EC and repealing Commission Decision 2009/77/EC.
262. https://www.esrb.europa.eu/home/html/index.en.html; established by Regulation (EU) No. 1092/2 010 of the European Parliament and of the Council of 24 Nov. 2010 on European Union macro-prudential oversight of the financial system and establishing a European Systemic Risk Board.
263. Cf. Art. 29 of the Solvency II Directive.
264. Cf. Art. 31(1) of the Solvency II Directive.

domestic and foreign reinsurance companies that operate in the Czech Republic,[265] (iii) persons to whom a performance of a certain activity has been entrusted by an insurance or reinsurance company pursuant to the provisions of § 7g of the IA, and (iv) other natural and legal persons, if so provided by the IA or another law.[266]

195. The object of insurance supervision (§ 85 IA) is, in the first place, compliance with IA and other legal regulations to the extent that they relate to the conduct of insurance and reinsurance activities, in particular:

- compliance of activities with the granted permit or right to establish branches or freedom to temporarily provide services;
- management of domestic insurance and reinsurance companies in terms of ensuring the fulfilment of their obligations (similarly for insurance and reinsurance companies from a third country in terms of ensuring the fulfilment of their obligations from their activities in the Czech Republic);
- amount, method of creation and use of technical provisions, compliance with the principle of prudent investment of assets, calculation of the SCR and MCR and adequacy of eligible capital of a domestic insurance company, third-country insurance company, domestic reinsurance company or third-country reinsurance company;
- fulfilment of duties imposed by the CNB;
- accountancy;
- management and control system;
- activities within the group (maintenance of usable capital at least in the amount of the group SCR, intra-group operations, concentration of group risks, compliance with the requirements for the management and control system at the group level, etc.);[267]
- compliance of the operated insurance activities with the statutory requirements for dealing with policyholders, insured persons and beneficiaries.

196. When exercising supervision in the form of on-site inspections, the relations between the CNB and supervised entities are governed by the Inspection Code,[268] unless otherwise provided by the IA (§ 94(1) IA).

---

265. While the supervision of the activities of a domestic insurance or reinsurance company (including its activities carried out through a branch or in the form of temporary provision of services) falls within the exclusive competence of the CNB (with the exception of supervision by the host Member State, *see* § 86(1) IA), an insurance and reinsurance company from another Member State which carries on its insurance or reinsurance business in the Czech Republic falls (with the exception of § 110 and § 111 of the IA) within the exclusive competence of the supervisory authority of its home Member State, without prejudice to the CNB's AML and CFT powers (§ 86(2) IA); in the case of insurance and reinsurance companies from third countries, the performance of supervision falls within the CNB's competence with regard to activities carried out in the Czech Republic, unless otherwise provided by the IA or an international agreement (§ 86(3) IA).
266. For example, insurance intermediaries according to AoDIR.
267. Cf. further §§ 87 et seq. IA.
268. Act No. 255/2012 Sb. on Inspection (Inspection Code).

197. In order to provide guarantees of impartiality, independence and absence of conflict of interest, the law stipulates certain restrictions for employees of the supervisory body who cannot perform supervision in the form of on-site inspections if they are vis-à-vis the inspected person in the position of a close person.[269]

198. Controllers are entitled, *inter alia*, to participate in meetings of the bodies of a domestic insurance or reinsurance company, to enter the premises of supervised persons and to request information and documents from them (§ 94(4) of the IA).

199. If the CNB discovers a breach of duties, it shall impose measures to remedy the deficiencies without undue delay and shall set a reasonable time limit. These remedial measures can take various forms depending on the breach of the duty in question (e.g., change of persons who no longer fulfil the conditions of eligibility and credibility, increase of technical provisions, change of auditor, preferential use of profit after tax to cover the unpaid loss or replenishment of the reserve fund or to increase the share capital etc.). All the above measures are primarily aimed at restoring the state of compliance with IA and other legislation.

200. A very detailed regulation in IA is devoted to situations where the fulfilment of the insurance or reinsurance company's obligations is endangered as a result of the identified deficiencies. In such a case, the CNB may, depending on the nature and extent of the deficiencies identified, take a number of measures, often with a significant impact on the activities of the supervised entity. Examples may be an obligation to submit a recovery plan (§ 98), a short-term financing plan (§ 98a), a suspension of the right to conclude insurance or reinsurance contracts (§ 102), an order to transfer an insurance or reinsurance portfolio (§§ 103 et seq.), restrictions or prohibitions of free disposal of assets, prohibition to pay out accessories, share in profit or similar performance resulting from the primary capital, increase of the SCR (§§ 95a et seq.), and, in the extreme case, introduction of compulsory administration (§§ 99 et seq.).

201. If the fulfilment of the insurance or reinsurance company's obligations is endangered, or if the conditions in the supervised person need to be adjusted temporarily, the CNB may also impose a preliminary measure consisting of a ban on concluding insurance or reinsurance contracts, restrictions or a ban on asset management without the CNB's consent, a ban on proceeding without the consent of the CNB pursuant to a decision of a statutory body, supervisory body, general meeting or a membership assembly, or in the suspension of the performance of a function to a person with a key function (§ 97 IA).

269. *See* § 45(2) of Act No. 6/1993 Sb., on the CNB; on the term 'close person', *see* § 22 CC.

202. Provision of § 95(10) IA explicitly enshrines the principle of opportunity, according to which the CNB may refrain from initiating proceedings to impose remedial measures.[270]

203. The extreme and toughest measure of the supervisory body is the revocation of the license to perform insurance or reinsurance activities (§§ 116 et seq. IA). The CNB withdraws the authorization immediately if:

- the insurance company is over-indebted (i.e., in a situation where the sum of the monetary expression of its liabilities exceeds the value of its assets);
- the remedial measure imposed did not restore its solvency;
- the insurance company obtained the authorization on the basis of incorrectly or incompletely stated decisive information or concealed such information;
- its financial situation does not guarantee the permanent fulfilment of its liabilities from insurance or reinsurance business;
- the insurance company has not complied with the MCR and has not submitted a short-term financing plan or such a plan has not been approved by the CNB;
- the insurance company has relocated its registered office outside the territory of the Czech Republic;
- the insurance company has not fulfilled the approved short-term financing plan within three months, or
- the insurance company requests so by its own decision.

204. The second paragraph of § 116 IA leaves the CNB some discretion in stipulating that the CNB may withdraw the authorization if the insurance company:

- does not meet any of the conditions for conducting insurance or reinsurance business;
- repeatedly or seriously breaches the IA duties, directly applicable regulation of the EU or a decision of the CNB;
- within one year from the date of entry into force of the decision granting it authorization to conduct insurance or reinsurance business, has not commenced an authorized activity; or
- does not conduct insurance or reinsurance business for more than six months.

205. Under similar conditions, the CNB also revokes the authorization of an insurance company from a third country, even in a situation where the authorization is revoked by a supervisory authority in another Member State due to its insufficient solvency or in its home state.

---

270. In particular if, due to: (i) the importance and extent of the breach or threat of a protected interest affected by the identified deficiency, (ii) the nature of the deficiency found, its consequence, the circumstances in which the deficiency occurred, or (iii) given the conduct of the domestic insurance or reinsurance company following the finding of the deficiency, it is clear that the purpose remedy has been already achieved.

206. As soon as the CNB's decision to withdraw the permit takes legal effect, the insurance company enters into liquidation, but even during this transitional period it follows IA, until the liabilities from its insurance activities are settled. However, it may no longer conclude insurance contracts, insurance intermediation contracts, extend insurance contracts already concluded or increase the sums insured or the limits of indemnity.

207. The rules of supervision in relation to the activities of an insurance or reinsurance company from another Member State operating in the Czech Republic (§§ 110–112 IA) and remedial measures in relation to the activities of insurance and reinsurance companies from a third country are specifically regulated (§§ 113–115 IA).

208. The IA defines the facts of offences in the insurance sector, separately for natural persons (§ 119), who may be fined up to CZK 1 million, and separately for legal entities and entrepreneurial natural persons (§ 120), for which the amount of the penalty can reach up to CZK 50 million. The administrative body competent to deal with offences under the IA is the CNB (§ 121).

209. The IA regulates the duty of confidentiality of persons authorized to perform supervision. They shall be bound by the obligation of professional secrecy with regard to the facts of which they have become aware in the course of their insurance supervision activities, with the exception of information provided in generalized or aggregated form from which it is not possible to identify the individual person concerned. This obligation continues even after the termination of the employment relationship. The obligation of professional secrecy also applies to members of advisory bodies and other persons involved in the exercise of supervision. The CNB may handle information obtained during the exercise of supervision only for the fulfilment of obligations under the IA.[271]

210. Specific analytical supervisory tools are regular stress tests of individual insurance companies, which the CNB uses to assess the resilience of financial institutions domiciled in the Czech Republic and the financial system as a whole. Scenarios for individual stress tests are prepared by the CNB; in the case of insurance companies, CNB also uses scenarios prepared by EIOPA. The stress test methodology is continuously updated and published in the Financial Stability Reports and on the CNB's website. The CNB has been conducting regular annual stress tests with selected domestic insurance companies since 2011. Every two years, European stress tests organized by EIOPA also take place, in which selected domestic insurance companies participate on an individual basis.[272] Every year, the CNB prepares and submits an informational report on financial market supervision to the Chamber of Deputies, the Senate, and the Government by 30 June, which also includes an

---

271. Further cf. Art. 64 of the Solvency II Directive.
272. For more details, *see* https://www.cnb.cz/en/financial-stability/stress-testing/insurance-sector/.

overview of discussed and sanctioned offences. The CNB publishes the financial market supervision reports on its website.[273]

211. The CNB cooperates in its supervision with the EIOPA. The establishment of this body was initiated by the so-called de Larosièr report,[274] prepared by a group of experts in response to the economic crisis of 2008. Based on their recommendations, the method of regulation of the EU financial sector was revised and a new system of European supervisory mechanisms was built, which in its new form began to operate in January 2011.

212. The European System of Financial Supervision (ESFS) consists of the ESRB, three European Supervisory Authorities – the EBA, the ESMA and the EIOPA and the supervisory authorities of each Member State. The European Supervisory Authorities shall be accountable to the European Parliament and the Council.

213. EIOPA was established by Regulation (EU) No. 1094/2010 of the European Parliament and of the Council of 24 November 2010. It is an EU body with legal personality, based in Frankfurt am Main. EIOPA covers insurance companies, reinsurance companies, insurance intermediaries, financial conglomerates and institutions for occupational retirement provision. Its main objective is to ensure, in cooperation with the other ESFS bodies, that the rules applicable to the financial sector are properly applied in order to preserve financial stability and ensure confidence in the financial system as a whole and effective and sufficient protection for financial services clients.

214. Within its respective competences, EIOPA shall contribute to the better functioning of the internal market, including in particular an efficient and consistent level of regulation and supervision, ensuring the integrity, transparency, efficiency and due functioning of financial markets, strengthening supervisory coordination at international level and preventing regulatory arbitrage. One of the main tasks of EIOPA is to contribute to the establishment of high-quality common regulatory and supervisory standards and practices, in particular by developing draft regulatory and implementing technical standards (adopted by the European Commission), guidelines, recommendations, and other measures, including opinions.

273. Available at https://www.cnb.cz/en/supervision-financial-market/aggregate-information-financial-sector/financial-market-supervision-reports.

274. The High-Level Group on Financial Supervision in the EU, Chaired by Jacques de Larosière (available at https://ec.europa.eu/economy_finance/publications/pages/publication14527_en.pdf).

§1. SOLVENCY CONTROL

215. As already mentioned, the main objective of insurance regulation and supervision is adequate protection of policyholders and beneficiaries.[275] The protection of policyholders presupposes that insurance and reinsurance companies are subject to effective solvency requirements[276] ensuring their long-term financial stability and contributing to the stability of the financial market as a whole.

216. In line with developments in risk management and in other financial sectors, Solvency II Directive introduced a new risk-oriented approach to the SCR and harmonized rules for valuing the assets and liabilities of insurance and reinsurance companies, including rules for the creation of technical reserves.[277]

217. The Solvency II regulatory framework is based on three pillars,[278] which include: (i) quantitative requirements, (ii) qualitative requirements for the establishment and maintenance of the internal control system, risk management and supervisory practices,[279] and (iii) rules for mandatory reporting and disclosure by insurance companies and reinsurance companies.[280]

218. From a solvency control point of view, the first pillar is based on quantitative requirements including procedures for calculating technical reserves[281] and capital requirements (SCR and MCRs), which are calculated either using a standard formula or (if the risk profile of the insurance or reinsurance company is not set to a standard formula) through a partial or complete internal model approved by the CNB. With regard to the very concept of solvency, IA defines solvency as the ability of an insurance or reinsurance company to ensure with its own resources the permanent fulfilment of liabilities from insurance or reinsurance activities (§ 3(2)(e) IA).

219. Pursuant to § 73 of the IA, a domestic insurance or reinsurance company are obliged to permanently maintain usable capital at least in the amount of the SCR, with regard to the entire scope of their activities. The rules for the calculation of SCR are regulated in detail in §§ 74 et seq. IA, in the CNB's implementing Decree No. 306/2016 Sb., and in the relevant EU delegated acts.[282]

---

275. Cf. point 16 of the recital and Art. 27 of Solvency II Directive.
276. Cf. point 14 of the recital of Solvency II Directive.
277. Cf. explanatory memorandum to Act No. 304/2016 Sb., amending the Insurance Act.
278. Similar to the banking regulations of Basel II.
279. It is assumed that quantitative solvency requirements cannot cover all the risks in the business of an insurance or reinsurance company and that certain risks should only be addressed by adequate management and control requirements; cf. explanatory memorandum to Act No. 304/2016 Sb.
280. This is done for the public, in the form of an annual report on solvency and financial condition, accessible free of charge in printed or electronic form (§§ 82 and 82a IA), and to the supervisory authority (§ 83 IA).
281. For more details, *see* Ch. 4. Technical Reserves and Investments.
282. Commission Delegated Regulation (EU) 2015/35 of 10 Oct. 2014 supplementing Directive 2009/138/EC of the European Parliament and of the Council on the taking-up and pursuit of the business of Insurance and Reinsurance (Solvency II); Commission Implementing Regulation (EU) 2016/

220. In calculating the SCR, the domestic insurance company is obliged to take into account all measurable risks to which it is exposed. It must include in the calculation all measurable risks arising from liabilities from existing contracts as well as contracts which it expects to be concluded within the next twelve months.

221. The SCR shall include, as a minimum, the underwriting, market, credit and operational risk (which includes legal risk excluding risk arising from strategic decisions and reputational risk) and shall correspond to the value of the primary capital risk of a domestic insurance or reinsurance company at the level of reliability of 99.5% and in time horizon of one year (§ 74 IA). In other words, the SCR is designated as the economic capital to be held by insurance and reinsurance companies to ensure that they are still able, with a probability of at least 99.5%, to meet their obligations to policyholders and beneficiaries over the next twelve months.[283] The domestic insurance or reinsurance company calculate the SCR at least once a year and continuously monitor the amount of usable capital and the SCR (§ 75 IA).[284]

222. The MCR is regulated in the provisions of §§ 79 et seq. IA. A domestic insurance or reinsurance company shall maintain a usable primary capital of at least the MCR calculated on a quarterly basis; the MCR corresponds to the amount of eligible primary capital below which policyholders and beneficiaries would be exposed to an unacceptable level of risk if the insurance and reinsurance company continued in their activities.

223. The decrease in the amount of usable capital below the MCR triggers the most serious intervention of the supervisory authority, which is the withdrawal of a permit to operate insurance, or reinsurance business.[285] The MCR ensures a minimum level below which usable capital should not fall. If the insurance company or reinsurance company has the capital in the amount of MCR, there is only 85% probability that it will be able to meet its obligations during the following year (compared to 99.5% for the SCR).

1630 of 9 Sep. 2016 laying down implementing technical standards with regard to the procedures for the application of the transitional measure for the equity risk sub-module in accordance with Directive 2009/138/EC of the European Parliament and of the Council; Commission Implementing Regulation (EU) 2015/2017 of 11 Nov. 2015 laying down implementing technical standards with regard to the adjusted factors to calculate the capital requirement for currency risk for currencies pegged to the Euro in accordance with Directive 2009/138/EC of the European Parliament and of the Council; Commission Implementing Regulation (EU) 2015/460 of 19 Mar. 2015 laying down implementing technical standards with regard to the procedure concerning the approval of an internal model in accordance with Directive 2009/138/EC of the European Parliament and of the Council, and others.

283. *See also* point 64 of the recital of Solvency II Directive.

284. Cf. *see also* Arts 100 et seq. of the Solvency II Directive.

285. Cf. § 116(1)(e) IA.

224. The MCR calculation is carried out according to a simple formula set out in Commission Delegated Regulation (EU) 2015/35, but at the same time it must not fall below the minimum amounts set out in § 79a IA and must be in the range of 25% to 45% of the SCR.[286]

§2. Supervision of Tariffs and Insurance Conditions

225. In accordance with Article 21 of the Solvency II Directive, Member States do not, in principle, require prior approval or regular notification of insurance conditions, premium rates or the technical documentation used to calculate them.[287]

226. Accordingly, the amount of premium rates and the content of insurance conditions[288] in the Czech Republic are not subject to prior approval, notification or revision by the supervisory authority.[289] However, the law sets out the basic criteria for determining the amount of insurance premiums. Pursuant to the provision of § 59 IA, a domestic insurance company and an insurance company from a third country are obliged to determine the premium amount on the basis of realistic actuarial assumptions and corresponding calculation methods so as to ensure the permanent fulfilment of all its liabilities from insurance business.

227. It is prohibited to use an aspect contrary to the principle of equal treatment when determining the amount of insurance premiums and for calculating insurance indemnity.[290] If the insurer uses nationality, racial or ethnic origin, pregnancy, maternity or other discriminatory aspects as a factor in determining the amount of premiums or for calculating the indemnity, no increase in premiums or reduction of indemnity is taken into account (§ 2769 CC).

---

286. Přikryl, Vladimír; Čechová, Jana. *Zákon o pojišťovnictví. Komentář.* § 79 [System ASPI]. Wolters Kluwer [cit. 2020-8-17]. ASPI_ID KO277_2009CZ. Available at system ASPI. ISSN: 2336-517X.]; identically the explanatory memorandum to Act No. 304/2016 Sb.; further cf. Arts 128 et seq. of the Solvency II Directive.
287. *See also* Arts 181 and 182 of the Solvency II Directive.
288. For the purposes of public regulation, insurance conditions mean contractual conditions prepared by the insurance company for concluding insurance contracts for individual insurance classes, for groups of these classes or for individual types of insurance concluded within the insurance class, especially general insurance conditions, special or supplementary insurance conditions (§ 3(2)(k) IA).
289. In this context, it is worth mentioning that prior to 31 Dec. 2008, an insurance company was obliged to submit the insurance conditions to the CNB upon its written request to check their compliance with legal regulations. If the CNB found that the insurance conditions did not comply with the legal regulation, it ordered the elimination of these deficiencies (§ 8(9) of Act No. 363/1999 Sb., Insurance Act, as amended with effect from 1 Apr. 2004). Prior to that, the content of the insurance conditions was even subject to the prior approval of the supervisory body, which was the Ministry of Finance (cf. in particular the provision of § 8(8) of Act No. 363/1999 Sb., as amended before 31 Mar. 2004, and even earlier provision of § 13(2) of Act No. 185/1991 Sb., on Insurance Business).
290. Compare closer Act No. 198/2009 Sb., on Equal Treatment and on the Legal Means of Protection against Discrimination.

228. Although, not expressly mentioned in § 2769 CC, following the judgement of the CJEU of 1 March 2011 in Case C-236/09, *Association belge des Consommateurs Test-Achats ASBL and Others v. Conseil des ministres*, which as of 21 December 2012, repealed Article 5(2) of Council Directive 2004/113/EC implementing the principle of equal treatment between men and women in the access to and supply of goods and services, the gender aspect, which was commonly used in insurance practice before, cannot be used to determine the amount of insurance or insurance benefits.

229. However, this does not affect the use of actuarial methods taking into account the gender factor for the assessment of insurance risk, the purpose of which is to ensure the fulfilment of liabilities from insurance or reinsurance activities, provided that this does not differentiate between premiums and claims by gender. Similarly, the use of age or health status in determining the amount of premiums and calculating claims for insurance risks, when the assessment of insurance risk is based on relevant actuarial methods and statistics, is not affected, if the difference in premiums are adequate (§ 59(2) IA).

230. If the insurance company fails to prove compliance with the above obligations for determining the amount of the premium at the request of the CNB, the CNB shall impose remedial measures on it (§ 59(4) IA).

231. In the context of the Czech insurance market, it is necessary to draw attention to the special regulation of § 3b MTPLIA, according to which the insurer is obliged to determine the premium in accordance with the conditions set by IA to ensure the permanent fulfilment of obligations arising from the operation of liability insurance for damage caused by the operation of a vehicle and the payment of Czech Insurers' Bureau (in Czech 'Česká kancelář pojistitelů') (CIB) contributions.

232. While the IA regulates the determination of the amount of premiums in general in relation to the insurance business as a whole, the MTPLIA regulates these rules explicitly and specifically in relation to the MTPL. This area has long been the object of increased interest from the CNB, as average premiums in this segment have long been on the verge of sufficiency, i.e., the ability to ensure the sustainability of liabilities arising from the operation of this sector, due to the highly competitive environment and steadily rising costs to fulfil obligations.[291]

291. For more details, *see* e.g., Silberová, Zuzana. *Dohled ČNB nad povinným ručením.* Pojistný obzor. 2017, No. 1, pp. 32–34; or CNB's Financial Market Supervision Report for 2018, p. 32 (available at https://www.cnb.cz/export/sites/cnb/cs/dohled-financni-trh/.galleries/souhrnne_informace_fin_trhy/zpravy_o_vykonu_dohledu/download/dnft_2018_cz.pdf).

Chapter 4. Technical Reserves and Investments

233. The adoption of the Act on Insurance Business of 1991[292] opened the insurance market in the Czech Republic and paved the way for the establishment of new insurance companies. Following these legislative changes, regulations on accountancy for insurance companies were adopted,[293] which stipulated the creation and location of technical reserves. Technical reserves are of undeniable importance in the management of insurance companies. Their creation is conditioned by the very meaning of insurance, which consists hugely in covering the negative consequences of accidental events.[294] The creation of technical reserves must be distinguished in particular for accounting purposes and for the solvency purposes.

234. The basic legal framework for the rules for calculating technical reserves is contained in the Insurance Act (§ 52 ff), and the detailed principles in directly applicable EU regulations.[295] According to that legal framework, any domestic insurance (or reinsurance) company[296] shall create technical reserves to settle liabilities from all insurance (or reinsurance) activities operated by it which are probable or certain, but their amount or the moment at which they arise is uncertain.[297] In other words, an insurance (or reinsurance) company must be able to meet its obligations at any time during its operations.

235. The technical reserves are usually determined by actuarial calculations. The value of technical reserves is equal to the sum of the value of the best estimate and the risk premium and corresponds to the amount that the insurance (or reinsurance) company would have to pay for immediate transfer of relevant liabilities from insurance (or reinsurance) activities to another insurance (or reinsurance) company. When calculating technical reserves, an insurance (or reinsurance) company shall calculate technical reserves in a prudent, reliable, and objective manner using information from financial markets and generally available data on underwriting risks and shall ensure the compliance of the calculation with such data and information.

292. Act No. 185/1991 Sb., on Insurance Business.
293. For example, Decree No. 502/2002 Sb. and Decree No. 503/2002 Sb., which implement certain provisions of Act No. 563/1991 Sb., on Accounting, for insurance companies.
294. *See*: Karfíková, Marie; Přikryl, Vladimír; Vybíral, Roman et al. *Pojišťovací právo*. 2nd revised ed. Praha: Leges, 2018; Karfíková, Marie; Přikryl, Vladimír, Čechová, Jana. *Základy pojišťovacího práva*. 1st ed. Praha: Orac, 2001; Řezáč, František; Oškrdalová, Gabriela et al. *Marketingové r˘í;zení; komerční; pojišťovny*. 1st ed. Brno: Masarykova univerzita, 2009.
295. *See* Arts 17–61 of Commission Delegated Regulation (EU) 2015/35 of 10 Oct. 2014 supplementing Directive 2009/138/EC of the European Parliament and of the Council on the taking-up and pursuit of the business of Insurance and Reinsurance (Solvency II).
296. An insurance (or reinsurance) company from another EU Member State which conducts insurance or reinsurance business in the Czech Republic shall create technical reserves to settle liabilities from this activity in accordance with the legislation of the home EU Member State (*see* § 52(2) IA).
297. This shall apply *mutatis mutandis* to an insurance (or reinsurance) company from a third country in relation to liabilities from insurance (or reinsurance) business conducted in the Czech Republic, unless an international agreement provides otherwise (*see* § 52(1) IA).

236. The value of the best estimate corresponds to the probability-weighted average of future cash flows, taking into account the time value of money using the relevant risk-free yield curve.[298] The calculation of the value of the best estimate is based on current and reliable information and realistic assumptions and is performed using appropriate actuarial and statistical methods. The cash flow projection used in the calculation of the value of the best estimate shall take into account all increases and decreases in cash necessary to settle liabilities from insurance or reinsurance activities, for the entire duration thereof. A domestic insurance (or reinsurance) company shall calculate the value of the best estimate without deducting receivables from the agreed reinsurance (§ 53 IA).

237. The value of the risk premium must be such as to ensure that the value of technical reserves corresponds to the amount that another insurance (or reinsurance) company could require to assume liabilities from insurance (or reinsurance) activities of insurance (or reinsurance) company.

238. The value of the best estimate and the risk premium shall be calculated separately.[299] In such case the risk premium shall be calculated as the cost of raising usable capital required to meet the SCR, which is related to relevant liabilities from insurance (or reinsurance) activities, and this throughout their duration. The rate used to determine the cost of raising such capital is determined by directly applicable EU regulation on the methods and assumptions of calculating the risk premium and is the same for all insurance (or reinsurance) companies.

239. Among other factors taken into account in the calculation of technical reserves (*see* § 55 IA) we should mention all costs related to the management of liabilities (obligations) from insurance (or reinsurance) activities, any increases in prices, costs and claims and all anticipated payments to policyholders and beneficiaries, including future non-guaranteed profit shares, with the exception of available bonus fund.[300]

240. When calculating technical reserves, the value of financial guarantees and contractual options contained in insurance and reinsurance contracts shall also be taken into account. Real assumptions based on current and reliable information are used to determine the probability of exercise of contractual options by policyholders, including early termination of contracts. These assumptions take into account,

298. A risk-free yield curve is used to discount future cash flows to their present value, the amount of which and its possible adjustments for each currency are determined by EIOPA; it can be adjusted through the so-called equalization adjustment or the volatility adjustment.

299. This does not apply if the future cash flows associated with insurance and reinsurance liabilities can be reliably replicated using financial instruments for which a credible market price is normally available. In such a case, the value of the technical reserves in relation to those future cash flows is determined on the basis of the market price of those instruments (*see* § 54(2) IA).

300. Retained earnings that were not intended to be distributed to policyholders and beneficiaries are considered an available bonus fund. This fund is not considered to be obligations from insurance or reinsurance activities.

implicitly or explicitly, the effects that future changes in financial and other conditions may have on the exercise of such options (§ 55(2) IA).

241. The law (§ 57 IA) requires the establishment of internal processes and procedures to ensure the suitability, completeness, and accuracy of the data used for the calculation of technical reserves[301] and to ensure the regular comparison of best estimates and assumptions with experience.[302] The adequacy of the level of technical reserves as well as the methods of their calculation (i.e., underlying statistical data are applicable and suitable for calculation) shall be proved to the CNB; if the rules are not respected, the CNB is entitled to increase these reserves.

242. The amount of technical reserves should also take into account the nature of the insurance pool as such. When conducting life insurance business, insurance companies usually create the following technical reserves:[303]

- Reserve for undeserved premiums (reflects the need for accrued income).
- Reserve for claims (reflects the need for accrued expenses).
- Life insurance reserve (intended to cover future liabilities).
- Reserve for premiums and discounts (if agreed).
- Life insurance reserve, if the investment risk is borne by the policyholder.
- Reserve for the fulfilment of liabilities from the applied technical interest rate and other numerical parameters.
- Non-life insurance premium reserve.
- and other reserves.

243. When conducting non-life insurance business, insurance companies usually create the following technical reserves:

- Reserve for unearned premiums.
- Reserve for insurance claims.
- Reserve for premiums and discounts.
- Equalization reserve (created in credit and guarantee insurance).
- Non-life insurance premium reserve.
- Reserve for the fulfilment of liability obligations for the obligations of the Czech Office of Insurers pursuant to the legislation regulating the motor vehicles liability insurance.
- and other reserves.

301. If it does not have sufficient data of reasonable quality to apply a reliable actuarial method when calculating technical provisions for part of its liabilities from insurance and reinsurance activities or claims on reinsurance contracts and for reinsurance special-purpose vehicles, it may use reasonable approximations, including individual approaches, to calculate the best estimate.

302. If, on the basis of this comparison, a systematic deviation between experience and the calculation of the value of the best estimate is identified, an insurance or reinsurance company shall adjust the actuarial methods or assumptions used in an appropriate manner.

303. Karfíková, Marie; Přikryl, Vladimír; Vybíral, Roman et al. *Pojišťovací právo*. 2nd revised edition. Praha: Leges, 2018, p. 133.

244. Financial stability and competitiveness of an insurance (or reinsurance) company is also affected by the ability of the insurance (or reinsurance) company to invest funds safely and profitably. There is no clear catalogue of concrete possible investments, nor an upper limit of the investment (as this would be contrary to the free movement of capital) but there are some rules to be followed.

245. Based on the precautionary principle and generally speaking, it is necessary that the investment be safe, liquid, and profitable with a suitably diversified portfolio of assets adapted to the nature and duration of insurance (or reinsurance) liabilities. A domestic (as well as third-country) insurance (or reinsurance) company (*see* § 60 IA):

- may invest only in assets whose risks it is able to properly identify, measure, monitor, manage, control and report and take due account of assessing its overall needs, and therefore continuously assess the impact of risk factors on its investments and all assets, in particular: invest assets to meet the SCR and MCR in such a way as to ensure the security, liquidity and profitability of the overall portfolio; the location of these assets must not at the same time restrict their availability;
- invests the assets to settle liabilities in a manner that is proportionate to the nature and duration of the insurance and reinsurance liabilities carried out and in the best interests of all policyholders and beneficiaries, taking into account the objective of any published investment policy; this must be ensured even in case of conflict of interest;
- diversifies its investments in such a way that there is no over-reliance on a particular asset, issuer, or group of persons or geographical area or excessive accumulation of risk in the portfolio as a whole, while investing in assets issued by the same issuer or issuers belonging to the same group risk concentration;
- in the case of investments in assets that are not traded on a European regulated market or a foreign market similar to a regulated market, does not exceed its prudent level; or
- enters into derivative contracts only on condition that the obligations arising therefrom contribute to reducing risks or facilitate efficient portfolio management.

246. Other special rules are stipulated for life insurance with the policyholder's investment risk (§ 61 IA). The insurance indemnity from the insurance belonging to the life insurance branches may have a direct link to the value of the investment fund's unit certificates or to the value of the assets of the insurance company's internal fund, which may be divided into units. The technical provisions relating to these liabilities must, as far as possible, be represented by those units or, if the units are not specified, by the assets of the internal fund. The indemnity from insurance falling within the life insurance branches may be directly linked to a share index or to a reference value other than the values specified above. In such a case, the technical reserves relating to these liabilities must be as much as possible represented by the shares corresponding to the reference value or, if the shares are not determined, by secured and marketable assets corresponding as much as possible to the assets on which the reference value is based.

247. Investment risks include, in particular, liquidity risk (if the insurance or reinsurance companies are unable to settle their investments and other assets when financial obligations are due) and concentration risk (exposure to all risks with a potential loss that is large enough to jeopardize solvency or financial condition); the diversification effect reduces both kinds of risks. The ability to meet its obligations is also affected by the currency in which the obligation is due.

248. EU law (implemented into national law – *see* § 62 IA) requires the keeping of special records of assets the source of which is technical reserves. A domestic (as well as third-country) insurance company shall keep records of assets intended for settlement of liabilities at the moment of the occurrence of a liability from its insurance or reinsurance activities, for the payment of which these assets are intended, and shall continuously update these records.

Chapter 5. Accountancy

249. As public interest entities, insurance and reinsurance companies are obliged to keep accounts in accordance with Act No. 563/1991 Sb., on Accounting (Accounting Act).[304] The accountancy of insurance and reinsurance companies is however further and concretely regulated in the implementing regulation – Decree No. 502/2002 Sb.,[305] focusing on entities that are insurance companies. The decree regulates in particular:

- the arrangement and designation of items in the financial statements and consolidated financial statements and the content of the items in those financial statements;
- the layout and content of the explanatory and supplementary information in the notes to the financial statements and consolidated financial statements;
- the methods of consolidating the financial statements and the procedure for including the entities in the consolidation group;
- accounting methods and their use;
- indicative chart of accounts of insurance and reinsurance company (including export insurance companies and the Czech Insurers' Bureau).

250. In accordance with general accounting regulations, all entities are required to keep accounts that are correct, complete, conclusive, comprehensible, clear, and in a manner that includes the permanence of accounting records. Accounting is correct as long as it does not contradict the law, is complete if all accounting cases for the given period are accounted for, is conclusive when individual records are conclusive and the entity has carried out all relevant inventories, and is understandable if it is allowed to determine, reliably and unambiguously, the exact content of individual accounting cases.[306]

251. Financial statements represent the accounting record (document) by which an insurance company presents its financial results to users who are primarily the insurance company's shareholders or its employees (e.g., the board of directors, management, creditors, investors or the interested public). An insurance (or reinsurance) company which prepares financial statements or consolidated financial statements in accordance with the Accounting Act is obliged to have these financial statements or consolidated financial statements verified by a statutory auditor or audit company (hereinafter the 'auditor') appointed by the insurance (or reinsurance) company in a way stipulated by the law regulating auditing activities.

---

304. To *see* the text (in Czech) consult: https://www.zakonyprolidi.cz/cs/1991-563/zneni-20180101.
305. To *see* the text (in Czech) consult: https://www.zakonyprolidi.cz/cs/2002-502.
306. For more details, *see* Karfíková, Marie; Přikryl, Vladimír; Vybíral, Roman et al. *Pojišťovací právo.* 2nd revised ed. Praha: Leges, 2018; Janasová, Marie. *Účetnictví pojišťoven v ČR.* 1st ed. Ostrava: VŠB – Technická univerzita Ostrava, 2006; Huleš, Jan; Hornigová, Jana. *Účetnictví pojišťoven.* 2nd updated and revised. Praha: Linde, 2009.

252. The selection of the auditor is up to the specific insurance (or reinsurance) company. The name of the designated auditor is then notified to the CNB, including information on their expertise, experience and the facts that could hinder the performance of duties.[307] The CNB has though the power to reject the auditor for reasons exhaustively defined by law.[308] If the CNB rejects the selected auditor, the insurance or reinsurance company must notify the CNB of the selection of a new auditor within thirty days of the delivery of the rejection.

253. The CNB may even order an insurance (or reinsurance) company to carry out an extraordinary audit if it considers that the audit of the financial statements or consolidated accounts has not been carried out in accordance with the law or if the auditor fails to comply with their reporting obligation set out in the law governing audit activities (§ 80a IA). Following the above, the auditor for the extraordinary audit is appointed by the CNB and the costs are also covered by the CNB. If the suspicions for which an extraordinary audit has been established are confirmed, then the costs must be borne by the original auditor, as in this case the error is imputable to them due to lack of expertise or diligence. The CNB may even eventually order the verification of the management and control system, in whole or in part, or the verification of the information published in the report on solvency and financial condition. A report on this verification is prepared by the auditor in accordance with CNB's Decree No. 306/2016 Sb., Implementing Certain Provisions of the Insurance Act.[309]

254. A very important aspect is the principle of transparency, which is also reflected here, especially thanks to the legally defined scope of the information obligation. Users are informed through obligation to publish the relevant documents (financial statements and annual reports – *see* below). The annual report is the second significant document (accounting record), which has a similar regime as the financial statements. However, it has a rather representative character towards the

---

307. The notification on the selection of the auditor shall contain (§ 80(4) IA):

- the name of the statutory auditor or the name of the audit company and the registration number assigned by the Chamber of Auditors of the Czech Republic;
- the time, scope and description of the auditor's current activities in the field of accounting for insurance (or reinsurance) companies;
- disciplinary measures taken by the Chamber of Auditors of the Czech Republic or another similar institution abroad against the auditor, if any; and
- a solemn declaration by the auditor that there is no interconnection with the insurance (or reinsurance) company in which it is to carry out the audit of the accounts or consolidated accounts.

308. The CNB shall reject the auditor if they are or have been a member of a statutory body, a supervisory body, an audit committee, a procurator or a branch representative, a key official or an employee of the insurance (or reinsurance) company in the last two years prior to the audit or consolidated accounts; or if their experience in the accounting of the insurance (or reinsurance) company or their previous experience in auditing an insurance (or reinsurance) company does not provide a precondition for a proper audit of the financial statements or consolidated accounts, given the scale and complexity of the activities carried out by the insurance (or reinsurance) company.

309. To *see* the decree (in Czech) consult: https://www.zakonyprolidi.cz/cs/2016-306.

public, presenting an insurance company's business and past and future developments. According to the Accounting Act, the financial statements are an integral document and consist of a balance sheet, a profit and loss statement, and an appendix. In addition, it may include a statement of cash flows or a statement of changes in equity. Entities are required to present information in the financial statements as of the end of the balance sheet date.

255. No later than four months after the end of the accounting period,[310] a domestic insurance (or reinsurance) company shall submit its annual report and consolidated annual report to the CNB in accordance with the Accounting Act, which includes audited financial statements, and publishes it via a remote access. If the general meeting or membership assembly of a domestic insurance (or reinsurance) company does not approve the financial statements or consolidated financial statements within that period, that insurance or reinsurance company shall send it to the CNB together with the reasons for which it was not approved.

256. An insurance (or reinsurance) company shall be obliged to publish information on themselves, the composition of shareholders and the structure of the group of which it is a part, to the extent, in the manner, and within the time limits fixed by the implementing decree.[311] An insurance (or reinsurance) company shall publish on its website both an annual report and a consolidated annual report for at least the last three accounting periods. Information on the legal, management and organizational structure, including an indication of all controlled entities and significant associates and branches belonging to the group, shall be disclosed annually at group level; this shall apply *mutatis mutandis* to an insurance holding company and a mixed financial holding company domiciled in the territory of the Czech Republic.[312]

257. An insurance (or reinsurance) company shall also publish a report on the solvency and financial situation and the nature and effects of significant changes in its activities after the approval by the competent authority, unless such information is provided as part of the group report on solvency and financial situation.[313]

258. The specific regulation applies to public health insurance governed by Act No. 48/1997 Sb., on Public Health Insurance, which sets out the conditions and

---

310. Unlike the general regulatory approach fixed in Act No. 90/2012 Sb., on Business Corporations, the deadline for convening a general meeting or membership assembly for the approval of regular financial statements is for the purpose of insurance business stipulated differently.
311. *See* §§ 24 and 25 of CNB's Decree No. 306/2016 Sb. The required data shall be published on its website at least in the Czech language in the form of an unlocked data file available for download in a suitable and commonly used format, namely *.pdf, *.doc, *.docx or *.odt. The numerical data contained herein are also published in an additional data file in a suitable and commonly used format, in *.xls, *.xlsx or *.ods. The required data shall be published as of the date of 31 Mar., 30 Jun. and 30 Sep. within six weeks after the end of the relevant calendar quarter and as of 31 Dec. within four months after the end of the calendar year.
312. *See* § 82(2) IA.
313. *See* § 82(3) IA.

scope of health care provided.[314] Health insurance companies have specific accounts, they have further defined special group of accounts that correspond to their purpose and specific activities. They do not create adjustments items or account for them unless stipulated by a special regulation. They only account for statutory reserves in accordance with applicable laws.

314. For more *see*: Vančurová, Alena; Klazar, Stanislav. *Sociální a zdravotní pojištění – úvod do problematiky*. 2nd ed. Praha: ASPI, 2008.

259. Insurance (or reinsurance) company is – as any legal entity – subject to corporate income tax. Corporate income tax[315] is enshrined in the second part of Act No. 586/1992 Sb., on Income Taxes (Income Tax Act)[316] starting from §§ 17 et seq.

260. Taxpayers are legal entities, organizational units of the state, mutual funds, sub-funds of a joint-stock company with variable share capital, trust funds, funds managed by pension companies, and other taxpayers specified by law.[317] Taxpayers are therefore all[318] legal entities, not only those created by registration in the Commercial Register, such as foundations and endowment funds which are listed in special public registers.

261. The Czech law divides all taxpayers into tax residents of the Czech Republic or tax non-residents. Taxpayers are tax residents of the Czech Republic if they have their registered office or headquarters in the territory of the Czech Republic, which means the address of the place from which the taxpayer is controlled. Tax residents have a tax liability that applies both to income from sources in the territory of the Czech Republic and to income from sources abroad. Taxpayers are tax non-residents if they do not have their registered office in the territory of the Czech Republic or if international agreements stipulate otherwise. Non-resident taxpayers have tax liability that applies only to income from sources in the Czech Republic.[319]

262. The corporate income tax period is defined as a calendar year, marketing year, the period from the record date of the merger or division of the corporation or transfer of assets to the shareholder until the end of the calendar year, or financial year in which the conversion or transfer of assets became effective, or the accounting period if that accounting period is longer than a continuous twelve-month period. At the same time, the marketing year is a twelve-month accounting period, which can only begin on the first day of a month other than January. The accounting period can be up to three months longer than the twelve months.[320]

---

315. The theoretical aspects of corporate income tax are analysed in detail in Czech doctrine. *See* particularly Bakeš, Milan; Karfíková, Marie; Kotáb, Petr; Marková, Hana et al. *Finanční právo.* 6th revised ed. Praha: C. H. Beck, 2012; Smržová, Petra; Mrkývka, Petr. *Finanční a daňové právo.* 2nd updated and supplemented ed. Plzeň: Aleš Čeněk, 2016.
316. To *see* the text (in Czech) consult: https://www.zakonyprolidi.cz/cs/1992-586.
317. *See* § 17(1) of Income Tax Act.
318. With some exceptions stipulated by law. One such exception is the CNB.
319. *See* § 17(3) and (4) of Income Tax Act.
320. *See* § 21a of Income Tax Act.

263. The subject of the tax is income or revenues, from all activities and from the disposal of all assets (property). Both monetary and non-monetary benefits[321] might represent income. Revenue generated by an exchange is assessed similarly to revenue generated by a sale.

264. The Income Tax Act also defines certain kinds of income that are not subject to tax. These legal exemptions apply, within the area of insurance business, only to health insurance companies. Exempt is the income of a health insurance company in the form of public health insurance premiums, fines imposed on policyholders or premium payers, penalties imposed on premium payers, surcharges to the insurance premium assessed by the employer, reimbursement of the costs of reimbursed health services incurred by the health insurance company as a result of the culpable unlawful conduct of a third party towards the insured, payments for occupational health services and specific health care from the employer, surety according to the legal regulation governing departmental, branch, company and other health insurance companies, repayable financial assistance from the state budget to cover the costs of provided paid services after the exhaustion of the reserve fund in the event of insolvency of General Health Insurance Company of the Czech Republic (in Czech 'Všeobecná zdravotní pojišťovna'), special-purpose subsidies from the state budget, receivables for reimbursed health services provided in the Czech Republic to foreign insured persons, which are natural persons for whom health services have been reimbursed in accordance with promulgated international social security agreements or directly applicable EU law.

265. The tax base is calculated as the difference by which income, with the exception of non-taxable income and income exempt from tax, exceeds expenses (costs), while respecting their material and temporal connection to the given tax period. The determination of the tax base for taxpayers who keep accounts is based on profit or loss, always without the influence of International Accounting Standards.[322]

266. The tax base might be further reduced by items deductible from the tax base exhaustively stipulated in § 34 of the Income Tax Act. Among the items that might be deductible from the tax base we should mention primarily a valid determined tax loss[323] and support of research and development or support of vocational

321. Non-monetary benefits are evaluated in accordance with Act No. 151/1997 Sb., on Property Valuation, unless the Income Tax Act provides otherwise.
322. *See* § 23 of Income Tax Act.
323. Such loss may be deducted from the tax base in the two tax periods immediately preceding the tax period or in the five tax periods immediately following after the period for which the tax loss is calculated.

education.[324] Furthermore, donations provided to municipalities, regions, organizational units of the state and legal persons in the Czech Republic, as well as legal persons that are organizers of public collections (for purposes stipulated by law) may be deducted from the tax base.[325]

267. Some statutory revenues are not included in the tax base as they form a separate tax base. The separate tax base includes all income from profit shares, settlement shares, shares in the liquidation balance or similar benefits, in the amount including tax withheld abroad, paid to taxpayers from sources abroad in the relevant tax period. The separate tax base does not include tax-exempt income.[326]

268. The corporate income tax rate is set at 19% (with exceptions below). The tax is calculated as the product of the tax base (reduced accordingly by items reducing the tax base and by deductible items) and the tax rate. The tax rate for the basic investment fund is 5%.[327] The tax rate of 15% applies to a separate tax base. So, the corporate income tax rate in the Czech Republic is differentiated.

269. The calculated tax may be further reduced by tax rebates (defined by the Income Tax Act). It is mainly the tax incentive for the employment of workers with altered working ability[328] or it can also apply the promise of investment incentives pursuant to Act No. 72/2000 Sb., on Investment Incentives.

270. Part Three of the Income Tax Act regulates common provisions for income taxes, lists expenses that are tax deductible[329] and describes expenses that cannot be recognized as tax expenses.[330]

---

324. If the deduction for research and development or the deduction for vocational training cannot be deducted due to a low tax base or tax loss, it may be deducted at the latest in the third period following the period in which it arose.
325. *See* § 20 of Income Tax Act.
326. *See* § 20b of Income Tax Act.
327. The tax rate is 0% for a fund of a pension company or a pension insurance institution. That the tax rate is set at 0% instead of the tax exemption, is chosen by the state deliberately in order to be able to monitor financial flows.
328. Tax is reduced by the amount of CZK 18,000 for each employee with a disability or the amount of CZK 60,000 for each employee with a severe disability (*see* § 35 of Income Tax Act).
329. *See* § 24 of Income Tax Act, e.g., depreciation of tangible assets, the residual value of tangible assets, membership fee to a legal person, if the obligation of membership arises from special legal regulations or is a necessary condition for the operation of the object of business or the performance of activities, the premiums paid by the taxpayer, in so far as they relate to income which is subject to tax and which is not exempt, and the premiums paid by the employer to the insurance company for insuring the risk of compensation of wages, salaries or remuneration; social security contributions and contributions to the state employment policy and public health insurance premiums paid by the employer; expenses provided to funds to ensure the competence of the Czech Insurers' Bureau defined by the MTPLIA, with the exception of expenses for the creation of the Loss prevention fund etc.
330. *See* § 25 of Income Tax Act, e.g., expenses (costs) for the acquisition of tangible assets and intangible assets; expenses for increasing the registered capital, including repayment of loans; insurance premiums paid for a member of the statutory body and another body of a legal entity due to liability for damage caused to the company in the performance of its function; paid profit shares; penalties, interest on arrears and fines; non-monetary benefits provided by the employer to employees

271. Tax depreciation plays an important role among tax-deductible items. Tax depreciation has a completely different function from accounting depreciation. The methods of tax depreciation take into account the fiscal interests of the state as well as the state's approach to stimulating the investment activity of business entities. The subject of the tax return is the depreciation of the tax, recognized as an expense to achieve, secure, and maintain income. The manner in which assets may be depreciated is determined exhaustively for tax purposes by the Income Tax Act. Tax depreciation means a certain part of the price of an asset for a tax period that can be claimed as a tax-deductible expense. For that purpose, the assets are divided into tangible and intangible.

272. Tangible assets are defined for the purposes of tax depreciation in the provisions of § 26 of the Income Tax Act. The basic rule is that tangible assets are individual movables or sets of movables with a separate technical and economic purpose, the entry price of which is higher than CZK 40,000 and which have operational and technical functions lasting longer than one year. Tangible assets are also buildings, houses or non-residential premises, as well as most buildings, permanent crops with a fertility period of more than three years, adult animals and their groups whose entry price is higher than CZK 40,000 and other property.

273. Tangible assets are depreciated from the so-called entry price (or sometimes also the increased entry price).[331] It means in particular:

- acquisition price, if the tangible assets are acquired for payment;
- own costs of own-account production;
- the value of an outstanding claim secured by a transfer of rights, in the case of tangible movable property which remains the property of the creditor; and
- reproduction acquisition price in other cases determined in accordance with the Property Valuation Act.

274. The residual value is therefore the difference between the entry price and the total depreciation of the asset. In the first year, a taxpayer classifies tangible assets into depreciation groups[332] for which the depreciation period is determined. The depreciation period varies from three to fifty years depending on the different depreciation group. The taxpayer can also choose between straight-line and accelerated depreciation. However, the method of depreciation cannot be changed during the depreciation period, i.e., it remains the same.

275. Thus, start-up costs, intangible research and development results, software, valuable rights and other assets that are accounted for as intangible assets defined by accounting regulations, if acquired for payment, by contribution of a partner or

---

in the form of a contribution to cultural programs, tours, sports events and printed books; the creation of reserve and other special-purpose funds; entertainment expenses, in particular entertainment, refreshments and gifts etc.

331. *See* § 29 of Income Tax Act.

332. *See* § 30 of Income Tax Act.

silent partner or a member of a cooperative, if acquired by transformation, donation or by inheritance, or created by own activity for the purpose of trading with it and its entry price is higher than CZK 60,000 and the useful life is longer than one year. The provision of § 32(4) of the Income Tax Act stipulates depreciation for intangible assets with the right to use for a definite period, so that the depreciation period is the same as the period of use. For other intangible assets that are depreciated, the law specifies the depreciation period in the range of eighteen to seventy-two months.

276. At the end of May 2019, the Czech Government approved a bill that would change the method of determining the tax deductibility of insurance companies' technical reserves with effect from 1 January 2020. Prior to 2019, insurance companies created technical reserves (which are tax deductible) according to the Accounting Act. Pursuant to the new tax legislation, the tax deductibility will be hereafter based on the technical reserves calculated according to the Solvency II rules which are lower than according to the Accounting Act.

Part II. The Insurance Contract: General

Chapter 1. Generalities (Characteristics, General Principles, Categories)

277. In practice, insurance is most often established on the basis of concluded insurance contract between the insurer and the policyholder. In accordance with the principle of contractual freedom of participants in private law, it is left to their discretion, firstly, whether they decide to conclude an insurance contract, but, of course, also under what conditions.[333]

278. The general regulation of an insurance contract, as one of the many types of contracts envisaged by law, is included in Book Four of the Civil Code among Relative Property Rights, specifically in Title II Obligations Arising from Juridical Acts, Chapter 15 Obligations Arising from Aleatory Contracts, Division 2 Insurance, provisions of §§ 2758–2872.

279. Historically, there has been repeated discussion over whether it is more appropriate to regulate private insurance under the Civil Code, or rather by a special law.[334] Although a number of arguments can be found in favour of a special law,[335] the approach chosen by the authors of the new Civil Code seems to be factually and systematically more appropriate, when they have moved the insurance regulation from a special law (which was the AIC until 31 December 2013) within the recodification of private law back to the Civil Code, as a comprehensive private law code.[336]

---

333. However, this does not fully apply to compulsory and statutory insurance, which was discussed in General Introduction, §6. Compulsory insurance.
334. The basic arguments for and against both solutions are clearly summarized with a historical excursion in the explanatory memorandum to the provisions of § 2758 CC.
335. For example, Jandová, Lucie. In: Jandová, Lucie; Šlauf, Petr; Svejkovský, Jaroslav. *Pojištění v novém občanském zákoníku. Komentář: [§ 2756-2872].* 1st ed. Praha: C. H. Beck, 2014, p. 5: 'The legal regulation of insurance is relatively detailed in comparison with the legal regulation of other obligations. The autonomy of the parties' will is also more limited in insurance compared to other types of contract. Moreover, private and public law elements intersect in insurance, and therefore the regulation of insurance in a special legal regulation has its justification (whether it is, e.g., the obligations of the insurer or compulsory insurance), so it is not a typical voluntary autonomous obligation of the parties.'
336. In which, moreover, it was included within the recodification of civil law in 1964, originally in the provisions of §§ 349 et seq., later in §§ 788 et seq. of Act No. 40/1964 Sb., Civil Code.

280. By an insurance contract, an insurer undertakes to provide the policyholder or a third person with insurance indemnity in the case of a random event covered by insurance (an insured event), and the policyholder undertakes to pay a premium to the insurer (§ 2758(1) CC). The parties of the insurance contract are therefore a person in the role of an insurer and a person in the role of a policyholder. The term 'insurer' must be distinguished from the term 'insurance company'. An insurance company is a concept of public law and means an entity conducting insurance business in the sense of Insurance Act. The term insurer, on the other hand, has a private law basis and refers to the contractual party of the insurance contract.[337]

281. The basic obligation characterizing the insurance contract is the obligation of the insurer towards the policyholder that in the event of an accidental (insured) event, he will provide him or a third person with insurance indemnity.

282. The insurer undertakes 'to provide' the insurance indemnity, not 'to pay'. The explanatory memorandum explains that it is not excluded that the insurer undertakes to provide the insurance indemnity in non-monetary form.

283. Multiple insurance obligations (insurance legal relationships) can be established by one insurance contract, and several types of insurance are often combined in one insurance contract. It is necessary to distinguish between insurance as a contractual relationship and an insurance contract as the juridical act that establishes the insurance. In practice, it is quite common for several insurances to be arranged in one insurance contract.[338] Thus, there is nothing to prevent for example, property and liability insurance from being arranged in one insurance contract. In practice, a common example may be a combination of MTPL and vehicle accident insurance. In business risks, an insurance contract is often negotiated as a comprehensive solution to the policyholder's insurance needs, regularly covering property and liability risks and possibly other types of insurance.

284. The policyholder is a natural or legal person who has concluded an insurance contract with the insurer and who agreed that for the service provided by the insurer, traditionally referred to as 'insurance coverage', to provide the insurer with a payment which the law designates as premiums. It is also a person for whom the law requires an insurable interest as a condition for the validity of the insurance contract and for the entire duration of the insurance, as a legitimate need of the policyholder to protect himself from the consequences of the insured event.[339]

---

337. *See also* Part I., Ch. 1. The Insurance Company: Its Form.
338. This was also approved by the Supreme Court in its decision of 7 Feb. 2012, file No. 32 Cdo 4034/2010, in which it stated that 'there was nothing to prevent one insurance contract from covering more than one types of insurance or from arranging more than one insured event within one type of insurance. Whether separate contracts are concluded for different types of insurance with differently arranged insured events, or whether one contract contains several types of insurance, is irrelevant to the effects of the juridical acts of the parties (including the effects of acts leading to the termination of the legal relationship established by the contract), unless mutual conditionality (connection) of individual (some) types of insurance resulted from a law or from a contract.'
339. For more details, *see* Ch. 2. Insurable Risk and Insurable Interest.

285. The position of the policyholder and his rights and obligations are given by the general insurance regulation in the Civil Code, the insurance contract and insurance conditions, and also to a large extent depends on whether the policyholder in a given relationship is a common legal entity, professional (e.g., an insurance intermediary), a natural person, a consumer, a weaker party, etc.

286. Another key subject of the legal relationship of insurance is the insured person, who may or may not be the same as the policyholder. Insured means a person whose life, health, property, liability or another insurable interest value is covered by the insurance (§ 2766 CC). He is therefore the bearer of the insurance risk in the general sense; the person who either represents a protected value in itself (if his life or health is insured) or owns, holds or administrates the protected value (if the property is insured), or he is obliged to compensate the damage caused to the protected value of another person (if his liability is insured).

287. The last necessary participant in the insurance relationship is the beneficiary, i.e., the person who becomes entitled to an insurance indemnity as a result of an insured event (§ 2770 CC). The beneficiary is a recipient of insurance indemnity and at the same time a person who has a locus standi to bring an action against the insurer.

288. There is no clear agreement in the domestic doctrine as to whether insurance is a synallagmatic contract or not. The explanatory memorandum to the Civil Code refers to it as synallagmatic.[340] So is the explanatory memorandum to the previous Act on Insurance Contract[341] and a significant part of the doctrine.[342] This view, although often repeated in the literature, is probably to be considered erroneous. If we understand the synallagmatic obligation as an obligation with a conditional performance,[343] it is necessary to state that in the insurance the performances of the insurer and the policyholder are not mutually conditioned, as the case law has already reached under the previous legislation.[344] It is therefore possible to side with

340. Cf. explanatory memorandum to § 2758 CC.

341. Cf. explanatory memorandum to AIC, General part.

342. For example, Jehlička, Oldřich; Švestka, Jiří et al. *Občanský zákoník. Komentář.* 4th ed. Praha: C. H. Beck, 1997, p. 790; Čechová, Jana; Přikryl, Vladimír. *Nový občanský zákoník: Zásadní změny v právní úpravě pojistné smlouvy – část I.* Pojistný obzor. 2012, No. 1, p. 4; Hulva, Tomáš. *Právní úprava pojistné smlouvy dle zákona č. 37/2004 Sb., o pojistné smlouvě (obecná ustanovení).* Právní rozhledy. 2005, No. 6, pp. 201 et seq.; Čechová, Jana; Přikryl, Vladimír. *Pojistná smlouva a její základní znaky.* Právní rozhledy. 2018, No. 10, p. 364.

343. Cf. § 1911 CC: 'Where the parties are to mutually perform at the same time, a discharge may only be required by the party which has already discharged the debt, or is willing and able to discharge the debt simultaneously with the other party.'

344. *See* resolution of the Supreme Court of the Czech Republic of 14 Apr. 2011, file No. 25 Cdo 194/2009: 'In the present case, it does not follow from the content of the contractual agreement of the participants and, moreover, from the very nature of the insurance relationship between the insurer and the policyholder that the performance obligation of one of them is tied to the mutual obligation of the other, on the contrary, the time of performance (maturity) of the obligation of each of them was agreed at a different point in time. The policyholder's obligation to pay the premiums to which he undertook by the insurance contract is not synallagmatically conditioned by the insurance company's obligation to pay the insurance indemnity in the event of an insured event and vice versa.'

authors who do not consider insurance for a synallagmatic obligation (unless mutual conditionality of performance is expressly agreed).[345]

289. Randomness is a key element of any insurance. This already follows from the legal definition of the insurance contract in the provision of § 2758 CC, by which the insurer undertakes to provide insurance indemnity in the case of a random event covered by insurance (an insured event). Therefore, as already mentioned, the insurance contract is classified into a group of aleatory contracts, which are characterized by the fact that the benefit or disadvantage of one or more contracting parties depends on uncertain (random) event.[346] Randomness may be that it is not certain whether an event will occur, and if it does occur, it is not known when (e.g., an accident or fire), or it is not certain whether the event will occur, and if it occurs, it is known when (reaching a certain age), or it is certain that the event will occur, but it is not known when (death).[347] If the element of randomness is missing, it cannot by definition be an insured event. The nature of the insurance contract precludes the application of provisions on change in circumstances (§§ 1764–1766 CC) or lesion (§§ 1793–1795 CC).[348]

290. If the occurrence of a random event is linked to the insurer's obligation to provide insurance indemnity to the beneficiary, we speak of an insured event. The insured event is the essential concept of the insurance relationship, as the occurrence of the insured event is associated with the activation of the insurer's obligation to provide insurance indemnity. An insured event is usually defined in the insurance contract both positively as a phenomenon defined by a certain cause and effect, and negatively by exclusionary conditions, the fulfilment of which does not give rise to the right to indemnity.

291. The possible cause of an insured event is traditionally referred to as an insurance peril. Insurance risk is usually understood as the degree of probability of the occurrence of an insured event.[349]

292. From the point of view of the basic contractual typology, an insurance contract can be characterized as:

---

345. *See* e.g., Jandová, Lucie. In: Jandová, Lucie; Šlauf, Petr; Svejkovský, Jaroslav. *Pojištění v novém občanském zákoníku. Komentář: [§ 2756-2872].* 1st ed. Praha: C. H. Beck, 2014, p. 12; or Wawerková, Magdalena. In: Hulmák, Milan et al. *Občanský zákoník VI. Závazkové právo. Zvláštní část (§ 2055–3014). Komentář.* 1st ed. Praha: C. H. Beck, 2014, p. 1293.

346. Cf. § 2756 CC: 'If the parties have stipulated that the benefit or detriment of at least one of the parties depends on an uncertain event, they have concluded an aleatory contract.'

347. The interpretation of the concept of randomness was given by the Supreme Court, e.g., in its resolution of 28 Nov. 2006, file No. 30 Cdo 427/2006.

348. *See* § 2757 CC.

349. However, the term 'risk' is commonly used in the insurance industry in many other senses; cf. e.g., Daňhel, Jaroslav et al. *Pojistná teorie.* 2nd ed. Praha: Professional Publishing. 2006, p. 18; or Řezáč, František. *Řízení rizik v pojišťovnictví.* 1st ed. Brno: Masarykova Univerzita, 2011, pp. 9 et seq.

- usually bilateral contract (although in practice it is common to encounter multilateral insurance contracts, for example, co-insurance contracts);
- named contract (as it is explicitly regulated as a contractual type in the provisions of §§ 2758 et seq. CC);
- onerous contract (both parties provide each other with performance of a certain money-expressible value – insurance premiums and insurance indemnity);
- causal contract (the economic reason is reflected in the insurance contract);
- consensual contract (its conclusion is perfected at the time of consent of the contractual parties);
- a synallagmatic contract (the performances of the insurer and the policyholder are not mutually conditioned – *see* explanation above);
- in most cases formal contract (for insurance contracts concluded for a period of one year and longer a mandatory written form is stipulated);[350]
- very often an adhesion contract (the conditions of the contract are determined by the stronger party (insurer), while the other party (policyholder) has only a very limited influence on defining the content of the contract and decides in fact only between its acceptance or non-acceptance – so-called take it or leave it contract).

293. A separate category is represented by insurance contracts concluded with the consumer, which fall under the regulation of so-called consumer contracts, specifically contracts on financial services pursuant to the provisions of §§ 1841 et seq. CC.

---

350. Cf. § 2758(2) and § 2773 CC.

Chapter 2. Insurable Risk and Insurable Interest

294. Czech law does not explicitly deal with the term 'insurable risk'.[351] Insurable risks are traditionally referred to as those risks that a commercial insurance company is able and willing to accept into insurance (to underwrite). From the point of view of private law, the insurance company is in principle not restricted in its underwriting process. What risks become the subject of insurance is left to the discretion of the parties.[352]

295. In the process of underwriting, the insurance company mainly takes into account actuarial, economic and public law factors. The insurance company only insures risks that meet certain criteria – in particular the risk must be: (i) accidental (the occurrence of a loss event must be accidental, unpredictable, unexpected), (ii) identifiable (the risk must be clearly identifiable, not interchangeable with other types of risks), (iii) estimable (it must be possible to calculate the probability of realization of the risk) and, last but not least, (iv) economically acceptable for the insurer (the insurer must be able to bear the risk, either within its own capacities or within the reinsurance programs).

296. However, the autonomy of the will of the parties to the insurance contract is to some extent limited by the concept of insurable interest. A necessary legal condition for the valid creation and duration of the insurance is the existence of the policyholder's insurable interest, as his legitimate need for protection against the consequences of an insured event (§ 2761 CC). The insurable interest is interpreted as a certain corrective, which is intended to prevent the insurance from being misused for speculative use.[353] This consideration is based on the idea that the policyholder should have a certain legitimate interest in the preservation or reparation of the value protected by the insurance, or a certain qualified relationship with the insured. If the policyholder lacks an insurable interest, this means de facto nothing more than that the consequences of the insured event do not directly affect him, he has no legitimate need to protect himself or the insured and the insurance thus becomes mere speculation – basically a bet.[354]

---

351. This term must be distinguished from the term 'insurance risk', which the legislation deals with and which expresses the degree of probability of the occurrence of an insured event caused by an insured peril.
352. With the very specific exceptions, such as e.g., the provision of § 54(3) AIC, which explicitly prohibited concluding insurance in the event of the death of a child occurring before the age of three, or in the event of a miscarriage or stillbirth. The explanatory memorandum stated, without further explanation, that such insurance would be contrary to ethics. This provision was no longer included in the new Civil Code, arguing that the ban was not common in historical and international comparisons.
353. Cf. explanatory memorandum to §§ 2761–2765 CC.
354. In practice, very borderline cases can be encountered. An example is the so-called hole-in-one insurance, in which the insurer undertakes to provide insurance benefits in the event that one of the participants in the golf tournament plays a hole on a single stroke. The insurance indemnity is then usually provided in the form of the costs of the prize (car, travel voucher, etc.). Although the obligation to give the winner a prize is undoubtedly linked to some interference with the tournament

297. The insurable interest represents one of the main defining elements of the legal relationship of insurance and distinguishes it from other related obligations, especially from betting and gaming, with which, on the contrary, a certain degree of speculation of participants is conceptually connected.[355]

298. The Civil Code has, in principle, taken over the definition of insurable interest from the previous legislation,[356] but in contrast to it, it explicitly associates the lack of insurable interest with invalidity of the insurance contract, or termination of the insurance (if the insurable interest extinguishes during the period of insurance).[357]

299. In the provisions of § 2762, the Civil Code defines in more detail the situation when the policyholder's insurable interest is given or presumed in the form of rebuttable legal presumptions.

300. The policyholder's insurable interest is always given if the subject of the insurance is his own life or health. In the form of a rebuttable legal presumption, the law stipulates that the policyholder has an insured interest in the life and health of another person if he proves to have an interest conditional on a relationship to that person, whether it is based on a family relationship[358] or it is conditional on a benefit or advantage arising if the person continues to be alive (§ 2762(1) CC). This may be, for example, a situation where the policyholder is dependent on the insured for maintenance, or where one of the spouses in the role of policyholder insures the life or health of the other spouse.

301. In the case of property insurance, the policyholder has primarily the insurable interest in his own property. A policyholder is presumed to also have an insurable interest in the property of another person if he proves that he would face a direct property loss without the existence and preservation of the property (§ 2762(2) CC). An example could be a situation where a parent company arranges

organizer's property, the question is to what extent the need for protection against the consequences of such insured event is justified and whether it is legitimate to arrange insurance for that purpose. It can be argued that the organizer can easily prevent this event by not organizing such a tournament at all. According to some authors, hole-in-one insurance is closer to a bet than insurance. In the literature, however, it is possible to meet a more liberal opinion, *see* e.g., Jandová, Lucie. In: Jandová, Lucie; Šlauf, Petr; Svejkovský, Jaroslav. *Pojištění v novém občanském zákoníku. Komentář.* 1st ed. Praha: C. H. Beck, 2014, p. 22.: 'If we start from the assumption that betting and gaming are legal obligations, which can be inferred at least with regard to their regulation by civil law, there is no reason to consider, e.g., insurance in case of fulfilment of such obligations as inconsistent with good morals. It can be assumed that e.g., today's well-known 'hole-in-one' insurance in golf would fall into this category.'

355. Cf. e.g., the explanatory memorandum to the provisions of § 2758 CC.
356. *See* § 3(n) AIC, in which the insured interest was defined as 'a legitimate need for protection against the consequences of an accident caused by an insured peril'.
357. Which was also inferred from previous legislation, that was based on the fact that in the absence of insurable interest, it is possible to invoke the invalidity of the insurance contract for conflict with good morals (cf. e.g., Bohman, Ludvík; Wawerková, Magdalena. *Zákon o pojistné smlouvě: komentář.* 2nd updated ed. Praha: Linde, 2009, p. 34).
358. Cf. § 771 CC.

insurance for a subsidiary, or where the employer insures the liability of his employees in the event of damage that employees may cause him in the course of their work.

302. The law allows to arrange property insurance even in situations where, at the time of concluding the insurance contract, the contracting parties know that the insurable interest does not yet exist, but it can be assumed that it will arise in the future (§ 2763 CC).

303. Finally, the law stipulates a rebuttable legal presumption that the policyholder's insurable interest is proven even if the insured has given his consent to the insurance (§ 2762(3) CC). But the insurable interest is an objective category. If the policyholder does not have an actual need for protection against the consequences of an insured event, the formal consent of the insured cannot establish the policyholder's insurable interest per se and such insurance could not validly arise despite the identical expression of the will of the parties to the insurance contract and the insured's consent.

304. It is significant that the list of rebuttable presumptions stated in the provisions of § 2762 CC cannot be considered exhaustive. The policyholder's insurable interest may be ad hoc proven by reference to the general clause of the insurable interest stated in the provisions of § 2761 of the CC.[359]

---

359. Identically e.g., Haas, Karel. In: Švestka, Jiří; Dvořák, Jan; Fiala, Josef et al. *Občanský zákoník: komentář. Svazek VI (§ 2521–3081).* § 2762 [ASPI System]. Wolters Kluwer [cit. 2020-9-15]. ASPI_ID KO89_f2012CZ. Available in the ASPI System. ISSN: 2336-517X.].

Chapter 3. Formation of the Insurance Contract

305. The process of concluding an insurance contract is regulated in the basic provisions of the Civil Code governing the insurance contract, especially in §§ 2758 and 2759 CC, which follow the general regulation of contracting in §§ 1731–1745 CC.

306. The insurance contract is concluded once the parties have stipulated its content (§ 1725 CC), which means timely acceptance of the proposal (an 'offer') by the other party. The contract is concluded when the acceptance of an offer becomes effective (§ 1745 CC), which is generally to be understood as the moment when the acceptance returns to the offeror. If the proposal for concluding an insurance contract does not specify by when it can be accepted, the law shall, in the alternative, set a time limit of one month (§ 2759(1) CC). If the conclusion of the contract is conditioned by a medical examination (typically in life insurance), the law extends this period to two months (§ 2759(1) second sentence CC). Where no time of the creation of insurance has been stipulated, the insurance is created on the first day following the date of the conclusion of the contract (§ 2772 CC).

307. A specificity of the insurance law is the possibility of accepting the insurer's offer by timely payment of the premium in the amount specified in the offer (§ 2759(1) second sentence CC). Thus, although the law does not require the policyholder's signature to accept the offer, the written form of the contract is considered to have been kept (§ 2758(2) second sentence CC). On the one hand, this opens up a large space for distance contracting using modern methods and digital technologies, on the other hand, one cannot lose sight of the fact that such a way of negotiation is also subject to the general legal regulation of consumer protection (if the client is a consumer), as well as to strict public law regulation of insurance distribution, which do not always sufficiently reflect the specifics of digital contracting.[360]

308. The above rules apply by analogy in the case of a proposal to amend an insurance contract (§ 2759(3) CC).

309. The law stipulates the obligatory written form for insurance contract, except in cases where the insurance is arranged for a period of less than one year (§ 2758(2) CC). The law also requires a written form for all juridical acts relating to insurance, unless the parties stipulate that such a form is not required (§ 2773(1) CC). However, the parties cannot use this option with regard to the mandatory written form of the insurance contract itself.[361] Notifications (this may be, for example,

360. Cf. e.g., the provisions of § 90(1) and (2) of the AoDIR, which prescribes the paper form of pre-contractual information in the first place and, only in the alternative, if the client chooses that way, allows the provision of information on another permanent data carrier or via a website.

361. Cf. explanatory memorandum to § 2773 CC; identically Jandová, Lucie. In: Jandová, Lucie; Šlauf, Petr; Svejkovský, Jaroslav. *Pojištění v novém občanském zákoníku. Komentář: [§ 2756-2872].* 1st ed. Praha: C. H. Beck, 2014, p. 62.

a change in the contact details of the policyholder) may be made in any form, unless the parties stipulate the written form (§ 2773(2) CC).

310. If the insurance contract is concluded in writing, it must contain the information specified in § 2777(1) CC, i.e., primarily: (a) the number of the insurance contract, (b) the identification of the insurer and the policyholder, (c) the identification of the beneficiary or a manner in which he will be determined, (d) definition of the insured event and insured peril, (e) determination of the premium amount, its maturity and information on whether it is a current or lump sum premium, (f) determination of the period for which the insurance is agreed (insurance period), and (g) any stipulations derogating from the insurance conditions.

311. If the contract has not been concluded in writing, the insurer shall state this information in the insurance certificate (in Czech 'pojistka'). The obligation to state these information is of a disciplinary nature and the possible failure to state any of them does not result in the invalidity of the insurance contract.[362]

312. An insurer shall provide the policyholder with the insurance certificate as a confirmation of the conclusion of the contract (§ 2775(1) CC). The insurer is obliged to issue the certificate to the policyholder always, regardless of the form of concluding the insurance contract. The law only distinguishes the amount of mandatory information stated in the certificate depending on whether the insurance contract was concluded in writing or not (*see* § 2777(1) and (2) CC).

313. By its nature, the insurance certificate is a unilateral declaratory confirmation of the insurer on the conclusion of the insurance contract and does not have the nature of juridical act. Under the previous regulation, it was common practice for the contracting parties to expressly agree in the insurance contract that the certificate is not issued separately and is replaced by the insurance contract. However, this practice is no longer possible, as the provision on the issuance of insurance certificate is peremptory (*see* § 2778 CC).[363]

314. The law also provides for the possibility that the right to indemnity is embodied in the insurance certificate in such a way that it cannot be successfully exercised or transferred without the insurance certificate. In such a case, the certificate is in the nature of a security and the insurer may require that the original insurance certificate be redeemed before issuing the duplicate (§ 2776 CC).[364]

---

362. Cf. explanatory memorandum to § 2777 CC; identically Jandová, Lucie. In: Jandová, Lucie; Šlauf, Petr; Svejkovský, Jaroslav. *Pojištění v novém občanském zákoníku.* Komentář. [§ 2756-2872]. 1st ed. Praha: C. H. Beck, 2014, p. 72.
363. Identically Haas, Karel. In: Švestka, Jiří; Dvořák, Jan; Fiala, Josef et al. *Občanský zákoník: komentář. Svazek VI (§ 2521–3081).* § 2775 [ASPI System]. Wolters Kluwer [cit. 2020-9-19]. ASPI_ID KO89_f2012CZ. Available in the ASPI System. ISSN: 2336-517X.].
364. However, this form of insurance certificate is rarely used in practice and only in specific areas of insurance, especially in international transport insurance.

315. A regular and substantial (but not obligatory) part of the matter of the insurance contract consists of insurance conditions, which define in particular the details of the creation, duration and termination of insurance, the insured event, exclusions from insurance and the scope of insurance indemnity and its maturity. The insurance conditions are nothing more than a special type of standard commercial terms regulated in §§ 1751 et seq. CC. Therefore, general provisions protecting the other – usually weaker – contracting party will apply.[365]

316. If the insurance contract refers to the insurance conditions, the insurer shall familiarize the policyholder with these conditions before concluding the contract (§ 2774 CC).[366] To become part of the insurance contract, the insurance conditions must be incorporated in the contract in manner provided by law. Above all, the insurance conditions must be transparently referred to in the insurance contract,[367] and the insurer must demonstrably acquaint the prospective policyholder with the insurance conditions before concluding the insurance contract.

317. The Supreme Court ruled on the nature of this insurer's obligation for example, in the judgement of 27 February 2018, file No. 23 Cdo 2865/2016: 'The provision of § 4(4) of the Act on Insurance Contract[368] constitutes a special legal regulation for the incorporation of indirect contractual arrangements for insurance contracts, while the Act on Insurance Contract chooses a stricter construction for these relationships. Indirect contractual arrangements which contain insurance conditions shall become part of the insurance contract only, if the policyholder is demonstrably acquainted with them before concluding the insurance contract (unless it is an exception pursuant to § 23(4) of the Act on Insurance Contract). In case of doubt, however, the person invoking them must prove that they were attached to the contract or that they were known to the other party. In the case of insurance conditions incorporated into the insurance contract pursuant to § 4(4) of the Act on Insurance Contract, the person who invokes the insurance conditions must prove that the policyholder was acquainted with this wording of the insurance conditions before concluding the insurance contract.'; and especially in the judgement of the Civil Law and Commercial Division of the Supreme Court of the Czech Republic of 13 February 2019, File No. 31 Cdo 1566/2017 (published in the Collection of Judicial Decisions and Opinions under No. 113/2019): 'It is unacceptable for the insurer to circumvent his legal obligation expressed in § 4(4) of the Act on Insurance Contract by incorporating part of the insurance conditions into other

365. Cf. § 1753 CC: 'A provision of the standard commercial terms which the other party could not have reasonably expected is ineffective, unless expressly accepted by that party; any stipulation to the contrary is disregarded.'; further also cf. legal regulation of adhesion contracts contained in §§ 1798–1801 CC.
366. This does not apply when concluding a distance contract, where the provision of § 1845 applies by analogy.
367. Cf. § 1799 CC: 'A clause in a contract of adhesion which refers to the terms stipulated outside the actual text of the contract is valid if the weaker party has been acquainted with the clause and its meaning or if it is proved that the meaning of the clause must have been known to him.'
368. It relates to the AIC, however, these conclusions also apply to contracts concluded under the Civil Code.

documents without demonstrably acquainting the policyholder with them, subsequently claiming that the policyholder had to be acquainted, as they are mentioned in the insurance contract or insurance conditions with which he was demonstrably acquainted. Such conduct cannot be afforded legal protection. … The next (second) level of insurance conditions must be incorporated into the insurance contract under the same conditions as the first. This conclusion cannot be interpreted as meaning that the only admissible way of acquainting the policyholder with the insurance conditions in accordance with § 4(4) of the Act on Insurance Contract is their submission before concluding the contract, but it is the most convincing, transparent and clear method for the contracting parties. If the insurer chooses a different procedure, it is up to him to prove that the policyholder was demonstrably acquainted with all insurance conditions before concluding the contract. … The information that the policyholder may view the insurance conditions at any time or that the insurance conditions are available at all insurer's points of sale cannot be considered as demonstrable acquaintance with the insurance conditions in the sense of § 4(4) of the Act on Insurance Contract.'

318. The insurance conditions are not subject to prior approval, notification or revision by the supervisory authority.[369]

369. For more details, *see* Part I., Ch. 3, §2. Supervision of Tariffs and Insurance Conditions.

Chapter 4. Obligations of the Policyholder and the Insured

§1. Description of Risk

319. With regard to the object of insurance (the insurable interest value), there is a certain information asymmetry within the insurance relationship. The person interested in insurance is usually better informed about his subjective risk and the characteristics of the object of insurance.[370] In order to reduce this information asymmetry, the law stipulates certain pre-contractual obligations on the contracting parties of the insurance contract. In addition to the general pre-contractual information obligation,[371] CC stipulates in § 2788 the explicit obligation of the prospective policyholder to answer truthfully and completely all written insurer's questions concerning facts that are relevant to the insurer's decision on how to evaluate the insurance risks, whether to insure them and under what conditions. The duty is considered to have been duly fulfilled if nothing substantial has been concealed in the response. This obligation also applies by analogy to the insured person (§ 2788(2) CC).

320. In practice, written questions from an insurer can take various forms. These are most often product questionnaires, which the person interested in insurance or the policyholder is obliged to fill in before concluding or changing the insurance contract, and which are subsequently one of the main inputs for the insurer's underwriting process. These may be questions concerning the health condition of the insured in personal insurance, the condition or fire safety of the building in property insurance, or the nature and scope of the insured's activities in liability insurance, etc.

321. Breaching this information duty may lead to a number of substantial legal consequences, including the insurer's right to a sanction reduction of the insurance indemnity pursuant to § 2800 CC, a sanction withdrawal from the insurance contract pursuant to § 2808(1) CC, or a sanction refusal of the indemnity pursuant to § 2809 CC.

322. Another manifestation of the effort to reduce the mentioned information asymmetry is the fact that in property insurance the maximum limit of indemnity is determined on the proposal of the policyholder as the sum insured in the amount equal to the insurance value of insured property at the time of conclusion of the contract (§ 2814(2) CC). Again, it is presumed that it is primarily a policyholder (or the insured), who has the appropriate information on the insured property value and who is therefore primarily responsible for the correct setting of the sum insured.

370. For more details, *see* e.g., Daňhel, Jaroslav. *Pojistná teorie.* 1st ed. Praha: Professional Publishing, 2005, pp. 21 et seq.

371. *See* particularly § 1728(2) CC, under which the contracting parties shall notify each other of all the factual and legal circumstances of which they know or must know, so that each of the parties can verify the possibility to conclude a valid contract and the interest of each party in concluding the contract is evident to the other party.

Incorrect determination of the sum insured has its consequences both in the inadequate setting of the insurance premium and, above all, in the form of the over-insurance or under-insurance.[372] For this reason, the insurer has the right to review the value of the insured property when concluding the contract.

§2. Payment of Premium

323. Insurance is a compulsory onerous legal relationship.[373] A key obligation on the client's side of the insurance contract therefore represents the policyholder's obligation to pay premiums to the insurer in the amount and in the manner agreed in the insurance contract.

324. The insurer is entitled to premiums for the duration of the insurance (§ 2782(1) CC). Here, the wording was specified in comparison with the previous § 13(1) AIC, which stipulated that the insurer is entitled to the premium for the insurance period, i.e., the period for which the insurance was agreed. The solution that the right to the insurance premium belongs to the insurer only for the period for which the insurance coverage is actually provided, i.e., for the duration of the insurance, seems to be more accurate. Exceptions to this rule may be stipulated by law.[374]

325. Insurance premium can be arranged as a current or lump sum premium.[375] Current premium is a premium that is determined by the insurance contract not for the entire period for which the insurance is agreed (in Czech 'pojistná doba'), but for a shorter period of time agreed in the insurance contract (in Czech 'pojistné období'). If this period is not explicitly agreed by the parties, the agreed insurance period is considered to be annual (§ 2783(2) CC in fine). The lump sum premium, on the other hand, is determined for the entire period for which the insurance is agreed. Payment of current and lump sum premiums can be arranged in instalments.[376]

---

372. For more details, *see* Ch.5, §1, I. Over – and under – Insurance.
373. Cf. § 2758 CC: '... the policyholder undertakes to pay a premium to the insurer.'
374. This is, e.g., a situation where the insurance extinguishes due to the termination of the insurable interest; in such a case, the insurer is entitled to the premium until the time when he learned of the termination of the insurable interest (§ 2765 CC); similarly, if the insurance extinguishes as a result of an insured event, the insurer is entitled to the premium until the end of the insurance period in which the insured event occurred, or to entire lump sum premium (§ 2782(2) CC).
375. Although CC did not take over the catalogue of legal definitions in the provisions of § 3 AIC, the substantive content of the terms current and lump sum premiums remains the same as they were defined in § 3(r) and (t) AIC.
376. By arranging the payment of a lump sum premium in instalments, such a lump sum premium does not lose its legal character and does not become a current premium (*see* Haas, Karel. In: Švestka, Jiří; Dvořák, Jan; Fiala, Josef et al. *Občanský zákoník: komentář. Svazek VI (§ 2521–3081).* § 2775 [ASPI System]. Wolters Kluwer [cit. 2020-9-19]. ASPI_ID KO89_f2012CZ. Available in the ASPI System. ISSN: 2336-517X.]).

326. Unless the parties agree otherwise, the insurer's right to a premium arises on the day of concluding the insurance contract (§ 2783(1) CC).[377]

327. The maturity of the premium is differentiated depending on whether a current or a lump sum premium has been agreed. A lump sum premium is due on the day of the commencement of the insurance. Current premium is due on the first day of the insurance period (§ 2783(2) CC). These provisions are, of course, dispositive and there is nothing to prevent the parties from arranging the maturity by way of derogation from the law.

328. Although the debtor of the obligation to pay premiums is the policyholder, the law stipulates the insurer's obligation to accept due premiums from the policyholder's mortgagee, the beneficiary or the insured, where these persons usually have a legitimate interest in the duration of insurance (§ 2784 CC).[378]

329. The insurer has the right to deduct receivable premiums or other insurance claims which are due from the insurance indemnity (§ 2787 CC). In contrary to the former provision of § 13(5) AIC, which used the term 'to set-off', the Civil Code uses the term 'to deduct', which is broader in meaning. While one of the preconditions for successful unilateral set-off is the reciprocity of the claims,[379] in the variability of insurance relationships this condition is often not met.[380] Therefore, instead of offsetting, the law confers on the insurer the right to reduce the insurance indemnity, i.e., to deduct his due receivables from the insurance indemnity. Due to the principle of the protection of victims, insurer cannot exercise this right in the compulsory insurance (§ 2787 second sentence CC).

330. The insurer determines premiums on the basis of actuarial assumptions and appropriate calculation methods, taking into account public law requirements, so as to ensure the permanent fulfilment of all its liabilities from the insurance business.[381] In determining the amount of the premium, the insurer may not use aspects contrary to the principle of equal treatment.[382] In accordance with the principle of

377. However, the insurance becomes effective in principle on the day following the conclusion of the insurance contract (§ 2772(1) CC).
378. The law does not regulate the relations between individual participants in such case, but it can be considered that this is a special provision for the general regulation of debt performance by a person other than the debtor (§§ 1936 et seq. CC) and general regulation of changes in the identity of a debtor (§§ 1888 et seq. CC).
379. Cf. §§ 1982 et seq. CC.
380. Typically, the insurer's right to the premium against the policyholder and the insurer's obligation to provide indemnity to the beneficiary does not have to be in a relationship of reciprocity, if the beneficiary differs from the policyholder.
381. For more details, *see* Part I, Ch. 3, §2. Supervision of Tariffs and Insurance Conditions.
382. *Ibid.*

protection of the weaker party, the law regulates the policyholder's right to request the insurer to communicate the principles for determining the amount of the premium (§ 2783(3) CC).[383]

331. Without an agreement with the policyholder, the insurer cannot unilaterally change the premium amount. However, the law allows for conditions to be agreed in the insurance contract, upon fulfilment of which the insurer has the right to adjust the new amount of the current premium for the next insurance period (§ 2785 CC). If the insurer adjusts the amount of the premium in this way, he shall notify the policyholder at least two months before the due date of the insurance premium for the insurance period in which the amount of premium is to be changed. If the policyholder disagrees with the change, he may express his disagreement within one month from the date on which he became aware of it; in that case the insurance is extinguished upon the expiry of the insurance period for which insurance premium has already been paid (§ 2786 CC).

332. It is necessary to distinguish from the above procedure a situation where the insurer and the policyholder agree in advance on the adjustment of the premium depending on the objective change in specific clearly defined parameters. Typically, it can be an automatic adjustment of premiums depending on the amount of claims (bonus/malus systems), or indexation of premiums in property insurance depending on the growth of real estate and construction work prices. Such an adjustment of the premium is then not a unilateral change of the premium by the insurer, but an automatic pre-agreed consensual change, which does not require further expression of the will of the parties and does not trigger the procedure under § 2786 CC.[384]

§3. Obligations in the Case of Insured Event

333. In the case of an event which the person who considers himself to be the beneficiary associates with a claim for insurance indemnity, the person shall notify the insurer accordingly without undue delay. At the same time, he is obliged to give the insurer a true explanation about the occurrence and extent of such an event, the rights of third persons, and any multiple insurance, and present the insurer with the necessary documents and proceed as stipulated in the contract. If the notifier is a person different from the policyholder or the insured, the policyholder and the insured also have these obligations (§ 2796(1) CC).

334. An insurer is not obliged to begin the investigation on its own initiative. The obligation to initiate an investigation is connected only with the notification of the insured event by an authorized person. This is primarily the one who considers

383. This obligation includes the communication of the general principles of the calculation of the premium, not of specific actuarial formulas or specific mathematical parameters of the calculation; this information as well as the insurer's tariffs are subject to the protection of business secrets (cf. § 504 CC).

384. Identically Jandová, Lucie. In: Jandová, Lucie; Šlauf, Petr; Svejkovský, Jaroslav. *Pojištění v novém občanském zákoníku. Komentář: [§ 2756-2872].* 1st ed. Praha: C. H. Beck, 2014, pp. 105–106.

himself to be the beneficiary, i.e., a person with the right to insurance indemnity. Compared to the previous legislation, however, the circle of persons qualified to initiate an insurer's investigation by their notification was expanded. In addition to the beneficiary (or the person who consider himself to be the beneficiary), the same notification can be made by any person who has a legal interest in the insurance indemnity (§ 2796(2) CC).[385]

335. The obligation to report the occurrence of the insured event must be fulfilled without undue delay. Late notification can bring a number of adverse consequences for insurance participants, including complicating and increasing the costs of investigation and thus establishing the insurer's right to reimbursement of these costs against the policyholder, insured or other person (§ 2797(3) CC), may lead to a sanction reduction of insurance indemnity pursuant to § 2800 CC, etc.

336. The provision of knowingly false or grossly distorted information concerning the scope of the notified event, or their concealment, may result in the insurer's right to reimbursement of costs reasonably incurred in the investigation of these facts (§ 2797(2) CC). The provision of false information may also fulfil the characteristics of the merits of the criminal offence of insurance fraud pursuant to § 210 of the Criminal Code.

337. The general provision of § 2796 CC is supplemented by several special provisions regulating the obligations of insurance participants in connection with the notification of the occurrence of the insured event. This is primarily the obligation of the beneficiary in property insurance to refrain from repairing the damaged property or removing the remnants of the destroyed property until consent is given by the insurer (§ 2851 CC), special information obligation of the insured in liability insurance about the fact that the victim has asserted his right to compensation against him, including the obligation to notify the insurer that proceedings before a public body or arbitration proceedings have been initiated against the insured in connection with the insured event (§ 2862 CC), or the obligation of the beneficiary to report the occurrence of the insured event in credit or guarantee insurance within the period agreed in contract, under the threat of non-recognition of the right to indemnity by the court as a result of the insurer's objection (§ 2869 CC).

385. Such a person can be, e.g., a mortgagee in property insurance or an injured party in liability insurance.

Chapter 5. Obligations of the Insurer

338. The fundamental obligation of the insurer is to provide the policyholder or a third party with the indemnity in the case of insured event.[386]

339. The insurer undertakes 'to provide' the insurance indemnity, not 'to pay', therefore it is not excluded that the insurer undertakes to provide the insurance indemnity in a non-pecuniary form (e.g., the provision of a certain service or performance).

340. The creditor of this obligation is the beneficiary, i.e., the person who, as a result of the insured event, acquires the right to indemnity. The right to indemnity arises in principle from events that occur during the term of the insurance. If the so-called retroactivity of the insurance is agreed and the insurance, at the will of the contractual parties, also covers the period before the day of concluding the insurance contract, the insurer is not obliged to provide indemnity if the policyholder was aware, or should and could have been aware, at the time the offer was made that the insured event had already occurred (§ 2772(2) CC).

341. The insurer is entitled to deduct receivable premiums, or other insurance claims which are due from the insurance indemnity, if it is not compulsory insurance (§ 2787 CC).[387] Breaching the obligations of the policyholder, the insured or the beneficiary may lead to a sanction in the form of a reduction of the indemnity (e.g., breach of the obligation to notify an increase in insurance risk pursuant to § 2793 CC, or a reduction of indemnity under § 2800(2) CC).

342. The insurer may refuse the indemnity where the insured event was caused by a fact of which he became aware only after the insured event occurred, which he could not have ascertained due to a culpable breach of the information duty of the policyholder or the insured, and the knowledge of which at the conclusion of the contract would have led him not to conclude the contract or to conclude it under other terms (§ 2809 CC). The insurance extinguishes on the date of rejection to provide insurance indemnity (§ 2810 CC).

343. The provision of the insurance indemnity is preceded by the process of investigating the insured event initiated by the notification of the occurrence of the loss event by the person who is considered to be the beneficiary, or another person with a legal interest in the insurance indemnity.[388]

344. The insurer is obliged to initiate an investigation without undue delay after such notification. The purpose of the investigation is to determine the existence and extent of insurer's duty to provide indemnity. The investigation is completed by notifying the person who asserted his right to insurance indemnity of its results. At

386. *See* the basic provision of § 2758 CC.
387. *See also* above Ch. 4, §2. Payment of Premium.
388. *See also* Ch. 4, §3. Obligations in the Case of Insured Event.

the request of this person, the insurer shall provide the person in writing with the justification of the amount of the insurance indemnity, or the reason for its dismissal (§ 2797(1) CC). The beneficiary may also exercise the right to inspect the insurer's claims file pursuant to the provisions of § 129a IA.[389]

345. The law provides that the investigation should normally be completed within three months. If it is not possible to complete the investigation within this period, the insurer shall inform the notifier of the reasons that prevent him from completing the investigation (§ 2798(2) CC).[390]

346. If the origin of the right to indemnity is not in dispute as to the reason and only its amount remains uncertain, the beneficiary may request a reasonable advance payment. This does not apply where there is a reasonable cause to refuse the provision of such an advance payment (§ 2798(2) CC in fine).

347. The maturity of the insurance indemnity is primarily the subject of a contractual agreement between the parties. If not agreed, the insurance indemnity is due within fifteen days from the date of completion of the investigation, i.e., within fifteen days from the notifying the person who asserted his right to insurance indemnity of the investigation results (§ 2798(1) in connection with § 2797(1) CC).

348. It is prohibited to take into consideration nationality, racial or ethnic origin, or any other consideration contrary to the principle of equal treatment when determining the amount of insurance indemnity. Any reduction in insurance indemnity for these reasons is disregarded (§ 2769 CC).

§1. Non-life Insurance

I. Over-and Under-Insurance

349. In Chapter 4, §1. Description of the risk, it was explained that it is primarily the policyholder who is responsible for the correct setting of the sum insured, as he has the information on the insured property value.

---

389. *See also* CNB's Supervisory opinion of 3 Sep. 2015, on Inspection of the Insurance Company's Claims File (available at https://www.cnb.cz/export/sites/cnb/cs/casto-kladene-dotazy/.galleries/stanoviska_a_odpovedi/pdf/nahlizeni_do_likvidacniho_spisu_pojistovny.pdf).

390. For more details on the insurer's obligations during the investigation, *see* in particular the CNB's Supervisory benchmark No. 1/2015, on the Process of Claims Handling according to the Civil Code (available at https://www.cnb.cz/export/sites/cnb/cs/dohled-financni-trh/.galleries/vykon_dohledu/dohledove_benchmarky/download/dohledovy_benchmark_2015_01.pdf), CNB's Supervisory benchmark No. 2/2013, on the Process of Claims Handling and Obligations of the Insurer according to § 16 of the Act on Insurance Contract (available at https://www.cnb.cz/export/sites/cnb/cs/dohled-financni-trh/.galleries/vykon_dohledu/dohledove_benchmarky/download/dohledovy_benchmark_2013_02.pdf), CNB's Supervisory benchmark No. 1/2012, on the Obligation of Insurers Providing Motor Third Party Liability Insurance (available at https://www.cnb.cz/export/sites/cnb/cs/dohled-financni-trh/.galleries/vykon_dohledu/dohledove_benchmarky/download/dohledovy_benchmark_2012_01.pdf).

350. Where the insurance value (i.e., the highest possible property damage that may occur as a result of an insured event) can be determined, the maximum limit of insurance indemnity is set up on the proposal of the policyholder as the sum insured in the amount equal to the insurance value of the insured property at the time of conclusion of the contract (§ 2814(2) CC).

351. However, if there is a situation where the agreed sum insured does not correspond to the insurance value of the insured property, or if there is a discrepancy between these values later during the term of the insurance (without the policyholder responding appropriately, for example, by a proposal to change the sum insured), either: (i) under-insurance, or (ii) over-insurance arises.

352. Due to the nature of the matter, both institutes are connected with non-life insurance against loss and damage, and their application in fixed-amount insurance is out of the question.

353. Under-insurance means a situation where the sum insured stipulated in the insurance contract is less than the actual insurance value of the insured property. If an insured event occurs in these circumstances, the insurer is entitled to reduce the indemnity in the same proportion as the ratio of the sum insured to the actual amount of the insurance value of the insured property (§ 2854 CC).

354. The amount of indemnity in the event of the existence of under-insurance is therefore determined on the basis of the following formula:[391]
math-figure

355. The reduction of indemnity due to under-insurance can be applied regardless of whether it is a partial or total damage. However, this is a right, not a duty of the insurer. The parties may agree that the under-insurance will not be applied at all, or that they will tolerate the difference between the sum insured and the insurance value up to a certain amount (usually up to about 10% in practice).

356. It is in the policyholder's interest to pay attention to the adequate setting of the sum insured, both when concluding the insurance contract and during the term of the insurance so that in time it always corresponds to the actual insurance value of the insured property.

357. On the other hand, over-insurance means the opposite situation, i.e., the sum insured exceeds the actual insurance value of the insured property. If a current premium has been agreed, in such a case both the policyholder and the insurer may propose to the other party an amendment to the contract consisting in a reduction of the sum insured while at the same time a proportional reduction of the premium for

391. Taken from Haas, Karel. In: Švestka, Jiří; Dvořák, Jan; Fiala, Josef et al. *Občanský zákoník: komentář. Svazek VI (§ 2521–3081).* § 2780 [ASPI System]. Wolters Kluwer [cit. 2020-9-20]. ASPI_ID KO89_f2012CZ. Available in the ASPI System. ISSN: 2336-517X.].

the following insurance period. If such a proposal is not accepted by the other party within one month, the insurance is extinguished (§ 2853(1) CC).

358. If lump sum insurance premium has been stipulated, the insurer has the right to claim a reduction in the sum insured under the condition that the insurance premium will also be proportionately reduced, and the policyholder has the right to claim a reduction in the premium under the condition that the sum insured will also be proportionately reduced. (§ 2853(2) CC).

II. Subrogation

359. Another of the key institutes of insurance law is inextricably linked with non-life insurance against loss and damage – insurer's right of subrogation. Subrogation means a statutory passage (cession) of the right of the beneficiary (or the insured, or the person who incurred the salvage costs) to compensation for damage or other similar right against a third party, to the insurer upon the payment of the insurance indemnity.

360. The purpose of this institute is to ensure a fair final redistribution of the economic costs of the insured event so that the costs are eventually borne by the primary tortfeasor who has caused the damage, and no unjust enrichment arises in the relations between the participants involved. If the institute of the subrogation did not exist, then the person who received the indemnity from the insurer would be enriched by providing him with insurance indemnity, without prejudice to his right to compensation or other similar right against the tortfeasor, or the tortfeasor would be enriched if his tortious obligation to compensate the injured party had automatically ceased to the extent of the indemnity paid.[392]

361. The subrogation is conceptually associated only with non-life insurance against loss and damage, in which the insurer's provides indemnity which shall, to the stipulated extent, compensate for the loss of property incurred as a result of an insured event (§ 2811 CC), and, on the contrary, has no place in fixed-amount insurance.

362. It is necessary to distinguish between the subrogation pursuant to the provision of § 2820 CC and the insurer's right to recourse against the insured. Right to recourse is a special original right of the insurer against the insured, which is characterized by its sanctioning nature, while as subrogation we refer to rights that pass to the insurer upon the payment of insurance indemnity and by which the reparation function predominates.[393]

392. Růžička, Hynek. In: Petrov, Jan; Výtisk, Michal; Beran, Vladimír et al. *Občanský zákoník: komentář.* 1st ed. Praha: C. H. Beck, 2017, p. 2768.

393. Cf. e.g., § 2866 CC and § 10 MTPLIA; *see also* e.g., the judgement of the Supreme Court of the Czech Republic of 30 Nov. 2000, file No. 29 Cdo 2941/99; resolution of the Supreme Court of the

363. The provision of § 2820(1) CC stipulates that if, in connection with an imminent or existing insured event, a beneficiary, an insured person or a person who incurred salvage costs became entitled to be compensated by another person for damage or another similar right, the claim, including accessories, security and other associated rights, passes to the insurer upon the payment[394] of the insurance indemnity, up to the amount of indemnity which the insurer lawfully paid to the beneficiary.

364. The condition for the cession of the right to the insurer is therefore the cumulative fulfilment of the following preconditions: (i) provision of insurance indemnity,[395] in connection with imminent or incurred insured event, and (ii) existence of right to compensation or other similar right of the beneficiary, the insured, or the person who incurred the salvage costs at the time of the provision of the insurance indemnity.

365. If this provision uses the wording 'or another similar right', it is to be understood, for example, as a right to the mutual settlement of jointly and severally liable tortfeasors (§ 2916 CC)[396] or the general right to recourse of a person liable to compensate for damage caused by another person (§ 2917 CC).[397]

366. The right passes to the insurer in the condition in which it was at the time of the provision of the insurance indemnity, up to the amount of the paid indemnity. Simultaneously with the claim, which is the subject of a statutory cession, its accessories, security and other associated rights also pass to the insurer.

Czech Republic of 22 Nov. 2011, file No. 32 Cdo 3266/2010; or judgement of the Supreme Court of the Czech Republic of 29 Mar. 2011, file No. 25 Cdo 4321/2008.

394. The lawmaker uses the imprecise term 'payment' here, although it has already been explained above that the insurance indemnity does not necessarily have to be provided in pecuniary form.

395. But also the provision of other insurance benefits, such as the provision of compensation for salvage costs.

396. *See* e.g., the historical judgement of the Supreme Court of the Czechoslovak Republic of 19 Oct. 1938, file No. Rv I 513/38 (Vážný, No. 17076/1938): 'If the insurer has paid the entire debt of the jointly and severally liable debtor, who was insured against the consequences of legal liability, to the injured third party, which the uninsured co-debtor was also obliged to pay, the insurer is entitled to claim compensation from the uninsured co-debtor for the share attributable to this co-debtor if the insured co-debtor assigned his recourse claim to the insurer.' Further *see* judgement of the Supreme Court of the Czech Republic of 15 Dec. 2015, file No. 23 Cdo 4210/2013, published in the Collection of Judicial Decisions and Opinions under No. 47/2017: 'The insurer of one of the persons who, together with other persons, is liable for damage caused in a traffic accident of motor vehicles, if he has provided the injured party with indemnity for the damage caused in full, resp. to the extent higher than the degree of participation of the insured person, has by the payment of such indemnity the right to settlement according to the degree of participation of individual persons in the traffic accident, directly against the insurers of other participants in the accident.'

397. Hass tried to comprehensively enumerate 'another similar rights' in Švestka, Jiří; Dvořák, Jan; Fiala, Josef et al. *Občanský zákoník: komentář. Svazek VI (§ 2521–3081).* § 2820 [ASPI System]. Wolters Kluwer [cit. 2020-9-20]. ASPI_ID KO89_f2012CZ. Available in the ASPI System. ISSN: 2336-517X.].

367. This change in the person of the creditor does not affect the running of the limitation period. If the right has become time-barred, the debtor may successfully invoke the statute of limitations also against the insurer.[398]

368. The original creditor of a ceded claim has to issue all necessary documents to the insurer, to inform him of everything necessary for the assertion of the claim and to ensure that the insurer can successfully assert the claim. If the creditor fails the passage of the right to the insurer, the Civil Code provides in § 2820(2) sanction in the form of the insurer's right to reduce the insurance indemnity by the amount he could have otherwise obtained (before the payment of the insurance indemnity), or the insurer's right to compensation up to the amount that the insurer could have otherwise obtained (after the payment of the insurance indemnity).

369. The second sentence of § 2820(1) CC stipulates an exception according to which there is no statutory cession if a debtor of the claim is person who lives in the same household as a beneficiary (insured person or a person who incurred salvage costs) or is dependent on him in maintenance. However, this exception does not apply if the insured event was caused intentionally. The Civil Code thus protects the property integrity of the common household as a community of persons living together, if they did not act with intent to cause damage.[399]

370. In contrast to the previous legislation, the lawmaker did not take over into the Civil Code the insurer's duty to apply with the necessary modifications the so-called moderation right of the court pursuant to the provisions of § 450 of the former Civil Code.[400] This can be considered a step in the right direction, as the insurer's duty as a private entity to apply an institute, the application of which is otherwise entrusted only to the court, appeared to be completely unsystematic.

III. Multiple Insurance

371. In practice, there are often situations where the same insurable interest value is insured against the same insurance peril and for the same period with several insurers. The law refers to such a situation as insurance with multiple insurers (§ 2816 CC), recognizing three possible variants: (i) co-insurance, (ii) concurrent insurance, and (iii) multiple insurance.

372. We speak of co-insurance if a contract has been concluded between the policyholder and multiple insurers represented by the leading insurer, and if the policyholder has undertaken to pay the premium to only one of them. Co-insurance is therefore characterized by the existence of a single insurance contract and a single

398. *See* e.g., the judgement of the Supreme Court of the Czechoslovak Republic of 21 Nov. 1974, file No. 3 Cz 66/74, published in the Collection of Judicial Decisions and Opinions under No. 24/1976.

399. Wawerková, Magdalena. In: Hulmák, Milan et al. *Občanský zákoník VI. Závazkové právo. Zvláštní část (§ 2055–3014). Komentář.* 1st ed. Praha: C. H. Beck, 2014, p. 1399.

400. Cf. § 33(2) AIC: 'If the right under the paragraph 1 has passed to the insurer, the provisions of § 450 of the Civil Code shall apply, with the necessary modifications, to its assertion.'

legal relationship of insurance, which, however, the policyholder arranges simultaneously with several insurers. The leading insurer specified in the contract pursuant to 2817(1) CC determines the insurance conditions and the amount of premiums, administers the co-insurance, receives claim notifications and carries out investigations necessary to determine the extent of the insurers' duty to provide insurance indemnity. If no other manner of premium income has been stipulated, the leading insurer shall also receive premiums.

373. The law also allows insurers to agree on a common approach to insuring certain insurance risks and to create a so-called pool.[401] Within the pool, similarly to ordinary co-insurance, the insurers may appoint the leading insurer, or create a special body for this purpose or entrust the performance of the leading insurer's duties to an insurance broker (§ 2817(2) CC).

374. The law also does not exclude the alternative that the policyholder concludes an insurance contract with only one insurer, who subsequently concludes a co-insurance contract with other insurers. Such a case is sometimes referred to as 'indirect co-insurance'. However, Haas rightly points out that in this case it is not co-insurance in the true sense of the word, as there is only one person on the insurer's side, while the defining feature of co-insurance under § 2817 CC is the plurality of insurers. An unnamed co-insurance contract concluded between insurers is, in fact, in the nature of a reinsurance contract, and the reinsuring insurer must have the appropriate authorization in this regard.[402]

375. The beneficiary asserts his right to the insurance indemnity against the leading insurer. Insurers then settle with each other according to their shares. Where no shares have been stipulated, they are conclusively presumed to be equal (§ 2817(3) CC). Provisions of § 2817(1) to (4) have a peremptory nature, it is possible to derogate from them only in the insurance of large insurance risks (§ 2817(5) CC).[403]

376. By concurrent insurance we mean the situation where the total of the sums insured does not exceed the insurance value of the insured property, or the total of the insurance indemnity limits does not exceed the actual amount of the damage incurred. The policyholder in the particular insurance contracts does not have to be the same person, the decisive factor is whether the object of the insurance, the insurance peril and the insurance period overleaps. However, in order to be a concurrent insurance, the insurance must be arranged with at least two different insurers (*see* § 2816 CC, the phrase 'with several insurers'). Unlike co-insurance, the policyholder (or more policyholders) pays separate premium for each particular insurance. The

---

401. For more details, *see* Part VIII, Ch. 3. Pooling.

402. Haas, Karel. In: Švestka, Jiří; Dvořák, Jan; Fiala, Josef et al. *Občanský zákoník: komentář. Svazek VI (§ 2521–3081).* § 2817 [ASPI System]. Wolters Kluwer [cit. 2020-9-20]. ASPI_ID KO89_f2012CZ. Available in the ASPI System. ISSN: 2336-517X.].

403. Cf. also 2872 CC.

law (in contrast to co-insurance and multiple insurance) defines concurrent insurance, but does not regulate it in any detail. This is because, in the concurrent insurance, there is no risk of unjust enrichment of the beneficiary, who cannot receive more than the insurance value of the insured property (more than the amount of damage incurred).[404]

377. Multiple insurance has exactly the same defining features as concurrent insurance, with the difference that the total of the sums insured exceeds the insurance value of the insured property, or the total of the insurance indemnity limits exceeds the actual amount of damage incurred. If multiple insurances arise, and if the policyholder is aware of this (because, as has been said, there may be more policyholders in particular insurances), he is obliged to notify each of the insurers concerned without undue delay. In the notification, he shall specify the other insurers and the sums insured or insurance indemnity limits stipulated under the other contracts (§ 2818(1) CC). The first insurer to receive a claim notification shall provide indemnity up to the sum insured or insurance the indemnity limit stipulated in the contract which is binding on the insurer (§ 2818(2) CC). The insurer shall also, without undue delay, notify this to the other insurers of which he became aware.

378. Insurers subsequently settle in the same proportion as the ratio of the sums insured or insurance indemnity limits stipulated in particular contracts which are binding on them (§ 2818 (3) CC). If the sum insured or the indemnity limit stipulated in the contract with the first insurer is not sufficient to compensate for the entire loss resulting from the insured event, the beneficiary may claim from the other insurers an insurance indemnity of up to the amount of compensation for the loss of property (§ 2818(2) second sentence CC).

§2. Life Insurance

379. Also life insurance[405] is defined on the one hand by the policyholder's obligation to pay premium to the insurer and on the other hand by the insurer's obligation to provide indemnity to the beneficiary[406] if an insured event occurs.

380. An insured event in life insurance may be the death of the insured, reaching a certain age or the day specified in the contract, or another fact related to a change in a person's personal status (e.g., wedding insurance, birth insurance, etc.).

381. It is absolutely crucial for the nature of the insurer's obligation in life insurance that the life insurance can only be arranged as a fixed-amount insurance (§ 2833 CC). Fixed-amount insurance obliges the insurer to provide a lump sum or

404. Bohman, Ludvík. In: Hulmák, Milan et al. *Občanský zákoník VI. Závazkové právo. Zvláštní část (§ 2055–3014). Komentář.* 1st ed. Praha: C. H. Beck, 2014, p. 1391.
405. Discussed in more details in Part V, Ch. 4. Life Insurance.
406. In death insurance, the person who acquires the right to indemnity is referred to as 'ultimate beneficiary' (*see* §§ 2829 et seq. CC).

repeated insurance indemnity in the stipulated amount in the case of an insured event. The amount determined on the proposal of the policyholder which the insurer is to pay in the event of an insured event, or the amount and frequency of payment of a pension, shall form the basis for determining the amount of premium and calculating the insurance indemnity (§ 2821 CC).

382. While the purpose of non-life insurance against loss and damage is to compensate for the loss of property caused by an insured event, the purpose of fixed-amount insurance is to obtain an amount, i.e., a certain financial sum, which is paid to the beneficiary in the event of an insured event. This amount is therefore completely independent of the occurrence or extent of any harm. The provision of indemnity from the fixed-amount insurance does not terminate the possible right to damages of the beneficiary against the tortfeasor (§ 2822 CC). The payment of the insurance indemnity does not lead to a statutory cession of the right to damages or another similar right to the insurer. Provision of § 2820 CC does not apply in the fixed-amount insurance.

383. If the reserve-making insurance is terminated prematurely, the policyholder acquires the right to a redemption (surrender value, in Czech 'odkupné') if the conditions of § 2842 CC (or the conditions stipulated in the insurance contract) are met. This surrender value represents the financial settlement of the policyholder and the insurer in the event of premature termination of the reserve-making insurance. It is the part of unused premiums stored by the insurer as a technical reserve calculated by actuarial methods as of the date of termination of the insurance. If the insured is different from the policyholder, the consent of the insured is required for the payment of the surrender value (§ 2826(3) CC). Unless otherwise agreed, the surrender value is due within three months after the date on which the request for its payment was delivered to the insurer. The insurance is extinguished upon the payment of the surrender value.[407] The payment of surrender value is not the provision of insurance indemnity, it has the nature of a so-called other insurance benefit.

407. In addition to this variant explicitly envisaged by law, where the surrender value is paid at the request of the policyholder and the insurance extinguishes upon the payment of the surrender value, in practice a variant is often agreed in which the right to surrender value arises as a result of previous termination of insurance, typically by notice of termination given by the policyholder.

Chapter 6. Insurance and Third Parties

384. An insurance contract is usually a bilateral juridical act of the insurer and the policyholder. In addition to these main subjects (contractual parties to the insurance contract), other persons often appear in the insurance relationship.

385. The essential subject of each insurance is the insured, who may or may not be the same as the policyholder. The insured is often identical to the beneficiary.

386. In addition to these essential participants, it is possible to meet other persons in the insurance, who are usually not included among the insurance participants in the strict sense, although they may have particular rights and obligations from the insurance. Such a person may be, for example, a person who has incurred salvage costs and claims against the insurer the right to compensation of them,[408] or the injured party without a right of direct action against the insurer.[409]

387. The above-mentioned categories of main participants may merge in one person, where the other contractual party stands against the insurer in the role of the policyholder, the insured and the beneficiary at the same time. On the other hand, different persons may be involved in all the roles mentioned, in various combinations, and it should be noted that in practice such situations are quite common. The following combinations are possible:[410]

(1) The person of the policyholder (A) is the same as the person of the insured (B) and the person of the beneficiary (C), i.e., one and the same person appears in all roles (A = B = C). This is insurance of one's own insurance peril for the policyholder's own benefit.
(2) The policyholder is the same as the insured but different from the beneficiary. In addition to the policyholder (and the insured at the same time), there is another person in the role of the beneficiary (A = B ≠ C). This is insurance of one's own insurance peril in favour of a third person.
(3) The policyholder is different from the insured, but he is the beneficiary. In addition to the policyholder (and the beneficiary at the same time), there is other person in the role of the insured (A = C ≠ B). This is insurance of another's insurance peril for the policyholder's own benefit.
(4) The policyholder is different from the insured and the beneficiary, and also the insured is different from the beneficiary. In addition to the policyholder, there are two other different persons – the insured and the beneficiary (A ≠ B ≠ C). This is insurance of another's insurance peril in favour of a third person.

---

408. Cf. § 2819(3) CC.
409. Cf. § 2863 CC, according to which the insurer has the right to request that the injured party provide the information under § 2777 (3) CC, which corresponds to the injured party's obligation to provide this information.
410. Inspired by Wawerková, Magdalena. In: Hulmák, Milan et al. *Občanský zákoník VI. Závazkové právo. Zvláštní část (§ 2055–3014). Komentář.* 1st ed. Praha: C. H. Beck, 2014, p. 1311.

(5) The policyholder is different from the insured and the beneficiary, and the insured is identical to the beneficiary. In addition to the policyholder, there is another person in the role of the insured and the beneficiary at the same time (A ≠ B = C). This is an insurance of another's insurance peril in favour of a third person, namely the insured.

388. Insurance of the insurance peril of another is specially regulated by law in the provisions of § 2767 CC. This provision covers the situation mentioned above ad (3), i.e., the policyholder is not identical to the insured and at the same time the insurance indemnity is concluded for the policyholder's own benefit. In such a case, the consent of the insured is required for the valid creation and duration of the insurance. If the policyholder fails to demonstrate the consent within the stipulated period, or otherwise within three months from the date of the conclusion of the contract, the insurance is extinguished upon the expiry of that period. If an insured event occurs during that period and no consent has been given, the right to the insurance indemnity is acquired by the insured person. The insured enters into the insurance on the day of the policyholder's death, or the policyholder's termination without a legal successor. If the insured notifies the insurer in writing within thirty days from the date of the policyholder's death or termination that he has no interest in the continuation of the insurance, the insurance is extinguished on the date of the policyholder's death or termination.

389. An insurance contract or a statute may stipulate that the right to indemnity in the case of the insured event is acquired by another person, different from the policyholder and the insured in one person. In these cases mentioned above ad (2), we speak of insurance or insurance contract in favour of a third person (§ 2768(1) CC). This is always in the case of the ultimate beneficiary, i.e., the beneficiary in the life insurance in the event of death, where conceptually the insured cannot be the same as the beneficiary.

390. The situation mentioned above ad (5), where the policyholder is a person different from the insured, but the insured remains the beneficiary, can also be described as insurance in the favour of a third person.[411]

391. Finally, a situation cannot be ruled out where the policyholder, the insured and the beneficiary are three different persons. Such a case, the above-mentioned ad (4), is referred to as insurance of another's insurance peril in favour of a third person, and the rules set out in § 2767 shall apply with necessary modifications (§ 2768(2) CC).

411. However, the law does not explicitly regulate this situation, which causes certain interpretation and application problems; for more details, *see* e.g., Jandová, Lucie. In: Jandová, Lucie; Šlauf, Petr; Svejkovský, Jaroslav. *Pojištění v novém občanském zákoníku.* Komentář. 1st ed. Praha: C. H. Beck, 2014, p. 41.

392. A specific category of third person in the insurance relationship is the injured party with a right of direct action against the insurer. In liability insurance,[412] the beneficiary is, in principle, identical to the insured person. The injured party usually has no locus standi to bring an action against the insurer and represents only the statutory determined place of performance. The provisions of § 2861(2) CC provide that the injured party becomes entitled to indemnity from the insurer only if it has been stipulated, or where provided by another statute. The injured party's right of direct action therefore constitutes an exception to the general rule and can only be established by a statute or a contract.[413]

393. The existence of the right of direct action of the injured party against the liability insurer does not cause the extinction of the right to damages against the tortfeasor. Both rights coexist, but are interdependent in the sense that, to the extent that one has been fulfilled, the other extinguishes. Therefore, if the insured compensates the damage or part of it himself, the direct claim of the injured party to the insurance indemnity against the insurer also extinguishes to this extent. Conversely, if the insurer provides the indemnity to the injured party, the injured party's right to compensation for damage against the tortfeasor extinguishes to that extent. This situation is referred to as false joint and several responsibility (in Czech 'nepravá solidarita').[414] The injured party is entitled to compensation only once, as it is a claim for identical performance, albeit on the basis of different legal reasons.[415]

394. A clear distinction must be made between these two rights. The provision of insurance indemnity to the injured party is not a performance due to the compensation for damage, as the person liable for compensation for damage remains the insured (tortfeasor). The insurer provides the indemnity that does not originate in the tortious relationship between the tortfeasor and the injured party, but in the insurance relationship established by the insurance contract. This distinction has important practical consequences, whether in terms of the territorial jurisdiction of the courts,[416] the different regime of statute of limitations,[417] or the procedural position of particular persons in court proceedings.

---

412. Discussed in more details in Part III, Ch. 4. Liability Insurance.
413. The contract here means primarily the insurance contract, so it is assumed that the right of direct action of the injured party may be established by an agreement between the insurer and the policyholder. However, it is necessary to realize that the right of direct action of the injured party may also be established by a contract between the tortfeasor and the injured party in the form of the assignment of the claim to indemnity to the injured party.
414. *See* judgement of the Supreme Court of the Czech Republic of 6 Apr. 2016, file No. 25 Cdo 222/2015; or judgement of the Supreme Court of the Czech Republic of 24 Jul. 2002, file No. 25 Cdo 499/2002.
415. Mimrová, Tereza. In: Petrov, Jan; Výtisk, Michal; Beran, Vladimír et al. *Občanský zákoník: komentář.* 1st ed. Praha: C. H. Beck, 2017, pp. 2790–2791.
416. *See* e.g., the resolution of the Municipal Court in Prague of 24 Apr. 2009, file No. 21 Co 139/2009, published in the Collection of Judicial Decisions and Opinions under No. 81/2011.
417. *See* e.g., the judgement of the Supreme Court of the Czech Republic of 12 Dec. 2007, file No. 25 Cdo 113/2006, published in the Collection of Judicial Decisions and Opinions under No. 93/2008.

395. A similar dependence can be found between the injured party's direct right to indemnity against the insurer and the insured's parallel right to have the insurer compensate the injured person for damage or other harm, because both the injured party with direct claim and the insured have a locus standi to bring an action against the insurer. Thus, in fact, it is a right to the same performance on the basis of the same legal reason, while two persons have locus standi to bring an action. The assertion of the right to indemnity by the injured party does not automatically terminate the insured's right to have the insurer to compensate the injured party's claim. Thus, these two rights coexist side by side with the fact that by satisfying the right of the injured party, the corresponding right of the insured also extinguishes to a given extent.

396. At present, the right of direct action of the injured party is established only by the provision of § 9(1) MTPLIA, which stipulates that the injured party has the right to make his claim for compensation with the respective insurer (or with the Czech Insurers' Bureau if it is a claim for a compensation from the Guarantee fund).

397. This is an important and very widely used provision in practice. For the first time, the direct claim of the injured party appeared in the Czech legal system in the early 1950s in the Decree of the Ministry of Finance of the Czechoslovak Republic No. 105/1951 Ú. l. I, on the Performance of Motor Third Party Liability Insurance. This decree established a direct claim of the injured party in cases where neither the person responsible for the operation of the motor vehicle nor another person liable for the damage was identified. This regulation was subsequently followed by Government Order No. 54/1953 Sb., on Road Traffic, and implementing decrees of the Ministry of Finance. With effect from 1 January 1992, Decree of the Ministry of Finance No. 492/1991 Sb., stipulated in the provision of § 7(1) that the insurance company pays indemnity to the injured party, however, the injured party does not have the right to indemnification against the insurance company, except in exhaustively enumerated cases. These were situations where the insured tortfeasor died or, in the case of a legal person, terminated without a legal successor, if the tortfeasor responsible for the harm caused to health or death was not identified, and if the insurance company refused in writing to compensate the injured party. With effect from 1 January 1998, also a situation in which the insured did not fulfil his obligation of notification regarding the occurrence of an insured event.

398. The fundamental change was brought about by MTPLIA, which came into full effect on 1 January 2000 and transformed the current statutory insurance system into a compulsory-contractual system, incorporating the relevant European legislation and enshrining the above-mentioned and widely applied provision of § 9(1) MTPLIA establishing the right of direct action of the injured party against the insurer.

399. The lawmaker thus complied with the requirements of European law in order to pave the way for the injured parties to compensation for their harm.[418] The direct claim of the injured party on the one hand eliminated the problem of the often difficult to enforce cooperation of the insured tortfeasor,[419] and on the other hand opened the way for the injured party to effectively obtain adequate reparation of the harm.

400. In addition to the aforementioned provision of § 9(1) MTPLIA, the right of direct action of the injured party may be met only in the statutory employer's liability insurance for damage in the event of an accident at work or an occupational disease, namely in the event that upon the termination of the employer, the rights and obligations from the employment relationship do not pass to another employer. In such a case, the injured party (or survivors) may assert his claims directly against the insurer of this employer.[420]

418. Kazda, Petr; Kazdová, Karolína. *Zákon o pojištění odpovědnosti z provozu vozidla. Komentář.* § 9 [ASPI System]. Wolters Kluwer [cit. 2020-10-12]. ASPI_ID KO168_p11999CZ. Available in the ASPI System. ISSN: 2336-517X.].
419. Bušta, Pavel; Přikryl, Vladimír. *Zákon o pojištění odpovědnosti z provozu vozidla s komentářem (ve znění 16 novel).* § 9 [ASPI System]. Wolters Kluwer [cit. 2020-10-12]. ASPI_ID KO168_1999CZ. Available in the ASPI System. ISSN: 2336-517X.].
420. Cf. § 205d(8) of the Act No. 65/1965 Sb., Labour Code, in connection with the provision of § 365(1) of the Act No. 262/2006 Sb., Labour Code.

Chapter 7. Termination of the Insurance Contract

401. Insurance, like other liabilities, extinguishes on the basis of legal facts with which the law or a contract associate this consequence. The insurance typically extinguishes as a result of juridical acts of the contractual parties (notice of termination, withdrawal from the contract, refusal of insurance indemnity) or on the basis of legal facts (expiration of the insurance period, death of the insured person).

402. In practice, these are mainly general reasons for the extinction of insurance defined in the provisions of §§ 2802–2810 CC:

- agreement of the insurer and the policyholder (§ 2802 CC);[421]
- expiration of the insurance period (§ 2803(1) CC);[422]
- vain expiration of the time limit set for the payment of premium in a qualified reminder from the insurer (§ 2804 CC);
- notice of termination within two months from the date of conclusion of the contract (§ 2805(a) CC);
- notice of termination within three months from the date of notification of the insured event (§ 2805(b) CC);
- notice of termination at the end of the insurance period (§ 2807 CC);
- notice of termination given by the policyholder due to the insurer's breach of duty to equal treatment (§ 2806(a) CC);
- notice of termination given by the policyholder due to the transfer of insurance portfolio or its part, or on the transformation of the insurer (§ 2806(b) CC);
- notice of termination given by the policyholder due to the withdrawal of the insurer's authorization (§ 2806(c) CC);
- withdrawal of the insurer or policyholder from the contract due to breach of duty to truthful communication (§ 2808(1) CC);
- withdrawal of the policyholder from the contract due to the insurer's breach of the duty to inform about the discrepancies between the insurance offered and the prospective policyholder's requirements (§ 2808(1) second sentence CC);[423]
- withdrawal of the policyholder from the distance contract (§ 2808(3) CC);
- rejection to provide insurance indemnity (§§ 2809 and 2810 CC in fine);
- extinction of the insurable interest (§ 2810 CC);
- extinction of the insurance peril (§ 2810 CC);
- death of the insured person (§ 2810 CC);

---

421. The parties are required to stipulate the manner of settlement in the agreement; *see also* the CNB's Supervisory information No. 1/2016, on Management of Legal Risk and the Risk of Financial Losses in Connection with the Termination of Insurance by Agreement (available at https://www.cnb.cz/cs/dohled-financni-trh/vykon-dohledu/dohledova-uredni-sdeleni-a-benchmarky/informace-dohledu-c.-1-2016-k-rizeni-pravniho-rizika-a-rizika-financnich-ztrat-v-souvislosti-s-ukoncovanim-pojisteni-dohodou/).

422. With the possibility of arranging the so-called automatic prolongation – *see* § 2803(2) CC.

423. The policyholder's right to withdraw from the contract for this reason, as well as the insurer's duty to inform the prospective policyholder about any discrepancies between the insurance offered and the policyholder's requirements (*see* § 2789(1) CC), were newly introduced by the Civil Code; AIC did not regulate similar right of the policyholder and a similar duty of the insurer.

– termination of the insured legal person without a legal successor (§ 2810 CC).

403. Above provisions do not constitute an exhaustive list of reasons for termination of insurance. Other ways of termination are regulated by the law, for example, in the provision of § 2786(2) CC (termination of insurance at the end of the insurance period for which the premium was paid, if the policyholder expressed disagreement with the change of premium for another insurance period), § 2793 CC (termination of insurance by insurer's notice of termination due to failure of the policyholder to notify the increase of the insurance risk), § 2812 CC (termination of property insurance upon notification of change of ownership or co-ownership of the insured property), § 2867 CC (termination of liability insurance related to ownership upon notification of change of ownership or co-ownership),[424] etc.

404. In addition to the mentioned reasons for the termination of the obligation specific to insurance and regulated within the insurance legislation, the insurance can of course also be affected by some general reasons for termination specified in the general provisions on obligations. An example could be withdrawal from the contract due to fundamental breach of contract (§ 2002 CC) or withdrawal from the contract for reasons agreed in the contract (§ 2001 CC).

405. When applying these general institutes, as well as when arranging other reasons for termination of insurance beyond the law, it is of course not possible to lose sight of restrictions specific to insurance (e.g., prohibition to terminate or withdraw from the insurance contract in compulsory insurance, unless permitted by a statute – *see* § 2781 CC), or general restrictions applicable to other types of obligations (consumer protection, adhesion contracts, etc.).

406. In practice, a situation may arise where several reasons for extinction envisaged by law or contract compete with each other. This is, for example, the termination of the insurance as a result of a notification of the change of ownership or co-ownership of the insured property (§ 2812 CC) in relation to the termination of the insurance due to the termination of the policyholder's insurable interest (§§ 2765 and 2810 CC).[425] In such a case, it is necessary to determine according to which provision the insurance extinguishes, whether according to the provisions of §§ 2765 and 2810 CC, or according to § 2812 CC. This is necessary because these provisions stipulate a different time of termination of the insurance – the moment of extinction of the insurable interest compared to the date of notification of the change of ownership. Similar situation is the concurrence of the termination of the insurance due to a change of ownership (§ 2812 CC) and due to the death of the insured or the termination of the insured legal person without a legal successor (§ 2810 CC). In both mentioned cases, it can be concluded that the provisions of § 2812 CC is *lex*

424. According to the AIC, the insurance extinguished in principle by a change of ownership or co-ownership, i.e., not by the notification of such change (cf. § 27(1) and § 43(4) AIC).

425. However, the change of ownership of the insured property does not always lead to extinguish of the insurable interest. Even if the owner changes, the policyholder's insurable interest may persist. If, e.g., the property was transferred from a parent (policyholder) to a child, the insurable interest of the parent undoubtedly continues.

specialis in relation to the general reasons for termination stipulated in § 2810 CC. Termination due to a change of ownership pursuant to § 1812 CC should therefore be applied in these cases as a matter of priority, and conversely the general reasons for termination referred to in § 2810 CC should apply only where there is no special rule for such situation.[426]

426. Identically Jandová, Lucie. In: Jandová, Lucie; Šlauf, Petr; Svejkovský, Jaroslav. *Pojištění v novém občanském zákoníku. Komentář.* 1st ed. Praha: C. H. Beck, 2014, pp. 331–332.

Part III. Property and Liability Insurance

Chapter 1. Fire Insurance

407. Fire insurance does not represent a separate type of insurance in domestic legislation. It is governed by the general legal regulation of property insurance against loss and damage[427] in the Civil Code. Fire is one of the basic and traditional insurance perils insured under property insurance. Fire insurance is associated with the beginnings of the Czech insurance industry.[428]

408. Fire insurance can be arranged separately, but more often it appears within the combined insurance peril 'FLEXA', which is the traditional summary designation for insurance risks of (F)ire, (L)ightning, (EX)plosion, and (A)ircraft. Fire insurance is also an integral part of property insurance arranged on the principle of all-risks coverage. This is one of the basic coverages that is negotiated in retail and business products. The object of this insurance can be both immovable and movable property (e.g., household equipment, supplies, etc.). A separate thing, a collective thing (*universitas rerum*)[429] or a set of things can be insured.

409. The term 'fire' is not defined by law for insurance purposes. The definition of fire is contained in the Decree of the Ministry of the Interior No. 21/1996 Sb., which implements some provisions of the Act of the Czech National Council on Fire Protection, according to which for the purposes of fire protection, a fire is considered to be any undesirable burning in which persons or animals have been killed or injured or material damage has been caused. Undesirable combustion in which persons, animals, or material values or the environment were immediately endangered is also considered to be a fire.

410. In the insurance policies, contractual definitions of fire are used, which are not completely uniform. In minor variations, a fire is usually defined as a fire in the form of a flame that accompanies burning and developed outside the designated fireplace or left such a fireplace and spread by its own power. Fire insurance usually also covers damage or destruction of the insured property by smoke and combustion products or extinguishing or tearing down when fighting a fire or removing its

427. Although the law allows property insurance to be arranged as a fixed-amount insurance, in practice it is, in the vast majority of cases, taken out in the form of insurance against loss and damage.
428. *See* General Introduction, §2. Historical Background of Insurance and Insurance Legislation.
429. Cf. § 501 CC.

consequences. However, a fire is usually not the glow and smouldering with limited access of oxygen, nor the effect of a utility fire and its heat, nor the effect of heat in the event of a short circuit in an electrical line or equipment, unless the flame created by the short circuit has spread.[430]

411. Fire insurance (property insurance in general) is usually arranged to full value, i.e., so that the sum insured corresponds to the insurance value. However, so-called first loss insurance (in Czech 'pojištění na první riziko') or fractional insurance is not excluded either.[431]

412. The insurance value may be expressed as:

(i) the replacement value (in Czech 'nová cena');
(ii) the actual cash value ('časová cena'); or
(iii) the usual value ('obvyklá cena').

413. Replacement value represents the sum that has to be spent to reinstate the thing of the same or comparable type, quality, and utility value in the new condition in the given place and time.[432]

414. The actual cash value is the value the thing had immediately before occurrence of the insured event; it is determined on the basis of the replacement value of the thing taking into account the level of wear and tear or another depreciation or appreciation of the thing resulting from its repair, modernization, or otherwise.[433]

415. Usual value means the price that would be reached when selling the same or similar thing within the common business relations in the given place and time.[434]

416. Where, in the case of property insurance, no insurance value has been stipulated, the insurance value is equal to the usual value of the property at the time at which its value is determined (§ 2849 CC).

---

430. Cf. e.g., the definition of fire in the insurance conditions of Generali Česká pojišťovna a.s., (VPP-BH-01-2020, available at https://www.generaliceska.cz/pojisteni-majetku); or Kooperativa pojišťovna, a.s., Vienna Insurance Group (M-100/17, available at https://www.koop.cz/dokumenty-ke-stazeni/dokumenty-k-pojisteni-majetku).
431. By the 'first loss insurance' (or first loss policy), it is understood a situation where it is not possible to determine in advance the insurance value of the insured property and the contractual parties stipulates a maximum threshold for insurance indemnity as the insurance indemnity limit. In practice, a conscious and agreed reduction of the sum insured below the insurance value of the insured property is also referred to as first loss insurance. In these cases, under-insurance is not applied. If the insurance covers only a part of the value of the insured property, we speak of 'fractional insurance' (cf. § 2814(3) CC).
432. Cf. former § 3(w) AIC.
433. Cf. former § 3(v) AIC.
434. Cf. § 492(1) CC, and § 2(2) of Act No. 151/1997 Sb., on Property Valuation, or e.g., the resolution of the Supreme Court of the Czech Republic of 28 August 2012, file No. 23 Cdo 500/2012.

417. The nature and amount of insurance risk, and thus the amount of the insurance premium, in fire insurance is influenced by a number of factors, including among others; building structure, building materials used, distance of individual buildings, installation of fire extinguishers, hydrants, automatic fire alarms, and other fire protection systems. In industrial insurance, these factors are evaluated by the risk engineers, who summarize their conclusions in a risk assessment report, which is an important basis for the underwriting process.

418. One of the basic terms found within fire risk assessment works with is 'fire complex'. A fire complex is a set of buildings for which, taking into account the given distances, the fire is expected to spread from one building to another. The minimum distance is considered to be the height of the building, but not less than 10 m, in the case of storeroom with flammable liquids it is at least 20 m. On the contrary, the spread of fire between individual fire complexes is not expected. An important parameter that is determined for a fire complex is the maximum possible damage. This is the highest possible damage that can be expected from one extraordinary event, provided that the function of external (fire brigade) and internal (fire safety equipment) fire protection systems is not considered.[435]

419. The maximum possible damage can be expressed as:

(i) Normal Loss Expectancy (NLE) – maximum expected damage potential if stable fire extinguishing systems work flawlessly and human intervention in fighting a fire has been successful.
(ii) Probable Maximum Loss (PML) – maximum expected damage potential if stable fire extinguishing systems are out of order, but the human factor is successful in fighting the fire, and fire walls prevent further spread of the fire.
(iii) Maximum Foreseeable Loss (MFL) – maximum expected damage potential in case the stable fire extinguishing systems are out of order, the human factor is not able to fight the fire, only properly executed fire walls prevent further spread of the fire.
(iv) Maximum Amount Subject (MAS) – under the given circumstances, the entire fire complex is destroyed, regardless of the existence of fire walls, the fire will not end until all combustible substances have burned.[436]

---

435. Šenovský, Michail; Šenovský, Pavel. *Metody hodnocení rizika průmyslových zón.* In: Červený kohout: sborník příspěvků, 13th year of the conference, Hluboká nad Vltavou, 2010.
436. Janata, Jiří. *Metodika přípravy rizikové zprávy pro pojistné trhy.* 1st ed. Praha: Professional Publishing, 2010, p. 90.

Chapter 2. Loss of Benefits Insurance

420. The special regulation of loss of benefits insurance (insurance of financial losses) is contained in a single provision of § 2871 CC, which gives the contractual parties considerable freedom in negotiating the conditions of this insurance. The Civil Code defines the insurance of financial losses only in a general way when it stipulates that the object of this insurance can be costs incurred as a result of a loss event, or loss of profit, or other financial losses stipulated in the contract. Unlike the former regulation of AIC, the Civil Code allows to arrange financial loss insurance as a fixed-amount insurance (§ 2871(2) CC).[437]

421. A typical insurance product of insurance of financial losses is business interruption insurance. Some authors[438] include credit insurance,[439] guaranty insurance,[440] and legal aid insurance,[441] which have their own special regulation in the Civil Code.

422. From the point of view of public law, this is a non-life insurance class according to point 16 of Part B of Annex 1 to the IA, according to which this insurance may cover financial losses resulting from:

- employment risks;
- insufficiency of income;
- bad weather;
- loss of benefits;
- continuing general expenses;
- unforeseen trading expenses;
- loss of market value;
- loss of rent or revenue;
- other indirect trading loss; and
- other forms of financial loss.

423. The above list is exhaustive, however, the last point provides the parties with a relatively wide scope for defining other financial losses that may be subject to this insurance. Within the broad definition of insurance of financial losses, the insurance may concern the actual property loss consisting in its real reduction (*damnum emergens*), the loss of profits, i.e., a loss consisting in non-increase of insured assets due to the insured event, which would occur in the regular course of things

437. Cf. explanatory memorandum to § 2871 CC.
438. For example, Ducháčková, Eva. *Pojištění a pojišťovnictví.* 1st ed. Praha: Ekopress, 2015, p. 199.
439. For more details, *see* Ch. 11. Credit and Guaranty Insurance.
440. *Ibid.*
441. *See* Ch. 6. Legal Aid Insurance.

(*lucrum cessans*), but also the insured's obligation to do something.[442] Financial losses according to the provision of § 2871 CC may represent any negative interference with the insured's assets.[443]

424. While property insurance serves primarily to cover direct material damage to the insured property, the business interruption insurance (also referred to in Czech as 'šomážní pojištění') is arranged to compensate subsequent damage caused by business interruption due to previous damage to property by natural or other events (e.g., closure due to epidemiological measures). In practice, the conclusion of this insurance is often conditioned by the simultaneous conclusion of property insurance.[444]

425. The business interruption insurance occurs on the market in several variants, most often as fire business interruption insurance (in connection with natural hazards insurance), or machinery business interruption insurance (with machine insurance), or advanced loss of profits insurance[445] (the so-called ALoP, supplementary to construction insurance).

426. The sum insured is usually derived from the gross profit, which includes both lost profits from the sale of products and services and fixed costs, which the insured is forced to incur regardless of business interruptions (wages and social security contributions, rent, including lease payments, taxes, insurance premiums, etc.). The subject of the insurance may also be other costs that the insured is forced to incur in connection with the business interruption (e.g., costs associated with the emergency operation, overtime pay, etc.).

427. The insurance indemnity is provided for the so-called indemnity period (in Czech 'doba ručení'), which means the agreed period of time during which the insurance company is obliged to provide insurance indemnity for financial losses resulting from the business interruption. The beginning of the indemnity period is usually the moment of material damage, or the moment of financial loss, and its duration is usually agreed in the order of months. The right to insurance indemnity is granted until the resumption of operations (as long as financial losses arise). If the business operation is not resumed, the right to indemnity expires at the latest with the expiration of the agreed indemnity period, or reaching the agreed maximum threshold of the insurance indemnity (sum insured). If so agreed, the indemnity period may exceed the duration of the insurance, i.e., the indemnity may be provided even after the termination of the insurance until the expiry of the agreed indemnity period.

---

442. Jandová, Lucie. In: Jandová, Lucie; Šlauf, Petr; Svejkovský, Jaroslav. *Pojištění v novém občanském zákoníku.* Komentář. 1st ed. Praha: C. H. Beck, 2014, p. 341.
443. Haas, Karel. In: Švestka, Jiří; Dvořák, Jan; Fiala, Josef et al. *Občanský zákoník: komentář. Svazek VI (§§ 2521–3081).* § 2871 [ASPI System]. Wolters Kluwer [cit. 2020-10-18]. ASPI_ID KO89_f2012CZ. Available in the ASPI System. ISSN: 2336-517X.].
444. Ducháčková, Eva. *Pojištění a pojišťovnictví.* 1st ed. Praha: Ekopress, 2015, p. 199.
445. Insurance of financial losses resulting from delays in construction or assembly due to material damage.

428. A typical feature of this product is the application of a time-based deductible, which represents the agreed period during which the insurer is not obliged to provide insurance indemnity. If the duration of the business interruption does not exceed the agreed period, the right to indemnity does not arise.

429. The arrangement of the so-called waiting period (in Czech 'čekací doba'), i.e., a certain period of time at the beginning of the insurance, during which the right to indemnity does not arise, is also frequent. The right to insurance indemnity arises only after the expiry of the waiting period. The purpose of the waiting period is to prevent the speculative arrangement of insurance by the policyholder at a time when, given the circumstances, it can already be expected that the business interruption will most likely occur (e.g., at the time of an incipient epidemic or flood).

Chapter 3. Transport Insurance

430. At the most general level, transport insurance can be defined as insurance against damage, destruction, or loss of a thing during transport. The basic insurance peril covered by transport insurance is the risk of an accident (vehicle accidents, marine accident or the sinking thereof aircraft crashes, etc.). However, transport insurance usually covers other risks, especially natural hazards and theft.[446]

431. The coverage is usually not limited to the relocation of the consignment, but also includes damage caused by related activities such as loading, unloading, intermediate storage of goods, etc. The subject of transport insurance are usually consignments transported on the basis of a contract of carriage. Consignments transported in-house are usually insured under comprehensive property insurance products.

432. Transport insurance can be divided into two main areas, namely: (i) property insurance of the transported consignment (cargo), (ii) liability insurance of the carrier and the freight forwarder. In addition to these main areas, specific types of insurance related to transport are also included in transport insurance – an example is the insurance of carrier's financial standing (in Czech 'pojištění finanční způsobilosti dopravce'). Some authors also include hull insurance of the means of transport (casco insurance).[447]

433. Transport insurance can be classified according to a number of other criteria, for example, according to the mode of transport (maritime, air, road, or rail transport), geographical aspects (inland or international transport), according to the insurance policy concept (single shipment insurance, insurance of all transports carried out within the agreed insurance period), etc.

434. Property insurance of the transported consignment (cargo) protects the consignment against risks that may occur during transport. The insurance contract can be concluded either by the owner of the transported cargo or by the carrier or freight forwarder as insurance of the insurance peril of another in favour of the insured owner of the cargo. In addition to the value of the cargo itself, related costs such as shipping, customs duties, or lost profits may also be subject to insurance. A significant advantage over liability transport insurance products is the fact that the right to indemnity arises regardless of whether the carrier, forwarder, or other person is liable for the damage caused to the cargo, and regardless of the possible limit of such liability. With regard the nature of this insurance, which is insurance against loss and damage, any right of the insured to damages shall pass to the insurer through the payment of the insurance indemnity pursuant to the provisions of § 2820 CC.

446. Ducháčková, Eva. *Pojištění a pojišťovnictví.* 1st ed. Praha: Ekopress, 2015, p. 194.
447. *Ibid.*

435. In international transport, certain standardized levels of insurance coverage have gradually formed:

- Free of Particular Average (FPA) – the basic level of insurance coverage, which includes only the complete destruction or loss of the consignment (not partial loss) as a result of serious accidents (sinking of the ship, damage to the consignment in the event of an earthquake, etc.).
- With Particular Average (WPA) – medium level of coverage, which, unlike FPA, also includes partial loss to the consignment, usually excluding damage caused by inherent nature of the goods (food spoilage, metal corrosion, ect.).
- Against All Risks (AAR) – the widest range of insurance coverage, which includes all usual risks, including partial loss and damage caused by the inherent nature of the goods, with the exception of risks expressly excluded (usually political risks, war risks, etc.).[448]

436. In the Czech insurance market, standardized wordings of international clauses in the field of marine insurance[449] – the so-called Institute Cargo Clauses (ICC)[450] – are widely used in practice:

- ICC C – the basic scope of insurance coverage covering the risk of fire, explosion, marine accident, sinking or capsizing of the ship, overturning or derailment of land conveyance, collision with any external object.
- ICC B – beyond the basic level C includes the risks of earthquake, volcanic eruption or lightning, washing overboard, entry of water into vessel, total loss of package lost overboard or dropped whilst loading on to, or unloading from, vessel.
- ICC A – the widest range of insurance coverage on the all-risks principle, i.e., insurance against all insurance perils, except for the expressly excluded.[451]

437. The INCOTERMS clauses[452] are also widely used in the practice of international transport, some of which explicitly include the obligation to arrange transport insurance – for example, CIP (Carriage and Insurance Paid to), or CIF (Cost, Insurance & Freight).[453]

448. *See* e.g., Machková, Hana; Sato, Alexej; Zamykalová, Miroslava et al. *Mezinárodní obchod a marketing.* 1st ed. Praha: Grada, 2002, pp. 168169; or Ducháčková, Eva. *Pojištění a pojišťovnictví.* 1st ed. Praha: Ekopress, 2015, p. 195 (note: in the latter source, it is necessary to point out a minor inaccuracy caused by the confusion of the abbreviations AAR and FPA in the descriptions).
449. The term 'marine insurance' originally referred only to maritime insurance but is now often used in practice in a broader sense as a synonym for transport insurance in general.
450. The wording of all clauses is available on the website of The International Underwriting Association of London, http://www.iuaclauses.co.uk/site/cms/contentDocumentLibraryView.asp?chapter=5.
451. Ducháčková, Eva. *Pojištění a pojišťovnictví.* 1st ed. Praha: Ekopress, 2015, p. 195.
452. Series of pre-defined commercial terms published by the International Chamber of Commerce in the area of international commercial law.
453. For more details, *see* https://iccwbo.org/resources-for-business/incoterms-rules/.

438. An alternative to property insurance of a consignment, which, however, cannot completely replace it, is carrier's liability insurance. A carrier means a person that carries out the transport of goods on the basis of a contract of carriage. By a contract for the carriage of a thing, a carrier undertakes to carry a consignor's thing as a consignment from the point of dispatch to the destination, and a consignor undertakes to pay freight to the carrier (§ 2555 CC). The carrier is liable for damage caused to a consignment between its receipt by the carrier and its surrender to the consignee, usually on the basis of the principles of strict liability, i.e., regardless of their fault. The substantive law of the contract of carriage, including the tort liability of the carrier, is to a large extent harmonized for individual modes of transport by multilateral international conventions.[454] A common feature of these conventions is that, under certain conditions, they limit the carrier's liability, usually by setting an upper limit on the carrier's compensation obligation, expressed in a certain amount of Special Drawing Right as defined by the International Monetary Fund (SDRs)[455] per kilogram of gross weight of the consignment. An example is the Convention on the Contract for the International Carriage of Goods by Road (CMR convention), which is widely applied in road freight transport practice, which according to Article 23(3), compensation may not exceed 8.33 SDRs (currently approximately CZK 273) per kilogram of gross weight short. As a general rule, those conventions also provide for the liberation reasons which allow the carrier to be relieved of its liability in certain circumstances.[456]

439. In relation to road freight transport, which in domestic conditions is currently the dominant mode of freight transport, it is necessary to draw attention to the recent significant legislative amendment made by Act No. 304/2017 Sb., which, with effect from 1 January 2019, added to Act No. 111/1994 Sb., on Road Transport, the new provision of § 9a, which relates the application of a substantial part of the CMR Convention to the field of inland transport, including the aforementioned limitation of the carrier's liability under Article 23 of the CMR Convention, which so far has had no parallel in national legislation.

440. Road freight carrier's liability insurance is arranged in the event of the carrier's obligation to compensate for damage caused to the transported consignment. In addition to the basic scope of coverage, the insurers offer a number of supplementary insurances – for example, insurance of the insured's obligation to compensate for damage incurred during loading or unloading, damage to the consignment caused by theft, damage caused by the subcontractor, etc. With the mentioned legislative amendment in the form of the application of the CMR Convention in the field of inland road freight transport, the demand for additional liability insurance

454. Among the most important can be mentioned the Convention on the Contract for the International Carriage of Goods by Road (CMR); Convention concerning International Carriage by Rail (COTIF); Warsaw and the subsequent Montreal Convention for the Unification of Certain Rules for International Carriage by Air; Hague-Visby Rules and later Hamburg Rules and Rotterdam Rules for sea freight transport; Budapest Convention on the Contract for the Carriage of Goods by Inland Waterway (CMNI), etc.

455. Special Drawing Rights as defined by the International Monetary Fund.

456. *See* e.g., Art. 17(2) and (4) of the CMR Convention.

to the full value of the consignment within the meaning of Article 24 of the CMR Convention is increasing. In this context though, it should be noted that even this additional insurance cannot fully replace the cargo insurance, as the insurance indemnity from liability insurance can be provided only in cases where the insured person is liable for damage and to the full value of the consignment only if all conditions stipulated in Article 24 are met.

441. In addition to carriers, freight forwarders play an irreplaceable role in transport and logistics. The freight forwarder's liability insurance is arranged in the event of the forwarder's obligation to compensate for damage caused to a consignment taken over in the arrangement of carriage. By a forwarding contract, a forwarder undertakes to arrange for a mandator, in the forwarder's name and on the mandator's account, the carriage of a consignment from a particular place to another particular place and, where applicable, also arrange or perform acts associated with carriage, and a mandator undertakes to remunerate the forwarder (§ 2471 CC). In practice, the scope of the forwarder's activities may be relatively wide and may include other tasks such as consolidation of shipments, packaging, storage, ensuring of adequate means of transport, completion of customs formalities, accompanying documents, or arranging insurance. In case damage is incurred to a consignment taken over in the arrangement of carriage, the forwarder has to compensate such damage unless they prove that they were unable to prevent it (§ 2478 CC). Unlike carriers, the freight forwarder's liability is not limited by law. However, a possible contractual limitation of liability is not excluded.[457]

442. In addition to material damage to the consignment, the forwarder's liability insurance also usually covers financial losses that may arise during the arrangement of carriage (e.g., additional costs for arranging alternative transport after incorrect determination of the place of delivery or dispatch of an incomplete consignment). Freight forwarder's liability insurance may also cover damage caused during the so-called self-entry (in Czech 'samovstup') of the forwarder. By self-entry is meant a situation where the carriage which a forwarder is to arrange is carried out by the forwarder himself (§ 2474 CC). In such a case, the freight forwarder assumes the role of the carrier, i.e., their possible liability is assessed in the regime of the contract of carriage (not forwarding contract), including the usual limitation of the carrier's liability. The forwarders may also enter such a position unwillingly if they fail to notify the mandator about the carrier with whom they have concluded the contract of carriage (§ 2461 CC). In such a case the mandator may assert his rights against the forwarder as a party obliged under a contract of carriage.[458]

443. The freight forwarder is obliged to insure the consignment only if it is stipulated in the forwarding contract (§ 2475 CC), however, as a transport organizer

457. Cf. § 2898 CC *a contrario*.
458. Cf. e.g., judgement of the Supreme Court of the Czech Republic of 26 Sep. 2007, file No. 32 Odo 1254/2005, published in the Collection of Judicial Decisions and Opinions under No. 74/2008, or judgement of the Supreme Court of the Czech Republic of 29 Apr. 2008, file No. 32 Cdo 1000/2007.

they should protect the mandator's interests and warn them of the need to arrange cargo insurance, especially if the value of the consignment exceeds the liability limit of the carrier.

444. A specific area of transport insurance is the insurance of carrier's financial standing. The offer of this insurance product responds to the existence of a statutory obligation of a road freight carrier operating transport by large vehicles (i.e., vehicles with a maximum permissible mass exceeding 3.5 tonnes), enshrined in the provisions of §§ 6 and 8 of Act No. 111/1994 Sb. on Road Transport, according to which a concession for the operation of such transport may be granted only to a person who meets, *inter alia*, the condition of financial standing, i.e., the ability of the carrier to meet its financial obligations. Financial standing can be demonstrated in the ways specified in the directly applicable regulation of the EU,[459] primarily by its own capital, bank guarantee or insurance. This insurance does not yet have a stable content on the market. The principle of guaranty insurance in the event of non-fulfilment of the insured's financial obligation is usually agreed on. In practice, however, some of the competent authorities accept the carrier's liability insurance as a proof of the carrier's financial standing.

459. Regulation (EC) No. 1071/2009 of the European Parliament and of the Council of 21 October 2009 establishing common rules concerning the conditions to be complied with to pursue the occupation of road transport operator and repealing Council Directive 96/26/EC.

Chapter 4. Liability Insurance

445. Liability insurance within commercially offered insurance products is one of the most frequent in the Czech insurance market, which is best illustrated by the fact that total gross written premiums from liability insurance products in the Czech Republic in 2019 amounted to more than CZK 42.5 billion.[460] Of this, MTPL together with general liability insurance, accounted for 32.5% of the market share in the non-life insurance in 2019.[461]

446. Liability insurance is characterized by a triangle of relationships between the insurer, the policyholder (insured), and the injured party. At the most general level, it can be defined as a legal relationship between the insurer and the policyholder, the essence of which is the insurer's obligation to provide in the case of an insured event, instead of the insured tortfeasor, performance compensating the damage to the stipulated extent, if the insured is liable and, by contrast, the policyholder's obligation to pay premiums to the insurer. This fully corresponds to the basic definition of liability insurance in the provisions of § 2861 CC, according to which an insured person has the right, in the event of an insured event, to have the insurer compensate the injured person for damage or other harm to the extent and in the amount prescribed by a statute or contract, if the insured person incurred the duty to provide compensation.

447. Liability insurance is primarily aimed at protecting the interests of the insured, who is (for a fee in the form of insurance premiums) protected from the negative economic consequences of the occurrence of their liability and obligation to damages to the injured party. At the same time, it fulfils a wider societal interest in the protection of injured parties (victims) by providing an additional financial source that increases the chances of victims to real compensation for their damage or other harm, regardless of the creditworthiness of the tortfeasor.

448. It is essential that in the case of an insured event, the insurer does not assume the role of a tortfeasor and the injured party does not, in principle, have the right to indemnity against the insurer. An exception in the form of a direct claim of the injured party against the insurer can be established only by a statute or a contract (§ 2861(2) CC).[462] The insurer does not become the subject of the liability obligation between the tortfeasor and the injured party, but bears the economic consequences of the damage instead of the insured person, to the extent, under the conditions and up to the limits agreed in the insurance contract.

---

460. CIA's Annual Report for 2019 (available at https://www.cap.cz/vyrocni-zpravy).
461. CNB's Financial Market Supervision Report for 2019 (available at https://www.cnb.cz/en/supervision-financial-market/aggregate-information-financial-sector/financial-market-supervision-reports/).
462. For more information on the injured party's direct claim, *see* Part II, Ch. 6. Insurance and Third Parties.

449. The tortfeasor's obligation to compensate the injured party is independent of the existence of liability insurance. The tortfeasor remains the one who is primarily obliged to compensate the injured party. A clear distinction must be made between the right of the injured party to compensation for damage against a tortfeasor and the right of the beneficiary to the insurance indemnity against the insurer.[463] To the extent of the indemnity provided by the insurer, the right of the injured party to compensation for damage against the tortfeasor extinguishes. If the entire damage is not compensated by the insurance indemnity, the tortfeasor remains obliged to compensate for the remaining extent. If the insured person compensated the damage or harm covered by insurance, they are entitled to be compensated by the insurer up to the amount of the indemnity which the insurer would have otherwise been obliged to provide to the injured party (§ 2865(1) second sentence CC).

450. The distinction between the injured party's right to compensation and the beneficiary's right to insurance indemnity has its practical consequences, for example, in limitation period,[464] where the right to indemnity and the right to compensation are time-barred separately and (to some extent) independently.[465]

451. Furthermore, for example, when assessing the territorial jurisdiction of the court, where, in relation to the right to insurance indemnity against the insurer, the choice of territorial jurisdiction under the provisions of § 87(b) CPC (i.e., the optional territorial jurisdiction according to the place where the event giving rise to the right to damages has occurred) cannot be applied.[466]

452. Finally, a fundamental aspect of the distinction between these two legal relationships is the fact that a decision of a court or other public authority on the right to compensation in a dispute between a tortfeasor and an injured party is not

463. Cf. e.g., judgement of the Supreme Court of the Czech Republic of 7 Jun. 2000, file No. 25 Cdo 1094/98; judgement of 12 Dec. 2007, file No. 25 Cdo 113/2006, published in the Collection of Judicial Decisions and Opinions under No. 93/2008; judgement of 21 Mar. 2014, file No. 25 Cdo 1002/2012; judgement of 28 Nov., file No. 32 Cdo 4765/2010; judgement of 27 Sep. 2016, file No. 25 Cdo 1896/2016, published in the Collection of Judicial Decisions and Opinions under No. 26/2018, and more.

464. Cf. judgement of 12 Dec. 2007, file No. 25 Cdo 113/2006, published in the Collection of Judicial Decisions and Opinions under No. 93/2008.

465. It is necessary to draw attention to § 635(2) CC, to which the Supreme Court gave an interpretation in the judgement of 28 Nov. 2019, file No. 25 Cdo 1976/2019, in which he stated that 'the right to insurance indemnity from liability insurance should not be actionable for longer than the right to compensation for the damage or injury covered by the insurance. It follows that the right to insurance indemnity may be time-barred before the expiration of the limitation period stipulated in the provision of § 626 of the Civil Code, by the expiration of the subjective limitation period for the assertion of the right to compensation for damage.'

466. *See* the resolution of the Municipal Court in Prague of 24 Apr. 2009, file No. 21 Co 139/2009, published in the Collection of Judicial Decisions and Opinions under No. 81/2011, or the resolution of the Supreme Court of the Czech Republic of 18 Aug. 2015, file No. 25 Cdo 2773/2015.

automatically binding on the liability insurer, as they are neither the (main) party to such proceedings nor the debtor of the tortious obligation to compensate for damage.[467]

453. A person who has a locus standi to bring an action against the insurer (i.e., the beneficiary) from liability insurance is the insured person.[468] The insurer provides the insurance indemnity to the injured party (§ 2861(1) CC), but the injured party is only the statutory determined place of performance; the insured remains the creditor of the claim for insurance indemnity.

454. In practice, the question arose as to whether the insured was entitled to sue the insurer in order to pay the injured party directly. The Supreme Court answered this question in the judgement of 12 December 2018, file No. 23 Cdo 5969/2017, published Collection of Judicial Decisions and Opinions under No. 9/2019, in which they stated that 'the law explicitly enshrines the right of the insured to demand that the insurer compensates the injured party instead of the insured in case of the insured event, for damage which the insured is liable for according to the law, up to the amount of the insurance indemnity limit stipulated in the insurance contract.'[469]

455. Unlike other types of insurance, the subject of liability insurance is not primarily life, health, or property, but an abstract legal relationship consisting in the liability obligation between the insured tortfeasor and the injured party. Liability insurance is therefore closely linked to the regulation of the legal liability and has significant overlaps beyond the insurance matters. The area of liability insurance therefore develops dynamically together with the development of the legislation on private tort law. If the tort law changes, the subject of liability insurance will change at the same time. This can be illustrated by the example of the recent recodification of the Czech substantive private law. While the regulation of liability insurance itself did not undergo significant changes, the system of private tort law was fundamentally rebuilt. The legal regulation of the tortfeasor's obligation to compensate for damage has changed significantly, i.e., the rules that determine who, to whom, in which cases, in what manner, and to what extent it is obliged to compensate for damage. At the turn of 2013 and 2014 (when the new Civil Code came into force), insurers were forced to respond to this with a comprehensive revision of their liability products and with a thorough analysis of changes in the subject of insurance and insurance risk in current insurance contracts.

---

467. Judgement of the Supreme Court of the Czech Republic of 30 Sep. 2009, file No. 25 Cdo 800/2008.

468. Jandová, Lucie. In: Jandová, Lucie; Šlauf, Petr; Svejkovský, Jaroslav. *Pojištění v novém občanském zákoníku. Komentář.* 1st ed. Praha: C. H. Beck, 2014, p. 306; Haas, Karel. In: Švestka, Jiří; Dvořák, Jan; Fiala, Josef et al. *Občanský zákoník: komentář. Svazek VI (§ 2521–3081).* § 2861 [ASPI System]. Wolters Kluwer [cit. 2020-9-20]. ASPI_ID KO89_f2012CZ. Available in the ASPI System. ISSN: 2336-517X.]; Wawerková, Magdalena. In: Hulmák, Milan et al. *Občanský zákoník VI. Závazkové právo. Zvláštní část (§§ 2055–3014). Komentář.* 1st ed. Praha: C. H. Beck, 2014, p. 1450.

469. Identically the judgement of the Supreme Court of the Czech Republic of 18 December 2018, file No. 23 Cdo 276/2018.

456. The law allows liability insurance to be arranged only as insurance against loss and damage (§ 2861(3) CC). In the case of insurance against loss and damage, the insurer provides insurance indemnity which, to the stipulated extent, compensates for the loss of property incurred as a result of an insured event (§ 2811 CC), up to the amount of the insurance indemnity limit, or to the full amount, if the limit of insurance indemnity has not been agreed. The relevant provision of § 2861(3) CC, which *a contrario* prohibits the contracting parties from arranging liability insurance as a fixed-amount insurance, is peremptory, which emphasizes the principle that liability insurance ultimately aims to the restitution of the injured party's damage or other harm, and do not lead to enrichment of the beneficiary. Wawerková adds that 'the Civil Code precludes liability insurance from being arranged as a fixed-amount. Otherwise, it would no longer be liability insurance, but, for example, financial loss insurance.'[470]

457. The insured event in liability insurance is not explicitly defined by law, however, it follows from the provision of § 2861(1) CC that the insured event in liability insurance is, in general, the occurrence of the insured's obligation to compensate the injured party. The Civil Code leaves the specific definition of the insured event in liability insurance to the discretion of the contracting parties to the insurance contract, or to special legal regulations. The definition of an insured event basically coincides with the definition of the scope of insurance,[471] i.e., the determination of which specific events and under what conditions the insurance covers. The scope of liability insurance can be defined by a combination of material (factual), time, and territorial criteria.

458. In terms of material scope, insurance can generally be constructed as 'named perils' or 'all-risks' insurance. In practice, liability insurance is arranged exclusively as insurance against the listed insurance risks.[472] Depending on their nature, insurance risks in liability insurance can be divided into: (i) risks covered in the basic scope of insurance coverage (e.g., risks within the scope of the so-called general liability insurance), (ii) risks insurable as a standard in the form of supplementary insurance (e.g., liability for damage to another's things assumed for the purpose of performing ordered activity, or insurance of a so-called consequential financial loss or pure financial loss), (iii) risks difficult to insure (e.g., liability caused by a particularly hazardous operation or environmental liability), and (iv) risks usually uninsurable (i.e., liability insurance for intentional damage or contractual liability beyond the liability stipulated by the law).[473]

---

470. Wawerková, Magdalena. In: Hulmák, Milan et al. *Občanský zákoník VI. Závazkové právo. Zvláštní část (§§ 2055–3014). Komentář.* 1st ed. Praha: C. H. Beck, 2014, p. 1451.

471. The term 'scope of insurance' is not defined by law, although it is used in some provisions (*see*, e.g., the provisions of § 2865(2) CC). However, the meaning of this term is steady in practice and well understood in ordinary language, on the contrary, its specific content must be assessed individually on the basis of a specific insurance contract and insurance terms and conditions.

472. Zárybnická, Jana. In: Zárybnická, Jana; Schelle, Karel. *Pojištění odpovědnosti za škodu (historie a současnost).* 1st ed. Ostrava: Key Publishing, 2010, pp. 137 et seq.

473. *Ibid.*

459. Another possible approach to the classification of individual types of liability insurance in terms of their material definition is their division according to individual types of liability as they result from tort law. It is therefore, in principle, a matter of determining which merits of tort liability are covered by the insurance. The insurance can thus cover a wide range of liability merits including liability arising from a breach of statutory or contractual duties (§§ 2910 and 2913 CC), liability for damage resulting from operating activities (§ 2924 CC), liability for damage caused by the operation of a means of transport (§ 2927 CC), or specific merits, such as the liability for damage caused by an animal (§§ 2933–2935 CC) or liability for damage caused by information or advice (§ 2950 CC), etc.

460. Of course, the insurance coverage does not have to be limited to the liability regulated by the Civil Code and can also be arranged in the case of employment liability or liability arising from another special legal regulation (e.g., Act No. 167/2008 Sb., on Prevention and Remedying Environmental Damage).

461. Furthermore, the scope of insurance coverage can be adjusted in terms of the nature of the damage or other harm to which the insurance applies. The parties to the insurance contract should always specify whether the insurance only covers harm to property (damage) or whether, and to what extent, it also covers non-pecuniary harm. From this point of view, liability insurance can be arranged, for example, in case of compensation for bodily harm and death (within which claims of pecuniary and non-pecuniary nature are covered), in case of damage to a thing caused by its damage, destruction, or loss, or in case of so-called consequential financial loss[474] or pure financial loss.[475] This division is also usually supplemented by a negative definition of the scope of insurance in the form of exclusions from insurance. Thus, non-pecuniary harm according to the provision of § 2971 CC,[476] or compensation for the sentimental value pursuant to the provision of § 2969(2) CC[477] is usually excluded from the scope of insurance.

462. Other exclusions from the liability insurance usually represent specific risks that the insurer does not accept into the insurance coverage for various reasons, whether with regard to their difficult predictability, unreasonably high probability of their occurrence, extent of their consequences, impossibility to control and influence, or with regard to conditions stipulated in reinsurance contracts.

463. Liability insurance traditionally excludes damage caused intentionally, contractual liability beyond the liability stipulated by the law, damage caused by nuclear energy, radiation of all kinds or electromagnetic fields, damage caused by

474. In insurance practice, by the term 'consequential financial loss' is understood a damage that arose in a causal connection with previous harm to life, health or property.
475. The term 'pure financial loss' refers to harm that is not preceded by damage to life, health, or property.
476. With regard to the assumptions of this liability, which include grossly negligent or intentional acts of the tortfeasor.
477. The precondition of compensation of the sentimental value is that the tortfeasor damages a thing out of caprice or maliciousness.

war, terrorist attacks, insurrections and riots, damage caused by state or official intervention, etc. Liability insurance also does not conceptually cover the rights arising from defective performance or default, or the insured's obligation to pay fines, penalties, or other contractual, administrative, or criminal sanctions.[478]

464. One of the key aspects in defining an insured event in liability insurance is determining which events are covered by the insurance in terms of the passage of time. In the construction of liability insurance products, three main approaches (so-called triggers) can be distinguished in terms of the time scope of insurance.

465. The first and historically older is the 'loss occurrence' trigger, in which the occurrence of the damage is the key moment for the occurrence of the insured event. If the insurance is arranged on the loss occurrence principle, it applies to the damage that arise during the term of insurance. In the pure conception of the of loss occurrence trigger, it is not decisive when the cause of the damage (typically a breach of a legal duty) occurred, which can thus precede the commencement of insurance. It is also irrelevant when the claim of the injured party was asserted and whether this happened before or after the termination of the insurance. Decisive is only the moment when the damage occurred. If the damage occurred during the insurance period, the beneficiary may, in principle, assert the right to insurance indemnity from such an event until the expiry of the limitation periods, regardless of the fact that the insurance has extinguished in the meantime. In practice, the loss occurrence trigger is most often used for so-called general liability insurance products, or in civil liability insurance. In the Czech insurance market, this principle is usually modified by the condition that during the term of insurance, not only must damage occur, but also the cause of such damage.

466. The second basic approach to the construction of liability insurance is the 'claims made' trigger. In the pure sense of this principle, insurance covers harms for which the injured party's claim was asserted during the term of insurance. In Czech insurance practice, this concept is usually used in a modified form, where the occurrence of an insured event assumes that during the term of insurance there is cumulatively the cause of damage, the damage itself, and the claim made by the injured party. Thus, the insurance conceived in this way does not cover causes that occurred before the commencement of the insurance, nor any claims made by the injured party after its termination. By a contractual arrangement between the insurer and the policyholder, the insurance may also cover causes or unmanifested harms from before the conclusion of the insurance contract (so-called retroactive cover)[479] or, conversely, claims asserted after the termination of the basic insurance (so-called

478. Insurance of fines or penalties imposed on the insured would probably have to be considered invalid due to contrary to good morals (similarly Bohman, Ludvík; Wawerková, Magdalena. *Zákon o pojistné smlouvě: komentář.* 2nd updated and revised ed. Praha: Linde, 2009, p. 216). However, it is not excluded that the subject of the liability insurance is liability for losses caused by imposing fines or penalties on another as a result of the insured's actions.

479. Usually with the condition that the cause of the damage was not or could not be at the date of concluding the insurance contract to the policyholder, or the insured, known.

run-off cover).[480] Claims made trigger is most often used in professional liability insurance products,[481] especially with regard to the nature of the activities in question, for which there may be a significant delay between the cause of the damage and the moment when the damage occurs (when it manifests).

467. The last trigger used in insurance practice is the 'act committed' trigger, in which the moment when the cause of the damage occurred (typically a breach of legal duty) is decisive for the occurrence of the insured event. The insurance therefore covers the damage, the cause of which occurred during the term of the insurance. On the contrary, it is not decisive when the damage itself occurred and when did the injured party file a claim. In this respect, the beneficiary is again limited in time only by the limitation period for the right to insurance indemnity.

468. The last of the criteria defining the scope of liability insurance is the determination of which events the insurance covers from a territorial (geographical) point of view. The territorial scope of the insurance should in principle correspond to the area in which the insured operates his activities, i.e., the area in which there is the greatest risk of injury or damage, which the insured could subsequently be obliged to compensate.

469. In the Czech insurance market, the territorial scope of liability insurance is most often offered in the variants: (i) territory of the Czech Republic, (ii) territory of Europe, and (iii) territory of the whole world (usually with the exclusion of the territory of the USA and Canada, which belong to the traditional reinsurance exclusions).[482] Eventual contractual limitation of the territorial scope of the coverage should be respective to the material scope of the insurance, the nature and scope of the insured activities and the nature and legal basis of the insured's potential liability.

480. Usually arranged upon termination of the insured's activities.

481. This is how the insurance of specific professions, for which the law imposes the obligation to conclude an insurance contract, is referred to. The most common ones include liability insurance for healthcare providers, auditors, tax advisors and accountants, legal professionals, authorized architects, engineers and technicians working in construction, insurance intermediaries, etc.

482. Zárybnická, Jana. In: Zárybnická, Jana; Schelle, Karel. *Pojištění odpovědnosti za škodu (historie a současnost).* 1st ed. Ostrava: Key Publishing, 2010, p. 178.

Chapter 5. Motor Vehicle Insurance (Pro Memoria)

470. Talking about motor insurance, we mean primarily two main areas – (i) motor hull insurance (casco),[483] and (ii) the compulsory MTPL.[484]

471. Both insurances can be arranged separately, but they are often arranged within one comprehensive insurance contract. In addition to these main insurances, there is a wide range of supplementary insurance on the market (e.g., accident insurance for vehicle crew, insurance for luggage transported in a vehicle, legal aid insurance for drivers) and assistance services (rescue and towing, vehicle repair at the scene of failure, provision of a replacement vehicle or accommodation, telephone advice, interpreting, etc.).

472. Motor vehicle insurance is one of the most important segments in the Czech Republic, as best evidenced by the fact that MTPL, together with motor hull insurance and other motor insurance, accounts for more than 45% of total non-life insurance premiums written.[485]

473. Motor hull insurance is not specifically regulated by law and is governed by the general regulation of property insurance against loss and damage in the Civil Code. The insurance contract and the insurance conditions of individual insurers play a decisive role in defining the rights and obligations in this type of insurance. The common denominator of all variants of this insurance is the coverage of property damage that occurs to the vehicle of the insured.

474. The basic insurance peril is an accident (impact damage). In addition, motor hull insurance allows the arrangement of a number of other risks such as theft, vandalism or natural hazards. In the Czech market, motor hull insurance products are often built on the modular principle, which allows to add or remove particular insurance peril according to the individual insurance needs of the client. The system of so-called packages is also widespread, where particular packages are usually graded according to the scope of insurance coverage, while wider packages also include the risks contained in packages with a lower scope.

---

483. Class of non-life insurance according to point 3(a) of Part B of Annex 1 to the IA.
484. Class of non-life insurance according to point 10(a) of Part B of Annex 1 to the IA; *see also* a group of non-life insurance according to Part C point (b) of Annex 1 to the IA.
485. CNB's Financial Market Supervision Report for 2019 (available at https://www.cnb.cz/en/supervision-financial-market/aggregate-information-financial-sector/financial-market-supervision-reports/).

475. In contrast, the compulsory MTPL is regulated in great detail by law and gives the parties to an insurance contract only relatively little space for individualization.[486] In terms of the volume of written premiums and socio-economic significance, this is one of the most important segments of the Czech insurance market.

476. The MTPL is constructed by law as a compulsory liability insurance, in which the emphasis is on the protection of the injured. A special regulation of this insurance is contained in Act No. 168/1999 Sb., on Motor Third Party Liability Insurance and on the Amendment to some other related Acts (MTPLIA), which also incorporates relevant EU legislation. Unless otherwise stipulated by this Act, the MTPL is governed by the Civil Code (§ 1(3) MTPLIA).

477. The MTPL applies to each person, who is liable for damage caused by the operation of a vehicle specified in an insurance contract (§ 6(1) MTPLIA). From this insurance, the insured has the right to have the insurer compensate the injured person for the damage or other harm for the extent and in the amount according to the Civil Code caused by the operation of the vehicle, to the extent specified in § 6 MTPLIA. Exclusions from insurance are stipulated in § 7 MTPLIA.

478. An important element unique in the environment of Czech insurance law is the injured party's direct claim to insurance indemnity against the insurer established by the provisions of § 9(1) MTPLIA.[487] In addition, the MTPLIA regulates in great detail a number of other aspects of this insurance, including minimum limits of insurance indemnity, insurer's right to recourse, termination of insurance, the institute of claims representatives, or the existence and activities of the Czech Insurers' Bureau and Guarantee fund.[488]

486. The contractual parties may derogate from Act No. 168/1999 Sb., on Motor Third Party Liability Insurance (MTPLIA), only if this does not reduce or limit the injured party's claims arising from the right to compensation for damage from liability insurance caused by operation of the vehicle (§ 3(1) MTPLIA).

487. For more details to the direct claim of the injured party, *see* Part II, Ch. 6. Insurance and Third Parties and Part IV, Ch. 2, §4. Direct Claim of the Injured Party.

488. For more information on both types of vehicle insurance, *see* Part IV. Motor vehicle insurance.

Chapter 6. Legal Aid Insurance

479. Legal aid insurance (legal expenses insurance)[489] is regulated in §§ 2856–2860 CC.[490] By the insurance contract on legal aid insurance, the insurer undertakes to pay, in the stipulated scope, the insured person's costs associated with the assertion of their rights, and provide associated services[491] (§ 2856 CC).

480. The subject of this insurance may be, in particular, costs of legal representation of the insured person, costs associated with conducting judicial or administrative proceedings (court fees, costs of witnesses or expert opinions, cash expenses of the party, etc.), costs associated with out-of-court dispute settlement (e.g., through a professional mediator), costs associated with the enforcement of decisions, etc. The legal relations to which legal aid insurance may cover may concern both the private and public law spheres.[492]

481. Legal aid insurance is often arranged as a supplementary to other insurance products (e.g., supplementary legal aid insurance for drivers within motor vehicle insurance), or to other financial products (e.g., legal aid insurance provided with a payment card). If legal aid insurance is stipulated under a comprehensive insurance contract (i.e., an insurance contract in which several separate legal insurance relationships are concluded), it must be – under penalty of invalidity – concluded separately in a separate special part of the policy stipulating the content and scope of the legal aid insurance, as well as the amount of insurance premium for this insurance (§ 2856(2) CC).[493] The law allows legal aid insurance to be arranged only as insurance against loss and damage (§ 2856(3) CC).

482. A legal aid insurance contract cannot restrict the insured's freedom to choose a legal representative.[494] Such a stipulation would be disregarded (§ 2857 CC).[495]

483. With regard to the special nature of this insurance, the law stipulates certain rules in an effort to minimize potential conflicts of interest in the settlement of

489. From the point of view of public law classification, this is the non-life insurance class listed in point 17 of Part B of Annex 1 to the IA.
490. For the most part, this is the transposition of Arts 16(2) and 198-205 of the Solvency II Directive (formerly regulated by Council Directive 87/344/EEC of 22 Jun. 1987 on the coordination of laws, regulations and administrative provisions relating to legal expenses insurance).
491. Here, therefore, the law explicitly provides for insurance indemnity in non-pecuniary form, which in practice means particularly the provision of legal advice and legal assistance.
492. Karfíková, Marie; Přikryl, Vladimír; Vybíral, Roman et al. *Pojišťovací právo.* 2nd revised ed. Praha: Leges, 2018, p. 351.
493. Cf. Art. 199 of the Solvency II Directive.
494. Cf. also § 2a of the Act No. 85/1996 Sb., on the Legal Profession, which enshrines the right to freely choose a lawyer.
495. *See* Arts 201 and 202 of the Solvency II Directive; also cf. judgement of the CJEU C-199/08 of 10 Sep. 2009, *Erhard Eschig v. UNIQA Sachversicherung AG,* ECLI:EU:C:2009:538.

claims arising from legal aid insurance.[496] The insurer shall ensure that: (i) none of their employees, which they have entrusted with the settlement of claims arising from legal aid insurance, at the same time perform similar activities in another class of insurance operated by the insurer; (ii) the settling of the claims arising from insurance is carried out by a person who is independent of the insurer and who is stipulated in the contract; or (iii) at the time when the right to insurance indemnity arises, the beneficiary has the opportunity to choose a representative to protect their interests (§ 2858 CC). In connection with the above-mentioned requirements to avoid conflicts of interest, it is common for legal aid insurance to be provided by specialized insurers.[497]

484. A specific regulation is stipulated by law for the case of resolving disputes between the insurer and the policyholder. Pursuant to the provisions of § 2859(1) CC, at the request of the policyholder, the insurer is obliged to conclude with the policyholder a contract for an arbitrator to settle disputes arising from the legal aid insurance. The insurer must notify the policyholder of the right to demand the conclusion of an arbitration agreement both in the insurance contract and if there is a conflict of interest or disagreement between the insurer and the policyholder.

485. The special regulation contained in §§ 2857–2859 CC does not apply to: (i) legal expenses insurance relating to the operation of sea-going vessels or insurance perils arising in connection with such an operation, (ii) representation of the insured person, if such an activity is simultaneously pursued under third-party liability insurance in the insurer's own interest, and (iii) legal expenses insurance provided by the insurer as a supplement to travel insurance (§ 2860 CC).[498]

---

496. For example, in the case of providing indemnity from the legal aid insurance of one client simultaneously with the claim settlement of an insured event from liability insurance of another client who caused damage to the first client, where the interests of both insured persons are clearly contradictory.

497. Ducháčková, Eva. *Pojištění a pojišťovnictví.* 1st ed. Praha: Ekopress, 2015, p. 209; in the Czech Republic, e.g., the insurance company D.A.S. Rechtsschutz AG, branch for the Czech Republic, specializes in legal aid insurance (https://www.das.cz/).

498. Cf. Art. 198(2) of the Solvency II Directive.

Chapter 7. Aviation and Space Insurance

486. As in the case of motor vehicle insurance, aviation insurance covers two main areas, namely: (i) aircraft hull insurance (casco), and (ii) aircraft liability insurance.[499] Accident insurance for persons transported by plane is often arranged as a supplementary insurance.

487. According to the provisions of § 2(2) of Act No. 49/1997 Sb., on Civil Aviation, an aircraft means a machine that can derive support in the atmosphere from the reactions of the air other than the reactions of the air against the earth's surface. On the contrary, it is not considered an aircraft if a model aircraft's maximum take-off weight does not exceed 20 kg. In addition to conventional aircraft, aircraft within the meaning of the above definition can also be helicopters, gliders, hot air balloons, and also drones with a take-off weight exceeding 25 kg.

488. Aircraft hull insurance is a parallel to motor hull insurance. It usually covers damage, destruction, or a missing aircraft and its accessories as a result of an accident, natural disaster, theft, vandalism, or other unavoidable event specified in the insurance contract. Unlike aircraft liability insurance, this is not compulsory insurance, so the law does not provide for any minimum coverage. Aircraft insurance is usually arranged either on the principle of insurance against selected insurance perils, or very often in the form of all-risks insurance, i.e., insurance against all risks except those that are explicitly excluded. Although the law does not preclude property insurance from being taken out as a fixed-amount insurance, aircraft insurance is usually arranged as an insurance against loss and damage. The Insurer will therefore provide the beneficiary with an insurance indemnity which, to the extent agreed, compensates for the loss of property incurred on the aircraft as a result of the insured event with the possible application of under-insurance, over-insurance, and other institutions associated with property damage insurance.

489. The aircraft liability insurance is regulated on the principle of compulsory insurance. The obligation to take out liability insurance for damage caused by the operation of an aircraft is stipulated in § 12(2)(d) of Act No. 49/1997 Sb., on Civil Aviation. The scope and conditions of aircraft liability insurance is determined by secondary legislation, unless a directly applicable regulation of the EU stipulates otherwise (§ 98(2) of Act No. 49/1997 Sb.). This directly applicable regulation is currently the Regulation (EC) No. 785/2004 of the European Parliament and of the Council of 21 April 2004 on insurance requirements for air carriers and aircraft operators.

490. The above Regulation applies to all air carriers and to all aircraft operators flying within, into, out of, or over the territory of a Member State to which the Treaty establishing the European Community (EU) applies. The Regulation does not

499. From the point of view of public law, these are the non-life insurance classes listed in points 5 and 11 of Part B of Annex 1 to the IA; together with luggage insurance, aviation insurance forms a group of non-life insurance according to Part C point d) of Annex 1 to the IA.

apply to State aircraft as referred to in Article 3(b) of the Convention on International Civil Aviation, signed at Chicago on 7 December 1944 (aircraft used in military, customs, and police services), model aircraft with a maximum take-off weight of less than 20 kg, foot-launched flying machines (including powered paragliders and hang gliders), captive balloons, kites, parachutes (including parascending parachutes), aircraft, including gliders, with a maximum take-off weight of less than 500 kg, and microlights, which are used for non-commercial purposes, or are used for local flight instruction which does not entail the crossing of international borders.

491. The minimum insurance indemnity limits for air carrier and aircraft operator liability insurance are set by the Regulation in respect of passengers (at least 250,000 SDRs per passenger[500]), baggage (at least 1,288 SDRs per passenger in commercial operations), and cargo carried by aircraft (at least 22 SDRs per kilogram in commercial operations) and, in relation to third parties, where minimum indemnity limits are set in the range of 0.75 to 700 million SDRs depending on the take-off weight of the aircraft.

492. Insurance against all damage to or loss of aircraft, and liability insurance for liability arising out of the ownership and use of aircraft, including carrier's liability, are always large insurance risks (§ 131(1)(a) IA).

493. Space insurance is not specifically regulated by law, it is not operated in the Czech Republic and none of the insurers' active on the Czech market currently offers such insurance.

500. For aircraft with a maximum take-off weight not exceeding 2,700 kg, used for non-commercial purposes, the minimum limit is 100,000 SDRs per passenger (within discretion of the Regulation used in § 31(5) of Decree of the Ministry of Transport and Communications No. 108/1997 Sb., which implements the Act No. 49/1997 Sb., on Civil Aviation).

Chapter 8. Theft and Embezzlement Insurance

494. Theft insurance is not regulated by law as a separate type of insurance. This is one of the usual insurance perils insured under property insurance, very often together with the insurance peril of vandalism.[501] It is characteristic of both mentioned insurance perils that the damage to property occurs as a result of intentional actions of a third party. Therefore, according to § 2820 CC, the insured's right to damages against the offender usually passes to the insurer through the payment of the insurance indemnity.

495. The scope of theft insurance is not specified by law and is left to the discretion of the parties to the insurance contract. Theft insurance is usually arranged both within retail products (typically household insurance) and within business insurance. Movable and immovable property (forcible theft of a building component) can be the subject of theft insurance. Items of a special nature or value (valuables, works of art, jewellery, antiques, etc.) may be excluded from the insurance, or insured under individual conditions.

496. The so-called simple theft, i.e., theft in which the perpetrator has not overcome any obstacle or used deception or violence, is usually excluded from the insurance. As a condition for the occurrence of an insured event from theft insurance, it is usually agreed that the offender must overcome a certain obstacle or measure protecting the insured property from theft. In addition to compensation for the stolen goods themselves, the insurance usually also includes other damage that the perpetrator causes when stealing from the insured property (broken lock, destroyed doors, damaged security systems, etc.).

497. Burglary and robbery are often distinguished in the insurance conditions of Czech insurance companies. Burglary is traditionally understood theft of an insured property after overcoming an obstacle in a way defined in the insurance contract – it can be, for example, intrusion into an enclosed space by making it accessible with a tool that is not designed to open it properly; overcoming an opening that is not used for entry (e.g., skylight or ventilation shaft); intrusion into an enclosed space by means of a key or a duplicate thereof, which the perpetrator has previously seized by burglary or robbery, etc. Robbery is usually understood as such conduct of the perpetrator in which they use provable violence or threats of immediate violence against the insured with the intention of seizing the insured property.[502]

501. Vandalism usually means the intentional damage or destruction of an insured property by a third person.
502. Theft and robbery are defined as the facts of criminal offences in the provisions of § 205 (theft) and § 173 (robbery) of Act No. 40/2009 Sb., Criminal Code. The term burglary is also defined by the Criminal Code, namely in the provision of § 121. For insurance purposes, however, it is not possible to proceed from the above criminal law definitions and the interpretation of these terms must be based primarily on the content of the insurance contract and agreed contractual definitions of these terms.

498. Premiums, or insurance indemnity limits, deductibles, etc., can be differentiated according to the level of security of the insured property. In principle, the higher the level of security measures that protect the insured property (security locks, security doors, alarms, monitoring systems, permanent security, etc.), the lower the insurance premiums or deductibles, or conversely the higher the indemnity limits, can be agreed.

499. The law in the provisions of § 2852 CC regulates the situation where the stolen (or lost) property is found after the insured event or the payment of the insurance indemnity. If the policyholder or beneficiary finds out after the insured event that the stolen property has been found, they are obliged to notify the insurer without undue delay. Property is not considered to have been found if possession of the property was lost and it either cannot be re-acquired, or it can be re-acquired only with unreasonable inconvenience or costs,[503] or the thing was damaged to the extent that it ceased to exist as such, or if it can be repaired only with disproportionate costs. If, after the insured event, the insurer provided the insurance indemnity, the ownership of the insured property does not pass to the insurer, but the insurer has the right to be given what they provided as the insurance indemnity.[504] The beneficiary may deduct the costs reasonably incurred in the removal of defects occurred at the time when the beneficiary was deprived of the opportunity to dispose of the property.

500. Embezzlement[505] insurance is one of the less frequented insurance products on the Czech market. As with theft insurance, it is not a separate type of insurance and the law does not specifically regulate it. In the Czech market, embezzlement insurance as a separate product can be found mainly in the form of insurance covering the risk of damage caused to the insured by the wrongful actions of their employees and other persons active for them (misuse of employer resources, fraudulent transfers of funds, intellectual property theft, extortion, etc.). Embezzlement insurance can also cover unlawful actions of third parties (cyber-attacks, loss of electronic data, payment by counterfeit payment instruments, etc.).

503. This may be the case, e.g., when it turns out that a stolen mobile phone was thrown into the lake by an escaping offender. Thus, although the victim knows where the stolen thing is, it is not realistic for him to regain possession.
504. This is the opposite rule to that laid down in the previous § 39 AIC, according to which in case the insured property was found after the payment of the insurance indemnity, the ownership of the property passed to the insurer ex lege, and the insurer was obliged to take over this property unless otherwise agreed in the insurance contract.
505. The criminal offence of embezzlement is defined in the provisions of § 206 of Act No. 40/2009 Sb., Criminal Code. As in the case of theft insurance, it is not possible to proceed from the criminal law definition and it is necessary to pay attention primarily to the contractual definition of this term in the insurance contract.

Chapter 9. Agricultural Insurance, Hail Insurance, Livestock Insurance

501. From the point of view of private law, agricultural insurance is not a special type of insurance.[506] This is non-life property insurance, for which specific products have been gradually set aside within the product offer of insurance companies. Within the scope of agricultural insurance: (i) crop insurance, (ii) livestock insurance, and (iii) forest insurance are arranged.

502. Crop insurance is property insurance that serves to cover property losses on crop production. Its basic type is the hail insurance, which covers only the risk of damage or destruction of crops by hail. A wider range of insurance coverage is offered in the so-called insurance against selected risks, which, in addition to hail, allows other insurance perils to be included in the insurance cover, such as floods, storms, or spring frost. The most comprehensive coverage within crop insurance is offered by the so-called crop yield insurance, which covers financial losses on crop production due to the whole set of influences. This type of insurance compensates for the failure to achieve the agreed standard crop yield per hectare. It is typical for crop insurance to negotiate a high deductible. In the Czech Republic, crop insurance is arranged primarily in the form of hail insurance or insurance against selected risks.[507]

503. Livestock insurance covers property losses related to the death, killing, or necessary slaughter of livestock. The subject of insurance can be both individual animals (a racehorse, a breeding bull, etc.) and sets of livestock (cows, sheep, horses, poultry, etc.). Usually agreed insurance perils include infection (infectious disease), natural hazards, injury or non-infectious diseases. Similar to crop insurance, due to the increased influence of subjective risks on the part of the insured, high deductibles, bonus/malus systems, etc. are applied.[508]

504. Forest insurance is usually arranged for the case of damage or destruction of forest stands and forest nurseries (grown planting material of forest trees) due to fire, hail, or other risks such as storms, snow, floods, landslides, etc. The insurance covers forest stands and other woody plants specified in the insurance contract, or harvested timber. Increased harvesting costs or reforestation costs may also be subject to the forest insurance.

---

506. In terms of public law classification, this is a class of non-life property insurance falling under points 8 and 9 of Part B of Annex 1 to the IA.
507. For more details, *see* Ducháčková, Eva. *Pojištění a pojišťovnictví.* 1st ed. Praha: Ekopress, 2015, p. 197; or Daňhel, Jaroslav. *Pojistná teorie.* 1st ed. Praha: Professional Publishing, 2005, p. 175.
508. *Ibid.*

505. Agricultural insurance in the Czech Republic is currently supported by the state in the form of subsidies for the price of insurance. The support is provided in the form of partial compensation of proven reimbursed costs for agricultural insurance (up to 65%), within the support programs of the Ministry of Agriculture, through the Support and Guarantee Agricultural and Forestry Fund.[509]

509. In Czech 'Podpůrný a garanční rolnický a lesnický fond, a.s.' (PGRLF), *see* https://www.pgrlf.cz/programy/podpora-pojisteni-2/podpora-pojisteni/.

Chapter 10. Catastrophe Insurance

506. 'From the point of view of disasters, the last period is characterized on the one hand by an increasing number of events with catastrophic impacts, especially natural disasters, but also huge damage resulting from non-natural influences. On the other hand, the increasing amount of damage in connection with these disasters.'[510]

507. Disasters can have their origin in natural activities, geophysical and other processes but might also be caused or provoked (either intentionally or negligently) also by humans (industrial ecological disasters, explosions, nuclear accidents, leakage of toxic substance, chemical leakage into the environment, huge traffic disasters, air accidents, arson, power failure and so on). Natural disasters can take different forms (blizzard, storm, lightning, hail, heat, extreme drought, tornado, tropical storm, hurricane, geological-landslide, rock collapses, volcanic eruption, avalanche, earthquake, tsunami, flood, fire etc.) and can cause varying types of damage with varying extent. While some natural catastrophic events are very rare, others can recur frequently. The damage from natural disasters can reach astronomical proportions and it would be difficult for an individual to cover it alone.[511]

508. Every year we witness several major natural disasters, most of which threaten the local population and cause significant property damage. The most common natural disasters in the Czech Republic – based on statistical insurance data[512] – include floods, hurricanes, hail, storms, snow and rarely earthquakes, etc. Law

---

510. Daňhel, Jaroslav. *Pojistná teorie.* 1st ed. Praha: Professional Publishing, 2005, p. 285.
511. For more *see also* Ducháčková, Eva. *Principy pojištění a pojišťovnictví.* 3rd updated ed. Praha: Ekopress, 2009; Vávrová, Eva. *Finanční řízení komerčních pojišťoven.* 1st ed. Praha: Grada, 2014; Vícha, Ondřej. *Základy horního a energetického práva.* Praha: Wolters Kluwer, 2015; Zuzaňák, Aleš; Šulcová, Jaroslava; Hora, Jan. *Příručka pro zprostředkovatele pojištění.* 2nd ed. Praha: Linde, 2011; Ducháčková, Eva. *Pojištění a pojišťovnictví.* 1st ed. Praha: Ekopress, 2015.
512. *See* statistical data published on website of ČAP: https://www.cap.cz/statistiky-prognozy-analyzy/mimoradne-zivelni-skody, According to published data, sorted chronologically, the most significant natural disasters with greater impact on insurance market were:

   - July 1997 – floods in Moravia. Insurance companies paid a total of CZK 9.7 billion to clients;
   - August 2002 – floods in Bohemia. Damage reached CZK 73 billion, of which insurance companies paid approximately half, which is significantly more than in the first case in Moravia;
   - March 2006 – spring floods in the Czech Republic caused 15,000 insured events with a total value exceeding CZK 1 billion;
   - January 2007 – hurricane Kyrill. The biggest wind disaster in the history of the Czech Republic affected the entire territory. It caused almost 80,000 insurance claims in the amount of almost CZK 2.25 billion;
   - March 2008 – hurricane Emma. Almost 38,000 claims in the total amount exceeding CZK 1.24 billion were reported throughout the Czech Republic;
   - June 2009 – floods caused about 17,000 insured events with total amount of damage CZK 0,6 billion;
   - September 2010 – floods caused over 1,900 insured events with total amount of damage CZK 113 million;
   - June 2013 – floods caused over 44,000 insured events with total amount of damage CZK 3.7 billion;

does not specifically define natural disaster insurance as independent insurance category. Natural risk insurance is therefore defined by the insurance conditions of a specific type of insurance. Within the given insurance, the water plumbing insurance risk can be also covered.

509. The insurance covers property damage caused by above-mentioned natural catastrophic events. Even in Czech context, the term FLEXA[513] is sometimes used. We can find it in some insurance conditions of domestic insurance companies, for example, as follows: 'Flexa means the sum of insurance risks of fire, direct lightning strike, explosion, aircraft crash and firefighting, tearing or evacuation resulting from any of these insurance risks.'[514]

510. The natural risks insurance is usually constructed on the principle of replacement value, the insurance indemnity is paid in the amount of the necessary repair, repurchase or re-establishment of the insured property that has been damaged, lost or destroyed.

511. We commonly define a natural disaster event as a large, usually sudden and unexpected occurrence of misfortune, destruction, devastation or damage caused by the natural element. By natural element, we habitually mean a violent, uncontrollable natural phenomenon or natural force, which usually has destructive effects, while their origin and course is difficult to influence by humans. It causes damage to property, nature, but harms also health and can result in death.

512. The size of the premium depends mainly on the stated value of the insured property, on the risk situation of the policyholder or insured. Taken into account is overall arrangement in terms of possible damage, while risk factors are the construction of the building, building materials used, distance of individual objects, implementation of hazardous activities such as chemical production etc., and the participation of the insured entity to cover incurred damage.

513. It is at the same time clear that it is not possible to solve the consequences of all eventual risks with natural risk insurance, so there are general criteria for insuring the risk, namely:[515]

- criterion of randomness (events do not depend on the will of the persons involved);

- October 2017 – hurricane Herwart caused about 45,000 insured events with total amount of damage CZK 368 million.

513. This concept comes from Anglo-Saxon insurance world. It is an abbreviation for a fire insurance contract that contains these insurance risks (Fire, Lightning, Explosion, Aircraft); *see also* above in Ch. 1. Fire Insurance.

514. *See* Special insurance conditions for electronics insurance (ZPP E 2005/01), Generali pojišťovna, a.s. https://www.generaliceska.cz/documents/20183/122618/pojistne-podminky-muj-majetek.pdf/bb765607-2395-41f5-a576-f81f855dd41a.

515. Ducháčková, Eva. *Pojištění a pojišťovnictví.* 1st ed. Praha: Ekopress, 2015, pp. 31–32.

- criterion of unambiguity (the risks are clearly descriptive, they must not be confused with another type of risk);
- criterion of predictability (there should be a detectable probability of realization of the relevant risk, damage should be therefore measurable);
- criterion of independence (the risk should be independent of each other – the probability of realization of one risk does not change with the input of another risk);
- size criterion (the insurer's ability to bear the risk);
- moral principles (insurance does not help to avoid administrative or criminal sanctions).[516]

514. The current increase in the number and amount of impacts from natural disasters might be bringing insurance and reinsurance companies into conflict with the size criterion. Increasing fluctuations in extents of damage come into conflict with the criterion of predictability. The current trend might be slowly getting us into a state of uninsurability, which is a highly socially undesirable state.

515. Liability for nuclear damage is regulated by special law (Atomic Act)[517] complemented by general regulation of liability for damage within the Civil Code[518] and also by the provisions of an international agreements.[519] The holder of a permit for the operation (or any activity related to the use) of a nuclear facility[520] or the holder of a permit for the transport of nuclear materials[521] is the operator who is held responsible for nuclear damage. In determining the scope and method of compensation for nuclear damage,[522] the provisions of the Civil Code in force at the time of the nuclear event shall apply.

---

516. *Ibid.*
517. Act No. 18/1997 Sb., on Peaceful Utilisation of Nuclear Energy and Ionising Radiation (Atomic Act), which was replaced in 2017 by Act No. 263/2016 Sb., the Atomic Act, but not in full. The issue of civil liability for damage caused by a nuclear incident (Ch. V) remains regulated in the original law.
518. The provisions of the Civil Code shall apply only unless an international agreement or Atomic Act provides otherwise.
519. Vienna Convention on Civil Liability for Nuclear Damage (Vienna Convention, 1963), Protocol to Amend the Vienna Convention (Revised Vienna Convention, 1997), Paris Convention on Nuclear Third-Party Liability (Paris Convention, 1960), Joint Protocol Relating to the Application of the Vienna Convention and the Paris Convention (Joint Protocol, 1988), Brussels Supplementary Convention (Brussels Convention, 1963).
520. If one person holds a permit for several nuclear installations located in the territory for which a joint internal emergency plan has been approved, these installations shall be considered for the purposes of liability for nuclear damage for one nuclear installation. However, several nuclear installations authorized by different persons cannot be considered as one nuclear installation in relation to liability for nuclear damage, even if these installations are directly linked to each other (§ 33(2) of the Atomic Act).
521. The State Office for Nuclear Safety shall issue a decree setting limits on the concentration and amount of nuclear material to which the provisions on nuclear damage in accordance with an international agreement do not apply. To *see* the decrees consult: https://www.sujb.cz/legislativa/atomove-pravo/.
522. Nuclear damage is also damage caused by incurring the costs of necessary measures to prevent or reduce exposure or to restore the original or similar state of the environment, if these measures were caused as a result of a nuclear event (§ 34(2) of the Atomic Act).

516. However, the liability of the license holder for nuclear damage caused by each individual nuclear incident is limited. In the case of nuclear facilities[523] for energy purposes, warehouses and repositories of spent nuclear fuel, or nuclear materials generated by the processing of this fuel, the legal limit for civil liability is the amount of CZK 8 billion. In the case of other nuclear facilities and transport, the legal limit is CZK 2 billion.[524]

517. The holder of a permit for the operation of a nuclear facility is obliged to arrange insurance for his liability for nuclear damage with an insurer authorized to it (*see* below) unless other financial security is stipulated in the event of the occurrence of the obligation to compensate for nuclear damage. Limit of insurance indemnity may not be lower than CZK 2 billion (in cases of nuclear facilities for energy purposes) and not less than CZK 300 million (in case of other nuclear facilities and transport of nuclear materials). Insurance is taken out separately for each nuclear facility or transport of nuclear materials (§ 36 of the Atomic Act). Detailed insurance conditions are set out in the general insurance conditions of the insurer approved by the state insurance supervision authority.

518. A specific feature of this civil liability is that the state provides a guarantee for the satisfaction of the granted claims for compensation for nuclear damage. This guarantee shall apply whenever the granted claims for compensation for nuclear damage are not paid from compulsory insurance or other specified financial security. The state guarantee is also limited up to the amount of CZK 8 billion after the exhaustion of the insurer's performance in the amount of CZK 2 billion in the case of nuclear facilities for energy purposes, and up to the amount of CZK 2 billion after the exhaustion of the insurer's performance in the amount of CZK 300 million in the case of other nuclear facilities and transport of nuclear materials. The recourse right of the state as a guarantor against the permit holder is not affected (§ 37 of the Atomic Act).

519. The right to compensation for nuclear damage shall lapse if the right to compensation for such damage has not been exercised within three years from the date on which the injured party became aware or could have learned of the event which led to the nuclear damage and who was responsible for it,[525] however, no later than ten years from the date on which such an event occurs; in the case of insurance, these periods begin to run after one year from the date of occurrence of the insured event.

---

523. Nuclear facilities include particularly nuclear power plants, nuclear fuel cycle facilities, small-scale research reactors, medical and industrial applications of radioisotopes, radioactive waste repositories, and radioactive waste storage facilities.

524. *See* § 35 of the Atomic Act.

525. In the event of a nuclear incident, the permit holder is obliged to notify in writing in the area affected by this incident, according to the State Office for Nuclear Safety's findings based on the activities of the national radiation monitoring network that he/she is obliged to compensate for nuclear damage caused by this incident. This written notice must be publicly available not only at the permit holder's place but also at the relevant regional authority and at all municipal authorities in this area (*see* § 38 of the Atomic Act).

520. In the Czech Republic, the relevant insurance is actively operated by the Czech Nuclear Insurance Pool[526] as a voluntary association of companies insuring or reinsuring risks connected with operation of nuclear installations and sources of ionizing radiation (including both Czech nuclear power plants – Dukovany[527] and Temelín[528]), established primarily for the purpose of insuring and hedging nuclear risks.[529] Czech Nuclear Insurance Pool currently offers several types (four) of Civil Liability Insurance:

- Civil Liability Insurance of a Nuclear Installation Operator for nuclear damage incurred to third parties as a consequence of operation of a nuclear installation or from transportation of nuclear material.[530] This Insurance is designed namely for holders of a license for operation of a nuclear installation, for any activity related to use of a nuclear installation, for transportation of nuclear material who are, in accordance with the Atomic Act, operators liable for nuclear damage on grounds of an international agreement (*see* above) to which the Czech Republic is a party.[531]
- Complementary insurance cover of the 'nuclear lockout' to the liability insurance for suppliers of equipment and services for the nuclear industry.[532]
- Insurance of operators of sources of ionizing radiation (radionuclide emitters), which is not obliged by the Atomic Act to take out liability insurance for nuclear damage caused to third parties, but who consider such insurance necessary to ensure the protection of their business activities (voluntary insurance).
- Supplementary insurance 'nuclear lockout' to insure the liability of members of the company's bodies.[533]

526. https://www.nuclearpool.cz/index.php/en/en-about-us-d.
527. The nuclear power plant with an installed capacity of 4 × 510 MW, put into operation in 1985–1988.
528. The nuclear power plant with an installed capacity of 2 × 1,000 MW (originally planned 4 × 1,000 MW), put into operation in 2002–2003.
529. International teams of engineers execute regular surveys of both of our nuclear power plants. Results of the surveys serve to assess the risks particularly for the use of insurers. Operators of power plants use recommendations of insurance experts in order to reduce the risk of operation of the nuclear installations. Czech Nuclear Insurance Pool operates within a worldwide community of national nuclear insurance pools and is actively contributing to the development of business and technical cooperation. The business exchange comprises of active (i.e., assumed) and passive (i.e., ceded) reinsurance business with more than twenty foreign national pools. The technical cooperation provides exchange of information, arranging of surveys on nuclear power plants as well as organization of assessment of insured losses. For more details, *see*: https://www.nuclearpool.cz/index.php/en/en-about-us/en-activities.
530. Kind of mandatory insurance – as required by Atomic Act in the wording effective from 1 Jan. 2017.
531. *See* https://www.nuclearpool.cz/index.php/en/en-third-party-liability.
532. This insurance is available only for clients who have concluded an insurance cover for the third-party liability for conventional (i.e., non-nuclear) damage; *see* https://www.nuclearpool.cz/index.php/en/en-third-party-liability.
533. This insurance can be arranged only for clients who have a valid liability insurance for conventional (i.e., non-nuclear) damage to members of the company's bodies; *see* https://www.nuclearpool.cz/index.php/en/en-third-party-liability.

Chapter 11. Credit and Guaranty Insurance

521. Credit insurance is stipulated to protect against consequences to property which the insured person may incur as a result of his debtor's failure to repay the funds he provided (*see* § 2868(1) CC). The essence of this insurance therefore lies in compensating for the loss of property that occurred to the insured, as the debtor did not repay the funds provided properly and on time. This insurance may include, for example, general insolvency, export credit, instalment credit, mortgage credit or agricultural credit.[534]

522. Credit insurance (as well as guarantee insurance) was introduced into our legal system by AIC. Now, it is regulated by Civil Code. The insured in this case is therefore the creditor, not the debtor. Unlike other insurances, this can only be arranged as insurance against loss and damage, as it is intended to compensate for the loss of property incurred in direct connection with the insured event. If the person who acquired the right to an insurance indemnity fails to inform the insurer of the loss event within the time limit stipulated in the contract, a court shall not grant such a right if the insurer invokes late notification of the loss event (§ 2869 CC).

523. Guaranty insurance is stipulated for the performance from an obligation arising from suretyship of the insured person, forfeiture of bail or security, or a performance provided under bail or security or for another similar stipulated reason (*see* § 2868(2) CC). In practice, this can be, for example, insurance of a guarantee for the proper execution of the work (Performance Bond), a guarantee for repairs during the warranty period (Maintenance Bond), a guarantee of a deposit (Advance Payment Bond).[535] Like credit insurance, guarantee insurance can only be arranged as insurance against loss and damage (§ 2868(3) CC).

524. Special insurance in case of bankruptcy of a travel agency is usually included under the guarantee insurance. This is an example of compulsory insurance, which is regulated in Act No. 159/1999 Sb., on Certain Conditions of Business and on the Performance of Certain Activities in the Area of Tourism.[536] This special insurance is not a standard liability insurance. The insurance covers only cases where the travel agency does not provide the customer with transport from the place of stay abroad back to the Czech Republic due to its bankruptcy (where the transport is part of the travel contract provided by the travel agency), or does not return the customer the deposit or price paid in case the tour did not take place or does not return to the customer the difference between the price paid for the tour and the price of the partially provided tour in the event that the tour took place in part.[537] Other obligation duties are not covered by the insurance.

534. *See* Annex 1 to the IA.
535. Jandová, Lucie. In: Jandová, Lucie; Šlauf, Petr; Svejkovský, Jaroslav. *Pojištění v novém občanském zákoníku. Komentář: [§ 2756-2872].* 1st ed. Praha: C. H. Beck, 2014, p. 333.
536. To see the text (in Czech) consult: https://www.zakonyprolidi.cz/cs/1999-159.
537. *See* § 6 of the Act No. 159/1999 Sb.

525. The travel agency is obliged to hand over to the client, together with the travel contract, a proof of guarantee insurance in the event of its bankruptcy issued by the insurance company, which must include, among other things, the method of notifying the insured event.[538] The insurance of non-repatriation by a travel agency is another special insurance, as the insurance company must provide transport, including the necessary accommodation. In the event that the customer arranges transport and necessities such as meals at his own expense, these costs will be reimbursed by the insurance company up to the amount that the insurance company would pay if it arranged the items for the client itself.[539]

526. The insurance contract may stipulate the period within which the beneficiary is obliged to notify the insurer of the occurrence of a loss event. If the event is not notified within the agreed period, this allows the insurer to use the objection of late notification of the event. This means that the insurer may choose not to use this objection and therefore can perform voluntarily without creating the unjust enrichment. If the period is not agreed by the contractual parties, the general regulation on the investigation of an insured event shall apply.[540]

527. Another special insurance is credit insurance with state support regulated by Act No. 58/1995 Sb., on Insuring and Financing Export with State Support.[541] This Act regulates state support for exports in the form of export credit risk insurance, which is understood as:[542]

- short-term export credit insurance against non-payment due to territorial or combined territorial and non-marketable commercial risks;
- insurance of long-term export credits and investment loans against non-payment due to territorial or combined territorial and non-marketable commercial risks, or non-payment due to non-marketable commercial risks;
- insurance of investments abroad against territorial risks, in particular against the risk of preventing the transfer of return on investment, expropriation or politically motivated violent damage;
- insurance against losses of exporters and investors associated with the preparation and implementation of business activities;
- insurance of credits granted to producers or exporters to finance production for export against the risk of non-payment of a loan due to the inability of a producer or exporter to fulfil the terms of an export contract;

538. *See* https://www.cap.cz/vse-o-pojisteni/pojisteni-zaruky-pro-pripad-upadku-cestovni-kancelare.
539. *See* § 7(1) of the Act No. 159/1999 Sb.
540. *See* § 2796(1) CC: 'In the case of an event which the person who considers himself to be the beneficiary associates with a claim for insurance indemnity, the person shall notify the insurer accordingly without undue delay and truthfully explain to the insurer the occurrence and extent of such an event, the rights of third persons, and any multiple insurance; at the same time, the person shall present the insurer with the necessary documents and proceed as stipulated in the contract. If he is not simultaneously the policyholder or the insured person, these duties are also incurred by the policyholder and the insured person.'
541. To *see* the text (in Czech) consult: https://www.zakonyprolidi.cz/cs/1995-58.
542. *See* § 1(2) of the Act No. 58/1995 Sb.

- insurance of bank guarantees or other services provided by the exporter's bank to a foreign person on behalf of the exporter against the risk of non-compliance with the exporter's contractual obligations under the export contract;
- insurance of risks of exchange rate loss of the CZK against foreign currencies arising in the case of indemnity as a result of the difference between the exchange rate valid at the time of concluding the insurance contract and the exchange rate valid at the time of indemnity payment;
- reinsurance activities consisting in the assumption of insurance risks (pursuant to points mentioned above) arranged by foreign credit insurance companies;
- reinsurance activities towards credit insurance companies in relation to export insurance against non-marketable territorial and non-marketable commercial risks;
- insurance and securing loans for small and medium-sized enterprises with permanent residence or registered office in the Czech Republic.

Chapter 12. Technical Insurance

528. Technical insurance is arranged in case of destruction of machines, machineries etc. Within the technical insurance, several types of insurance are used, which include in particular machinery insurance, assembly insurance, construction insurance, and electronic equipment insurance.[543]

529. Machinery insurance, sometimes referred to as machine risk insurance, is insurance against sudden damage and destruction of a machine by any accidental event limiting or excluding its functionality (caused either by working, improper or incorrect operation, maintenance, repair or installation etc.), but not as a result of natural wear or corrosion, not as a result of a natural disaster, theft or loss of machine parts.[544] The basis for calculating the premium is the replacement value, i.e., the reduction price of the machine.[545]

530. Machinery insurance can be modelled into the following forms:[546]

- classical machinery insurance (following the natural disaster insurance and covering only the insured risk of accident of machines and machinery);
- mechanical insurance of mobile machines and machinery (covering not only purely mechanical hazards but also insurance hazards of a natural elements with regard to the needs of more comprehensive coverage of insurance hazards for mobile machinery);
- insurance of electronic equipment.

531. Assembly risk insurance covers all risks associated with the assembly of machines and machinery. It can be conceived on the principle of all-risks insurance or in such a way that the covered insurance risks will be precisely listed. This insurance usually includes natural and machine risks, but also, for example, liability risks.[547]

532. Construction risk insurance covers all risks of damage to construction parts and materials during the whole period of construction. It is often combined in one product as construction and assembly insurance. Such combined insurance covers property damage caused by construction and assembly activities, by activities leading to the reversal of the imminent insured event, mitigation of the consequences of the insured event or removal of the insured property (if the obligation to do so is for hygienic, ecological or safety reasons) as well as liability for damage caused to another entity involved in the construction or installation.

543. Ducháčková, Eva. *Principy pojištění a pojišťovnictví.* 3rd updated ed. Praha: Ekopress, 2009, p. 148.
544. Zuzaňák, Aleš; Šulcová, Jaroslava; Hora, Jan. *Příručka pro zprostředkovatele pojištění.* 2nd ed. Praha: Linde, 2011, p. 24.
545. http://www.czechinsurance.cz/portfolio/stroje/.
546. Ducháčková, Eva. *Principy pojištění a pojišťovnictví.* 3rd updated ed. Praha: Ekopress, 2009, p. 149.
547. *Ibid.*

533. Construction risk insurance usually does not cover indirect damage and damage caused by design, construction, material defects or incorrectly performed work. Sometimes it might be supplemented by the warranty insurance, which covers machine risks during the warranty period.[548]

548. *Ibid.*

Part IV. Motor Vehicle Insurance

Chapter 1. Motor Hull Insurance

534. With a total written premium of almost CZK 22 billion and a share of 21.1% of the total written premium in non-life insurance in 2019, the motor hull insurance[549] is one of the most important segments of the Czech insurance market.[550]

535. The subject of motor hull insurance (casco insurance), as the name suggests, is the hull of vehicle, i.e., the vehicle itself. While MTPL covers damage caused by the operation of the vehicle to other persons, hull insurance covers damage caused to the vehicle itself. Motor hull insurance is a type of property insurance and is not specifically regulated by law. Unlike the MTPL, this is not compulsory insurance and the law therefore does not stipulate any minimum scope of this insurance or more detailed requirements for its content. The scope of hull insurance is left to the discretion of the contracting parties to the insurance contract.

536. The subject of the motor hull insurance can be both passenger cars and commercial or truck vehicles over 3.5 tonnes. Insurance companies offer product solutions for retail and also corporate clients (fleet insurance). Under individual conditions, insurance of luxury vehicles, sport cars, motorcycles, veterans, driving school vehicles, etc. may be arranged. Specialized hull insurance products also exist for working machines such as harvesters, tractors, excavators, bulldozers, cranes, etc.

537. The basic insurance peril is an accident (impact damage). In addition, motor hull insurance allows to arrange a number of other risks such as theft, vandalism, or natural hazards. The usual supplementary insurances also include car windows insurance, temporary replacement car costs, cargo and luggage insurance or passenger injury coverage. Insurance companies also offer a wide variety of assistance services including for example, rescue and towing, vehicle repair at the scene of failure, provision of a replacement vehicle or accommodation, telephone advice, interpreting, etc.). The basic territorial scope of insurance usually covers the geographical territory of Europe, including the Asian part of Turkey.

549. Which has already been generally introduced in Part III, Ch. 5. Motor Vehicle Insurance.
550. CIA's Annual Report for 2019 (available at https://www.cap.cz/vyrocni-zpravy).

538. Particular insurance risks can be included in the insurance on the basis of all-risks coverage or on the principle of named perils insurance. Motor hull insurance products are often constructed on the so-called modular principle, which allows the inclusion of individual risks in the insurance according to the individual needs of the insured.[551] The system of so-called packages is widespread, where particular risks are grouped into certain pre-defined units (packages), which allows clients to choose a broader or narrower scope of coverage according to their individual needs and, depending on that, also adjust the amount of premiums paid.

539. Pricing in hull insurance is influenced by a number of factors – usually the type and brand of the vehicle, purchase price, age of the vehicle, selected scope of insurance, selected deductible, method and frequency of payment, previous loss record, etc.[552]

540. In the event of complete destruction of the vehicle (total loss[553]), the insurance indemnity is usually provided in the amount of the usual value (or actual cash value) of the vehicle. For new vehicles (or vehicles up to a certain age) there is a possibility on the market to arrange the so-called GAP (Guaranteed asset protection) insurance, which allows to cover the difference between the indemnity paid from the primary hull insurance and the agreed sum insured for GAP insurance in the amount of the purchase price. This insurance therefore covers the financial loss caused by the difference between the purchase price of the vehicle and the amount of the insurance indemnity from the hull insurance in the amount of the usual value (or actual cash value) of the vehicle.[554]

541. A certain limited alternative to hull insurance is the so-called direct settlement service provided to the MTPL. Direct settlement relates to damage to the insured vehicle (or other harms) caused by the operation of another vehicle to the extent that the operator of this other vehicle is liable for such damage. Direct settlement therefore allows the injured party to turn to his insurer, who will provide insurance indemnity instead of the tortfeasor's liability insurer. Subsequently the right of the insured person against the tortfeasor and his liability insurer shall pass to the insurer who thus provided the insurance indemnity (in accordance with § 2820 CC).

542. The recent trend is to determine the amount of insurance premiums in hull insurance (or in MTPL) depending on the number of kilometres actually travelled ('pay as you go'). This approach makes it possible to take into account the different insurance risk arising from the different use of individual vehicles. At its core is the simple reasoning that a vehicle that travels fewer kilometres has generally a lower

---

551. Ducháčková, Eva. *Pojištění a pojišťovnictví.* 1st ed. Praha: Ekopress, 2015, p. 190.
552. *Ibid.*, p. 191.
553. Total loss in insurance practice means a situation where the vehicle was damaged so that it is irreparable or when the repair is uneconomical, because the repair costs exceed the usual value of the vehicle (or approaches this value when they exceed a certain agreed limit, e.g., 85% from the usual vehicle value).
554. Ducháčková, Eva. *Pojištění a pojišťovnictví.* 1st ed. Praha: Ekopress, 2015, p. 191.

risk exposure than a vehicle that travels more on the road. This system allows clients to achieve lower premiums if they use their vehicle less. Original product solutions required the installation of telematics monitoring devices in the vehicle. At present, products are already appearing on the market for which it is sufficient to document the condition of the odometer of the insured vehicle on annually basis without the need to install monitoring device. The obvious disadvantage of fixed monitoring devices is that they represent a significant invasion of the privacy of the insured persons and place more demanding requirements for compliance with legal regulations for the protection of personal data. On the contrary, the advantage is that these systems (so-called black box technologies) make it possible to monitor and evaluate, in addition to the number of kilometres travelled, other data such as driver behaviour. Thus, they make it possible to reward a careful driving style and compliance with traffic regulations in the form of a discount on the premium, and, conversely, to penalize risky behaviour such as speeding or aggressive driving style. Alternatively, they may include other functions such as automatic emergency call in the event of an accident, etc.

Chapter 2. Motor Third Party Liability Insurance

§1. MTPL: Generalities

543. MTPL[555] represents one of the most important segments of the Czech insurance market. The total number of concluded insurance contracts is approaching 8 million, the number of insured vehicles has already exceeded this limit and amounts to approximately 8.4 million (of which approximately 5.6 million are passenger vehicles). The total written premium reached almost CZK 26 billion in 2019, which represents approximately 24.3% of the total volume of written premium in non-life insurance.[556]

544. The basic source of MTPL regulation in the Czech Republic is Act No. 168/1999 Sb., on Motor Third Party Liability Insurance and on the Amendment to some other related Acts (MTPLIA), and the Decree of the Ministry of Finance No. 205/1999 Sb., on Implementing Certain Provisions of the Motor Third Party Liability Insurance Act.

545. MTPLIA incorporates the relevant EU regulations[557] and regulates compulsory liability insurance for damage caused by operation of a vehicle (MTPL)[558]

555. For a general introduction, *see* Part III, Ch. 5. Motor Vehicle Insurance; for more details *see* in particular Jandová, Lucie; Vojtek, Petr. *Zákon o pojištění odpovědnosti z provozu vozidla. Komentář.* 2nd ed. Praha: C. H. Beck, 2019; Bušta, Pavel; Přikryl, Vladimír. *Zákon o pojištění odpovědnosti z provozu vozidla s komentářem (ve znění 16 novel).* 5th ed. Praha: Venice Music Production, 2014; Kazda, Petr; Kazdová, Karolína. *Zákon o pojištění odpovědnosti z provozu vozidla. Komentář.* 1st ed. Praha: Wolters Kluwer. 2016; Bušta, Pavel. *Nové smluvní pojištění odpovědnosti z provozu vozidla.* Pojistný obzor, 1999, No. 6; Horník, Jiří. *Leasing vozidel a nový systém tzv. 'povinného ručení'.* Pojistný obzor. 2000, No. 10, pp. 10–12; Karfíková, Marie. *Pojištění odpovědnosti z provozu vozidla.* Daně. 1999, No. 11; Karfíková, Marie; Přikryl, Vladimír; Vybíral, Roman et al. *Pojišťovací právo.* 2nd revised ed. Praha: Leges, 2018; Mesršmíd, Jaroslav. *K přípravě pojišťovnictví na členství ČR v Evropské unii.* Pojistný obzor. 1998, No. 4; Schelle, Karel. *Vývoj právní úpravy pojišťovnictví.* 1st ed. Brno: Masarykova univerzita, 1994; Schelle, Karel; Hradec, Michal. *Historie právní úpravy pojišťovnictví.* 1st ed. Praha: Eurolex Bohemia, 2006; Vostatek, Jaroslav. *Odpovědnostní pojištění motorových vozidel: quo vadis?* Finance a úvěr. 1996, No. 4 and 5; Přikryl, Vladimír; Čechová, Jana. *Revize motorové směrnice.* Pojistný obzor. 2018, No. 4, pp. 9–15; Žulavská, Lucie. *Revize motorové směrnice ve světle zprávy Výboru pro vnitřní trh a ochranu spotřebitele.* Pojistný obzor. 2018, No. 4, pp. 16–17.

556. CIA's Annual Report for 2019 (available at https://www.cap.cz/vyrocni-zpravy); CIB's Annual Report for 2019 (available at https://www.ckp.cz/o-nas/vyrocni-zpravy); CNB's Financial Market Supervision Report for 2019 (available at https://www.cnb.cz/en/supervision-financial-market/aggregate-information-financial-sector/financial-market-supervision-reports/).

557. This area is harmonized primarily by EU directives; these are in particular:

- Council Directive 72/166/EEC of 24 Apr. 1972 on the approximation of the laws of Member States relating to insurance against civil liability in respect of the use of motor vehicles, and to the enforcement of the obligation to insure against such liability.
- Second Council Directive 84/5/EEC of 30 Dec. 1983 on the approximation of the laws of the Member States relating to insurance against civil liability in respect of the use of motor vehicles.

and the establishment of the Czech Insurers' Bureau, its legal status, organization and subject of activity (§ 1(1) MTPLIA).

546. Although the MTPL is exceptional in many respects (especially in terms of the scope and details of the special regulation), it is still, in its essence, liability insurance as regulated in §§ 2861–2867 CC. So, in principle, everything that has been said above in Part III, Chapter 4. Liability insurance, applies to MTPL. Unless otherwise stipulated by MTPLIA, the MTPL is governed by the Civil Code (§ 1(3) MTPLIA).

547. The law regulates MTPL in the form of compulsory insurance.[559] Only a person whose liability for damage caused by operation of a vehicle is insured in accordance with the MTPLIA is permitted to operate a vehicle on a highway, a road, a local road or special-purpose road, with the exception of special-purpose roads that are not publicly accessible.[560] In the case of a vehicle registered in the Registry of motor vehicles pursuant to the act regulating the conditions of operation on roads,[561] the obligation of liability insurance pursuant to the MTPLIA must be fulfilled for the entire period when the vehicle is registered in the Registry of motor vehicles (§ 1(2) MTPLIA).

- Third Council Directive 90/232/EEC of 14 May 1990 on the approximation of the laws of the Member States relating to insurance against civil liability in respect of the use of motor vehicles.
- Directive 2000/26/EC of the European Parliament and of the Council of 16 May 2000 on the approximation of the laws of the Member States relating to insurance against civil liability in respect of the use of motor vehicles and amending Council Directives 73/239/EEC and 88/357/EEC (Fourth motor insurance Directive).
- Directive 2005/14/EC of the European Parliament and of the Council of 11 May 2005 amending Council Directives 72/166/EEC, 84/5/EEC, 88/357/EEC and 90/232/EEC and Directive 2000/26/EC of the European Parliament and of the Council relating to insurance against civil liability in respect of the use of motor vehicles.

Above directives were subsequently published in a consolidated version in the form of Directive 2009/103/EC of the European Parliament and of the Council of 16 Sep. 2009 relating to insurance against civil liability in respect of the use of motor vehicles, and the enforcement of the obligation to insure against such liability.

558. In the Czech Republic, MTPL is often referred to as 'mandatory suretyship' (in Czech 'povinné ručení'). However, this designation, used mainly by the general public, is conceptually completely incorrect and does not correspond to the nature of this legal relationship (for more details, *see* e.g., Jandová, Lucie. In: Jandová, Lucie; Vojtek, Petr. *Zákon o pojištění odpovědnosti z provozu vozidla. Komentář.* 2nd ed. Praha: C. H. Beck, 2019, p. 42).
559. In general, on compulsory insurance, *see* General Introduction, §6. Compulsory insurance.
560. Operating or leaving a vehicle on the road without MTPL insurance is a misdemeanour under the provisions of § 16(1) MTPLIA, for which a fine from CZK 5,000 to CZK 40,000 may be imposed.
561. Act No. 56/2001 Sb., on the Conditions of Operating Vehicles on Roads.

548. The insurance arises on the basis of an insurance contract concluded between the policyholder and the insurer (§ 3(1) MTPLIA). The owner of a domestic vehicle[562] or the driver of a foreign vehicle is obliged to conclude an MTPL insurance contract, unless otherwise stipulated by MTPLIA (§ 3(2) MTPLIA). Exceptions to this obligation have, for example, the bodies of the Integrated Rescue System, the Police of the Czech Republic, the Security Information Service, the General Inspectorate of Security Forces, customs authorities, etc. (*see* § 5 MTPLIA).[563]

549. A certain specificity is that the law imposes a contractual obligation on the insurer, i.e., the obligation to conclude an MTPL insurance contract if the proposal for its conclusion does not contradict MTPLIA, the law regulating the insurance contract (Civil Code) or the insurer's insurance conditions (§ 3(1) second sentence MTPLIA).

550. The insurance contract must contain the requirements specified in § 3(4) MTPLIA.[564] The contracting parties may derogate from the MTPLIA insofar as it does not reduce or restrict the injured party's claims arising from the MTPL (§ 3(1) MTPLIA).[565]

551. The law allows MTPL to be arranged as insurance of the insurance peril of another (cf. § 2767 CC). However, after negative experiences with the so-called open fleets,[566] the law restricts the possibility of insuring more vehicles at the same time with one insurance contract. This is only possible if the vehicles have the same owner or operator, if the policyholder has an insurable interest based on the provision of a loan or other similar financial service for the purpose of acquiring ownership of the vehicle, or if the owner or operator of the vehicle and the policyholder are part of the same concern (§ 3(2) MTPLIA).

---

562. If the vehicle is co-owned by several persons, the obligations under the MTPLIA shall be performed by the co-owner who has obtained written authorization from the other co-owners. If none of the co-owners have been authorized, all co-owners perform the duties jointly and severally (§ 26(1) MTPLIA).
563. Compensation for damage caused by the operation of vehicle exempted from MTPLIA, shall be provided by the Ministry of Finance (§ 11 MTPLIA). The compensation on the part of the Ministry is not an insurance indemnity, but a damages. The scope of compensation is thus not limited by the provisions of § 6 MTPLIA or the insurance indemnity limits and is governed by the Civil Code.
564. Cf. also § 2777 CC.
565. Cf. also § 2779(1) CC.
566. In the motor vehicle insurance, specific groups were previously formed, usually led by an insurance intermediary acting in the role of policyholder, where primary motivation of these groups was to achieve a lower insurance premium and thus a competitive advantage. Although the insurance needs of the individual insured persons were realized by such contract, the policyholder's legitimate need for protection against the consequences of an insured event was completely missing. As a result of the pressure on low premiums, these agreements began to deform the market. The insurance companies themselves, the Czech Insurers' Bureau and the CNB gradually opposed this practice; for more details, *see* e.g., Bušta, Pavel; Přikryl, Vladimír. *Zákon o pojištění odpovědnosti z provozu vozidla s komentářem (ve znění 16 novel).* § 3 [ASPI System]. Wolters Kluwer [cit. 2020-10-30]. ASPI_ID KO168_1999CZ. Available in the ASPI System. ISSN: 2336-517X.].

552. Immediately after concluding the insurance contract relating to the domestic vehicle, the insurer shall issue a 'green card'[567] to the policyholder (§ 3(3) MTPLIA), i.e., an international certificate proving the fact that the MTPL insurance contract has been concluded in relation to the vehicle.[568]

553. The insurance contract must be concluded so that this insurance, upon an indivisible premium, is valid in the territory of all Member States and other states mentioned in a list specified in a decree to be issued by the ministry.[569] The insurer is obliged to specify this scope of validity of the insurance in the green card (§ 6(5) MTPLIA).

554. When operating the vehicle on the road, its driver is obliged to carry a green card or a frontier insurance certificate[570] and present it to a member of the Police of the Czech Republic upon request (§ 17(1) MTPLIA).[571]

§2. Scope of Insurance

555. The MTPL applies to each person, who is liable for damage caused by the operation of a vehicle specified in an insurance contract (§ 6(1) MTPLIA). According to the provisions of § 2(f), the insured means a person to whose liability for damage the liability insurance applies. MTPL thus covers the liability of each person for damage caused by the operation of the vehicle specified in the insurance contract, not only if he is the vehicle operator, but also a different person who drove the operator's vehicle at the time of the accident and is liable for the damage. MTPL therefore covers both the liability of the vehicle operator pursuant to §§ 2927 et seq. CC, as well as the persons liable for damage according to § 2910 CC, typically a driver of the vehicle.[572]

556. Vehicle for the purposes of the MTPLIA (i.e., a vehicle subject to the obligation to conclude the MTPL insurance contract) means a road vehicle, a special

567. International Motor Insurance Certificate (IMIC).
568. Based on the decision taken during the 2019 Council of Bureaux General Assembly, as of 1 Jul. 2020 national Bureaus are allowed on a voluntary basis to issue the IMIC in black on white and allow the interested insurance markets to send PDF files directly and electronically by e-mail or any other facility to their policyholder. Subsequently, the policyholders can print the IMIC in black on white (for more details, *see* https://www.cobx.org/sites/default/files/cob_file_folder/FAQ-Website-Consumers-colour-of-the-IMIC.pdf).
569. Cf. § 4 of the Decree of the Ministry of Finance No. 205/1999 Sb.
570. Cf. § 14 MTPLIA.
571. Failure to present the green card at the request of the Police is a misdemeanour pursuant to § 16(2) of the MTPLIA, for which a fine of CZK 1,500 to CZK 3,000 may be imposed, or by an on-the-spot order up to CZK 1,500.
572. Cf. e.g., resolution of the Supreme Court of the Czech Republic of 5 Feb. 2008, file No. 25 Cdo 1957/2006.

vehicle and a trolleybus.[573] On the other hand, a wheelchair for handicapped, an animal drawn vehicle and a non-motorized vehicle drawn or pushed by a pedestrian, a bicycle and a scooter (unless they are approved as a type of motorcycle) are not considered to be vehicles (§ 2(a) MTPLIA).

I. Civil Liability in Respect of the Use of Motor Vehicles

557. Liability for damage caused by the operation of a vehicle, which is the subject of MTPL insurance, is regulated by the Civil Code. The liability of the tortfeasor may be based on the principle of general liability for fault according to § 2910 CC, as well as the strict liability of the vehicle operator according to § 2927 CC.

558. The general liability according to § 2910 CC is based on the principle of presumed fault (cf. § 2911 CC) and its basic conditions are: (i) wrongfulness (a breach of a statutory obligation), (ii) the occurrence of harm, (iii) the causal relationship (causal nexus) between them, and (iv) the existence of fault. The tortfeasor can be released from liability (exculpated) if he proves that he did not cause the harm even through negligence.[574]

559. Special regulations on liability for damage caused by the operation of a means of transport are contained in §§ 2927–2932 CC. It is not a *lex specialis* in relation to the general liability under § 2910 CC, but separate liability merits that may stand side by side and affect different tortfeasors (typically the operator of a vehicle liable under § 2927 CC and the driver liable under § 2910 CC).[575]

560. The liability of the vehicle operator is based on the principle of strict liability, i.e., liability regardless of the fault of the tortfeasor. No breach of a statutory obligation is required for the occurrence of liability pursuant to § 2927 CC.

561. It is assumed that the operation of a means of transport is inherently associated with an increased risk of harm, and that the person who operates the means of transport should be principally liable for such damage. The law therefore stipulates that a person who operates transport shall compensate the damage caused by the specific nature of such an operation (i.e., undesirable manifestations of such characteristics of the vehicle that are typical for its operation and result from its nature as a means of transport, which usually moves by motor speed and may, by its own movement or heavy braking, or other associated manifestations, such as steering failure, malfunction, separation of a part of the vehicle, collision with a stone and its ejection, cause an adverse effect on persons inside the vehicle or on

573. Cf. §§ 2 and 3 of the Act No. 56/2001 Sb.

574. For more details, *see* e.g., Hulmák, Milan a kol. *Občanský zákoník VI. Závazkové právo. Zvláštní část (§ 2055–3014). Komentář.* 1st ed. Praha: C. H. Beck, 2014, pp. 1537 et seq.

575. Cf. e.g., judgement of the Supreme Court of the Czech Republic of 17 Jan. 2008, file No. 32 Cdo 2837/2007, or resolution of 4 Sep. 2007, file No. 25 Cdo 271/2007.

persons or objects, which it comes into contact with).[576] Another operator of a vehicle, vessel or aircraft has the same duty, unless such a means of transport is driven by human power (§ 2927(1) CC).

562. The terms 'operation of a vehicle' and 'special nature of operation' are not defined by law and their definition is thus left primarily to the decision-making practice of the courts. According to case law, a vehicle is in operation not only when it is moving, but also when it is stationary, but its engine is running. The operation of the vehicle is also preparation for driving and immediate performance after the end of the ride, as well as the performance needed to maintain the vehicle. The starting of the engine itself belongs to the operation of the motor vehicle, regardless of whether the vehicle is moving and whether or not it happened on the road, or in another place accessible to the public or still in the garage, and whether the engine started the operator himself or his employee.[577]

563. The operation can also be a spontaneous movement of a vehicle standing on a slope after releasing the parking brake without starting the engine.[578] A motor vehicle is in operation even if, as a result of a driver failure, it creates an obstacle for other road users, regardless of whether the vehicle's engine is running at the time of the accident. Driver failure means any free or involuntary conduct that is causally related to the damage, from intentional conduct (suicide attempt, vehicle-ramming attack, intentional damage to the vehicle), through negligent conduct (common accidents caused by traffic offences), to uncaused acts (failure to cope with a complex traffic situation, health ailments).[579] The strict liability of the vehicle operator may also be based on a defect in the electrical installation of a car parked in the garage, which resulted to the car catching fire and the subsequent fire of the building.[580]

564. The CJEU's case law also has a significant impact on the understanding of the content of the concept of operation of vehicle and on the definition of the range of vehicles to which the MTPL should apply. Recently, it is possible to mention especially decisions in cases Vnuk,[581] Andrade,[582] Torreiro,[583] or Juliana,[584] which probably does not need to be presented in more detail here. The forthcoming revision of the motor directive is responding not only to these decisions. The European

576. Vojtek, Petr. In: Jandová, Lucie; Vojtek, Petr. *Zákon o pojištění odpovědnosti z provozu vozidla. Komentář.* 2nd ed. Praha: C. H. Beck, 2019, p. 104.
577. Judgement of the Supreme Court of the Slovak Socialist Republic of 27 Oct. 1971, file No. 1 Cz 42/71, published in the Collection of Judicial Decisions and Opinions under No. 9/1972.
578. Opinion of the Supreme Court of the Czech Socialist Republic, file No. Cpj 10/83, published in the Collection of Judicial Decisions and Opinions under No. 3/1984.
579. Judgement of the Supreme Court of the Czech Republic of 18 Mar. 2015, file No. 25 Cdo 3925/2013, published in the Collection of Judicial Decisions and Opinions under No. 71/2015.
580. Judgement of the Supreme Court of the Czech Republic of 31 Aug. 2017, file No. 25 Cdo 3485/2016, published in the Collection of Judicial Decisions and Opinions under No. 10/2018; similarly Judgement of the CJEU C-100/18 of 20 Jun. 2019, *Línea Directa Aseguradora SA v. Segurcaixa Sociedad Anónima de Seguros y Reaseguros*, ECLI:EU:C:2019:517.
581. Judgement of the CJEU C-162/13 of 4 Sep. 2014, *Damijan Vnuk v. Zavarovalnica Triglav d. d.*, ECLI:EU:C:2014:2146.

Commission adopted a proposal for a new version of the motor directive on 24 May 2018.[585] Changes can be expected, among other things, in the definition of the operation of the vehicle and the definition of vehicle itself, where the trend in the CJEU case law is the gradual extension of the interpretation of these concepts.[586]

565. The operator cannot be released from liability if the damage was caused by circumstances originating from the operation. Otherwise, the operator can release from the liability if he proves that he could not have prevented the damage despite having exerted all the efforts which may have been required (§ 2927(2) CC). The ground for release is fulfilled either by an unavoidable event coming from an external intervention (e.g., a natural event, a third party or animal intervention) which caused a harmful effect during operation of the means of transport, which could not be prevented by the operator, or an event related to the operation, which could not have been prevented even by using the available measures.[587] However, liberation is not possible if the damage was caused by circumstances originating from the operation (§ 2927(2) first sentence CC).[588]

566. In the provision of § 2932 CC, the law regulates the so-called collision of operations, i.e., the situation where the operations of two or more operators collide.[589] In such a case, the operators settle between themselves according to their contribution to the damage caused.[590]

582. Judgement of the CJEU C-514/16 of 28 Nov. 2017, *Isabel Maria Pinheiro Vieira Rodrigues de Andrade and Fausto da Silva Rodrigues de Andrade v. José Manuel Proença Salvador and Others*, ECLI:EU:C:2017:908.
583. Judgement of the CJEU C-334/16 of 20 Dec. 2017, *José Luís Núñez Torreiro v. AIG Europe Limited, Sucursal en España a Unión Española de Entidades Aseguradoras y Reaseguradoras (UNESPA)*, ECLI:EU:C:2017:1007.
584. Judgement of the CJEU C-80/17 of 4 Sep. 2018, *Fundo de Garantia Automóvel v. Alina Antónia Destapado Pão Mole Juliana a Cristiana Micaela Caetano Juliana*, ECLI:EU:C:2018:661.
585. *See* https://ec.europa.eu/info/law/better-regulation/have-your-say/initiatives/1407-REFIT-review-of-the-Motor-Insurance-Directive.
586. For more details on this topic, *see* e.g., Přikryl, Vladimír; Čechová, Jana. *Revize motorové směrnice.* Pojistný obzor. 2018, No. 4, pp. 9–15; Žulavská, Lucie. *Revize motorové směrnice ve světle zprávy Výboru pro vnitřní trh a ochranu spotřebitele.* Pojistný obzor. 2018, No. 4, pp. 16–17.
587. Vojtek, Petr. In: Jandová, Lucie; Vojtek, Petr. *Zákon o pojištění odpovědnosti z provozu vozidla. Komentář.* 2nd ed. Praha: C. H. Beck, 2019, p. 111.
588. Cf. e.g., judgement of the Supreme Court of the Slovak Socialist Republic of 23 Apr. 1975, file No. 2 Cz 20/75; decision of the Municipal Court in Prague of 10 Jan. 1968, file No. 6 Co 675/67, published in the Collection of Judicial Decisions and Opinions under No. 16/1969; opinion of the Supreme Court of the Czech Socialist Republic, file No. Cpj 10/83, published in the Collection of Judicial Decisions and Opinions under No. 3/1984; resolution of the Supreme Court of the Czech Republic of 30 Aug. 2006, file No. 25 Cdo 638/2005; resolution of the Supreme Court of the Czech Republic of 29 Mar. 2011, file No. 25 Cdo 948/2010; or decision of the Supreme Court of the Czechoslovak Socialist Republic of 23 Sep. 1969, file No. 3 Cz 21/69, published in the Collection of Judicial Decisions and Opinions under No. 24/1970.
589. A collision of operations can occur even without an actual contact of vehicles, e.g., due to glare, throwing out a stone, tearing off and flying off part of the vehicle, leakage of operating fluid on the road, etc. (cf. e.g., opinion of the Supreme Court of the Czech Socialist Republic, file No. Cpj

II. Scope of Insurance Indemnity

567. From the MTPL insurance, the insured has the right to have the insurer compensate the injured person for damage or other harm for the extent and in the amount according to the Civil Code caused by the operation of the vehicle, to the extent specified in § 6 MTPLIA. This key provision regulates the scope of insurance indemnity and exhaustively[591] determines what claims the insurer is obliged to pay to the injured party instead of the insured tortfeasor.

568. The insurer is obliged to provide insurance indemnity to the following extent:

(i) the harm caused by personal injury or death (§ 6(2)(a) MTPLIA);
(ii) reasonably incurred costs associated with health care of the wounded animal and damage caused by impairment, destruction or loss of a property, as well as for damage incurred by a loss of property if a natural person lost the capability to take care of it (§ 6(2)(b) MTPLIA);
(iii) loss of profit (§ 6(2)(c) MTPLIA);
(iv) reasonably spent costs related to legal representation when making claims under points (i) to (iii); in connection with the damage referred to in points (ii) or (iii) only in case of futile expiration of the period pursuant to § 9(3) MTPLIA or unjustified refusal or unjustified reduction of the insurance indemnity by the insurer (§ 6(2)(d) MTPLIA); above points (i) – (iv) under the condition that the injured party has asserted and proved his claim and if the loss event from which the harm arose, and from which the insured is obliged to compensate the harm, occurred during the term of liability insurance;
(v) claim asserted and proven by the health insurance company for reimbursement of costs incurred for health care paid for by public health insurance (§ 6(4) MTPLIA);
(vi) recourse compensation prescribed for payment to the insured under the law governing sickness insurance (§ 6(4) second sentence MTPLIA);

10/83, published in the Collection of Judicial Decisions and Opinions under No. 3/1984; or opinion of the Civil Law and Commercial Division of the Supreme Court of the Czechoslovak Socialist Republic of 15 Nov. 1972, file No. Cpjf 93/71, published in the Collection of Judicial Decisions and Opinions under No. 64/1972).

590. For more details on liability in respect of the use of motor vehicles, collision of operations, contribution of the injured party and other related topics, *see* e.g., Jandová, Lucie; Vojtek, Petr. *Zákon o pojištění odpovědnosti z provozu vozidla. Komentář.* 2nd ed. Praha: C. H. Beck, 2019, pp. 94 et seq.

591. Cf. e.g., judgement of the Supreme Court of the Czech Republic of 11 Apr. 2017, file No. 25 Cdo 4112/2017, published in the Collection of Judicial Decisions and Opinions under No. 64/2019: 'It follows from the cited provisions that the insurance indemnity provided from motor third party liability insurance is not unlimited and does not cover all damage incurred by the injured party as a result of a loss event, but only claims exhaustively stipulated in § 6(2) of this Act.'

(vii) reimbursement of costs of the fire brigade or units of volunteer fire departments of the municipalities (§ 6(4) second sentence MTPLIA).[592]

569. Unless otherwise stipulated, the insurer shall provide insurance indemnity to the extent and in the amount pursuant to § 6(2) MTPLIA in money up to the indemnity limit stipulated in the insurance contract.

570. Following the European law,[593] MTPLIA sets minimum limits of insurance indemnity in the provisions of § 3a. The limit of insurance indemnity shall be at least:

(i) for harm caused by personal injury or death at least CZK 35,000,000 for each injured or killed, including reimbursement of costs incurred for health care paid for by public health insurance and recourse claims pursuant to § 6(4);
(ii) for property damage and loss of profit at least CZK 35,000,000, regardless of the number of victims; if the sum total of the claims asserted by more injured parties exceeds the limit of insurance indemnity stipulated in the insurance contract, the insurance indemnity to each of them shall be reduced in proportion of this limit to the sum total of the claims of all the injured parties.

571. Indemnity provided for damage caused by the operation of the vehicle, to the extent that the insured is obliged to compensate for this damage and which the injured party has duly proved, cannot be refused or reduced, except in the cases specified by law (§ 7(4) MTPLIA).

572. In the provision of § 7, MTPLIA exhaustively regulates exclusions from the MTPL insurance. For example, the insurer does not compensate for:

(i) harm sustained by the driver of the vehicle by operation of which the harm was caused;
(ii) costs incurred by the provision of health care, health insurance benefits or pensions from pensions insurance as a consequence of personal injury or death sustained by the driver of the vehicle by operation of which this harm had caused;
(iii) damage to property and loss of profit, which the insured person is obliged to compensate for his or her spouse or persons who lived in the same household with the insured at the time of the occurrence of the loss event (with the exception of loss of profit due to personal injury);

592. In detail on particular claims, with a comprehensive excursion into the area of tort law and compensation for damage under the Civil Code, including related case law, given the considerable scope of this matter, full reference can be made here to the exhaustive commentary on § 6 MTPLIA in Jandová, Lucie; Vojtek, Petr. *Zákon o pojištění odpovědnosti z provozu vozidla. Komentář.* 2nd ed. Praha: C. H. Beck, 2019, pp. 116 et seq.
593. Cf. Art. 9 of the Directive 2009/103/EC.

(iv) damage to the vehicle by operation of which the damage was caused as well as to the cargo transported by this vehicle (with the exception of the damage to things which the person transported by this vehicle had on or in his custody);
(v) damage caused by manipulation with the load of a non-moving vehicle;
(vi) damage caused by the operation of vehicle during its participation in an organized motor race or competition, with the exception of the damage caused in the course of such participation if the driver during this race or competition is obliged to observe road traffic rules;
(vii) damage caused by operation of a vehicle during an act of terrorism or war event, if such an operation is in direct connection with this act or event, etc.[594]

573. The insurer is obliged to perform the investigation of a loss event without undue delay. Within the period of three months following the day of asserting the claim for compensation from liability insurance by the beneficiary, the insurer is be obliged to (§ 9(3) MTPLIA):

(i) complete the investigation of the insured event and inform the injured party of the amount of indemnity by individual claims, including the method of determining its amount, if the insurer's obligation to provide indemnity has not been questioned and the injured party's claims have been proven; or
(ii) notify the injured party with a written explanation of those claims which have been rejected by the insurer or which have been reduced, or which it was not possible to complete the investigation within the specified period.[595]

574. Failure to fulfil the above duties is sanctioned by the obligation to pay interest on arrears at a special rate regulated in the provisions of § 9(4) MTPLIA. The breach of the above duties is also linked to the insurer's obligation to reimburse the injured party for the reasonably incurred costs associated with legal representation in asserting claims for indemnity in the extent of property damage and loss of profit (§ 6(2)(d) MTPLIA).

575. The due date of the insurance indemnity is stipulated in certain respects differently from the general regulation of CC,[596] as it may be based on two different facts. In accordance with the general regulation, the MTPLIA stipulates that the indemnity is due within fifteen days as soon as the insurer has completed the investigation necessary to determine the extent of its obligation to provide indemnity.

594. For a complete list of exclusions, *see* § 7 MTPLIA.
595. *See also* CNB's Supervisory benchmark No. 1/2012, on the Obligation of Insurers Providing Motor Third Party Liability Insurance (available at https://www.cnb.cz/export/sites/cnb/cs/dohled-financni-trh/.galleries/vykon_dohledu/dohledove_benchmarky/download/dohledovy_benchmark_2012_01.pdf), cf. also Art. 22 of the Directive 2009/103/EC.
596. Cf. § 2798(1) CC.

Alternatively, however, the said fifteen-day period may be based on the moment when the insurer has received a final court decision on its obligation to provide insurance indemnity (§ 9(2) MTPLIA).

§3. Obligation of the Insured

576. The insured is obliged, without undue delay, to notify the insurer in writing that a loss event took place and state the factual situation as regards this event, to produce necessary documents, and in the course of investigation related to the loss event to proceed in compliance with the instructions of the insurer. At the same time he is obliged to state that: (i) the right for compensation has been asserted against him and to comment on the compensation requested and the amount thereof, (ii) administrative or criminal proceedings have been initiated against him in connection with the loss event and inform the insurer about its progress and result, without undue delay, (iii) the injured party has exercised his right to damages by filing the claim with a court or another relevant authority, if the insured learns of this fact (§ 8(1) and (2) MTPLIA.[597]

577. The insured is also obliged to provide cooperation to the injured party and to provide him, at his request, with the information defined in the provisions of § 8(3) MTPLIA necessary for the assertion of the right to the insurance indemnity.

578. In the event of a traffic accident not subject to notification to the Police of the Czech Republic,[598] the insured is obliged to provide evidence in the form of a joint record of the traffic accident[599] and submit it to the insurer without undue delay (§ 8(4) MTPLIA).

§4. Direct Claim of the Injured Party

579. In Part II, Chapter 6. Insurance and third parties, and Part III., Chapter 4. Liability insurance, it was explained that in liability insurance, the beneficiary is, in principle, identical to the insured person. The injured party usually has no locus

597. Cf. also §§ 2862 and 2796 CC.

598. The obligation to report a traffic accident to the police and to remain at the scene of the accident until the arrival of the police officer arises for the participant in the traffic accident in the event that:

- a person has been killed or injured;
- material damage probably exceeds the amount of CZK 100,000 on one of the participating vehicles, including the transported cargo;
- there is damage to the property of a third party;
- the road component or accessory is damaged or destroyed;
- the participants in a traffic accident cannot themselves, without making a disproportionate effort, ensure the restoration of traffic flow on the road (*see* § 47(4) and (5) of the Act No. 361/2000 Sb., on Road Traffic).

599. Cf. § 47(3)(g) of the Act No. 361/2000 Sb., on Road Traffic.

standi to bring an action against the insurer and represents only the statutory determined place of performance. The injured party becomes entitled to indemnity from the insurer only if it has been stipulated, or where provided by another statute (§ 2861(2) CC). The injured party's right of direct action therefore constitutes an exception to the general rule and can only be established by a statute or a contract.

580. Such an exception established by a statute is represented in the current Czech legislation by direct claim of the injured party according to provisions of § 9(1) MTPLIA,[600] which, in accordance with European law,[601] stipulates that the injured party has the right to assert his claim for insurance indemnity with the respective insurer (or with the Czech Insurers' Bureau if it is a claim for a compensation from the Guarantee fund). This is an important and very widely used provision in practice, which is one of the pillars of the current MTPL legislation based on the principle of protection of victims.

581. The right of direct action of the injured party is not in the nature of a claim for damages. The insurer does not become the person liable for the damage instead of the tortfeasor. A clear distinction must be made between these two rights. This distinction has important practical consequences, whether in terms of the territorial jurisdiction of the courts,[602] the different regime of statute of limitations,[603] or the procedural position of particular persons in court proceedings.

582. The existence of the direct claim against the liability insurer does not cause the extinction of the right to damages against the tortfeasor. Both rights coexist, but are interdependent in the sense that, to the extent that one has been fulfilled, the other extinguishes. This situation is referred to as false joint and several responsibility (in Czech 'nepravá solidarita').[604]

583. A similar dependence can be found between the injured party's direct claim and the insured's parallel right to have the insurer compensate the injured person for the caused harm. In fact, it is a right to the same performance on the basis of the same legal reason, while two persons have locus standi to bring an action.[605] These two rights coexist side by side. By satisfying the right of the injured party, the corresponding right of the insured extinguishes to a given extent.

---

600. Briefly on the history of the legal regulation of direct claim in MTPL insurance, *see* Part II, Ch. 6. Insurance and Third Parties.
601. Cf. Art. 18 of the Directive 2009/103/EC.
602. *See* e.g., the resolution of the Municipal Court in Prague of 24 Apr. 2009, file No. 21 Co 139/2009, published in the Collection of Judicial Decisions and Opinions under No. 81/2011.
603. *See* e.g., the judgement of the Supreme Court of the Czech Republic of 12 Dec. 2007, file No. 25 Cdo 113/2006, published in the Collection of Judicial Decisions and Opinions under No. 93/2008.
604. *See* judgement of the Supreme Court of the Czech Republic of 6 Apr. 2016, file No. 25 Cdo 222/2015; or judgement of the Supreme Court of the Czech Republic of 24 Jul. 2002, file No. 25 Cdo 499/2002.
605. For the locus standi of the insured person in liability insurance, *see* the explanation in Part III., Ch. 4. Liability insurance and the judgement of the Supreme Court of the Czech Republic of 12 Dec. 2018, file No. 23 Cdo 5969/2017, published Collection of Judicial Decisions and Opinions under No. 9/2019, or judgement of 18 Dec. 2018, file No. 23 Cdo 276/2018.

584. As a result of the passage of the right pursuant to § 2820 CC, the direct claim to insurance indemnity may also be in favour of the insurer of one of the jointly and severely liable tortfeasors, if such insurer provided the injured party with insurance indemnity to a greater extent than corresponds to the participation of his insured person. In such a case, this insurer has the right to settlement in proportion to the participation of individual persons in causing the damage, directly against the insurers of other participants in the accident.[606]

§5. Insurer's Right to Recourse

585. The principle of protection of injured parties is reflected in the provision of § 7(4) MTPLIA, which stipulates that insurance indemnity for damage caused by operation of a vehicle, to the extent that the insured is obliged to compensate for such damage and which the injured party has duly proven, cannot be refused or reduced. In certain cases, in the event of a flagrant breach of obligations by the insured, it could be considered fair for the insurer to refuse the insurance indemnity provided in favour of the insured tortfeasor (in the sense that it relieves the insured of his obligation to compensate for the injured party). However, as the interest in compensating the injured party prevails, the insurer is still forced to provide the indemnity. In these justified cases, it is legitimate for the financial costs of the insurance indemnity to be passed on to the insured tortfeasor, who should ultimately be the one to bear the negative consequences of the insured event.

586. Provision of § 10 MTPLIA therefore enshrines the insurer, in certain situations, the right to reimbursement of what he has fulfilled from the insurance. This right of the insurer is usually referred to as a recourse.

587. It is necessary to distinguish between the insurer's right to recourse and the subrogation pursuant to the provisions of § 2820 CC. Right to recourse is a special original right of the insurer against the insured, which is characterized by its sanctioning nature, while as subrogation is referred to rights that pass to the insurer upon the payment of insurance indemnity and by which the reparation function predominates.[607]

588. The conditions for the claim to recourse are regulated only by the mentioned provision and cannot be supplemented by other preconditions stipulated for the claim for damages. This is not a right to damages and the application of tort law is excluded. The application of the provisions of the Civil Code on liability for damage is relevant only for the determination of the insured, i.e., the person whose liability for damage is covered by liability insurance.[608]

---

606. *See* judgement of the Supreme Court of the Czech Republic of 15 Dec. 2015, file No. 23 Cdo 4210/2013, published in the Collection of Judicial Decisions and Opinions under No. 47/2017.
607. *See also* Part II, Ch. 5, §1, II. Subrogation.
608. *See* e.g., resolution of the Supreme Court of the Czech Republic of 22 Nov. 2011, file No. 32 Cdo 3266/2010.

589. The right to recourse becomes time-barred in the general three-year limitation period (§ 619 in connection with § 629(1) CC), not in the periods of limitation given for claiming damages (§ 636 of the Civil Code), which apply to the injured party's claims for damages against the tortfeasor.[609]

590. The insurer has the right against the insured to get a refund for the indemnity provided, if he proves that the insured (§ 10(1) MTPLIA):

(i) caused the damage deliberately;
(ii) without a justifiable reason, has failed to fulfil the obligation to draw up a joint record of a traffic accident or to report a traffic accident which is a loss event, and, as a result, the possibility of a proper investigation by the insurer or the possibility of the insurer to assert this right to recourse has been made more difficult or impossible;[610]
(iii) without a justifiable reason he left the scene of the accident or otherwise made it impossible to investigate the actual cause of the accident;
(iv) caused the damage by the operation of vehicle which the insured used illegitimately;
(v) without a justifiable reason, he failed to meet the obligations pursuant to § 8(1) to (3) of the MTPLIA and, as a result, the possibility of a proper investigation of the insurer was made more difficult or impossible;
(vi) refused to obey, without a justifiable reason, as a driver, the request of the Police of the Czech Republic to undergo a test detecting alcohol, narcotic or psychotropic drugs or medicament marked with prohibition to drive a motor vehicle;
(vii) was driving a vehicle without necessary driving license (with the exception of driving a vehicle by a person learning to drive the vehicle or in the process of passing a driving examination and that always only in the presence of an authorized instructor or of an individual schooling trainer-driver);
(viii) was driving at the time when he was prohibited from driving;
(ix) was driving a vehicle under the influence of alcohol, narcotics or psychotropic substances or a medicament marked with prohibition to drive a motor vehicle;[611]

609. Cf. e.g., judgement of the Supreme Court of the Czech Republic of 22 Apr. 2008, file No. 25 Cdo 799/2006.
610. The mere fact that the insured has escaped from an accident and has not fulfilled the obligation to report a traffic accident, does not a priori establish the insurer's right to recourse for what he provided (resolution of the Supreme Court of the Czech Republic of 20 Sep. 2010, file No. 23 Cdo 3349/2009).
611. The existence of a mere breach of the basic road traffic obligation not to drive under the influence of alcohol does not automatically give rise to a recourse claim for what the insurer has provided on behalf of the insured, as it must be established that the breach was causally related to the occurrence of damage for which the insured is liable (resolution of the Supreme Court of the Czech Republic of 18 May 2011, file No. 23 Cdo 1583/2010); Recourse right applies not to the driver who, as an employee of the insured, caused damage to the injured party in intoxication, but the insured, even though he is a legal entity, as the employer of the driver who used this driver to perform his working tasks within the employment relationship (judgement of the Supreme Court of the Czech Republic of 28 Mar. 2007, file No. 32 Odo 1397/2005).

(x) entrusted the driving of the vehicle to a person specified in (vii), (viii) and (ix).

591. MTPLIA in § 10(3) establishes joint and several liability of the vehicle operator in cases where the vehicle was driven by a person referred to in points (vii) to (x), i.e., a person different from the operator. However, the operator may be released from his liability if he proves that he could not influence the actions of this person.

592. The insurer also has the recourse right against the insured, if he proves that the insured has breached the basic road traffic rules by operating the vehicle (§ 10(2) MTPLIA):

(i) which design and technical condition do not meet requirements of safety of traffic on roads, of safety of persons handling the vehicle, transported persons and property; or
(ii) which technical capability for being operated has not been approved, and at the same time this breach was in a causal connection with the occurrence of damage, which the insured is liable for.

593. A specific recourse right of the insurer directed not against the insured, but against the policyholder, is regulated in the provisions of § 10(4) MTPLIA. The insurer has against the policyholder the right to get a refund for the sum he had provided for damage caused by the operation of vehicle if the damage was caused by a fact, which the insurer could have not ascertained due to deliberately untrue or incomplete answers at the time of negotiating the insurance, and which was essential for the conclusion of the insurance contract.[612]

594. In addition to the recourse right, the insurer has the right against the insured to reimbursement of costs associated with the investigation of the insured event or other costs caused by the breach of duty pursuant to § 8(1) to (3) MTPLIA.

595. Of course, the sum of the required refund must not be higher than the provided insurance indemnity (§ 10(5) MTPLIA).

§6. Termination of Insurance

596. MTPLIA contains in the provision of § 12 a special regulation of the termination of the MTPL insurance. According to the above provision, the insurance extinguishes:

612. Cf. § 2788 CC.

(i) on the day when the policyholder, his heir, legal successor, or vehicle owner, if he is a person different from the policyholder, notified the insurer of a change in the ownership of a domestic vehicle;[613]
(ii) on the day a vehicle which is not subject to registration physically ceased to exist as a vehicle;
(iii) on the day of decommissioning of a domestic vehicle in accordance with the Act on the Conditions of Operating Vehicles on Roads;
(iv) when a vehicle has been stolen (if it is impossible to determine the exact date of the theft, a vehicle is considered as stolen as soon as the Police of the Czech Republic was notified of the theft of the vehicle);
(v) on the day following the vain expiry of a time limit set forth by the insurer in a reminder for payment of the premium or a part thereof delivered to the policyholder;[614]
(vi) upon notice of termination pursuant to a special legal regulation;[615]
(vii) by mutual agreement of the insurer and the policyholder;
(viii) upon the expiry of the insurance period;
(ix) on the day of registration of the termination of physical existence of a vehicle in the Registry of motor vehicles in case of vehicles subject to registration (or the day of the irreversible change preventing the operation of the vehicle, if it is not possible to submit the application for registration the termination of physical existence of a vehicle).

597. The policyholder is obliged to notify the insurer of the facts referred to in points (i) to (iv) without undue delay. After the termination of the MTPL insurance, the policyholder is obliged to return the green card to the insurer without undue delay, if it has been issued.

598. After the termination of the insurance, the insurer is obliged to issue to the policyholder, on the basis of his written request, within fifteen days from the date of its delivery, a confirmation of the duration of MTPL insurance and its loss record, the details of which shall be determined by the Decree of the Ministry of Finance.[616]

---

613. *See also* CNB's Supervisory benchmark No. 3/2013, on the Right of the Insurance Company to Demand Proof of a Change of Vehicle Owner upon Termination of the Insurance according to § 12 (1) point a) of the Motor Third Party Liability Insurance Act (available at https://www.cnb.cz/export/sites/cnb/cs/dohled-financni-trh/.galleries/vykon_dohledu/dohledove_benchmarky/download/dohledovy_benchmark_2013_03.pdf).
614. This time limit may not be shorter than one month and the insurer's reminder must contain a warning concerning extinction of the insurance in case of non-payment of the overdue premium and the insurer shall also notify the person specified in the insurance contract as the owner of the domestic vehicle if he is different from the policyholder. The time limit set forth by the insurer in the reminder may be extended by mutual agreement prior to expiry of the time limit.
615. MTPLIA refers here to the general options for terminating the insurance contract by a notice of termination regulated in the Civil Code (cf. also § 2781 CC).
616. Cf. § 3 of the Decree of the Ministry of Finance No. 205/1999 Sb.; *see also* CNB's Supervisory benchmark No. 2/2012, on the Obligation of the Insurer to Issue a Certificate on the Duration of

599. If the insurance extinguishes before the expiry of the period for which it was agreed, the insurer is entitled to the premium until the end of the calendar month in which the insurance extinguished. The insurer is obliged to refund the remaining portion of the paid premium.

600. If the MTPL insurance extinguished without a new insurance contract being concluded in relation to the given vehicle within fourteen days of its termination, the municipal authority shall decommission such a road vehicle. The owner of the road vehicle is obliged to submit to the municipal authority that decommissioned the road vehicle within ten days from the date of entry into force of the decision to decommission the road vehicle a certificate of registration of the road vehicle and all issued plates with assigned registration mark, submit a technical certificate of the road vehicle to mark the record of its decommissioning, and if the decommissioning of the vehicle lasts longer than twelve consecutive calendar months, notify the address of the place where the decommissioned road vehicle is located and the purpose of its use (§ 12 of the Act No. 56/2001 Sb., on the Conditions of Operating Vehicles on Roads).

601. It is possible to agree with Jandová[617] that the list of ways of termination in § 12 of the MTPLIA is not exhaustive. In addition to the ones explicitly regulated, some general reasons for termination of insurance according to the Civil Code may also apply in the alternative.

§7. Claims Representatives

602. European legislation[618] is based on the idea that the parties injured as a result of a motor vehicle accident and occurring in a State other than that of their residence should be entitled to claim in their Member State of residence against a claims representative appointed there by the insurance undertaking of the responsible party. This solution enables damage suffered by injured parties outside their Member State of residence to be dealt with under procedures which are familiar to them. The institute of claims representatives is therefore intended to facilitate for victims to assert their claims in the event of harm to their health or property suffered as a result of a traffic accident during their stay in the EU outside their place of residence or domicile. The injured party should be able assert his claims at the claims representative of an insurer established in another Member State in his home Member State without having to assert his claims in a complicated way across the border in another country.

Liability Insurance for Damage Caused by the Operation of the Vehicle and its Loss Record (available at https://www.cnb.cz/export/sites/cnb/cs/dohled-financni-trh/.galleries/vykon_dohledu/dohledove_benchmarky/download/dohledovy_benchmark_2012_02.pdf).

617. Jandová, Lucie. In: Jandová, Lucie; Vojtek, Petr. *Zákon o pojištění odpovědnosti z provozu vozidla. Komentář.* 2nd ed. Praha: C. H. Beck, 2019, p. 317.

618. Cf. points 34 et seq. of the recital and Art. 21 of the Directive 2009/103/EC.

603. In accordance with Article 21(1) of the Directive 2009/103/EC, the appointment of claims representatives by a domestic insurance company in each Member State is one of the conditions for obtaining the authorization to provide MTPL insurance (§ 13(6)(l), § 19 (1)(c) IA). Similarly, the appointment of a claims representative for the Czech Republic is one of the conditions for the provision of MTPL insurance in the Czech Republic by an insurance company from another Member State in the form of temporary provision of services (§ 30(2)(d) IA). Also, an insurance company from a third country is obliged to appoint a claims representative in the Czech Republic and in other Member States if it intends to obtain the authorization to provide an MTPL (§ 32(6)(i) IA).[619]

604. The main task of a claims representative is to quickly and effectively deal with and settle claims with an international element asserted by the injured party in his home state. The possibility to assert claims against the claims representative does not prevent the injured party of the possibility to assert claims directly against the tortfeasor's liability insurer or the tortfeasor himself.

605. A claims representative may be active for several insurers. He must be entitled to represent the insurer in relation to the injured party, to settle the injured party's claims in full and to be able to act in the official language of the injured party's Member State of residence or domicile. The insurer notifies the details of claims representatives to the Czech Insurers' Bureau, which shall ensure that this information is forwarded to the relevant information centres of the Member States.

606. The appointment of a claims representative does not constitute the opening of a branch of an insurance company and the activity of a claims representative is not regarded as an establishment in the territory of another Member State.

607. It must be emphasized that, in principle, a claims representative cannot be directly sued for the insurance indemnity (unless this option is expressly established by the relevant national law).[620]

608. MTPLIA distinguishes several types of claims representatives:

(i) a claims representative of a domestic insurer (or a third-country insurer providing the MTPL insurance in the Czech Republic) for other Member States (§ 9a MTPLIA);
(ii) a claims representative of an insurer from another Member State for the Czech Republic, if this insurer provides MTPL insurance in the territory of the Czech Republic on the basis of the freedom to provide services temporarily (§ 9b MTPLIA);

619. Cf. also Arts 151 and 152 of the Solvency II Directive.
620. *See* Judgement of the CJEU C-558/15 of 15 Dec. 2016, *Alberto José Vieira de Azevedo and Others v. CED Portugal Unipessoal, Lda and Instituto de Seguros de Portugal – Fundo de Garantia Automóvel*, ECLI:EU:C:2016:957.

(iii) claims representatives of the insurer authorized in another state to provide the MTPL insurance who does not provide such insurance in the Czech Republic (§ 9c MTPLIA);
(iv) claims representative determined on the basis of a rebuttable legal presumption (§ 9d MTPLIA):
   - if the insurer provides MTPL insurance in the territory of the Czech Republic on the basis of the freedom to establish branches, it is considered that the obligations of the claims representative according to § 9c(1) to (3) MTPLIA shall be fulfilled by the head of this branch in the Czech Republic;
   - if the insurer provides MTPL insurance in the territory of the Czech Republic on the basis of the freedom to provide services on a temporary basis, it is considered that the obligations of the claims representative according to § 9c(1) to (3) MTPLIA shall be fulfilled by the claims representative referred to in point (ii).

§8. Czech Insurers' Bureau

609. MTPLIA in the provisions of §§ 18 et seq. regulates the establishment of the Czech Insurers' Bureau (CIB)[621] and determines its legal status, organization, and scope of its activities.

610. Insurers' bureaux in individual states are professional organizations associating insurance companies that are authorized to provide MTPL insurance. At the international level, the bureaux are associated in the umbrella organization of the Council of Bureaux.[622]

611. CIB is a sui generis legal entity, registered in the Commercial Register, with its registered office in Prague, which is authorized to conduct activities to the extent specified by the MTPLIA. The provisions of the Insurance Act shall apply, with the necessary modifications, to the activities of the CIB.

612. CIB performs in particular the following tasks (§ 18(2) MTPLIA):

(i) administers the Guarantee fund and the Loss prevention fund;
(ii) carries on frontier insurance and runs the information centre;
(iii) guarantees execution of tasks related to its membership in the Council of Bureaux;
(iv) enters into agreements with the insurers' bureaux and guarantee funds of other states, information centres, and bodies authorized in other Member States to handle claims for substitute compensation, and executes tasks arising from such agreements;
(v) cooperates with state authorities in matters pertaining to MTPL insurance;

621. https://www.ckp.cz/en/.
622. https://www.cobx.org/.

(vi) keeps records and statistics for the purposes of MTPL insurance;
(vii) participates in the prevention of loss events in road traffic and in the prevention of insurance frauds related to the operation of vehicles.

613. The structure and competence of the CIB bodies are determined in the provision of §§ 19 et seq. MTPLIA. The bodies of the CIB consist of the Members' Assembly (the supreme body of the Bureau – for more details, *see* § 20 MTPLIA), the Board of Directors (five-member statutory body – for more *see* § 21 MTPLIA), the Supervisory Board (supervisory body supervising the activities of CIB – for more details, *see* § 22 MTPLIA) and Chief Executive (exercising the competence of CIB on a day-to-day basis in the period between meetings of the Board of Directors – *see* § 23 MTPLIA).[623]

614. Membership in the CIB incepts for the insurer on the day the CNB's decision granting the insurer authorization to conduct MTPL insurance takes effect, or on the day the insurer from another Member State commences operation of MTPL insurance in the Czech Republic.

615. Insurers associated in the CIB are obliged to pay financial contributions. Contributions may be used for ensuring the CIB's competency only. The members of the CIB are also liable as sureties for its debts for which the CIB has not created adequate assets, in the same proportion as their share in the total amount of contributions of all members.

616. A necessary precondition for the functioning of the MTPL system is the establishment and maintenance of the necessary information base with data on concluded insurance contracts, insured vehicles and other facts, and the sharing of this information with the relevant state authorities (Ministry of Transport). The CIB keeps records of data on MTPL insurance in accordance with the provisions of § 18(2)(f) MTPLIA. Insurers are obliged to submit to the CIB data on MTPL insurance from insurance contracts they have in their insurance portfolio. The scope of the communicated data is determined by the Decree of the Ministry of Finance No. 205/1999 Sb.

617. The key tasks are performed by the CIB in relation to the injured parties. In addition to providing compensation from the Guarantee fund (which will be discussed below), the CIB operates an information centre[624] in order to provide the information necessary for assertion of claims of the injured parties. Through the information centre, the CIB ascertains and stores data on the domestic vehicle registration plates, insurers, numbers of insurance contracts relating to MTPL insurance for domestic vehicles and the dates of inception and termination of insurance,

623. Current organization chart is available at https://www.ckp.cz/images/clanky/en/about_us/about_cib/organigram_ckp_aj.pdf.
624. https://ic.ckp.cz/ICwww/servlet?_page=info&lngID=2.

green card numbers, claims representatives, etc. (§ 15a MTPLIA). This is supplemented by the explicit obligation of the CIB to provide the injured parties, at their request, with the data necessary for the assertion of their claims under the conditions of § 18a MTPLIA.

618. The CNB supervises the administration of the Guarantee fund and other CIB activities in accordance with the Insurance Act. In exercising supervision, the CNB may impose remedial measures on the CIB in order to eliminate the identified deficiencies. If the CIB does not comply with the imposed remedial measures or if these deficiencies are repeated in its activities, the CNB may impose a fine of up to CZK 10 million on the CIB (§ 25 MTPLIA).

I. Guarantee Fund

619. Pursuant to Article 10(1) of the Directive 2009/103/EC, each Member State shall set up or authorize a body with the task of providing compensation, at least up to the limits of the insurance obligation for damage to property or personal injuries caused by an unidentified vehicle or a vehicle for which the insurance obligation has not been satisfied.

620. In the Czech Republic, the CIB, which administers the Guarantee fund for this purpose (§§ 24 et seq. MTPLIA), performs the function of such body. The Guarantee fund is formed from the premium for frontier insurance pursuant to § 14, from the insurers' contributions pursuant to § 18(5), from the compensations received pursuant to § 24(7) and (9) and from the contributions received pursuant to § 4 MTPLIA.

621. The CIB provides from the Guarantee fund to the injured (§ 24(2) MTPLIA):

(i) compensation for personal injury or death caused by operation of an unidentified vehicle for which an unidentified person is liable; material damage and lost profit is compensated only in case of simultaneous heavy personal injury and only if the material damage and lost profit exceed CZK 10,000;
(ii) compensation for harm caused by operation of a vehicle without MTPL insurance;
(iii) compensation for harm caused by operation of a domestic vehicle insured with an insurer that is unable to pay the compensation due to his bankruptcy;
(iv) compensation for harm caused by operation of a foreign vehicle insured by frontier insurance;
(v) compensation for harm caused by operation of a foreign vehicle whose driver is exempted from the obligation to conclude frontier insurance when operating this vehicle in the territory of the Czech Republic;
(vi) substitute compensation as per § 24a and 24b MTPLIA;
(vii) compensation for damage caused by operation of a vehicle which was dispatched from one Member State to the Czech Republic as a country of its final

destination, if the vehicle in question was not insured against MTPL and the accident occurred within a period of thirty days after the acceptance of delivery by the purchased, even though the vehicle has not formally been registered in the Czech Republic.

622. CIB provides these compensations to the injured party under the same conditions as the insurer provides insurance indemnity (§ 24(6) MTPLIA), i.e., to the extent stipulated in § 6(2), with the application of exclusions under § 7 or with the possible occurrence of the right to recourse according to § 10 MTPLIA. Claims for compensations under the above points (ii), (iii) and (vii) may be asserted by the injured party against the CIB under the same conditions under which he could assert a claim for insurance indemnity against the insurer, which means in particular that the right of direct action of the injured party in the sense of § 9(1) MTPLIA is established here in relation to these claims.

623. The maximum threshold of the compensation in one loss event are the limits of insurance indemnity stipulated in § 3a(2) MTPLIA (with the exception of compensation for damage caused by the operation of a foreign vehicle and substitute compensation).

624. The CIB is entitled to refund for one-third of what it has paid to the injured party pursuant to § 24(2)(a), (b) and (g), but not more than CZK 300,000.[625] The joint and several debtors of this claim are the operator and the driver of the vehicle whose operation caused the damage; the driver only if he has liable for such damage. If the vehicle operator cannot be identified, the joint and several debtor is the owner of the vehicle. If the conditions for assertion of the recourse right pursuant to § 10 MTPLIA are met, the CIB is entitled to reimbursement of the amount paid without restriction, similarly to the MTPL insurer.

625. MTPLIA imposes on the CIB the duty to demand refund of compensation provided from the Guarantee fund at the foreign guarantee fund, or foreign insurers' bureau, if it is compensation under § 24(2)(e), substitute compensation under § 24a(1)(c), or § 24b MTPLIA.

625. The mentioned refund limit was introduced with effect from 1 Jan. 2018 by an amendment made by Act No. 293/2017 Sb., in connection with the reintroduction of a mandatory contribution pursuant to § 4 of the MTPLIA in the event of a breach of obligation to insure a vehicle. According to the explanatory memorandum to this law, the CIB's recourse claims often are amounts in the order of millions of CZK, which the liable person may be unable to pay at all during his life and which are liquidating for him. This negative impact is also given in the event that the breach of the obligation pursuant to § 1(2) occurs due to omission. The new adjustment of the contribution according to § 4 MTPLIA should ensure sufficient income into the Guarantee fund so that the expenses of the Guarantee fund are adequately covered. The CIB's recourse is therefore limited to one-third of the compensation provided, but not more than CZK 300,000. The amount of CZK 300,000 was determined according to the experience of CIB as an amount that can be realistically recovered and the payment of which does not have liquidating social effects on the person concerned.

626. Substitute compensation from the Guarantee fund pursuant to § 24a and 24b MTPLIA is provided by the CIB to the injured party on the basis of his written request, unless court proceedings have already been initiated against the insurer in the given case. In general, it can be stated that the substitute compensation from the Guarantee fund is provided in cases where there is a person (in addition to the tortfeasor) against which the injured party can assert his claims, but for some reason the real achievement of compensation is complicated for the injured party. CIB thus provides compensation from the Guarantee fund, for example, if the insurer has not fulfilled his obligations in investigating a loss event pursuant to § 9(3) MTPLIA, or if the insurer domiciled in another Member State has not appointed a claims representative for the Czech Republic. CIB is entitled to refund of the paid compensation from the body authorized to provide substitute compensation in the state of the insurance company that does not provide MTPL insurance in the Czech Republic (according to § 9c), which took out MTPL insurance for the vehicle. With the payment of the substitute compensation, the right of the injured party against the tortfeasor or his insurer passes to the CIB.

627. Furthermore, the CIB provides substitute compensation from the Guarantee fund to the injured party resident or having the seat in the Czech Republic, if: (i) it is impossible to identify the vehicle, the operation of which caused the damage in the territory of a Member State other than the Czech Republic, or (ii) it is impossible, within two months following the damage caused by operation of a vehicle in the territory of other Member State, to identify the insurance company liable to provide insurance indemnity for such a damage. CIB is entitled to reimbursement from the guarantee fund of the Member State concerned in which the damage occurred or in whose territory the vehicle whose operation caused the damage has its habitual location.

628. With effect from 1 January 2018, the obligation of the owner and operator of the vehicle to pay the specified mandatory contribution to the Guarantee Fund was returned to MTPLIA in the event that the obligation to arrange compulsory vehicle insurance was not met.[626] The obligation to pay the contribution is a logical result of the fact that from the Guarantee fund is provided, among others, compensation in the event of damage caused by an uninsured vehicle. When looking for sources of financing of the Guarantee fund, it is therefore reasonable that persons who operate a vehicle without proper insurance should primarily participate in its financing. Therefore, the owner of a domestic vehicle and its operator are jointly and severally obliged to pay to CIB a contribution for each day that the vehicle is operated without MTPL insurance in violation of the law. The obligation to pay the contribution does not apply if the vehicle has been stolen. The amount of the allowance is calculated as the product of the number of days the vehicle was operated without

626. The mandatory contribution in case of uninsured vehicles has already been introduced in the past in the MTPL legislation (from 1 Jan. 2009 by Act No. 137/2008 Sb. – cf. § 24c MTPLIA as amended from 1 Jan. 2009 to 14 Jan. 2015); subsequently, with regard to some practical problems associated with its enforcement, it was cancelled with effect from 15 Jan. 2015 by the Act No. 354/ 2014 Sb.

insurance and the amount of the daily rate according to the type of vehicle set by the Decree of the Ministry of Finance No. 205/1999 Sb. The obligation to pay the contribution expires within a preclusive period of one year from the date of inception of the obligation to pay the contribution, unless the CIB sends a request for payment of the contribution to the liable person. Payment of the contribution does not affect the obligation to take out an MTPL insurance.

II. Loss Prevention Fund

629. The Loss prevention fund was established with effect from 1 January 2014. In accordance with the provisions of § 23a MTPLIA, the CIB constitutes a Loss prevention fund, which collects financial contributions from insurance companies to finance the equipment of the Integrated Rescue System of the Czech Republic,[627] as well as other loss prevention projects relating to damage arising from the operation of vehicles in the Czech Republic.

630. The Loss prevention fund consists of levies on premiums received from MTPL, income from the investment of temporarily available financial means of this fund, subsidies from CIB financial means or levies from the Guarantee fund.

631. Member insurance companies are obliged to pay to the Loss prevention fund at least 3% of the annual premium received from MTPL for each calendar year.

632. The financial means of the Loss prevention fund are earmarked to cover costs associated with: (i) acquisition of equipment or material resources necessary for the operation of the basic components of the Integrated Rescue System, (ii) technology modification and operation of operational and information centres of the Fire Rescue Service in connection with providing necessary assistance to motorists, (iii) implementation of projects focusing on road safety according to program priorities approved by the government, (iv) implementation of other programs approved by the Commission established pursuant to § 23b MTPLIA, (v) administrative and organizational support of Commission activities.[628]

633. The Commission draws up an annual report on its activities and on the use of the Loss prevention fund, which it publishes in a way that allows remote access.[629]

---

627. The basic components of the Integrated Rescue System are the Fire Rescue Service of the Czech Republic, fire protection units within the district coverage by fire protection units, providers of emergency medical service and Police of the Czech Republic (§ 4(1) of the Act No. 239/2000 Sb. on the Integrated Rescue System).
628. For more details on the functioning of the Loss prevention fund and on the individual approved programs, *see* https://www.fondzabranyskod.cz/.
629. Annual reports are available at https://www.fondzabranyskod.cz/o-fondu/vyrocni-zpravy.

Part V. Insurance of the Person

634. Personal insurance is currently regulated dominantly by the Civil Code (§§ 2824–2848)[630] and partially by public law regulations such as IA, which regulates the conditions for the operation of insurance and reinsurance activities and the performance of supervision in the insurance industry. This act contains special provisions for life insurance with the policyholder's investment risk.[631] Another public law regulation represents Act No. 586/1992 Sb., on Income Taxes, which lays down the conditions for tax deductibility.

635. Life insurance is specifically defined for private and public law. This dichotomy has not only theoretical significance, but also some practical implications. For instance, the public law definition is decisive for the scope of the insurance company's authorization for insurance activities, the amount of share capital or its reporting, whereas the private law definition is important for the correct application of the relevant provisions of the Civil Code or for the competencies of the Financial Arbitrator.[632]

636. Within the scope of personal insurance, a wide range of risks can be covered: a person may be insured against the risk of death, of reaching a certain age or date contractually agreed as the end of insurance, against sickness, accident or another fact related to health or change of personal status[633] of the person insured (§ 2824 CC). Either a lump sum indemnity or a pension might be agreed upon. The insurance may also include a gradual accumulation of the financial amount, which is paid out at the end of the insurance, for example, as a retirement security. The

630. This new regulation replaced a partial previous legislation in the Act No. 37/2004 Sb., on Insurance Contract.
631. *See* § 61 of the Insurance Act: '(1) The insurance indemnity from the insurance belonging to the life insurance branches may have a direct link to the value of the investment fund's unit certificates or to the value of the assets of the insurance company's internal fund, which may be divided into units. The technical reserves relating to these liabilities must, as far as possible, be represented by those units or, if the units are not specified, by the assets of the internal fund. (2) The insurance indemnity from the insurance belonging to the life insurance branches may be directly linked to the share index or to a reference value other than the values specified in paragraph 1. In that case, the technical reserves relating to those liabilities must, as far as possible, be represented by shares corresponding to the benchmark or, if the shares are not set, by secured and marketable assets corresponding as far as possible to the assets on which the benchmark is based.'
632. Karfíková, Marie; Přikryl, Vladimír; Vybíral, Roman et al. *Pojišťovací právo.* 2nd revised ed. Praha: Leges, 2018, p. 321.
633. It could be, e.g., wedding insurance, which is still not clearly defined in theory.

above-mentioned is supported by the state, for example, in the form of tax deductibility, for contracts concluded before the age of 65 years of the insured person, the same applies for pension products. The characteristic feature is longevity and variability. In the case of personal insurance, the insured risk might be an accident, illness, adverse change in the state of health or another fact affecting the life of the insured. As already mentioned, the insured person can only be a natural person, however a beneficiary (or ultimate beneficiary) can also be a legal entity.

637. If a policyholder concludes a contract in favour of an ultimate beneficiary, the consent of the insured person is also required to conclude the contract.[634] Where a policyholder's descendant who lacks full legal capacity is to be the insured person, no special consent is required if the policyholder himself is the legal representative of the insured person (§ 2826(1) CC). Where the consent[635] of the insured person or their legal representative is required and the policyholder fails to demonstrate the consent within the stipulated period, or otherwise within three months from the date of the conclusion of the contract, the insurance is extinguished upon the expiry of that period. If an insured event occurs during that period and no consent has been given, the right to the insurance indemnity is acquired by the insured person (§ 2826(2) CC). If the insured event is the death of the insured person, the right is acquired by the insured person's spouse, and in their absence by the insured person's children; in the absence of a spouse or children, the rights to the insurance indemnity are acquired by the insured person's parents, and in their absence by the insured person's heirs (§ 2831(2) CC).

638. If insurance covers the members of a particular group or their families and their dependants (group insurance), the contract does not have to contain the names of the insured persons if the insured persons can be identified without any doubts no later than at the time of the insured event.[636] It is, though, necessary to specify in the insurance contract the key according to which the members of the group will be finally determined. Consent is not required here, as it cannot actually be given, if we imagine the contract made in favour of participants in public transport, visitors to a sports match, or employees of a certain company.

639. Where there are reasons related to determining the level of insurance risk, the amount of premiums or the investigation of an insured event, the insurer may require information on the health condition (§ 2828 CC), and the determination of the health condition or cause of death of an insured person if the insurer was given

634. The ultimate beneficiary must be identified clearly, intelligibly and unambiguously, their written consent is required (unlike group insurance – *see* further) according to the provisions on concluding a contract in favour of a third party – *see* § 1767 CC.
635. Such consent is also required to change the ultimate beneficiary, change the shares in the insurance indemnity where multiple ultimate beneficiaries have been designated, and to pay the surrender value; if consent is not granted, all such changes are disregarded (§ 2826(3) CC).
636. Speaking about group insurance, the policyholder is usually a legal entity (an employer, association, organizer of a sports event etc.), which concludes a single insurance contract. A larger number of persons is insured, and these persons must be indicated with sufficient determination so that they can be safely identified, it does not necessarily have to be a specification by their names.

consent to do so by the insured person. An investigation is conducted on the basis of reports and medical records requested from treating physicians by the person operating the healthcare facility authorized by the insurer and, if necessary, by an examination conducted by the healthcare facility.

640. When the death of the insured person is the insured event, the policyholder may determine the ultimate beneficiary by their name or by their relationship to the insured person. Prior to the occurrence of the insured event, the policyholder may change the ultimate beneficiary; the change becomes effective on the date on which the notification is delivered to the insurer (§ 2829 CC). Determination of the ultimate beneficiary can take place in several hypotheses (§§ 2830–2831 CC):

(a) If the policyholder has designated irrevocably their spouse to be the ultimate beneficiary, its effects are extinguished upon divorce or invalidation of the marriage.
(b) If the policyholder has designated irrevocably their ancestor or descendant as the ultimate beneficiary, its effects are extinguished when the ultimate beneficiary or policyholder becomes adopted.[637]
(c) If the ultimate beneficiary was not designated at the time of the insured event, or if they did not acquire the right to the insurance indemnity, the right is acquired by the insured person's spouse, and in their absence by the insured person's children. In the absence of them, the rights to the insurance indemnity are acquired by the insured person's parents, and in their absence by the insured person's heirs.
(d) If several persons acquire the right to an insurance indemnity, their shares are presumed to be equal.

641. The ultimate beneficiary shall acquire the right to an insurance indemnity upon the occurrence of the insured event. Before the ultimate beneficiary acquires that right, the policyholder may freely dispose of the rights arising from the insurance (§ 2832 CC), especially to pledge or assign them, as well as to change the designation of the ultimate beneficiary. However, in the case of a pension insurance, the consent of the insurer is required to change the ultimate beneficiary, otherwise the change is not binding on the insurer.

637. This also applies if the insured person's adopted child or adopted parent has been irrevocably determined as the ultimate beneficiary, and the adoption was cancelled.

Characteristics of basic types of personal insurance[638]

Characteristics	Types of personal insurance				
	risk life and accident	capital life	universal flexible life	investment life	retirement
Risk coverage	Yes	Yes	Yes	Yes	-
Capital value creation	-	Yes	Yes	Yes	Yes
Actively influencing revenues	-	-	-	Yes	-
Guaranteed appreciation	-	Yes	Yes – only for selected tools	Yes – only for selected tools	Yes
Flexibility	Yes	Yes	Yes	Yes	-
Tax deductibility	-	Yes	Yes	Yes	Yes

638. Inspired by the CIA's Product factsheet – accident insurance (available at http://www.cap.cz/vse-o-pojisteni/pojisteni-osob/pojisteni-urazu).

Chapter 1. Workmen's Compensation and Occupational Disease

642. Protecting employees from the consequences of accidents at work and occupational diseases takes many forms in different countries, based mainly on historical contexts. In Austro-Hungarian Empire, compulsory labour insurance was introduced by Act No. 1/1888 Sb., on Insurance of Workers in the Event of an Accident, of 28 December 1887. The main reason was the development of mechanical engineering and the associated significant increase of bodily injuries. A worker who was injured and became permanently or temporarily incapable of working was mostly dependent on a 'begging bag'. Although it was possible to claim compensation in private law, the employee would have to prove direct fault of the employer which was not easy (however proving fault is not easy even today). This was even more problematic if the death occurred or the injury was caused by the employee's carelessness. The law therefore imposed an obligation on the employer to compensate every employee's injury, regardless of whether it was the fault of others or a pure accident (without anyone's fault), except with the intentional behaviour of the employee. The insurance companies at the time were operating on the capital principle, which meant for them to hold assets intended to pay indemnities. At about the same time, health insurance was introduced as well.[639]

643. The described reality lasted until September 1948, when the previous system was replaced by the social insurance system introduced by Act No. 99/1948 Sb., on National Insurance. This was followed by several amendments. One of them (made in 1992 by the amendment to Act No. 65/1965 Sb., Labour Code), which introduced the so-called statutory insurance of the organization (later called more suitably employer), has survived to this day. This regulation is followed by the Decree of the Ministry of Finance No. 125/1993 Sb.[640] The regulation, originally intended as transitional, has survived to the present day. In the context of adopting the new Labour Code in 2006 (Act No. 262/2006 Sb.), another act was adopted, focusing directly on Accident Insurance of Employees (Act No. 266/2006 Sb.). This enactment assumed the transformation of the above said statutory insurance into the social security system. However, it never came into force and was finally abolished in 2014.[641]

644. The introduction of statutory liability insurance for employers in the event of an accident at work or an occupational disease occurs through an amendment (Act No. 37/1993 Sb.) to the former Labour Code, namely its § 205d. The creation of this insurance was encouraged by the international obligations of the Czech Republic (ILO conventions). Statutory insurance arises with the establishment of an employment relationship and lasts for the entire period of employment.

---

639. Karfíková, Marie; Přikryl, Vladimír; Vybíral, Roman et al. *Pojišťovací právo.* 2nd revised ed. Praha: Leges, 2018, p. 416.
640. Decree of the Ministry of Finance No. 125/1993 Sb., Stipulating the Conditions and Premium Rates of the Statutory Employer's Liability Insurance for Damage in Relation to Work Accident or Occupational Diseases.
641. Karfíková, Marie; Přikryl, Vladimír; Vybíral, Roman et al. *Pojišťovací právo.* 2nd revised ed. Praha: Leges, 2018, p. 417.

645. According to the current legislation contained in §§ 365 et seq. of the Labour Code, the statutory liability insurance of the employer for damage in the event of an accident at work or an occupational disease is governed by the provisions of § 205d of Act No. 65/1965 Sb. and Decree No. 125/1993 Sb., until the entry into force of another legal regulation. The administrative costs of insurance companies in this insurance amount to 4% of the total amount of accepted premiums paid by the employer in a given calendar year.

646. An accident at work can be defined as a health disorder caused during the performance of a work task or in direct connection with it, independently of employee's will, by the sudden, violent, and short-term action of external influences that results in a health disorder.[642]

647. Occupational disease,[643] in turn, can be defined as damage to health caused by prolonged exposure to external influences, regardless of the will of the employee. Sometimes it occurs due to a single effect of external influences (such as lead poisoning).[644] The legal definition is that it is a disease caused by the adverse effects of chemical, physical, biological or other harmful effects, if they arose under the conditions listed in the list of occupational diseases. Occupational diseases also include acute poisoning caused by the adverse effects of chemicals.

648. Statutory insurance is established by law, on the day of the creation of an employment relationship with the employer, and lasts for the entire period of the employer's existence. If the rights and obligations do not pass from one employer to another in case of termination of employers' activities, then the injured party can claim its right directly against the insurance company. In the Czech market, the insurance is provided by two insurance companies – Generali Česká pojišťovna a.s.[645] and Kooperativa pojišťovna, a.s., Vienna Insurance Group.[646] The statutory insurance is operated in the form of ongoing financing, i.e., the indemnities are paid from the premiums collected in a given year, regardless of the time of their occurrence.

649. If the insurance company suffers – due to the above-mentioned procedure – any property damage, it is entitled to compensation from the state budget. Statutory insurance does not cover the full conceivable range of the employer's liability for damage caused to the employee, but only liability for damage caused by work accident or occupational disease. The employer has the right to have the insurance

642. Hradec, Milan; Zárybnická, Jana; Křivohlávek, Václav. *Pojištění a pojišťovnictví.* 1st ed. Praha: Vysoká škola finanční a správní, 2005, p. 35.
643. For the National Register of occupational diseases in the Czech Republic, *see* https://www.uzis.cz/index.php?pg=registry-sber-dat--narodni-zdravotni-registry--narodni-registr-nemoci-z-povolani#publikace; for the list of occupational diseases, *see* http://www.ceskyfocalpoint.cz/wp-content/uploads/2014/08/Seznam-nemoc%C3%AD-z-povolán%C3%AD-2015.pdf.
644. Hradec, Milan; Zárybnická, Jana; Křivohlávek, Václav. *Pojištění a pojišťovnictví.* 1st ed. Praha: Vysoká škola finanční a správní, 2005, p. 37.
645. https://en.generaliceska.cz/.
646. https://www.koop.cz/en.

company compensate for the damage and non-property damage caused to the employee by an accident at work or an occupational disease, to the extent that the employer is liable for it under the Labour Code.

650. The insured event is the occurrence of the employer's obligation to pay for damage or injury. If the case is subject to judicial review and the court agrees, the insured event is deemed to have occurred on the day of the legal force of the judgement in question. The insurance company also covers the costs of court and out-of-court proceedings, if so agreed. On the contrary, no pecuniary damage and non-pecuniary damage is compensated, if the employer undertook to pay it beyond the scope of the legal regulation.

651. In connection with the prevention and occurrence of an insured event, the employer is mainly obliged to ensure that no harmful event even occurs and to notify (without undue delay to the insurance company in whose district the employer has its registered office) any increase in risk which the employer is aware of and which has occurred since the insurance contract was concluded. In case the damage event occurs, the employer not only has to make a notification that such event has occurred, but also must make comments on the required compensation and its amount, or has to authorize the insurance company to follow the legal action. The employer is obligated to inform the insurance company that criminal proceedings have been instituted against the employee or a third person in connection with the damage event, and to inform the insurance company about the course and outcome of such proceedings. The employer also has to notify that the injured party exercises the right to compensation in court. In civil proceedings for damages, the employer has to respect the instructions of the insurance company, in particular the employer is not allowed to make a court settlement without the consent of the insurance company.[647]

652. If the employer breaches the previously said duties, the insurance company is entitled to adequate compensation. The insurance company has the same right against the employer if the damage was caused by a culpable breach of obligations in the employment relationship, but only up to the amount that the employer is entitled to claim. In the case of an employer who was in delay with the payment of insurance premiums at the time of payment of the indemnity, the insurance company is entitled to reimbursement from such employer up to the amount of indemnity paid due to insured events occurring at the time for which the insurance premium was not paid.

653. If the insurance company has compensated the damage for the employer, the employer's right to compensation from the person who is liable to the injured party for these damages are passed to the insurance company. The employer is obliged to provide the insurance company with all needed cooperation.

---

647. Karfíková, Marie; Přikryl, Vladimír; Vybíral, Roman et al. *Pojišťovací právo.* 2nd revised ed. Praha: Leges, 2018, p. 420.

654. The duty to pay insurance premiums arises for the employer if they employ at least one employee. The employer is obliged to notify this to the insurance company and to provide necessary identification data. The basis for calculating the premium is based on Act No. 589/1992 Sb., on Social Security Premiums and Contributions to the State Employment Policy. The minimum premium for a calendar quarter is CZK 100. The employer is obliged to prove to the insurance company the payment of the insurance premium for the entire period and duration of the insurance and the correctness of its calculation; otherwise, it is considered that it has not been paid. If the premium has not been paid properly and in due time, it is increased by 10% of the amount due for each month started. However, the insurance company may refrain partially or completely from recovering the increased premium; in cases above the amount of CZK 250,000 only with the consent of the Ministry of Finance.

Chapter 2. Bodily Injuries

655. (Personal) accident insurance can be arranged as a lump sum insurance or damage insurance; in practice, it is usually arranged as a lump sum insurance. Not only special provisions for accident insurance apply to it, but also general provisions on personal insurance and provisions on lump sum and damage insurance. It is up to the contractual parties to determine the insured event, i.e., to define what the accident is. The definition of the accident depends purely on the contractual agreement of the parties, so it is always necessary to check how the accident is actually defined. The insured event must be duly determined, not only due to the provision of the insurance indemnity, but also due to the beginning of the limitation period. Contractual exclusions then represent a negative definition of an accident.

656. The previous legislation[648] defined an accident as an unexpected and sudden action of external forces or one's own physical force, regardless of the will of the insured person, which occurred during the insurance period and which caused the insured person damage to health or death. Traditionally, personal accident insurance contains a number of additions and contractual exclusions that specify what an accident is or is not. Exclusions can be divided into general ones, relating to other insurances, and exclusions relating specifically to accident insurance. The last mentioned constitute *via facti* a negative definition of an accident. For example, the sudden spinal disc syndromes, infectious disease, fatigue fractures, bodily harm resulting from a suicide attempt, self-harm etc. are not considered a bodily injury.[649]

657. Sometimes the insured event is defined in such a way that it is not only an accident itself, but also a manifestation of its consequences (either at the time of insurance or at an agreed time). Accident insurance is – according to the literature – most often concluded:[650]

- in the event of death resulting from an accident, and may contain other subtypes, such as death caused by a traffic accident;
- in the event of total disability resulting from an accident, if the disability pension has been approved for the third degree of disability[651] or a degree determined by the contractual conditions;

648. Act No. 37/2004 Sb., on Insurance Contract, §§ 60 et seq.
649. Jandová, Lucie. In: Jandová, Lucie; Šlauf, Petr; Svejkovský, Jaroslav. *Pojištění v novém občanském zákoníku. Komentář: [§ 2756-2872].* 1st ed. Praha: C. H. Beck, 2014, p. 269.
650. Karfíková, Marie; Přikryl, Vladimír; Vybíral, Roman et al. *Pojišťovací právo.* 2nd revised ed. Praha: Leges, 2018, pp. 337–338.
651. The 3rd degree disability pension (called the full disability pension prior to 31 Dec. 2009) is a benefit from the pension system, which is intended to ensure a citizen's income in the event of a decline in their ability to work. In order for a citizen to be recognized as disabled in the 3rd degree of disability, the ability to work must decline by at least 70%. The health condition is assessed in accordance with the Decree on the Assessment of Disability No. 359/2009 Sb., which implements the Pension Insurance Act. Disability is recognized for the one disease (disability), which has the most

- in the event of permanent consequences of the accident, if no improvement is possible, the insurer will pay the insurance indemnity determined according to the evaluation tables.

658. Permanent consequences are those consequences of a bodily injury that are no longer able to be improved, i.e., permanent effects on physical and mental functions. The insurance indemnity for these accidents is most often determined according to the so-called evaluation tables, which are part of the insurance contract. For the evaluation of permanent consequences, they contain a summary of permanent consequences and the evaluation assigned to them according to the degree of severity. The calculation differs according to the insurance variants. Based on the valuation tables, the amount of daily compensation for the period of treatment of the accident is also determined:

- In the case of medical treatment of health consequences of an accident, the insurance premium is paid in connection with the accident itself and the duration of its treatment, usually determined as a multiplication of the amount and duration of the necessary treatment of the bodily injury. This insurance includes other subtypes, such as daily compensation for the period of treatment of the enumerated injuries.
- In the event of incapacity to work or hospitalization of the insured in a medical facility due to an accident, the insurance premium is paid depending on the length of incapacity to work or length of hospitalization in the medical facility. The calculation of the insurance indemnity is determined as the product of the agreed sum insured for one day and the number of days.

659. The Civil Code describes situations when the insurance indemnity will not be provided or will be reduced. The insurer has the right to refuse to provide insurance indemnity in the case of an accident of the insured person in connection with a criminal offence for which the insured person was found guilty of intentional criminal offence, or by which they deliberately harmed their health (§ 2845 CC).

660. Furthermore, the insurer has the right to reduce the insurance indemnity down to one half if the injury was caused as a result of the insured person having consumed alcohol or an addictive substance or a product containing such a substance, if justified by the circumstances under which the injury occurred. However, if such an accident resulted in the death of the insured, the insurer has the right to reduce the indemnity only if the accident occurred in connection with the insured person's act whereby they caused severe bodily harm or death to another person (§ 2846(1) CC).[652] Decisive for the determination of the reduction are the specific circumstances of the accident, when it is possible to reduce the indemnity by up to

---

significant effect on the decline in the person's ability to work. A medical examiner has the opportunity to increase the percentage rating of the decline in the ability to work by up to 10 percentage points, depending on other diseases (disabilities) or according to the complexity of the profession of the assessed pension applicant.

652. The insurer shall not have the mentioned right if alcohol or addictive substance was contained in a medicinal product which the insured person took in a manner prescribed by their physician, and

50%. An exception is an accident resulting in death, when it is possible to reduce it only if the accident occurred in connection with the act of the insured, such as a car accident. If the insured dies without the death or injury of other persons, the insurer must pay the insurance in full.

661. If the insured person dies as a result of an accident, the insurer will pay the indemnity to the ultimate beneficiary, if the death occurs at a certain time, regardless of whether the insurance still lasts or not. The amount of accident insurance depends on many factors in addition to the health status and age, it depends for example, on the classification of the insured into a risk group based on their work, hobbies, and sports activities. A change in such activities of the insured may entail the obligation to report this change to the insurer.

---

if the insured person had not been warned by the physician or producer of the medicinal product that it was prohibited to carry out the activity which resulted in the injury under the influence of the medicinal product (§ 2846(2) CC).

Chapter 3. Private Health Insurance

662. Private health insurance – in terms of the Czech Civil Code the sickness insurance – is not a very common type of insurance, but it can be sometimes a suitable complement to public health insurance. The legal regulation is only fragmentary[653] and therefore the concrete nature of such insurance very much depends on the contractual arrangements. An insured event itself can be arranged in a wide variety of ways. In general, an insured event might be an illness, injury, or any act related to the health condition of the insured, especially in connection with their illness, injury, pregnancy and preventive[654] or dispensary care.[655]

663. The law binds the payment of insurance benefits with health care arising from illness or injury. Insurance can be arranged as a lump sum insurance as well as damage insurance, thus covering the real medical costs or the agreed amount spent on health care. The illness is characterized as interventions in human health that are either felt subjectively or are medically detectable.

664. Another basic term is health care,[656] which is defined more narrowly than the term healthcare services. Healthcare services mean not only provision of health care pursuant to Act No. 372/2011 Sb., on Health Services and on Conditions of their Provision (Health Services Act), by healthcare workers as well as activities performed by other professional staff, if these activities are performed in direct connection with the provision of health care (*see* above), but also other services like consultancy services,[657] handling of the deceased's body including the transport of the deceased's body to a pathological-anatomical autopsy or medical autopsy and from a pathological-anatomical autopsy or from a medical autopsy performed by the

653. *See* § 2847 CC.

654. *See* § 5(2)(a) of the Health Services Act: The purpose of preventive care is the early detection of factors that are causally related to the onset of illness or deterioration of health, and the implementation of measures aimed at eliminating or minimizing the impact of these factors and preventing their occurrence.

655. *See* § 5(2)(c) of the Health Services Act: The purpose of dispensary care is active and long-term monitoring of the health status of a patient endangered or suffering from an illness or deterioration of health, for which a change in health status can be reasonably expected according to the development of the disease, early detection of which can significantly affect further treatment and development.

656. Health care means – according to the Health Services Act – a set of activities and measures carried out on persons for the purpose of the prevention, detection and elimination of a disease, defect or medical condition, maintenance, restoration or improvement of health and functional condition, sustaining and prolonging life and alleviating suffering, aid for reproduction and childbirth, health assessment, preventive, diagnostic, curative, curative rehabilitation, nursing or other medical procedures performed by medical staff, professional medical examination according to Act No. 65/2017 Sb., on the Protection of Health against the Harmful Effects of Addictive Substances.

657. The purpose of consultancy service is to assess the individual treatment procedure, or to propose an amendment or supplement, and other consultations to support a patient's decision-making on the provision of health services by another healthcare provider or a healthcare professional whom the patient chose – *see* § 2(2)(b) of the Health Services Act.

provider pursuant to the Funeral Services Act, emergency medical service, activity of the transfusion service facility or blood bank, and also anti-alcohol and anti-drug detention service.

665. The insured services are defined in the law demonstratively, so the final scope of insurance depends on the concluded contract. The entitled person is also listed and specified in the insurance contract.

666. The Civil Code also regulates the maximum length of the so-called waiting period, i.e., the contractually agreed period during which the insurer does not have to provide insurance indemnity. The purpose of the waiting period is to prevent possible speculation and misuse of insurance in situations when the insured knows that health care is virtually inevitable. For example, a person interested in an insurance has a toothache and comes to insure the costs of dental care, or a woman in a high degree of pregnancy comes to insure childbirth, etc. The general waiting period can be a maximum of three months; in the case of childbirth, psychotherapy, dental and orthopaedic prostheses it can be up to eight months and in the case of nursing care even up to three years from the date of commencement of insurance (§ 2848 CC). If the concluded waiting period exceeds the maximum duration limit, the provisions of §§ 586[658] and 577[659] of the Civil Code shall apply. Consequently, an objection to an invalid waiting period arrangement may be raised only by the person for whose protection the invalidity of such legal action is stipulated.

667. Unlike the (personal) accident insurance, a change in insurance risk during insurance is not linked to an information duty and the insurer is not allowed to change insurance. This insurance has a whole range of subtypes, for example, insurance in the event of a hospital stay, insurance of above-standard care, insurance in the event of disability, etc. An example of insurance expressly stipulated by special law[660] is the travel health insurance for foreigners, serving to cover the costs of necessary and urgent medical care provided to foreigners in the Czech Republic and also to cover the repatriation of a foreigner or their remains back to their country of origin. This special law also stipulates other parameters of insurance, such as minimum limits of insurance indemnity, territorial scope, or excludes the arrangement of co-participation of the insured.

658. If the invalidity of a juridical act is determined to protect the interest of a person, invalidity may only be invoked by that person. Unless an entitled person invokes invalidity of a juridical act, the juridical act is considered valid.
659. If the reason for invalidity only consists in an unlawful determining of quantitative, temporal, spatial or other scope, a court shall change the scope so that it is consistent with an equitable arrangement of rights and duties of the parties; in doing so, the court is not bound by the parties' motions, but shall consider whether a party would have made the juridical act had the party ascertained its invalidity in time.
660. Act No. 326/1999 Sb., on the Residence of Foreign Nationals in the Czech Republic.

Chapter 4. Life Insurance

668. In accordance with the previous legislation, there are two definitions of life insurance, namely for public law regulation and private law regulation. According to the Civil Code, this is insurance in the event of death, in the event of reaching a certain age or age specified by the insurance contract as the end of the insurance, it also means insurance in the event of another fact concerning a change in one's personal status. The insured can only be a person, i.e., a natural person, but the policyholder or the beneficiary can be both a person (natural person) and a legal entity. Life insurance is purely risk insurance, or reserve-making insurance, and can only be arranged as a fixed-amount insurance, i.e., it cannot be arranged as insurance against loss and damage. Its purpose is to provide for the insured or their family in cases when their income is reduced, or to provide for the family in the event of the death of the insured. Reserve-making insurance is divided into capital insurance, where the financial reserve is valued at the technical interest rate, and investment insurance, where the financial reserve is invested in mutual funds according to the policyholder's instructions.

669. There are two insured events, namely death or survival to a certain age or day determined by the insurance contract (so-called insurance with a savings clause). Very often, life insurance is combined with death insurance, in which case an insured event always occurs, and it is therefore necessary to create reserves.

670. Life insurance is divided into:[661]

- Insurance in the event of death, in which the insured event is the death in the duration of the insurance. It is therefore risk insurance, where the premium is consumed during the insurance period and no reserve is created. For this reason, there is no right to a redemption payment. Furthermore, a low premium is typical compared to the sum insured. As an option, it can be understood as insurance for funeral costs.
- Insurance in the event of survival is insurance with the so-called savings clause. The reason for the conclusion may be the retirement security or the child's security upon reaching the age of majority.
- Insurance in the event of survival to a specified age or earlier death is included among reserve-making insurance. Also, in theory this kind of insurance is referred to as a mixed insurance because it is combined with death insurance.
- Pension insurance, for which the insured event is survival to the end of the insurance period or death, if a survivor's pension is arranged. Either paid as a recurring indemnity or a lump sum indemnity. Not to be confused with public pension insurance.
- Investment life insurance combines insurance protection and the possibility of investing. The insurer usually uses the paid premiums to purchase units of offered

661. Karfíková, Marie; Přikryl, Vladimír; Vybíral, Roman et al. *Pojišťovací právo.* 2nd revised ed. Praha: Leges, 2018; Mesršmíd, Jaroslav; Kovář, Bedřich; Bohumský, Petr. *Životní pojištění.* 1st ed. Praha: Grada Publishing, 2002, pp. 326–329.

funds in the allocation ratio chosen by the policyholder. The purchase will be made at the current purchase price of the unit. Purchased units are registered on the client's individual account. Fees for initial costs and insurance administration costs are deducted from it.

- Wedding insurance is insurance in case of a change in one's personal status. Also referred to as dowry insurance.
- Study insurance works on the same principle.

671. The life insurance premium that the policyholder pays for insurance coverage may be agreed on in the insurance contract either as a single premium, which is paid all at once at the conclusion of the insurance contract, or as a regular premium, which is paid repeatedly at the beginning of the agreed period, for example, monthly, quarterly, semi-annually or annually. The size of genuine insurance is determined on the basis of the sum insured, risk assessment and technical interest rate.

672. There may be situations in life that the law shall reflect explicitly. If the insured person and the ultimate beneficiary die at the same time or under circumstances that prevent the determination of which of them died first, the insured person is considered, for insurance purposes, to have been determined to have survived the ultimate beneficiary.[662] The above-mentioned is important also for the payment of insurance premiums (similarly in the issue of inheritance). Furthermore, the insurer is not obliged to provide insurance indemnity in the event of suicide of the insured, as suicide precludes death as an accident if it happens within two years from the conclusion of the contract (§ 2837 CC).

673. Unlike in the previous legislation, the ban on insurance in the event of the death of a child under 3 years of age and the ban on insurance in the event of abortion or the birth of a stillborn child were not adopted. According to the explanatory memorandum to the Civil Code, these were not taken over because these prohibitions are not usual from both historical and international point of view.

674. The date of birth is a key figure for this type of insurance, it is not surprising that the law explicitly addresses some of the consequences associated with incorrect indication of date of birth. Where an incorrect date of birth of the insured person has been provided, the insurer has the right to withdraw from the contract if it is proven that, given the insurance conditions in force at the time the contract was concluded, the insurer would not have concluded the contract.[663]

662. *See* § 2836 CC.

663. If the insurer fails to assert the right to withdraw from the contract during the life of the insured person and within three years after the date of conclusion of the contract, but no later than two months after they became aware of the incorrect information, their right is extinguished (§ 2835 CC).

675. Some other situations establish (in addition to the right to withdraw from the contract in the event of incorrect indication of the date of birth) also the possibility to reduce the insurance indemnity. If the insurer has erroneously determined premiums, the period of insurance, the premium payment period or the sum insured because the policyholder had provided an incorrect date of birth or sex of the insured person, the insurer has the right to reduce the insurance indemnity in the proportion of the amount of insurance premiums that have been paid to the amount of insurance premiums that would have been paid had the policyholder provided the correct date of birth or sex of the insured person.[664]

676. Failure to pay the insurance premium results in the termination of the insurance, unless it is a reserve-forming insurance with insurance payment for individual insurance periods.[665] For example, in the case of insurance in the event of death concluded for a precisely defined period for ordinary insurance premiums, the law stipulates that the right to reduction does not arise and the insurance expires with non-payment, as this insurance is risky. As this is a risk insurance, the right of redemption arises only if it is expressly agreed, the same applies to pension insurance. If sufficient value has accumulated in the provisioning insurance, its further duration is possible without further payment of premiums.

677. Usually we talk about the reduction or transfer of insurance to a reduced level. When reducing the sum insured, the procedure is based on actuarial calculations. Simply put, in the event that the standard insurance is not paid during the insurance period and at the same time sufficient funds have been accumulated for a sufficiently long period specified in the insurance contract, the insurance automatically changes to insurance with a reduced sum insured and at the same time there is no obligation to pay other current premiums if sufficient reserve has been reached. The reduction occurs the day after the insurance would have expired.

678. During the reduction, all supplementary insurances usually expire, but since the insurance is based on the contractual principle, it can be agreed otherwise. In connection with the already mentioned, it is also possible to agree on a limit below which the reduced sum insured (pension) must not fall. If, after the reduction, the reduced amount is too low, the law allows the insurance period to be reduced instead of the sum insured being reduced. Shortening the insurance period is, in contrast to reducing the insured amount, a dispositive arrangement.

---

664. If, as a result of providing incorrect information (indicated above), higher premiums were paid, the insurer shall adjust their amount starting from the insurance period following the insurance period in which the insurer received the correct information. Insurance premiums paid for the subsequent insurance periods are reduced by the overpaid premiums; in the case of a lump sum premium, the insurer shall refund the overpayment to the policyholder without undue delay (§ 2834(2) CC).

665. *See* § 2838 CC which contains special legislation in relation with § 2804 CC. § 2838 CC stipulates that: (1) If the current premium for insurance was paid for the period stipulated in the contract and if, after this period, further current premium was not paid within the agreed time limit, such insurance shall change into insurance with a reduced sum insured (reduction of the sum insured) or into reduced annual pension, without the duty to pay the current premiums. (2) If the reduced sum insured or reduced annual pension is less than the limit stipulated in the contract, the period of insurance is reduced.

679. The situation described above, when a reduction occurs, may not be irreversible. It is possible to arrange the conditions under which everything will return to its original state. The basic condition is the payment of the unpaid insurance premiums for a given period and from then it is necessary to pay the specified insurance premiums properly and on time. The payment of the premium for the period when the premium was reduced does not mean that the insurer is obliged to provide the originally agreed amount for insured events occurring during this period.

680. It is also necessary to mention the redemption (surrender value, in Czech 'odkupné'), i.e., the financial settlement of the insurer with the policyholder in the event of early termination of the reserve-making life insurance. This is a part of the unused premiums, which is stored as a technical reserve. The reason for which the insurance was terminated is not decisive for the payment (of course, except for the occurrence of the insured event). The insurer is obliged to pay the surrender the value at the policyholder's request within the period stipulated by law (i.e., within three months from the date of delivery of the request). The insurance expires with the payment of the surrender value to the policyholder. It is possible to arrange the moment of the payment of the surrender value as the moment of entering the order to make the payment by the payment service provider (similarly for payment by payment voucher).

681. If the policyholder is different from the insured person, the written consent of the insured person is required for the payment, otherwise the surrender value will not be paid. In addition to the payment of the surrender value, during the insurance period it is possible to request the so-called partial redemption of the surrender value which will be reflected in the reduction of reserves.

682. It is typical for life insurance that it is supplemented by non-life risk coverage. Typically, supplementary insurance is arranged in various forms, in particular as an accident insurance, disability insurance, health insurance, long-term care insurance or serious illness insurance.

683. If insurance covers the members of a particular group or their families and their dependants (group insurance), where applicable, the contract does not have to contain the names of the insured persons if the insured persons can be identified without any doubts no later than at the time of the insured event. The consent of the insured persons is not required. This applies by analogy if the policyholder has assigned the contract. A breach of the duty to truthfully and completely respond to the questions of the insurer shall, in the case of a group insurance, only affect the insurance of those persons involved in the breach of this duty (§ 2827 CC).

Chapter 5. Pension Funds

684. The right to adequate material security in old age, guaranteed by Article 30(1) of the Charter, is exercised in the Czech Republic primarily through the dominant first pillar of the pension system, which is a state-organized and operated pension insurance system, based on the principle of compulsory and ongoing (pay as you go) financing, from which retirement pensions are provided. Due to the unfavourable demographic development, the aging of the population and the related long-term unsustainability of the primary pension system, the last decade has been characterized by efforts to find a political consensus on its reform. Supplementary pension systems operating beyond the first pillar have experienced relatively rapid developments in the Czech Republic in the last two decades.

685. The State-Contributory Supplementary Pension Insurance (in Czech 'penzijní připojištění se státním příspěvkem') was introduced as a supplementary pension system in the Czech Republic in 1994,[666] which was transformed into the SPS system (in Czech 'doplňkové penzijní spoření') in 2012 and 2013.[667] In general, these can be characterized as supplementary pension schemes with dominant elements of the third pillar, based on the individualistic principle, voluntary membership, and fund financing. At its core stands a voluntary private contractual relationship between a pension company and a natural person who, for a long time, deposits funds with a pension company in order to preserve, enhance, and provide additional resources for the post-productive age. The system is financially supported by the state through the state contributions. In addition to the participant itself, third parties can also contribute,[668] especially employers who are motivated by tax relief (contributions can be included in their expenses for income tax purposes). Early withdrawal of funds is sanctioned by the loss of state contributions and revenues from them.

686. Although the original system of the State-Contributory Supplementary Pension Insurance has not completely disappeared and the legal relations established under the effectiveness of the former legislation continue (although the later rules set out in Act No. 427/2011 Sb. apply in part to them), it is no longer possible to negotiate new contractual relations in the original scheme. Therefore, the following explanation will be given on the current form of the third pillar – the system of SPS (which, however, has a number of common features with the original Supplementary Pension Insurance).

687. As already mentioned, the SPS system was established by the Act No. 427/2011 Sb., on SPS. According to its basic provision § 1(1), the mentioned act regulates SPS with a pension company, rights and obligations from SPS, claims from

---

666. Act No. 42/1994 Sb., on State-Contributory Supplementary Pension Insurance.
667. Act No. 427/2011 Sb., on Supplementary Pension Savings.
668. There is a certain overlap with the second pillar system, which is characterized by collective financing by employers.

SPS, provision of the state contribution, activities of a pension company, transformation of the pension fund and the state supervision in the area of SPS. The SPS itself are defined in paragraph 2 as the collection and placement of the participant's contributions, contributions paid on behalf of the participant by their employer and state contributions to participation funds managed by the pension company, and payment of benefits from SPS to ensure supplementary income in old age or disability.

688. SPS emerge on the basis of a contract on SPS between the participant and the pension company on the day specified in this contract (§ 4(1) SPS). In principle, a participant may enter into only one SPS contract with one pension company (§ 4(3) SPS). A participant may be any natural person who has entered into an SPS contract with a pension company (§ 2 SPS).[669] The SPS contract cannot be concluded by a participant of the original State-Contributory Supplementary Pension Insurance.

689. By an SPS contract, the pension company undertakes to collect and manage the participant's financial means in the participation fund or several participation funds in accordance with the SPS and the agreed savings strategy, and to pay benefits under the conditions and manner specified by the SPS and the contract. The participant, on the other hand, undertakes to pay the participant's contribution under the conditions, in the amount and in the manner specified by the SPS and the contract (§ 5(1) SPS). A mandatory written form is set for the SPS contract (§ 5(2) SPS). In the contract the participant determines the savings strategy – the method of distribution of financial means in the participation funds,[670] which may be changed by the participant during the term of the contract (§ 5(7) SPS). In the event of the participant's death, the participant may specify in the contract one or more natural persons (called 'designated person') who, upon meeting the conditions stipulated by law, will be entitled to a lump sum settlement (§ 24 SPS) or to a termination settlement (§ 25 SPS). Participation in SPS is voluntary. The participant may terminate their SPS at any time. On the other hand, termination by the pension company is possible only for exhaustive reasons stipulated by law (§§ 6 and 7 SPS). Otherwise, the contract may terminate only in cases stipulated by law (§ 8 SPS).

690. The participant's financial means managed by the pension company consist of the participant's contributions, the contributions paid by their employer, state contributions, and their appreciation and depreciation.[671] The amount of the participant's contribution is determined for a calendar month and may not be lower than CZK 100 (§ 9(1) SPS). The participant is entitled to change the amount of the contribution (§ 9(3) SPS). With the consent of the participant, the contribution or its part may be paid by the employer on behalf of the participant. The participant is obliged to notify the pension company of this fact in advance in writing (§ 10(1)

669. Prior to the end of 2015, the arrangement of supplementary pension savings was allowed only to persons over 18 years of age (cf. § 2 SPS, as amended prior to 31 Dec. 2015).
670. *See* § 3(a) SPS.
671. *See* § 3(c) SPS.

SPS). No state contribution is provided to the employer's contribution (§ 10(2) SPS). In the choice of a pension company, employees must not be restricted by the employer and the employer's contribution cannot be conditioned by concluding a contract with a specific pension company. The employer may not influence the employee in the choice of the pension company, they may not accept remuneration, reward or non-monetary or non-monetary advantage in connection with the provision of the employer's contribution (§ 10(3) SPS). The participant may deduct the payment of their contributions from the income tax base, up to the amount of the total contributions paid for the SPS by the taxpayer in the tax period reduced by CZK 12,000. The maximum amount of CZK 24,000[672] can be deducted in this way for the tax period. Therefore, if the contributions paid by the taxpayer do not exceed CZK 12,000 in the tax period, they cannot be used to reduce the tax base. Employer's contributions represent an employee's income from dependent activities (i.e., employment), which is exempt from income tax up to CZK 50,000 per year.[673] In relation to the employer, the contributions paid by them represent a tax-deductible expense (cost) that can be deducted from the employer's tax base.[674]

691. The state, through the Ministry of Finance, provides a state contribution from the state budget for the benefit of the participant, to the contributions paid by the participant (§§ 12 et seq. SPS). Entitled to the state allowance is a participant who has a permanent residence in the territory of the Czech Republic or resides in the territory of a Member State, and at the same time is:

- a participant in the state-organized pension insurance system according to the Czech legislation;
- a recipient of a pension from the state-organized pension insurance; or
- a participant in the public health insurance in the Czech Republic.

692. For each calendar month, a participant who meets the set conditions and has paid the contribution of at least CZK 300 properly and on time is entitled to a state contribution. If the amount of the participant's monthly contribution:

- is CZK 300 to CZK 999, the amount of the monthly state contribution is CZK 90 and 20% of the amount exceeding CZK 300;
- is CZK 1,000 and more, the amount of the monthly state contribution is CZK 230.

693. The state contribution does not apply to the contribution paid by the employer.

694. The participant's funds can be used for the payment of the following benefits (§ 19 SPS):

672. *See* § 15(5) of Act No. 586/1992 Sb., on Income Taxes.
673. This limit is set collectively for the employer's contributions to the supplementary pension savings (or former supplementary pension insurance) and to the premiums for private life insurance; for more details, cf. § 6(9)(p) of Act No. 586/1992 Sb., on Income Taxes.
674. *See* § 24(2)(j)(5) of Act No. 586/1992 Sb., on Income Taxes.

- retirement pension for a specified period;
- disability pension for a specified period;
- lump sum settlement;
- termination settlement;
- payment of a single premium for life pension; or
- payment of a single premium for pension for a precisely defined period with a precisely determined amount of the pension.

695. Retirement and disability pension benefits for a specified period, lump sum settlement and termination settlement are provided by the pension company. Lifetime pension and pension for a precisely defined period with a precisely determined amount of pension is provided by the insurance company. In this case, the pension company will pay a single premium on behalf of the participant on the basis of the submission of a concluded insurance contract that meets the conditions set by the SPS (§ 23 SPS). Conditions giving rise to individual claims are regulated in detail in §§ 20 et seq. SPS.

696. The pension company is regulated in the provisions of §§ 29 et seq. SPS. A pension company is a joint-stock company with its registered office in the Czech Republic, whose business is to collect participant contributions, employer's contributions and state contributions for the purpose of placing them in mutual funds, managing assets in mutual funds and paying SPS benefits (§ 29(1) SPS). The performance of this activity is conditioned by permission being granted by the CNB. In addition to its main activity, the pension company may also perform activities pursuant to § 35 (if registered)[675] or § 74 SPS.[676] The business name of a pension company must contain the designation 'pension company' and at the same time it is forbidden to use this designation to other entities (§ 30 SPS). The initial capital of a pension company must be at least CZK 50 million (§ 37 SPS). The SPS stipulates in great detail other conditions for the performance of the pension company's activities, including minimum capitalization requirements (§§ 37 and 38), managers (§§ 39 and 40), management rules, including rules for prudent conduct of business (§§ 49 and 50), outsourcing (§ 51), staffing (§ 53), accounting (§ 56) or mandatory disclosure of information on the activities of a pension company (§§ 57–59). Supervision of pension companies is performed by the CNB (§§ 141 et seq. SPS).

697. Participation funds, in which the participant's financial means are accumulated, are regulated in the provisions of §§ 93 et seq. SPS. A participation fund is a set of assets, that belongs to all participants and other persons, to whom the right to the payment of the participation funds has been transferred, in proportion to the number of pension units. The nature of the participation funds precludes the application of the general provisions on co-ownership to the participation fund, the assets

675. These are activities consisting in the provision of related services on the financial market, in particular the intermediation of life insurance contracts or educational activities in the area of supplementary pension savings.
676. The intermediation of supplementary pension savings.

in the fund, the management of the assets in the fund, and other rights and obligations relating to the participation fund. Neither the participant nor any other person has the right to request the division of assets in the participation fund or the cancellation of the participation fund (§ 93(2) SPS). The assets in the participation fund are managed by the pension company in its own name and on behalf of the participants. The assets in the fund are not part of the assets of the pension company that manages them (§ 93(3) SPS). The participation fund has no legal personality. The obligation imposed by the SPS on the participation fund is the obligation of the pension company that manages it. The right granted by SPS to a participating fund is the right of the pension company that manages it (§ 93(4) SPS). The pension company always creates and manages one mandatory participation fund, namely the mandatory conservative fund (§ 98 SPS). In addition, the pension company may create and manage other participation funds (§ 94 SPS). The participant can choose whether to place their funds in the mandatory conservative fund or in other participation funds created by the pension company. The creation of a participation fund is subject to the permission of the CNB (§ 96 SPS). Each participation fund must have a statute – a document that contains in an understandable form information on how the participation fund is invested, an explanation of risks associated with SPS and other information necessary for a participant to accurately and correctly assess their decision to invest in the participation fund (§ 97 SPS). Furthermore, the participation fund cannot exist without a depositary, which records assets in the fund and checks whether the pension company disposes of assets in the fund in accordance with the law, the depositary agreement, agreements with participants and the statute (§§ 88 et seq. SPS). The SPS sets out very detailed rules for the method of investment of participation funds (§§ 98 et seq. SPS). The pension company maintains a personal pension account for each participant or other recipient of the benefit, in which it records the participant's financial means and the participant's pension units in individual participation funds (§§ 120 and 121 SPS). Within one month after the end of each calendar year, the pension company is obliged to send the participant a statement for the past calendar year, which must include, among other information, the movements of the participant's financial means in the cash sub-account for the period since the last statement, credited and depreciated pension units in the property sub-account, the value of the participant's share in the fund, which is calculated by multiplying the current value of the pension unit of the participation fund as of the date of the statement and the number of pension units of the participation fund credited to the property sub-account by that date, and other data specified in § 125 SPS.

698. In addition to the State-Contributory Supplementary Pension Insurance, followed by SPS, there was another supplementary pension system in the Czech Republic during 2013–2015, and that was the Retirement Savings (in Czech 'důchodové spoření').[677] It was a hybrid model called the second pillar of the pension system,[678] based on the principle of fund financing with the possibility of voluntary

677. Act No. 426/2011 Sb., on Retirement Savings, and Act No. 397/2012 Sb., on Premiums for Retirement Savings.

678. However, employers did not contribute to its financing.

entry, but with the impossibility of exit. Retirement savings were based on the transfer of 3% of premiums (the so-called opt-out) from the state-organized pension insurance system to the private pension accounts of retirement savings participants with pension companies, provided that the participant contributes another 2% of their resources. Act No. 376/2015 Sb., on Termination of the Retirement Savings Scheme, abolished this system due to public lack of interest, an adverse impact on the state budget, and an uncertain degree of real appreciation of long-term deferral, with effect from 1 January 2016.[679]

699. Although at present there is no supplementary pension system of the second pillar in place in the Czech Republic, there is a legislative framework for the operation of institutions of occupational supplementary pension schemes, in the form of Act No. 340/2006 Sb., on Activities of Institutions for Occupational Retirement Provision. This act constitutes a transposition of Directive 2003/41/EC of the European Parliament and of the Council of 3 June 2003 on the activities and supervision of institutions for occupational retirement provision. Based to this Act, occupational pension insurance may be offered in the Czech Republic by institutions that have the authorization of the home supervisory authority from EU countries for the given activity in accordance with the principles of the single internal market. The act also regulates the conditions for the operation of occupational pension insurance by institutions established in the Czech Republic. At the same time, the act stipulates in the provision of § 10h, with regard to the current non-existence of the second pillar, that an institution of occupational pension insurance may not be established in the territory of the Czech Republic. Although the conditions for the activities of institutions for occupational retirement provision are regulated by law, the operation of this activity is currently not permitted in the Czech Republic.[680]

700. On 25 July 2019, Regulation (EU) 2019/1238 of the European Parliament and of the Council of 20 June 2019 on a pan-European Personal Pension Product (PEPP) was published in the Official Journal of the EU. The PEPP Regulation aims to promote the stability and sustainability of national pension systems and to complement (not replace or harmonize) them with another supplementary personal pension product based on voluntary participation, which is simple, safe, affordable, transparent, customer-friendly and transferable throughout the Union. This should, *inter alia*, increase its attractiveness as a product, particularly to young people and mobile workers, and will help to further facilitate the right of Union citizens to live and work across the Union.[681] The PEPP Regulation lays down the single set of rules for the registration, creation and distribution of personal pension products which are distributed in the EU under the designation 'PEPP' and for the supervision of these products. The PEPP is designed to give Union citizens another choice when it comes to saving money for the post-productive age period, and can be

679. Lang, Roman; Voňšek, Vladimír. In: Koldinská, Kristina; Tröster, Petr et al. *Právo sociálního zabezpečení*. 7th substantially revised ed. Praha: C. H. Beck, 2018, p. 192.

680. This solution was adopted by Act No. 260/2011 Sb. in response to Judgement C-343/08 of 14 Jan. 2009, *European Commission v. Czech Republic*, ECLI: EU:C:2010:14.

681. *See* especially points 3–10 of the recital of the PEPP Regulation.

offered by a wide range of financial institutions from credit institutions, insurance companies, institutions for occupational retirement provision to investment companies.[682] It is a product of non-occupational insurance for individuals based on a voluntary basis. As it should serve for the long-term accumulation of capital, the possibilities of early withdrawal of funds can be limited and might be penalized.[683] The PEPP Regulation harmonizes the basic framework and parameters of the PEPP, but in certain areas (e.g., in the accumulation and pay-out phase) it presupposes a wide discretion of national regulations.[684] In accordance with Article 74 the PEPP Regulation shall apply twelve months after the publication of the relevant delegated acts. At the end of 2019, the Ministry of Finance of the Czech Republic prepared a public consultation on the adaptation of Czech legislation to the PEPP Regulation with focus on the opinions and suggestions of market participants and the professional public on the use of discretions in the PEPP Regulation. The preparation of the draft of the adaptation law is included in the government's legislative work plan for 2020, which also envisages the completion of delegated acts at the European level, the drafts of which EIOPA is required to prepare and submit to the Commission by 15 August 2020.[685]

682. *See* Art. 6(1) of the PEPP Regulation.
683. *See* point 20 of the recital of the PEPP Regulation.
684. *See* Arts 47, 57, and 58 of the PEPP Regulation.
685. *See also*, e.g., Mesršmíd, Jaroslav. *PEPP a důchodový systém.* Pojistné rozpravy. 2019, No. 36, pp. 3–4; Kubátová, Irena. *Nařízení o panevropském osobním penzijním produktu.* Pojistný obzor. 2019, No. 2, pp. 18–21. Kunertová, Tereza. *PEPP: Jaké změny přinese nový panevropský penzijní produkt?* Pojistný obzor. 2019, No. 2, pp. 10–11.

Part VI. Private Insurance: Social Security

701. Social security contributions in the Czech Republic include payments for sickness insurance, pension insurance, and contribution to the state employment policy. Pension and sickness insurance are based on the insurance principle, i.e., on the regular payment of the insurance premium. The insurance premium (collected by the Czech Social Security Administration[686]) in accordance with Act No. 589/1992 Sb., on Social Security Premiums and Contributions to the State Employment Policy,[687] is a revenue of the state budget.

702. Employers, employees who participate in public health insurance, self-employed persons, and people who have taken out voluntary pension insurance are obliged to pay insurance premiums.[688] Employers pay insurance premiums for their employees.

703. Social security insurance can be supplemented by various social funds, which can be compulsory or voluntary, and which supplement compulsory social security insurance with new or higher benefits under state supervision.[689]

686. The Czech Social Security Administration (ČSSZ) is the largest financial administrative institution, which manages the agenda of more than 8.9 million clients, of which approximately 2.9 million are pensioners. It pays out over 3.5 million pensions and an average of around 280,000 sickness insurance benefits per month. The contribution of the ČSSZ to the state budget is more than one-third of all revenues. The competencies of the ČSSZ are regulated by the Act of the Czech National Council No. 582/1991 Sb., on the Organization and Implementation of Social Security. Pursuant to the provisions of § 5 of this Act, the ČSSZ performs especially the following tasks: decides on pension insurance benefits, arranges the payment of these benefits, decides on the obligation of a citizen to return a pension insurance benefit provided incorrectly or in the wrong amount, decides on the obligation of the organization to replace unduly paid amounts in the pension insurance benefit, decides on appeals in cases in which the district social security administration has ruled in the first instance, decides on the elimination of the hardships that would occur in the implementation of social security in individual cases and collects social security contributions and contributions to the state employment policy according to a special law. For more, *see* https://www.cssz.cz/.

687. https://www.zakonyprolidi.cz/cs/1992-589.

688. The premium is calculated as a specified percentage of the assessment base for the relevant period. This is the calendar month for employees for which the premium is paid. For self-employed persons this is a calendar year and the assessment base for insurance premiums is the amount that they determine themselves, but no less than 50% of the tax base.

689. Koldinská, Kristina; Tröster, Petr et al. *Právo sociálního zabezpečení.* 7th substantially revised ed. Praha: C. H. Beck, 2018, p. 12.

704. From a general and global perspective, the pension system usually consists of three parts (pillars):

- the first pillar is general, compulsory and organized by the state (state scheme);
- the second pillar is based on the principle of collective security through employers (collective scheme);
- the third pillar is the individual security of citizens through their own investment activities in the form of life insurance, participation in investment funds, etc. (individual scheme).[690]

705. However, the specific regulation of the supplementary pension system differs from country to country and depends on tradition, historical, and social development, on the regulation of the basic pension insurance etc.

706. After January 2013, the pension system in the Czech Republic consisted of the three pension pillars. In addition to the compulsory first pillar (pension insurance), the second pension pillar (pension savings) and the reformed third pension pillar including SPS and supplementary pension insurance were already completed. Supplementary pension insurance is a system operated through transformed funds, which is nevertheless the largest fund system in the Czech Republic in terms of the number of participants. Supplementary pension insurance was closed for new participants at the end of 2012. In 2014, the government decided – via special law on the termination of pension savings[691] – to end the second pillar (pension savings).[692]

707. Supplementary pension insurance and SPS are both based on the civic principle, i.e., on the relationship between a pension company and an individual citizen. The supplementary pension system in the Czech Republic is characterized by these principles, namely voluntariness, transferability, long-term, security, financial support from the state and the participation of third parties.[693]

708. Although the supplementary schemes are primarily of a private law nature, as they are based on a contractual relationship, they also bear important public law features, to what extent contractual freedom is limited by a number of mandatory provisions and when the very establishment and operation of pension companies and pension funds is subject to strict regulation[694] and extensive state supervision.

---

690. *Ibid.*, p. 153.
691. Act No. 376/2015 Sb., on Termination of the Retirement Savings Scheme (available at https://www.zakonyprolidi.cz/cs/2015-376).
692. https://www.mfcr.cz/cs/soukromy-sektor/soukrome-penzijni-systemy/zakladni-informace.
693. Koldinská, Kristina; Tröster, Petr et al. *Právo sociálního zabezpečení.* 7th substantially revised ed. Praha: C. H. Beck, 2018, p. 179.
694. A pension fund may not be established on the basis of a public offering of shares, it may only issue registered shares of the same nominal value and may not issue shares on favourable terms for employees and preference shares. The value of the registered capital of a pension fund must be at least CZK 50,000,000. The share capital must consist of only cash deposits, which must be repaid

709. Supplementary pension insurance, regulated by Act No. 42/1994 Sb., on State-Contributory Supplementary Pension Insurance,[695] is the collection of funds from members of the supplementary pension scheme ('participant')[696] and from the State provided for the benefit of the participants. Supplementary pension insurance may actually not be provided by persons other than pension funds. The amendment, effective from 2013, brought tax benefits, deepened the long-term nature of insurance, introduced measures in favour of system security and supported the tendency towards a higher concentration of participants in a smaller number of stronger pension funds.

710. SPS, regulated by Act No. 427/2011 Sb., on SPS,[697] is a system based on the collection and placement of a participant's funds, contributions paid for the participant by their employer, and state contributions to participant funds managed by a pension company and payment of benefits. Participation is voluntary.

711. A participant can be a person of any age who has entered into an SPS contract. Minors do not require the consent of the court (it is considered a common matter of property administration). It is possible to conclude principally only one contract with one pension company, another contract only under the conditions of § 4(2) SPS.[698]

712. The contract specifies the savings strategy, i.e., it determines the participating fund or funds. It is possible to identify the person(s) to whom the funds will go in the event of the participant's death. The contract can expire only under the conditions of the law,[699] the most common form is termination. It is also possible to terminate the contract by transferring funds to another pension company.[700]

---

before the creation of the fund. An increase in the registered capital may not be made by non-monetary deposits. New shares may not be offered for subscription on the basis of a public offer to subscribe for shares. For the transfer of pension fund shares in the amount of more than 10% of the pension fund's share capital, performed in one or more operations to any person or more persons acting in concert, and for the offer to subscribe for shares in more than 10% of the share capital pension fund to a selected applicant requires the prior consent of the CNB. Pension fund shares, which represent a shareholding of shareholders in a pension fund, may not be used to secure liabilities etc.

695. https://www.zakonyprolidi.cz/cs/1994-42/zneni-20170701.

696. A participant may be a natural person over 18 years of age with permanent residence in the Czech Republic who concludes a written contract on supplementary pension insurance with the pension fund. A participant may also be a natural person residing in the territory of another Member State of the European Union, if he participates in pension insurance or is a recipient of Czech pension insurance or participates in public health insurance in the Czech Republic who concludes with a pension fund relevant contract. *See* § 2 of Act No. 42/1994 Sb., on State-Contributory Supplementary Pension Insurance.

697. https://www.zakonyprolidi.cz/cs/2011-427.

698. A contract on supplementary pension savings before the termination of a supplementary pension savings from another contract may be concluded if the payment of the benefit to the participant was started, at the earliest on the first day of the calendar month immediately following the day of the start of the payment of the benefit from all the participant's funds.

699. The supplementary pension savings of the participant expire on termination of the payment of the retirement pension for a specified period or the disability pension for a specified period from all

713. SPS can only be used for the following benefits: retirement pension for a specified period, disability pension for a specified period, one-off settlement, severance pay, payment of a lump sum premium for a life pension, payment of a lump sum pension premium for a precisely defined period with a precisely determined amount of the pension.[701]

714. The conditions for the entitlement to the retirement pension for a specified period are either the minimum age of 60 years or meeting the conditions for the so-called pre-retirement. The conditions for the pre-retirement pension (paid from SPS) are the following: the participant must have been contributing for at least sixty calendar months (including the period of participation in supplementary pension insurance), and must reach at least the age of five years less than the age required for the entitlement to the retirement pension from the state pension insurance, and have a sufficient amount saved so that the monthly pension payment is at least 30% of the average wage and the pension is paid continuously for at least two years.[702]

715. The condition for the disability pension for a specified period is receiving the disability pension of the third degree and the contributing period must have lasted for at least thirty-six months (other rules are similar to the previous described pension).[703]

716. The conditions for a one-off settlement are the age of 60 years and the duration of contributions of at least sixty calendar months. It is also possible to choose a combination of a one-off settlement and the payment of a pension for a certain period of time. It belongs to both the participant and the designated person (if determined), if the participant died after the day on which he became entitled. A one-off settlement becomes the object of inheritance.[704]

717. The severance pay belongs to the participant in the event of termination of the SPS by notice or by an agreement and if the savings period lasted for at least twenty-four calendar months. The severance pay belongs to the designated person if the participant died and was not entitled to another benefit. If there is no person designated, then it becomes the object of inheritance. In connection with persons under the age of 18, partial severance pay has been introduced, which can be obtained before the age of 18.[705]

---

funds of the participant, on the day of payments of a one-off settlement from all funds of the participant, payment of a one-off premium for a life pension or a one-off premium for a pension for a precisely defined period with a precisely determined amount of the pension from all funds of the participant, on the day on which the participant and the pension company have agreed in writing, by expiry of the notice period or by the death of the participant. *See* § 8 SPS.

700. Under the conditions of § 27 in conjunction with §§ 61 and 62 SPS.

701. *See* § 19 SPS.

702. https://www.mfcr.cz/cs/soukromy-sektor/soukrome-penzijni-systemy/iii-pilir-doplnkove-penzijni-sporeni-a-p/zakladni-informace.

703. *See* § 20(2) SPS.

704. *See* § 20(1) SPS.

705. *See* § 25 SPS.

718. Payment of a lump sum premium for a life pension and payment of a lump sum premium for a pension for a precisely defined period with a precisely determined amount of pension are based on the condition of concluding a contract with an insurance company; the conditions of payment might be differing. Before concluding the contract, the insurance company is obliged to communicate in writing the amount guaranteed to the participant. If the conditions are clearly defined, we are talking in practice about pre-retirement pension (as described above), that allows the possibility to draw up to five years before the retirement age and its purpose is to bridge the period that may not be financially favourable for the participant.

719. A participant may not pay their contribution to SPS to more than one pension company at the same time. The amount of the participant's contribution is set for a calendar month and may not be less than CZK 100. The participant's contribution is payable by the end of the calendar month for which it is paid. The participant is entitled to change the amount of the participant's contribution; but not retroactively.[706]

720. The participant's contribution or part of it may be paid by the employer if the participant agrees.[707] The participant is obliged to notify the pension company of this fact in advance in writing. No state contribution shall be provided for the employer's contribution. The employer may not influence the employee in the choice of the pension company, they may not accept a fee, remuneration or a non-monetary advantage in connection with the provision of the employer's contribution.

721. The participant is entitled to defer payment under legal and contractual conditions (stipulating the maximum deferral). It is also possible to interrupt the payment of the contribution. However, the period of interruption of the payment of the participant's contribution to the SPS is not included in the savings period.[708] The advantage is that the payment of these contributions is subject to a tax deduction.[709]

722. The Ministry of Finance shall provide a state contribution to the participant from the state budget. The pension company is obliged to register state contributions provided for the benefit of individual participants. For each calendar month, a

706. *See* § 9 SPS.
707. It is not contrary to the principle of equal treatment to provide a different amount of the employer's contribution depending on the risk, difficulty or effort of the work performed, if this is agreed in the collective agreement or stipulated in the employer's internal regulations. *See* § 10 SPS.
708. *See* § 11 SPS.
709. A contribution in the total amount of a maximum of CZK 24,000 paid by the taxpayer for their supplementary pension insurance with a state contribution, supplementary pension savings according to the contract on supplementary pension savings may be deducted from the tax base in the tax period. *See* § 15(5) and § 38h(6) of the Income Tax Act.

participant who meets the statutory conditions and who has paid a contribution of at least CZK 300 shall be entitled to a state contribution.[710]

723. As already mentioned, this activity can only be performed by pension companies. Pension companies are joint-stock companies domiciled in the Czech Republic, whose business is to collect participant contributions, employer's contributions and state contributions for the purpose of placing them in mutual funds, managing assets in mutual funds and paying SPS benefits.[711] This activity can be performed in the Czech Republic only by a pension company licensed by the CNB.[712] In addition to granting operating licenses, the CNB also supervises the activity of pension companies in accordance with §§ 141 et seq. SPS.

724. Pension companies put the monetary contributions into mutual funds. A participant mutual fund is a set of assets that belongs to participants according to the number of pension units. Permission to create this fund is again granted by the CNB. A personal account is maintained for each participant, in which funds and units are recorded. Within the mutual fund, the law also gives the possibility to invest under the conditions specified in the provisions of §§ 99 to 108 SPS. The pension company is entitled to remuneration for its services.

725. In conclusion, it should be noted that even if the second pension pillar is not currently in place in our country, it is still possible to establish an employee supplementary pension scheme in the Czech Republic, based on the judgement of the Court of Justice C-343/08,[713] which responded to the lack of transposition of Directive No. 2003/41/E.

726. Based on this judgement, the Czech Republic introduced, by an amendment to Act No. 340/2006 Sb., on Activities of Institutions for Occupational Retirement Provision,[714] the more precise conditions for operating supplementary employee pension insurance (*see* § 10a to 10 g of the Act). The pension insurance is operated on the principle of fund management, established separately for the purposes of pension benefits, authorized in the state of the EU in which the institution has its registered office. It is necessary for the institution to have the permission of the competent authority of the home state, the consent of the state where it operates is not required. Supervision is performed by the CNB to a minimal extent, the institutions are primarily being supervised by home institutions.

---

710. If the amount of the monthly contribution of the participant is CZK 300 to 999, the amount of the monthly state contribution is CZK 90 and 20% of the amount exceeding CZK 300. If the amount of the monthly contribution of the participant is CZK 1,000 and more, the amount of the monthly state contribution is CZK 230. *See* § 14 SPS.
711. *See* § 29 SPS.
712. *See* § 31 SPS.
713. https://eur-lex.europa.eu/legal-content/CS/TXT/?uri=CELEX%3A62008CJ0343.
714. https://www.zakonyprolidi.cz/cs/2006-340.

Part VII. Insurance Intermediaries

727. The area of insurance distribution in the Czech Republic underwent significant changes at the turn of 2018 and 2019. Following Directive (EU) 2016/97 of the European Parliament and of the Council of 20 January 2016 on insurance distribution (IDD), Act No. 170/2018 Sb., on the Distribution of Insurance and Reinsurance (AoDIR) was adopted. AoDIR incorporates the relevant regulations of the EU and regulates the activities of persons authorized to intermediate insurance or reinsurance, including the activities of such persons abroad, rights and obligations in distributing insurance or reinsurance and competences of public authorities in the field of insurance or reinsurance distribution.[715]AoDIR came into force on 1 December 2018, when it replaced the previous Act No. 38/2004 Sb., on Insurance Intermediaries and on Independent Loss Adjusters.[716]

728. The aim of the AoDIR was, among other things, to unify the basic principles of regulation with other segments of the financial market, eliminate interproduct regulatory arbitrage, strengthen and clarify the responsibilities of individual actors in the distribution chain, consolidate consumer protection rules, strengthen clients' awareness of insurance conditions and facilitate information comparability across financial products, reduce the excessively high number of insurance intermediaries on the market and set up an effective system of verification and regular deepening of professional competence of persons involved in insurance distribution, strengthen administrative punishment tools, improve and streamline supervision, and thus generally increase the credibility of the sector and enhance the level of services provided.[717]

729. It should be emphasized that, unlike the previous legislation, AoDIR does not only regulate the area of insurance and reinsurance intermediation, but in compliance with the objective of the IDD, it applies its rules in general to all forms of insurance and reinsurance distribution. Within the general concept of insurance distribution, AoDIR distinguishes between 'insurance intermediation' (typically the

715. In general, *see also* General Introduction, §3. Sources of insurance law.
716. For more details on the previous Act, *see* Škopová, Věra; Musilová, Radoslava; Krupičková, Hana. *Zákon o pojišťovacích zprostředkovatelích a samostatných likvidátorech pojistných událostí a předpisy související. Komentář.* 1st ed. Praha: C. H. Beck, 2006.
717. Cf. Explanatory Memorandum and Final Regulatory Impact Assessment Report to the AoDIR (both available in Czech at https://www.psp.cz/sqw/text/tiskt.sqw?O=8&CT=48&CT1=0), or e.g., Beran, Jiří; Indra, Milan; Urbanec, Jan. *ZDPZ: Účinnější ochrana spotřebitele a cesta k vyšší kredibilitě sektoru.* Pojistný obzor. 2018, No. 4, pp. 18–22.

conclusion of an insurance contract by an insurance intermediary acting on behalf of the insurer or the client) and the 'provision of insurance' (typically the direct sale of insurance by an insurance company).[718]

730. In addition to the broad discretions of IDD, the Czech lawmaker also used the adoption of the new law to regulate areas not regulated by IDD – it is worth mentioning the regulation of the so-called fleet insurance in § 4 AoDIR, which applies to policyholders' activities consisting in offering the opportunity to become insured if this activity is operated in business way.[719] Although IDD does not regulate this activity in any way and it is not the intermediation or provision of insurance, some of the obligations regulated by AoDIR shall apply, with the necessary modifications, to its performance.[720]

731. Section 3(1) of the AoDIR defines certain areas of activities that are excluded from the scope of the law. This includes, for example, the provision of general information on insurance or reinsurance; distribution of insurance, if the insurer is a person who does not perform their activity as an entrepreneur; comparison of insurance, if it does not allow negotiating or changing insurance; provision of information and recommendations in the course of the activities of lawyers or notaries; or claims handling.[721] Other activities excluded from the scope of the law also include the so-called tipping, consisting in a general assessment of the client's possible interest in negotiating insurance and then passing the contact ('tip') regarding the client to the insurance company or insurance intermediary.[722]

---

718. Cf. the definition of the terms 'insurance intermediation' and 'provision of insurance' in § 2 AoDIR.
719. But not necessarily only in vehicle insurance, as the name might suggest.
720. For more details, *see* CNB's Supervisory benchmark No. 1/2020, on Some Obligations of the Insurance Company and the Policyholder in Offering the Possibility to Become Insured (available at https://www.cnb.cz/export/sites/cnb/cs/dohled-financni-trh/.galleries/vykon_dohledu/dohledove_benchmarky/download/dohledovy_benchmark_2020_01.pdf), CNB's Supervisory opinion of 3 Jun. 2020, on the Interpretation of the Policyholder's Obligations pursuant to § 4 of the Act on the Distribution of Insurance and Reinsurance (available at https://www.cnb.cz/export/sites/cnb/cs/casto-kladene-dotazy/.galleries/stanoviska_a_odpovedi/pdf/k_povinnosti_pojistnika_podle_zakona_o_distribuci_pojisteni_a_zajisteni.pdf), CNB's Supervisory opinion of 29 Nov. 2018, on the Distribution of Insurance Cover by the Policyholder according to § 4 AoDIR (available at https://www.cnb.cz/export/sites/cnb/cs/casto-kladene-dotazy/.galleries/stanoviska_a_odpovedi/pdf/distribuce_pojistne_ochrany_flotilove_pojisteni.pdf); in relation to the latter opinion, it is necessary to draw attention to the amendment to the provisions of § 4(7) AoDIR, which, with effect from 1 May 2020, revoked the requirements for the existence of the so-called qualified insurable interest of the fleet policyholder and amended the wording of the conditions under which fleet insurance can be provided; also cf. e.g., Šmotková, Michaela. *Změny ve flotilovém pojištění a výklad souvislosti s prodejem zboží a poskytováním služby.* Pojistný obzor. 2020, No. 4, pp. 20–23; Kult, Alexandr; Škrabka, Jan. *Regulace flotilového pojištění po novele v reflexi názorů ČNB.* Pojistné rozpravy. 2020, No. 37, pp. 58–64.
721. The activity of independent loss adjusters is newly – in contrast to the previous Act No. 38/2004 Sb. – excluded from the scope of AoDIR and subject to the general trade regulation regime.
722. For more details, *see* CNB's Supervisory opinion of 10 May 2011, on Defining the Difference between Tipping and Insurance Intermediation (available at https://www.cnb.cz/export/sites/cnb/cs/casto-kladene-dotazy/.galleries/stanoviska_a_odpovedi/pdf/k_vymezeni_hranice_mezi_tiparstvim.pdf).

732. In accordance with Article 1(3) and (4) IDD, AoDIR defines in § 3(2) a specific exception from its scope for persons whose main activity is not insurance distribution, but who in their main activity may additionally distribute insurance (the so-called intermediary of supplementary insurance). These might be, for example, travel agencies that can offer travel insurance or sellers of consumer goods who can offer insurance for defects, damage or loss of the goods they supply. Given the complementary nature of such activities, it would be disproportionate for these persons to be fully subject to the regulation of insurance distribution. Therefore, only certain obligations exhaustively enumerated in § 3(2) AoDIR apply to the intermediation of insurance by these persons if the conditions stipulated by law are met.

733. Persons performing the activity of an insurance intermediary according to AoDIR are subject to registration. The register of insurance intermediaries is kept in electronic form[723] and is managed and operated by the CNB (§ 40 AoDIR).

723. Available at https://apl.cnb.cz/apljerrsdad/JERRS.WEB07.INTRO_PAGE?p_lang=en.

Chapter 1. Law of Establishment and Supervision

734. In accordance with § 2(i) of the AoDIR, an insurance intermediary is a person who, as an entrepreneur, intermediates insurance or reinsurance. The provisions of § 5 of the AoDIR exhaustively stipulate that to intermediate the insurance or reinsurance as an entrepreneur may only:

(a) an independent intermediary;
(b) a tied agent;
(c) a supplementary insurance intermediary;
(d) an insurance intermediary with a home Member State other than the Czech Republic;
(e) an insurance company (as regards insurance intermediation);
(f) a reinsurance company (as regards reinsurance intermediation).

735. The position of an independent intermediary is regulated in §§ 6 et seq. of the AoDIR. An independent intermediary means a person who is authorized to intermediate insurance or reinsurance on the basis of an authorization granted by the CNB. The CNB will grant the authorization if the conditions exhaustively enumerated in § 7 are met. The application is submitted electronically via the REGIS application.[724] If the CNB grants the application in full, it will enter an independent intermediary in the register. The decision takes legal effect at the moment of registration. The full requirements of the application are set out in the secondary legislation, which is the CNB's Decree No. 196/2018 Sb., on Applications under the Act on the Distribution of Insurance and Reinsurance. The authorization lasts until the end of the calendar year following the calendar year in which the independent intermediary was entered in the register (§ 9 AoDIR) and may be always extended for another twelve months after the payment of the administrative fee.[725] The authorization expires for the reasons stated in § 11 AoDIR. An independent intermediary may act either as: a) an 'insurance agent' (who intermediates insurance for an insurance company), or b) an 'insurance broker' (who intermediates insurance for a client) (§ 12 AoDIR). § 76 of the AoDIR prohibits an independent intermediary from intermediating individual insurance simultaneously as an insurance agent and an insurance broker. Therefore, within one specific insurance relationship, an independent intermediary may not act both on behalf of an insurance company (as an agent) and on behalf of the client (as a broker).[726] By way of derogation from the general

---

724. For more details, *see* the CNB's methodological materials on individual types of applications (https://www.cnb.cz/en/supervision-financial-market/conduct-of-supervision/licensing-and-approval-proceedings/licensing-and-approval-proceedings-insurance-intermediaries-and-independent-loss-adjusters/).
725. Which currently amounts to CZK 2,500 (item 65(11)(g) of the tariff of fees in the annex to Act No. 634/2004 Sb., on Administrative Fees).
726. Cf. also CNB's FAQ – answer of 9 Jun. 2008, on Concurrence of Activities of an Insurance Broker and an Insurance Agent within one Insurance Contract (available at https://www.cnb.cz/cs/casto-kladene-dotazy/Soubeh-cinnosti-pojistovaciho-maklere-a-pojistovaciho-agenta-v-ramci-jedne-pojistne-smlouvy-9.6.2008).

rules on tortious liability under the CC,[727] AoDIR expressly provides that if an insurance or reinsurance company uses an independent intermediary in its activities, it is not liable for the damage caused by that intermediary, and the independent intermediary is liable themselves. The insurance or reinsurance company shall bear the consequences of the unlawful act of the independent intermediary only indirectly and only if it has not carefully selected or supervised the independent intermediary (*culpa in eligendo* or *culpa in custodiendo*).[728] Therefore, an independent intermediary must be insured for the entire period of performance of their activities for damage caused by a breach of their obligations during the distribution of insurance (§ 13 AoDIR).[729]

736. The conditions for the authorization for the activity of a tied agent are regulated by §§ 15 et seq. AoDIR. A tied agent means a person who is authorized to intermediate insurance or reinsurance on the basis of the record of a tied agent in the register (§ 15(1) AoDIR). A tied agent enters into a contract with the represented person, which must be in writing. The contract may be concluded with only one representative (§ 15(2) AoDIR). A tied agent shall be entered in the register on the basis of an electronic notification submitted by the represented person, which may be an insurance or reinsurance company, an independent intermediary, or an insurance intermediary with a home Member State other than the Czech Republic.[730] CNB shall register the person (without delay, but no later than within five working days from the day when the notification was received) on the basis of an electronic notification pursuant to § 17 AoDIR submitted by the represented person, if the data on the registered person correspond to the data in the basic register, and this person is not yet registered as an insurance intermediary (§ 16(1) AoDIR). The authorization arises from the record of the tied agent in the register (§ 18(1) AoDIR) and lasts until the end of the calendar year following the calendar year in which the entry was made (§ 18(3) AoDIR). The CNB will always extend the authorization for another twelve months after the payment of the administrative fee,[731] which is paid by the represented person. The authorization expires for the reasons stipulated in § 20 AoDIR. As the represented person is principally liable for the breach of obligation of the tied agent, the tied agent does not have to be insured.

727. Cf. §§ 167, 1935 and 2914 CC.
728. Cf. Explanatory Memorandum to the provisions of § 14 AoDIR; a similar construction is applied if the damage is caused by a tied agent or a supplementary insurance intermediary used in the activities of an independent intermediary – cf. §§ 23 and 32 of the AoDIR and the explanatory memorandum to these provisions.
729. The minimum limits of insurance indemnity are set by the directly applicable EU regulation, which is currently the Commission Delegated Regulation (EU) 2019/1935 of 13 May 2019 amending Directive (EU) 2016/97 of the European Parliament and of the Council with regard to regulatory technical standards adapting the base Euro amounts for professional indemnity insurance and for financial capacity of insurance and reinsurance intermediaries.
730. *See* § 2(j) AoDIR.
731. Currently CZK 500 (item 65(11)(h) of the tariff of fees in the annex to Act No. 634/2004 Sb., on Administrative Fees).

737. A supplementary insurance intermediary means a person who is entitled to intermediate insurance on the basis of the record of a supplementary insurance intermediary for the given represented person in the register (§ 24(1) AoDIR). A supplementary insurance intermediary may intermediate only insurance which is a supplementary service to the goods supplied or services provided, and only as its ancillary activity (§ 24(2) AoDIR). These can be, for example, a car dealer who intermediates MTPL. It is necessary to distinguish the supplementary insurance intermediary from the so-called intermediary of a supplementary insurance in the sense of the exception specified in the provision of § 3(2) AoDIR. While the said exception applies to persons who, although they intermediate insurance within the meaning of the definition given in § 2(f) of the AoDIR, are not insurance intermediaries within the meaning of § 5 of the AoDIR, and the regulation of insurance distribution applies on their activities only partially, the supplementary insurance intermediary is one of the types of insurance intermediaries regulated in § 5 AoDIR, and is subject to registration as well as in principle to all obligations under the AoDIR.[732] CNB shall register the person (without delay, but no later than within five working days from the day when the notification was received) on the basis of an electronic notification pursuant to § 26 AoDIR submitted by the represented person, if the data on the registered person correspond to the data in the basic register, and this person is not yet registered as an insurance intermediary. In view of the fact that a supplementary insurance intermediary may be active for more than one represented person, registration shall not be prevented if the person is already registered as a supplementary insurance intermediary for another represented person. The authorization to operate as a supplementary insurance intermediary for a given represented person is established by record in the register and lasts until the end of the calendar year following the calendar year in which the record was made (§ 27(1) and (2) AoDIR). CNB will always extend the authorization for another twelve months if the administrative fee is paid by the represented person.[733] The authorization expires for the reasons stipulated in § 29 AoDIR.

738. An insurance intermediary with a home Member State other than the Czech Republic may operate in the territory of the Czech Republic within the scope to which they are entitled to do so in their home Member State, on the basis of freedom of establishment or freedom to provide services on a temporary basis, under the conditions specified in the §§ 33 et seq. of the AoDIR.

739. If the insurance is intermediated by an insurance company, the provisions of the AoDIR concerning an independent intermediary shall apply by analogy, with the exceptions enumerated in § 5(2) of the AoDIR.

---

732. *See also* CNB's FAQ – On Some Provisions of the Act on the Distribution of Insurance and Reinsurance (available at https://www.cnb.cz/cs/casto-kladene-dotazy/K-nekterym-ustanovenim-zakona-o-distribuci-pojisteni-a-zajisteni/).

733. Currently CZK 500 (item 65(11)(i) of the tariff of fees in the annex to Act No. 634/2004 Sb., on Administrative Fees).

740. Part Five of the AoDIR generally regulates the personnel prerequisites for the operation of insurance intermediaries. Insurance distributors and their workers[734] must permanently meet the conditions of professional competence pursuant to § 56, which includes both general knowledge and professional knowledge and skills necessary for the distribution of insurance or reinsurance. General knowledge is proven by a high school diploma or proof of higher education. The acquisition of professional knowledge and skills for the distribution of insurance is evidenced by a certificate of successful completion of a professional examination in accordance with AoDIR. The administration of the exams is provided by accredited persons,[735] i.e., persons authorized to organize professional examinations and continuing education programs on the basis of accreditation granted by the CNB (§§ 61 et seq. AoDIR).[736] The scope of professional knowledge and skills according to particular groups of expertise (set out in § 57 AoDIR), and other issues related to professional examinations, is determined by a secondary legislation, which is the CNB's Decree No. 195/2018 Sb., on Professional Qualifications for the Distribution of Insurance.[737] In addition to professional competence, the second key prerequisite for the performance of the activities of an insurance intermediary is the trustworthiness regulated in § 70 AoDIR. A natural person who is fully independent and gives a precondition for the proper operation of activities pursuant to the AoDIR is considered trustworthy. In the case of a legal entity, a person whose current activity presupposes the proper operation of the activity pursuant to the AoDIR is considered trustworthy. The requirements for the trustworthiness and professional competence of persons operating in the field of financial services are specified in the official communication of the CNB of 5 August 2020, on the Interpretation of the Concepts of Trustworthiness and Professional Competence.[738]

741. The area of insurance and reinsurance distribution is supervised by the CNB. Insurance companies, reinsurance companies, insurance intermediaries, the policyholder in the so-called fleet insurance within the meaning of § 4 of the AoDIR, and accredited persons are subject to supervision. The supervision is not limited to the fulfilment of the obligations stipulated by the AoDIR, but also to the

734. A worker means a person who is in an employment relationship with an insurance company, reinsurance company or insurance intermediary, or a member of their statutory body, or another person with similar powers or a corporate agent, if they are directly involved in, or responsible for the distribution of insurance or reinsurance (*see* § 2(k) AoDIR).

735. Accredited persons are registered in the register kept by the CNB, their current list is available at https://apl.cnb.cz/apljerrsdad/JERRS.WEB07.INTRO_PAGE?p_lang=en.

736. A set of exam questions and further information on the professional exams are available at https://www.cnb.cz/cs/dohled-financni-trh/vykon-dohledu/povolovaci-a-schvalovaci-rizeni/povolovaci-a-schvalovaci-rizeni-pojistovaci-zprostredkovatele-a-samostatni-likvidatori-pojistnych-udalosti/Zkousky-dle-zakona-c.-170_2018-Sb.-o-distribuci-pojisteni-a-zajisteni/.

737. To consult the text, *see*: https://www.cnb.cz/export/sites/cnb/cs/legislativa/.galleries/vyhlasky/vyhlaska_195_2018.pdf.

738. To consult the text, *see*: https://www.cnb.cz/export/sites/cnb/cs/legislativa/.galleries/Vestnik-CNB/2020/vestnik_2020_18_22320560.pdf.

obligations stipulated by other legislation to the extent that they relate to the distribution of insurance or reinsurance,[739] as well as the obligations set out in directly applicable EU rules. The general interpretation given in Part I. Chapter 3. Supervision applies *mutatis mutandis* to supervision in the field of insurance and reinsurance distribution set out in detail in Part Seven of the AoDIR.

739. For example, secondary legislation to the AoDIR, relevant provisions of the Civil Code, Act No. 634/1992 Sb., on Consumer Protection, Act No. 253/2008 Sb., on Selected Measures against Legitimisation of Proceeds of Crime and Financing of Terrorism, etc.

Chapter 2. Insurance Intermediaries and the Insurance Contract

742. Insurance intermediation according to AoDIR includes activities related to the concluding of an insurance contract as well as activities that precede it (offer of insurance, submitting proposals, insurance comparison, and other preparatory work aimed at negotiating, changing, or terminating insurance). In addition, the activities of an insurance intermediary include assistance in the administration of insurance and in the exercise of insurance rights.[740]

743. When negotiating insurance, the insurance intermediary acts either on behalf of the insurer (tied agent, supplementary insurance intermediary, independent insurance intermediary in the position of the insurance agent) or on behalf of the client (independent insurance intermediary in the position of insurance broker). An independent intermediary, who can act both on the client side of the contract as well as on the side of the insurance company, cannot act in both of these roles at the same time in intermediating one specific insurance relationship (§ 76 AoDIR). Intermediaries perform their activities on the basis of a contract with a represented person or a client, for which the law stipulates a mandatory written form (§ 12(2), § 15(2) and § 24(3) AoDIR). The requirements for the contract are not regulated by AoDIR, so the general regulation of the Civil Code will apply. In practice, these may be different types of contracts – especially in the regime of general contractual representation (§§ 441 et seq. CC), or one of the mandate-type contracts, typically a commercial agency contract regulated in §§ 2843 et seq. CC.

744. In relation to the process of concluding an insurance contract, and more generally to the dealings of insurance distributors with a client, AoDIR sets out very detailed rules in its Part Six. These are particularly general requirements for professional care (§ 71), qualification, honesty, transparency, clarity, truthfulness and comprehensibility of the distributor's actions (§§ 72 and 73), including the regulation of the so-called incentives (§ 75), duty of confidentiality (§ 74), up to a very detailed regulation of pre-contractual and other information obligations (§§ 82 et seq.), the obligation to provide the client with recommendations (§ 77) or, in the case of reserve-making insurance, an advice (§ 78), the obligation to make record of negotiation, rules for storing documents, etc. If the contract is concluded with a consumer, the regulation of consumer contracts in the Civil Code also applies.[741] The insurance company or an independent insurance intermediary is liable for damage caused during the distribution of insurance according to the rules mentioned in the previous Chapter.

740. Cf. definition of intermediation in § 2(e) AoDIR.

741. *See also* General introduction, §5 Consumer protection.

Part VIII. Reinsurance, Co-insurance, Pooling

Chapter 1. Reinsurance

745. Reinsurance plays an irreplaceable role in private insurance system, as its main role is to facilitate the distribution of insurance and reinsurance risks, especially at the international level, and to enable insurance and reinsurance companies to increase their insurance and reinsurance capacity and reduce their capital costs. Reinsurance has a relatively long tradition associated with industrialization, which creates the potential for greater risks, which often exceed the capabilities of a single insurer and in some cases the capabilities of the entire insurance market in the region. The connection of the international reinsurance market in expanding the capacity of insurance companies plays an important role in quantitative terms and at the same time enables easier and faster introduction of new insurance products. It significantly helps to diversify the potential risks.[742]

746. According to the CIA, reinsurance represents, in brief, insurance of company insurance, i.e., insurance of the risk taken over by the insurer. It creates the contractual relationship between the insurer and the reinsurer.[743] Reinsurance does not reduce the extent of the damage but makes its financial consequences more economically viable.[744]

742. *See* namely Karfíková, Marie; Přikryl, Vladimír, Čechová, Jana. *Základy pojišťovacího práva.* 1st ed. Praha: Orac, 2001; Ducháčková, Eva. *Pojištění a pojišťovnictví.* 1st ed. Praha: Ekopress, 2015; Bokšová, Jiřina. *Účetnictví komerčních pojišťoven – specifika v ČR.* 1st ed. Praha: Wolters Kluwer, 2010; Janasová, Marie. *Účetnictví pojišťoven v ČR.* 1st ed. Ostrava: VŠB – Technická univerzita Ostrava, 2006; Drdla, Miloš; Martinovičová, Dana. *Bankovnictví a pojišťovnictví.* Brno: Brno International Business School, 2005; Vávrová, Eva. *Finanční řízení komerčních pojišťoven.* 1st ed. Praha: Grada, 2014; Zuzaňák, Aleš; Šulcová, Jaroslava; Hora, Jan. *Příručka pro zprostředkovatele pojištění.* 2nd ed. Praha: Linde, 2011; Karfíková, Marie; Přikryl, Vladimír; Vybíral, Roman et al. *Pojišťovací právo.* 2nd revised ed. Praha: Leges, 2018; Cipra, Tomáš. *Zajištění a přenos rizik v pojišťovnictví.* 1st ed. Praha: Grada Publishing, 2004.

743. A reinsurance contract can be defined as aleatory, as it contains future obligation duties that cannot be precisely determined at the time of its conclusion. It must always be in writing.

744. https://www.cap.cz/slovnik-pojmu/1354-zajisteni?highlight=WyJ6YWppXHUwMTYxdFx1MDExYm5cdTAwZWQiXQ==.

747. More precisely, according to the Insurance Act,[745] reinsurance in the broad sense means activities assuming insurance risks on the basis of concluded contracts, by which the reinsurance company undertakes to provide the insurance company in the agreed scope and monetary performance if an accidental event specified in the contract occurs, and the insurer undertakes to pay the reinsurer a specified part of the premium from insurance contracts concluded by the insurer, which are the subject of the reinsurance contract. Reinsurance activities also include activities directly arising from permitted reinsurance activities, especially activities related to its administration, investing, providing statistical or actuarial consultancy (advice) in the insurance industry, analysis and research of insurance risks, activities of the holding company and activities in the financial sector pursuant to the Act regulating the supplementary supervision of financial conglomerates.[746]

748. The purpose of reinsurance therefore lies in the possibility for insurance companies to provide insurance even in cases where the insurance company, with regard to its capital capabilities, has to transfer part of its risks or sums exceeding its capacity, in the form of reinsurance to another company (reinsurance company). This is a key element in ensuring the level of financial health and stability of insurance market and the financial system as a whole, as it allows insurance companies to underwrite risks that significantly exceed their insurance capacity or gives space for the introduction of new insurances for which there are not enough statistical data.

749. It is necessary to proceed in such a way that the fulfilment of insurance obligations is not jeopardized. If so, the CNB may require the insurance company to adequately secure the receivables, in particular in the form of a pledge or guarantee, or to order a reduction of the reinsurance company's share in the insurance company's liability, within a period appropriate to the change.

750. By a reinsurance company we mean, in accordance with the Czech legislation, a domestic reinsurance company, a reinsurance company from another Member State or a reinsurance company from a third country, with the exception of a reinsurance company which is excluded from the scope of the EU Directive on the taking-up and pursuit of the business of Insurance and Reinsurance.[747]

751. By captive reinsurance company we mean a reinsurance company which is controlled by an entity in the financial sector other than an insurance or reinsurance company (or other than an insurance holding company or a mixed-activity insurance holding company) or which is controlled by another entity who is not in the

745. *See* § 3(1)(l) IA.
746. Act No. 377/2005 Sb., on Supplementary Supervision of Banks, Savings and Credit Cooperatives, Electronic Money Institutions, Insurance Companies and Securities Dealers in Financial Conglomerates (Financial Conglomerates Act), https://www.zakonyprolidi.cz/cs/2005-377.
747. *See* § 3(1)(g) IA.

financial sector if the activity of this reinsurance company is exclusively limited to reinsurance of insurance risks of an entity connected with it.[748]

752. In order to obtain a license to operate a reinsurance company, a significant amount of capital is required, among other things, in the minimum amount of CZK 1,000,000,000 (in words: one billion CZK). On 8 August 2008, the CNB granted the first license to the domestic reinsurance company VIG RE zajišt'ovna, a.s.[749]

753. Reinsurance premium is usually determined as a percentage of the total gross insurance portfolio or as a fixed amount. Like an insurance company, a reinsurance company can transfer part of its risks to another reinsurance company, in which case we speak of retrocession. A reinsurer who has taken over part of the risks from the first insurer, may pass their part on to another reinsurer or reinsurers.

754. Reinsurance can be classified according to various criteria. We present here both the classification from the point of view of the subject (insurance or reinsurance company) and the classifications according to the nature of the reinsurance contract.

755. If we look at reinsurance from the point of view of insurance and reinsurance companies, we distinguish between active and passive reinsurance. Reinsurance is active (taken over), if the risk is taken over into reinsurance (either via cessation – from insurance companies, or via retrocession – from another reinsurance company) and is therefore performed by the reinsurance company. On the other hand, passive reinsurance means that the risk is transferred to reinsurance company and therefore is performed by the insurance company. The person who transfers the insurance risk is marked as the assignor and the person who accepts the insurance risk for reinsurance is marked as the assignee. In all cases covered by the contract, the assignee shares the fate of the assignor. As a guarantee that the assignee will fulfil all their obligations to the assignor, the assignor usually retains a certain part of the security in a special account in the form of a deposit.

756. In terms of the relationship between the assignor and the assignee, in other words, according to the distribution of rights and obligations, four variations of reinsurance contract can occur:

(1) facultative – facultative. This kind of relationship is characterized by free and on a case-by-case basis decision whether to offer the insurance risk for reinsurance, and free decision whether to take over, i.e., both entities have the right

---

748. *See* § 3(1)(k) IA.
749. https://www.vig-re.com/about/; VIG Re is a reinsurance company based in the Czech Republic that provides risk and capital management solutions to more than 350 insurance companies in 38 countries, with a focus on Austria and the CEE region. It was founded in 2008. The company headquarter is located in Prague and in 2017 a branch office was established in Frankfurt a. M.

to assign/not assign, or to accept/ not accept the concrete risk. Each reinsurance relationship is concluded individually which in turn means higher transaction costs what usually makes the whole operation more expensive;

(2) facultative – obligatory. This scheme is binding on one party only (the reinsurer). Whereas the first insurer freely decides on reinsurance, the reinsurer is obliged to take over every risk that the first insurer hands over to them; a scheme suitable for reinsurance of those risks that the assignor knows they will occur but does not know when or to what extent.

(3) obligatory – obligatory. Such scheme is binding on both parties, usually concluded for a longer period and typically takes the form of a framework reinsurance agreement covering all transactions of the same risk for a number of recurring cases of reinsurance. For example, household insurance, i.e., for the entire insurance portfolio, where the reinsurance parameters are precisely agreed.

(4) obligatory – facultative. According to this modality, the insurer is obliged to assign part of each risk assumed but the reinsurer may or may not assume the offered part of the risk. This scheme is used in special cases, usually between affiliate companies; for instance, an insurance company may undertake in this way to its affiliated reinsurance undertaking to offer it insurance risks to reinsurance as a matter of priority, and it is up to the reinsurance undertaking to decide whether to cover that risk.[750]

757. In terms of the manner of reinsurance, we distinguish between proportional and non-proportional (damage) reinsurance.

758. A proportional reinsurance contract is an agreement that obliges the assignor company to assign and the reinsurer to accept a share of the risks from the agreed insurance covered by the contract. The reinsurer contributes proportionally to the premium, as well as to the damages and certain expenses incurred by the assignor company. Proportional reinsurance is further divided into quota reinsurance[751] and excess reinsurance.[752]

---

750. For more details, *see* Karfíková, Marie; Přikryl, Vladimír, Čechová, Jana. *Základy pojišťovacího práva.* 1st ed. Praha: Orac, 2001, p. 119; Karfíková, Marie; Přikryl, Vladimír; Vybíral, Roman et al. *Pojišťovací právo.* 2nd revised ed. Praha: Leges, 2018; Cipra, Tomáš. *Zajištění a přenos rizik v pojišťovnictví.* 1st ed. Praha: Grada Publishing, 2004; Ducháčková, Eva. *Pojištění a pojišťovnictví.* 1st ed. Praha: Ekopress, 2015; Zuzaňák, Aleš; Šulcová, Jaroslava; Hora, Jan. *Příručka pro zprostředkovatele pojištění.* 2nd ed. Praha: Linde, 2011.

751. Quota reinsurance contract – the assignor company is obliged to assign and the reinsurer is obliged to accept a fixed part of each risk accepted by the assignor company. The reinsurer participates proportionally in all damages and receives the same share of the premium. However, the reinsurer must pay the assignor company the agreed commission. https://www.cap.cz/slovnikenc

752. Excess reinsurance contract (Surplus Contract) is an agreement in which the assignor company undertakes to assign to the reinsurer and the reinsurer is obliged to accept the part of the risk that is beyond the set framework, which covers the insurance company itself. An assignor company has the right to decide how much of its own debit it wants to keep for each individual risk. The contract stipulates the maximum amount of own debit and the total capacity of the existing contract.

759. Non-proportional reinsurance is divided into reinsurance of the second risk, excess of loss reinsurance, and reinsurance of the annual excess of claims. A non-proportional reinsurance contract is an agreement according to which the reinsurer pays all damages that exceed a certain limit of its own debit specified by the assignor company (excess of damages). In the case of reinsurance of the excess of damages, the reinsurer participates in the compensation of damages only if the damages exceed the agreed limit, up to a specified amount. This amount is called the layer. Three basic factors are important, namely the frequency of claims incurred in a specified period, the amount of insurance benefits within an individual claim case, and the deviation of the benefits paid from the average.

760. Starting in 2010, the Single European Passport also applies to reinsurance companies, which allows them to operate in the territory of EU, either on the basis of the right to establish their branches or on the basis of freedom to temporarily provide services within the scope of authorization. European law has a significant impact on national regulation on insurance and reinsurance activities. By implementing Directive (EU) 2016/97 of the European Parliament and of the Council of 20 January 2016 on insurance distribution (IDD), the categories of intermediaries were newly determined in the Czech Republic (diminishing from the original six to four), the insurance agents and brokers fall into the group of independent insurance intermediaries, a new category of tied agents and supplementary insurance intermediaries is also emerging.[753] A new time limit for the validity of the brokerage authorization has also been introduced, to a maximum of two years, which can be extended by twelve months, via an application to the CNB.[754]

This is determined by the maximum number of multiples of its own debit that can be assigned to the reinsurance. Any risk that is less than the debit itself is fully covered by the insurer https://www.cap.cz/slovnikenc

753. *See also* Part VII. Insurance Intermediaries.

754. *See* § 9 AoDIR.

Chapter 2. Co-insurance

761. Co-insurance represents the distribution of insurance risks among several insurers and is historically older than reinsurance. The principles 'one for one, no one for another' apply (Lloyd's insurance company).[755] It is especially advantageous for large insurance risks which exceed the capabilities of one insurer, or if the insurer does not want to bear the insurance risk itself.[756]

762. Co-insurance in terms of Czech private law represents a type of multiple insurance[757] that arises if an insurance contract has been concluded between the policyholder on the one hand and more insurers represented by the leading insurer on the other, and if the policyholder has undertaken to pay a single premium for the entire co-insurance. It is important that the right to premiums arises only to the leading insurer; insurers then settle with each other. The right to the insurance indemnity is asserted against the leading insurer; insurers shall mutually settle according to their shares and where no shares have been stipulated, they are conclusively presumed to be equal.[758]

763. The leading insurer acts in the name of other insurers and exercises all rights and duties arising from the co-insurance contract, in particular sets the insurance conditions and the amount of premiums, manages the co-insurance, receives claim notifications of insured events and carries out investigations necessary to determine the extent of the insurers' duty to provide insurance indemnity etc. If no manner of premium income has been stipulated, the leading insurer shall also receive premiums.[759]

764. Within a co-insurance relationship, a contract may also be concluded between the policyholder and several insurers who stipulated, in the name and on the account of all the insurers, a common approach when insuring certain insurance perils, and who determined the leading insurer or, where applicable, entrusted a joint body created for this purpose or an insurance agent qualified for a higher level of professional competence with performing the leading insurer's duties.[760]

765. It should be noted that co-insurance can arise both with the knowledge of the policyholder and even without it. A typical example is reinsurance, where there

755. *See* Drdla, Miloš; Martinovičová, Dana. *Bankovnictví a pojišťovnictví.* Brno: Brno International Business School, 2005, p. 190.
756. Vávrová, Eva. *Finanční řízení komerčních pojišťoven.* 1st ed. Praha: Grada, 2014; Jandová, Lucie; Šlauf, Petr; Svejkovský, Jaroslav. *Pojištění v novém občanském zákoníku. Komentář: [§ 2756-2872].* 1st ed. Praha: C. H. Beck, 2014; Haas, Karel. In: Švestka, Jiří; Dvořák, Jan; Fiala, Josef et al. *Občanský zákoník: komentář. Svazek VI (§ 2521–3081).* 1st ed. Praha: Wolters Kluwer ČR, 2014.
757. *See also* Part II, Ch. 5, §1, III. Multiple Insurance.
758. § 2817(3) CC.
759. § 2817(1) CC.
760. § 2817(2) CC.

is only a contract between the insurer and the policyholder, which means that there is no contractual relationship between the policyholder and other insurers (i.e., an indirect co-insurance).[761]

766. In the case of co-insurance, there may also be another form of cooperation between the insurers. They may create a pool on the co-insurance side (*see* below).

761. K. Haas draws attention to the incorrectness of subordinating indirect co-insurance to the current legal regulation of co-insurance in the Civil Code. He states that such a concept is in direct conflict with the wording of the Civil Code on plural insurance pursuant to § 2816. For more, *see* Haas, Karel. In: Švestka, Jiří; Dvořák, Jan; Fiala, Josef et al. *Občanský zákoník: komentář. Svazek VI (§ 2521–3081).* 1st ed. Praha: Wolters Kluwer ČR, 2014, pp. 633 et seq. Similarly, Růžička, Hynek. In: Petrov, Jan; Výtisk, Michal; Beran, Vladimír et al. *Občanský zákoník: komentář.* 1st ed. Praha: C. H. Beck, 2017. p. 2766.

Chapter 3. Pooling

767. Pool insurance takes place within an association of several insurance institutions to cover for risks of an excessively dangerous nature, such as nuclear or radiation risks, war risks and risks in air transport. The essence lies in the fact that all participants bring in all their insurances of a certain type, which newly creates a larger insurance pool. Pool participants then receive a fixed share, which usually corresponds to their contribution. The administration is usually entrusted to one of the members or to the 'pool office', both entitled to the agreed remuneration. It is created on the basis of an agreement between a larger number of contractual partners. A characteristic feature is the transfer of own insurance business to the pool and, on the other hand, the takeover of the business of other members of the pool into reinsurance.

768. It is usually a complex arrangement of relations between members, which are most often established to cover risks of a specially defined nature (nuclear and war risks, risks of liability of pharmaceutical manufacturers and aviation or space risks). Members can be divided into three categories: transmitting and receiving pool trade, transmitting only, and receiving only.[762]

769. An example of pool insurance in the Czech Republic can be the Czech Nuclear Insurance Pool, which has been operating since 1995 in the form of pool insurance for liability insurance for damage from the operation of nuclear facilities. It is an association of companies insuring and reinsuring the risks associated with the operation of nuclear facilities and with the transport of nuclear materials. Nuclear facilities covered by the pool include nuclear power plants, nuclear fuel cycle facilities, small-scale research reactors, medical and industrial applications of radioisotopes, radioactive waste repositories, radioactive waste storage facilities and other facilities.

770. At present, the Czech Nuclear Insurance Pool participates in the insurance and reinsurance of more than 386 nuclear power plants worldwide, including both of the Czech nuclear power plants Dukovany and Temelín. Regular risk inspections of both Czech nuclear power plants performed by international teams of engineers are designed primarily to assess risks for insurance purposes. The recommendations of specialists are also used by power plant operators to reduce the risk of operating these nuclear facilities. The Czech Nuclear Insurance Pool operates within the global community of national nuclear pools, with which it actively develops business and technical cooperation. Within the framework of trade exchange, it cooperates on the basis of active (i.e., taken over) and passive (i.e., handed over) reinsurance with more than twenty foreign national pools.[763]

---

762. *See also* Drdla, Miloš; Martinovičová, Dana. *Bankovnictví a pojišťovnictví.* Brno: Brno International Business School, 2005; Vávrová, Eva. *Finanční řízení komerčních pojišťoven.* 1st ed. Praha: Grada, 2014; Haas, Karel. In: Švestka, Jiří; Dvořák, Jan; Fiala, Josef et al. *Občanský zákoník: komentář. Svazek VI (§ 2521–3081).* 1st ed. Praha: Wolters Kluwer ČR, 2014, pp. 631 et seq.
763. https://www.nuclearpool.cz/index.php/cs/cz-o-nas/cz-cinnost.

Part IX. Taxation of Insurance

771. Premiums paid under an insurance contract are private law in nature, which is why we sometimes call them private insurance premiums, while premiums where the obligation to pay is imposed directly by law, and these premiums are revenue of public budgets, are referred to as public insurance premiums.

772. Public insurance premiums are typically social security contributions and public health insurance premiums. Public premiums are non-refundable, involuntary, conditionally equivalent and non-punitive pecuniary benefits imposed by law, administered by the state or other persons performing financial public administration (such as health insurance companies), which are public revenues of public budgets, namely revenues usually purposeful, regular, periodic and planned.[764]

773. The tax legislation defines a large group of incomes that are exempt from tax. According to the provisions of § 4 of the Income Tax Act, income obtained in the form of a benefit from sickness insurance, pension insurance, financial assistance to victims of crime, social security, benefits from the application of state employment policy instruments and public health insurance, benefits from insurance contracts on pension insurance and benefits from foreign compulsory insurance of the same type are exempt from tax; however, in the case of income in the form of a regularly paid pension, a maximum of thirty-six times the minimum wage applicable on 1 January of the calendar year shall be exempt from tax on such income for the tax period not included.[765]

774. Furthermore, income from disability pension from supplementary pension insurance with a state contribution for a definite period, disability pension for a specified period and lump sum pension insurance premiums, payment of funds of a pension savings upon termination of pension savings and other benefits from personal insurance[766] are exempt from income tax.

764. Karfíková, Marie. *Teorie finančního práva a finanční vědy.* 1st ed. Praha: Wolters Kluwer, 2017.
765. *See* § 4(1)(h) of the Income Tax Act.
766. With the exception of one-off benefits, severance payments or surrender benefits and pensions from pension insurance and life insurance, namely life insurance, death or survival insurance, pension insurance and supplementary pension savings, which are defined by the period of their receipt, and with the exception of other income from personal insurance, which is not an insurance benefit and does not constitute the termination of the insurance contract. – *see* § 4(1)(l)(4) of the Income Tax Act.

775. Conversely, the following income concerning the insurance and premiums is subject to income tax (as income from dependent activity): payment by an employer in the total amount of a maximum of CZK 50,000 per year as:

(i) the contribution to the supplementary pension insurance with the state contribution remitted to the account of its employee with the pension company, an employer's contribution to the SPS remitted to the account of its employee with the pension company;
(ii) a pension insurance contribution paid in favour of its employee to a pension insurance with a pension insurance institution, on the basis of a contract concluded between the employee and the pension insurance institution, or on the basis of an otherwise agreed employee's participation in the pension insurance, provided that the payment of benefits from pension insurance was concluded up to sixty calendar months and at the same time not earlier than the year of reaching the age of 60, and provided that the employee is entitled to benefits from the pension insurance and, in the event of the employee's death, another person, except the employer who paid the pension contribution;
(iii) a contribution to insurance premiums paid by an employer to the insurance company on behalf of the employee for their life insurance or death or survival insurance, or to pension insurance, even when arranging earlier benefits in the event of entitlement to a retirement pension or disability pension for a third-degree disability, or in the event that the insured person becomes disabled in the third degree, or in the event of death, provided that the payment of insurance benefits is agreed in the insurance contract only after 60 calendar months from the conclusion of the contract and at the earliest in the calendar year during which the insured reaches the age of 60.

776. The premiums paid by a taxpayer for private life insurance can be deducted.[767] A maximum of CZK 24,000 can be deducted for the tax period, regardless of how many insurance contracts with various insurance companies the taxpayer has concluded.

777. The supplementary pension insurance benefit with a state contribution is considered to be the tax base after reduction by paid contributions and state contributions. The pension insurance benefit is considered to be the tax base after

767. Provided that the payment of insurance benefits (pension or a lump sum) is agreed in the insurance contract only after sixty calendar months from the conclusion of the contract in a calendar year during which the taxpayer reaches the age of 60 and that according to the terms of the insurance contract the payment of other income that is not an insurance benefit and does not constitute termination of the insurance contract is not allowed. In the case of an insurance contract with a fixed sum insured in the event of survival, additionally provided that the insurance contract with a fixed sum insured for life with an insurance period of five to fifteen years inclusive has an agreed sum of at least CZK 40,000 and an insurance contract with a fixed life the sum insured for the event of survival with an insurance period of more than fifteen years has an agreed sum insured of at least CZK 70,000. In the case of pension insurance, the agreed sum insured is considered to be the corresponding one-off indemnity. In the case of a one-off premium, the premium paid is proportionally calculated for the tax period according to the duration of the insurance with an accurate account of days. *See* § 15(6) of the Income Tax Act.

deduction of contributions paid. The SPS benefit is considered to be the tax base after deduction of contributions paid and state contributions. In the case of pensions, contributions to supplementary pension insurance, state contributions to supplementary pension insurance, contributions to pension insurance, contributions to SPS and state contributions to SPS are spread over a defined period of receiving a pension.

778. Lump sum compensation or redemption (severance payment) from supplementary pension insurance with state contribution for the determination of the tax base is not reduced by contributions paid to the pension company by an employer for employees after 1 January 2000. A lump sum pension insurance benefit or a benefit paid upon early termination of pension insurance is not reduced by contributions paid by an employer for the benefit of the employee. Lump sum compensation or redemption (severance pay) from SPS for the determination of the tax base is not reduced by contributions paid to the pension company by an employer for employees, except for contributions to supplementary pension insurance with state contribution paid to the pension fund by an employer for employees before 1 January 2000 in the event that the participant's funds have been transferred from the supplementary pension insurance with a state contribution to the participant's SPS, from which the lump sum compensation or severance pay is paid.[768]

779. Benefits from private life insurance are considered to be the tax base (as an income from capital assets) but after the deduction of premiums paid. Other income from personal insurance, which is not an insurance benefit and does not constitute the termination of the insurance contract, is considered to be the tax base after reduction of the premium paid on the date of payment, up to the amount of this income. The severance pay is principally reduced by the premium paid to determine the tax base.[769]

780. A contribution in the total amount of a maximum of CZK 24,000 paid by the taxpayer may be deducted from the tax base in the tax period if such contribution was paid towards:

(i) supplementary pension insurance with a state contribution under a contract concluded between the taxpayer and the pension company; the amount that can be deducted in this way is equal to the sum of the parts of the monthly contributions which, in the individual calendar months of the tax period, exceeded the amount from which the maximum state contribution is applicable;
(ii) pension insurance under a pension insurance contract concluded between the taxpayer and the pension insurance institution, provided that the payment of pension insurance benefits was agreed after sixty calendar months and at the same time not earlier than the year of reaching the age of 60; the amount that

768. *See* § 8(6) of the Income Tax Act.
769. *See* § 8(7) of the Income Tax Act.

can be deducted in this way is equal to the sum of the contributions paid by the taxpayer to their pension insurance for the tax period;

(iii) SPS according to the contract on SPS concluded between the taxpayer and the pension company; the amount that can be deducted in this way is equal to the sum of the parts of the monthly contributions which, in the individual calendar months of the tax period, exceeded the amount from which the maximum state contribution is applicable.[770]

781. With regard to insurance companies and their income, there are further exemptions of monetary payments from the corporate income tax base in the actual Czech tax legislation. Nevertheless, these exemptions are only in regard to a health insurance company. None of the following are subject to income tax: any income of a health insurance company in the form of public health insurance premiums, fines imposed on policyholders or premium payers, penalties imposed on premium payers, surcharges to the insurance premium assessed by an employer, reimbursement of the costs of health services incurred by the health insurance company as a result of the culpable unlawful conduct of a third party towards the insured, payments for occupational health services and specific health care from an employer, deposit according to the legal regulation governing departmental, branch, company and other health insurance companies, repayable financial assistance from the state budget to cover the costs of provided paid services after the exhaustion of the reserve fund in the event of insolvency of General Health Insurance Company,[771] special-purpose subsidies from the state budget, receivables for reimbursed health services provided in the Czech Republic to foreign insured persons which are natural persons for whom health services have been reimbursed in accordance with promulgated international social security agreements approved by the Parliament and by which the Czech Republic is bound, or directly applicable EU law.[772]

770. If a taxpayer's supplementary pension insurance with state contribution, pension insurance or supplementary pension savings expired without the right to a pension, one-off settlement or lump sum benefit from the pension insurance and at the same time the taxpayer was paid a severance pay related to the termination of the pension insurance, the right to deduct the non-taxable part of the tax base expires. *See* § 15(5)(c) of the Income Tax Act.

771. https://www.vzp.cz/.

772. *See* § 18(2)(e) of the Income Tax Act.

Part X. Risk Management and Prevention

782. The insurance company is obliged to establish, maintain and apply an effective management and control system for the entire period of its activities, which includes, *inter alia*, risk management (§ 7(1) IA).[773] The risk management system shall include the reporting strategies and procedures necessary for the continuous identification, measurement, monitoring, management and internal reporting of risks to which an insurance undertaking is or may be exposed. It must enable the assessment of risks individually and in their aggregate, including the evaluation of their interdependencies. The risk management system must be appropriately integrated into the organizational structure of the insurance company and persons with key functions must duly respect it in decision-making processes (§ 7b(1) IA).

783. For the area of risk management, the insurance company must have a written concept approved by its statutory body, the functionality of which is regularly, at least once a year, reviewed (§ 7(3) IA). The person responsible for risk management of the insurance company is one of the persons with a key function (§ 3(6)(k) IA).

784. There is no uniformly recognized definition of 'risk'. In the insurance industry, risk is usually defined as a negative deviation from the normal, which can manifest itself in damage, destruction or loss of life, health or property of the insured. The insurable risk must be identifiable, the occurrence of the event must be accidental, the risk and the damage arising from it must be quantifiable and the risk must be economically acceptable.[774] A summary of the risks to which the insurance company is exposed represents the risk profile of the insurance company. Risk management, taking over risks from clients and working with risk in general is the essence of insurance.[775]

---

773. On topic of risk management and prevention in the insurance industry, *see* e.g., Cipra, Tomáš. *Riziko ve financích a pojišťovnictví: Basel III a Solvency II.* 1st ed. Praha: Ekopress, 2015; Vávrová, Eva. *Finanční řízení komerčních pojišťoven.* 1st ed. Praha: Grada Publishing, 2014; Řezáč, František. *Řízení rizik v pojišťovnictví.* 1st ed. Brno: Masarykova Univerzita, 2011; Přikryl, Vladimír; Čechová, Jana. *Zákon o pojišťovnictví. Komentář.* 1st ed. Praha: Wolters Kluwer, 2017.

774. *See also* Part II, Ch. 2. Insurable risk and insurable interest; for a comprehensive overview of particular definitions of 'risk' *see* e.g., Řezáč, František. *Řízení rizik v pojišťovnictví.* 1st ed. Brno: Masarykova Univerzita, 2011, pp. 9 et seq.

775. Vávrová, Eva. *Finanční řízení komerčních pojišťoven.* 1st ed. Praha: Grada Publishing, 2014, p. 55.

785. The classification of risks to which commercial insurance companies are exposed in their activities is very diverse.[776] It can be usually distinguished:

- own (internal) risks – risks related to the insurance company's own business activities;
- extraneous risks – risks that the insurance company takes over from its clients.[777]

From another point of view, risks can be divided as follows:[778]

- insurance (insurance-technical) risk – risks associated with underwriting risks, calculation of insurance premiums and creation of technical reserves;
- market risk – expresses the effect of volatility on the future value of investments in the financial market (including credit risk, currency risk, equity risk, commodity risk, credit spread risk and correlation risk);
- credit risk – the risk that a partner will not fully meet its financial obligations;
- liquidity risk – the risk of inability to monetize the investments and other assets in order to repay debts due;
- operational risk – the risk of loss caused by failure of persons, systems or due to external events (usually including legal and tax risks, the risk of non-compliance with legislation, the risk of fraud, business risks, misselling, etc.).

786. Risk management itself is a complex of actions aimed at finding and assessing the most significant risks, deciding which risks can be taken and turned into chances and which must be rejected, and to mitigate or eliminate risks systematically by appropriate instruments. The basic goal of risk management is to achieve the safest possible operation of the economic activity of a commercial insurance company while minimizing the costs of ensuring this security.[779]

787. For the effective setting up of the risk management system, it is appropriate that the risk analysis includes the following steps:[780]

- risk identification – risk factor recognition;
- risk classification – sorting risk into defined groups;
- creation of a list of risks;
- risk assessment – determining the probability of occurrence of a risk and the scope of its impact on the insurance company.

---

776. Cf. Řezáč, František. *Řízení rizik v pojišťovnictví.* 1st ed. Brno: Masarykova Univerzita, 2011, pp. 13 et seq.
777. Vávrová, Eva. *Finanční řízení komerčních pojišťoven.* 1st ed. Praha: Grada Publishing, 2014, pp. 55 et seq.
778. Cf. Majtánová, Anna; Daňhel, Jaroslav; Ducháčková, Eva; Kafková, Eva. *Pojišťovnictví – Teorie a praxe.* 1st ed. Praha: Ekopress, 2006, p. 224; Cipra, Tomáš. *Riziko ve financích a pojišťovnictví: Basel III a Solvency II.* 1st ed. Praha: Ekopress, 2015, pp. 235 et seq.; *see also* legal definition of risks in the provision of § 3 (7) IA.
779. Vávrová, Eva. *Finanční řízení komerčních pojišťoven.* 1st ed. Praha: Grada Publishing, 2014, p. 75.
780. *Ibid.*, p. 76.

788. As part of the risk management process, emphasis must be placed primarily on prevention.[781] Measures in the field of prevention, reduction and mitigation of risks may include in particular:[782]

- preventive activities – direct financing of preventive measures through loss prevention funds,[783] awareness-raising activities leading to the reduction of risk realization, certain elements within the construction of insurance products (bonus/malus systems, deductible, etc.);
- reinsurance – transfer of risk or its part to another entity, i.e., reinsurer (usually another insurance or reinsurance company);[784]
- deductible – expresses the part of the damage, the reparation of which the client ensures from its own resources;
- risk sharing – co-insurance, i.e., horizontal distribution of risk between several insurers;[785]
- risk pooling – associations of insurers for the joint coverage of certain types of risks;[786]
- risk retention – financing the consequences of acceptable (tolerable) risks from the insurance company's own resources;
- securitization of insurance risks – merging of assets into a tradable unit in order to obtain additional insurance or reinsurance capacity (e.g., catastrophe bonds).

789. Control and monitoring play a crucial role in the risk management process. Insurance companies should continuously monitor all changes in risk factors and should also constantly assess the effectiveness of established risk management systems. If a new risk arises, insurance companies should have plans in advance on how to respond to the risks and what management procedures to apply.[787]

781. Prevention of damage and mitigation of their consequences is an immanent part of insurance business – cf. § 3(1)(f) IA.
782. According to Řezáč, František. *Řízení rizik v pojišťovnictví.* 1st ed. Brno: Masarykova Univerzita, 2011, pp. 34 et seq.
783. For example, the Loss prevention fund managed by the Czech Insurers' Bureau, established pursuant to § 23b MTPLIA.
784. For more details, *see* Part VIII., Ch. 1. Reinsurance.
785. For more details, *see* Part II., Ch. 5, §1, III. Multiple insurance.
786. For more details, *see* Part VIII., Ch. 3. Pooling.
787. Vávrová, Eva. *Finanční řízení komerčních pojišťoven.* 1st ed. Praha: Grada Publishing, 2014, p. 79.

Selected Bibliography

Monographs and Commentaries

Bahýľová, Lenka; Filip, Jan; Molek, Pavel; Podhrázký, Milan; Suchánek, Radovan; Šimíček, Vojtěch; Vyhnálek, Ladislav. *Ústava České republiky.* 1st ed. Praha: Linde, 2010. ISBN 978-80-7201-814-7.

Bakeš, Milan; Karfíková, Marie; Kotáb, Petr; Marková, Hana et al. *Finanční právo.* 6th revised ed. Praha: C. H. Beck, 2012. ISBN 978-80-7400-440-7.

Basedow, Jürgen; Birds, John; Clarke, Malcolm; Cousy, Herman; Heiss, Helmut; Loacker, Leander (ed.). *Principles of European Insurance Contract Law (PEICL).* 2nd expanded ed. Köln: Verlag Dr. Otto Schmidt KG, 2016. ISBN 978-3-504-08002-0.

Bohman, Ludvík; Wawerková, Magdalena. *Zákon o pojistné smlouvě: komentář.* 2nd updated ed. Praha: Linde, 2009. ISBN 978-80-7201-755-3.

Bokšová, Jiřina. *Účetnictví komerčních pojišťoven – specifika v ČR.* 1st ed. Praha: Wolters Kluwer, 2010. ISBN 978-80-7357-521-2.

Bříza, Petr. *Volba práva a volba soudu v mezinárodním obchodě.* 1st ed. Praha: C. H. Beck, 2012. ISBN 978-80-7179-606-0.

Bříza, Petr; Břicháček, Tomáš; Fišerová, Zuzana; Horák, Pavel; Ptáček, Lubomír; Svoboda, Jiří. *Zákon o mezinárodním právu soukromém. Komentář.* 1st ed. Praha: C. H. Beck, 2014. ISBN 978-80-7400-528-2.

Bušta, Pavel; Přikryl, Vladimír. *Zákon o pojištění odpovědnosti z provozu vozidla s komentářem (ve znění 16 novel).* 5th ed. Praha: Venice Music Production, 2014. ISBN 978-80-9042-705-1.

Cabada, Ladislav; Kubát, Michal et al. *Úvod do studia politické vědy.* 1st ed. Plzeň: Aleš Čeněk, 2007. ISBN 978-80-7380-076-5.

Cabada, Ladislav; Šanc, David. *Český stranický systém ve 20. Století.* 1st ed. Plzeň: Aleš Čeněk, 2005. ISBN 80-86898-50-4.

Cipra, Tomáš. *Riziko ve financích a pojišťovnictví: Basel III a Solvency II.* 1st ed. Praha: Ekopress, 2015. ISBN: 978-80-87865-24-8.

Cipra, Tomáš. *Zajištění a přenos rizik v pojišťovnictví.* 1st ed. Praha: Grada Publishing, 2004. ISBN 80-247-0838-8.

Cousy, Herman. *Changing Insurance Contract Law*: An *Age-Old*, Slow and *Unfinished Story*. Palgrave Macmillan Insurance Regulation in the European Union. Solvency II and Beyond; 2017, pp. 31–57. ISBN: 978-3-319-61215-7.

Daňhel, Jaroslav et al. *Pojistná teorie.* 2nd ed. Praha: Professional Publishing, 2006. ISBN 80-86946-00-2.

Dobiáš, Petr. *Pojištění podnikatelů ve vztazích s mezinárodním prvkem.* 1st ed. Praha: Leges, 2019. ISBN: 978-80-7502-348-3.

Drdla, Miloš; Martinovičová, Dana. *Bankovnictví a pojišťovnictví.* Brno: Brno International Business School, 2005.

Ducháčková, Eva. *Pojištění a pojišťovnictví.* 1st ed. Praha: Ekopress, 2015. ISBN 978-80-87865-25-5.

Ducháčková, Eva. *Principy pojištění a pojišťovnictví.* 3rd updated ed. Praha: Ekopress, 2009. ISBN 978-80-86929-51-4.

Ducháčková, Eva; Daňhel, Jaroslav. *Teorie pojistných trhů.* 1st ed. Praha: Professional Publishing, 2010. ISBN 978-80-7431-015-7.

Dvořák, Jan; Švestka, Jiří; Zuklínová, Michaela et al. *Občanské právo hmotné. Svazek 1. Díl první: Obecná část.* 1st ed. Praha: Wolters Kluwer, 2013. ISBN 978-80-7478-326-5.

Eliáš, Karel et al. *Nový občanský zákoník s aktualizovanou důvodovou zprávou a rejstříkem.* 1st ed. Ostrava: Sagit, 2012. ISBN 978-80-7208-922-2.

Fenyves, Attila; Kissling, Christa; Perner, Stefan et al. *Compulsory Liability Insurance from a European Perspective.* Berlin: De Gruyter, 2016. ISBN 978-3-11-048469-4.

Filip, Jan. *Ústavní právo České republiky: 1 Základní pojmy a instituty. Ústavní základy ČR.* 4th revised and supplemented ed. Brno: Masarykova univerzita, Doplněk, 2003. ISBN 80-210-3254-5.

Gerloch, Aleš; Hřebejk, Jiří; Zoubek, Vladimír. *Ústavní systém České republiky.* 2nd revised and supplemented ed. Praha: Prospektrum, 1996. ISBN 80-7175-041-7.

Holländer, Pavel. *Filosofie práva.* 1st ed. Plzeň: Aleš Čeněk, 2006. ISBN 80-86898-96-2.

Hradec, Milan; Zárybnická, Jana; Křivohlávek, Václav. *Pojištění a pojišťovnictví.* 1st ed. Praha: Vysoká škola finanční a správní, 2005. ISBN 80-86754-48-0.

Huleš, Jan; Hornigová, Jana. *Účetnictví pojišťoven.* 2nd updated and revised ed. Praha: Linde, 2009. ISBN: 978-80-7201-753-9.

Hulmák, Milan et al. *Občanský zákoník VI. Závazkové právo. Zvláštní část (§ 2055–3014). Komentář.* 1st ed. Praha: C. H. Beck, 2014. ISBN 978-80-7400-287-8.

Janasová, Marie. *Účetnictví pojišťoven v ČR.* 1st ed. Ostrava: VŠB – Technická univerzita Ostrava, 2006. ISBN 80-248-1147-2.

Janata, Jiří. *Metodika přípravy rizikové zprávy pro pojistné trhy.* 1st ed. Praha: Professional Publishing, 2010. ISBN 978-80-7431-032-4.

Jandová, Lucie; Šlauf, Petr; Svejkovský, Jaroslav. *Pojištění v novém občanském zákoníku. Komentář: [§ 2756-2872].* 1st ed. Praha: C. H. Beck, 2014. ISBN 978-80-7400-530-5.

Jandová, Lucie; Vojtek, Petr. *Zákon o pojištění odpovědnosti z provozu vozidla. Komentář.* 2nd ed. Praha: C. H. Beck, 2019. ISBN 978-80-7400-765-1.

Jehlička, Oldřich; Švestka, Jiří et al. *Občanský zákoník. Komentář.* 4th ed. Praha: C. H. Beck, 1997. ISBN 80-7179-147-4.

Karfíková, Marie. *Teorie finančního práva a finanční vědy.* 1st ed. Praha: Wolters Kluwer, 2017. ISBN 978-80-7552-935-0.

Karfíková, Marie; Přikryl, Vladimír et al. *Pojišťovací právo.* 1st ed. Praha: Leges. 2010. ISBN 978-80-87212-45-5.

Karfíková, Marie; Přikryl, Vladimír, Čechová, Jana. *Základy pojišťovacího práva.* 1st ed. Praha: Orac, 2001. ISBN 80-86199-27-4.

Karfíková, Marie; Přikryl, Vladimír; Vybíral, Roman et al. *Pojišťovací právo.* 2nd revised ed. Praha: Leges, 2018, ISBN: 978-80-7502-271-4.

Kazda, Petr; Kazdová, Karolína. *Zákon o pojištění odpovědnosti z provozu vozidla. Komentář.* 1st ed. Praha: Wolters Kluwer. 2016. ISBN 978-80-7552-259-7.

Klíma, Karel, et al. *Komentář k Ústavě a Listině.* 2nd extended ed. Plzeň: Aleš Čeněk, 2009. ISBN 978-80-7380-140-3.

Koldinská, Kristina; Tröster, Petr et al. *Právo sociálního zabezpečení.* 7th substantially revised ed. Praha: C. H. Beck, 2018, ISBN 978-80-7400-692-0.

Kučera, Zdeněk; Pauknerová, Monika; Růžička, Květoslav et al. *Mezinárodní právo soukromé.* 8th ed. Plzeň – Brno: Aleš Čeněk – Doplněk. 2015. ISBN 978-80-7380-550-0.

Kurka, René; Paříková, Anežka. *Subjekty finančního trhu. Vybrané aspekty likvidace a insolvence.* 1st ed. Praha: C. H. Beck, 2014, ISBN 978-80-7400-277-9.

Kysela, Jan. *Deset let Ústavy České republiky: východiska, stav, perspektivy.* 1st ed. Praha: Eurolex Bohemia, 2003. ISBN 80-86432-45-9.

Lavický, Petr et al. *Občanský soudní řád (§ 1 – 250l). Praktický komentář.* 1st ed. Praha: Wolters Kluwer, 2016. ISBN 978-80-7478-986-1.

Lavický, Petr et al. *Občanský zákoník I. Obecná část (§ 1–654). Komentář.* 1st ed. Praha: C. H. Beck. 2014. ISBN 978-80-7400-529-9.

Machková, Hana; Sato, Alexej; Zamykalová, Miroslava et al. *Mezinárodní obchod a marketing.* 1st ed. Praha: Grada, 2002. ISBN: ISBN 80-247-0364-5.

Majtánová, Anna; Daňhel, Jaroslav; Ducháčková, Eva; Kafková, Eva. *Pojišťovnictví – Teorie a praxe.* 1st ed. Praha: Ekopress, 2006. ISBN 80-86929-19-1.

Marvan, Miroslav; Chaloupecký, Josef. *Dějiny pojišťovnictví v Československu. 2. díl, Dějiny pojišťovnictví v Československu (1918-1945).* 1st ed. Bratislava: Alfa Konti, 1993. ISBN 80-88739-01-2.

Marvan, Miroslav; Chaloupecký, Josef. *Dějiny pojišťovnictví v Československu. 3. díl, Dějiny pojišťovnictví v Československu (1945-1992).* 1st ed. Praha: Česká pojišťovna, 1997. ISBN 80-238-8592-8.

Marvan, Miroslav; Patoprstý, Ján et al. *Dějiny pojišťovnictví v Československu, 1. díl, Dějiny pojišťovnictví v Československu do roku 1918.* Praha: Novinář, 1989.

Mesršmíd, Jaroslav. *Regulace pojišťovnictví v EU.* 1st ed. Praha: Professional Publishing, 2015. 978-80-7431-146-8.

Mesršmíd, Jaroslav; Kovář, Bedřich; Bohumský, Petr. *Životní pojištění.* 1st ed. Praha: Grada Publishing, 2002. ISBN 80-247-0146-4.

Novák, Miroslav; Lebeda, Tomáš et al. *Volební a stranické systémy. ČR v mezinárodním srovnání.* 1st ed. Dobrá Voda: Aleš Čeněk, 2004. ISBN 80-86473-88-0.

Novotný, Petr; Koukal, Pavel; Záhořová, Eva. *Nový občanský zákoník. Náhrada škody.* 1st ed. Praha: Grada Publishing, 2014. ISBN 978-80-247-5165-8.

Otavský-Hermann, Karel. *Soukromé pojišťovací právo československé podle zákona z 23. prosince 1917.* Praha: Česká akademie věd a umění, 1921.

Petrov, Jan; Výtisk, Michal; Beran, Vladimír et al. *Občanský zákoník: komentář.* 1st ed. Praha: C. H. Beck, 2017. ISBN 978-80-7400-653-1.

Plender, Richard; Wilderspin, Michael. *The European Private International Law of Obligations.* 3rd ed. London: Sweet & Maxwell, Thomson Reuters. 2009. ISBN 978-04-2195-490-8.

Přikryl, Vladimír; Čechová, Jana. *Zákon o pojišťovnictví. Komentář.* 1st ed. Praha: Wolters Kluwer. 2017. ISBN 978-80-7552-546-8.

Řezáč, František. *Řízení rizik v pojišťovnictví.* 1st ed. Brno: Masarykova Univerzita, 2011. ISBN 978-80-210-5637-4.

ŘEzáč, František; OS'Krdalová, Gabriela et al. *Marketingové ří;zení; komerční; pojišťovny.* 1st ed. Brno: Masarykova univerzita, 2009. ISBN 978-80-210-4799-0.

Rozehnalová, Naděžda; Valdhans, Jiří; Drličková, Klára; Kyselovská, Tereza. *Mezinárodní právo soukromé Evropské unie (Nařízení Řím I, Nařízení Řím II, Nařízení Brusel I).* 1st ed. Praha: Wolters Kluwer. 2013. ISBN 978-80-7478-016-5.

Schelle, Karel. *Vývoj právní úpravy pojišťovnictví.* 1st ed. Brno: Masarykova univerzita, 1994. ISBN 80-210-1014-2.

Schelle, Karel; HRADEC, Michal. *Historie právní úpravy pojišťovnictví.* 1st ed. Praha: Eurolex Bohemia, 2006. ISBN 80-86861-52-X.

Schelleová, Ilona; Schelle, Karel, et al. *Soudnictví: historie, současnost a perspektivy.* 1st ed. Praha: Eurolex Bohemia, 2004. ISBN 80-86432-65-3.

Schlossberger, Otakar. *Platební služby.* 1st ed. Praha: Management Press, 2012. ISBN 978-80-7261-238-3.

Škopová, Věra; Musilová, Radoslava; Krupičková, Hana. *Zákon o pojišťovacích zprostředkovatelích a samostatných likvidátorech pojistných událostí a předpisy související. Komentář.* 1st ed. Praha: C. H. Beck., 2006. ISBN 80-7179-476-7.

Sládeček, Vladimír; Mikule, Vladimír; Suchánek, Radovan; Syllová, Jindřiška. *Ústava České republiky. Komentář.* 2nd ed. Praha: C. H. Beck. 2016. ISBN 978-80-7400-590-9.

Sládeček, Vladimír; Mikule, Vladimír; Syllová, Jindřiška. *Ústava České republiky. Komentář.* 1st ed. Praha: C. H. Beck, 2007. ISBN 978-80-7179-869-9.

Smržová, Petra; Mrkývka, Petr. *Finanční a daňové právo.* 2nd updated and supplemented ed. Plzeň: Aleš Čeněk, 2016. ISBN 978-80-7380-639-2.

Spirit, Michal. *Pojistné právo.* 1st ed. Praha: Vysoká škola ekonomická, 2000. ISBN 80-245-0109-0.

Svejkovský, Jan et al. *Nový občanský zákoník: srovnání nové a současné úpravy občanského práva.* 1st ed. Praha: C. H. Beck, 2012. ISBN 978-80-7400-423-0.

Švestka, Jiří, Spáčil, Jiří; Škárová, Marta; Hulmák, Milan et al. *Občanský zákoník I. Komentář. § 1-549.* 1st ed. Praha: C. H. Beck, 2008. ISBN 978-80-7400-004-1.

Švestka, Jiří; Dvořák, Jan; Fiala, Josef et al. *Občanský zákoník: komentář. Svazek VI (§ 2521–3081).* 1st ed. Praha: Wolters Kluwer ČR, 2014. ISBN 978-80-7478-630-3.

Svoboda, Karel. *Historický vývoj pojišťovnictví.* Praha: Sdružení československého úřednictva ústavů peněžních, 1910.

Tomášek, Michal; Týč, Vladimír et al. *Právo Evropské unie.* 1st ed. Praha: Leges, 2013. ISBN 978-80-87576-53-3.

Vančurová, Alena; Klazar, Stanislav. *Sociální a zdravotní pojištění – úvod do problematiky.* 2nd ed. Praha: ASPI, 2008. ISBN: 80-7357-102-1.

Vávrová, Eva. *Finanční řízení komerčních pojišťoven.* 1st ed. Praha: Grada, 2014. ISBN 978-80-247-4662-3.

Velich, Roman. *Právní úprava pojištění odpovědnosti.* Rigorózní práce. Univerzita Karlova, 2019.

Zárybnická, Jana; Schelle, Karel. *Pojištění odpovědnosti za škodu (historie a současnost).* 1st ed. Ostrava: Key Publishing, 2010. ISBN 978-80-7418-061-3.

Zuzaňák, Aleš; Šulcová, Jaroslava; HORA, Jan. *Příručka pro zprostředkovatele pojištění.* 2nd ed. Praha: Linde, 2011. ISBN 978-80-7201-838-3.

Articles

Bakeš, Milan; Vybíral, Roman. *ZDPZ: Subrogace v oblasti pojišťovnictví se zaměřením na mezinárodní prvek.* AUC Iuridica 2020, No. 3, pp. 9-14.

Beran, Jiří; Indra, Milan; Urbanec, Jan. *ZDPZ: Účinnější ochrana spotřebitele a cesta k vyšší kredibilitě sektoru.* Pojistný obzor. 2018, No. 4, pp. 18–22.

Bušta, Pavel. *Nové smluvní pojištění odpovědnosti z provozu vozidla.* Pojistný obzor. 1999, No. 6.

Čechová, Jana; Přikryl, Vladimír. *Nový občanský zákoník: Zásadní změny v právní úpravě pojistné smlouvy – část I.* Pojistný obzor. 2012, No. 1, pp. 4–7.

Čechová, Jana; Přikryl, Vladimír. *Nový občanský zákoník: Zásadní změny v právní úpravě pojistné smlouvy – část II.* Pojistný obzor. 2012, No. 2, pp. 6–9.

Čechová, Jana; Přikryl, Vladimír. *Pojistná smlouva a její základní znaky.* Právní rozhledy. 2018, No. 10, pp. 364–366.

Čechová, Jana; Přikryl, Vladimír. *Vymezení vozidla pro účely pojištění odpovědnosti z provozu vozidla.* Pojistné rozpravy. 2018, No. 35, pp. 84–91.

Daňhel, Jaroslav; Ducháčková, Eva. *Pojistný trh roku 2018 se ponese ve znamení intenzivnější regulace.* Pojistný obzor. 2018, No. 1, pp. 12–13.

Dobiáš, Petr. *Autonomie vůle stran při uzavírání mezinárodních pojišťovacích a zajišťovacích smluv.* Sborník Dny práva 2016. Masarykova univerzita. Brno. 2017, pp. 7–27.

Dobiáš, Petr. *Evropské právo: Aplikace nařízení Řím I, Řím II a Brusel Ibis.* Pojistný obzor. 2016, No. 1, pp. 38–41.

Dobiáš, Petr. *Principles of European Insurance Contract Law in Comparison with Czech Law on Insurance Contracts.* Sborník Czech Yearbook of International Law 2010. Huntington, New York: Juris Publishing, 2010, pp. 111–125.

Dobiáš, Petr. *Vývoj právní úpravy pojistné smlouvy v rakouském Všeobecném zákoníku z roku 1811.* Sborník 200 let Všeobecného občanského zákoníku. Praha: Wolters Kluwer, 2011, pp. 612–622.

Ducháčková, Eva. *Výstupy z projektu k vývoji českého pojistného trhu.* Pojistné rozpravy. 2017, No. 34, pp. 4–10.

Horník, Jiří. *Leasing vozidel a nový systém tzv. 'povinného ručení'.* Pojistný obzor. 2000, No. 10, pp. 10–12.

Hulva, Tomáš. *Právní úprava pojistné smlouvy dle zákona č. 37/2004 Sb., o pojistné smlouvě (obecná ustanovení).* Právní rozhledy. 2005, No. 6, pp. 201–210.

Jandová, Lucie. *Aktuální vývoj judikatury v oblasti pojištění a náhrady škody.*

Pojistné rozpravy. 2018, No. 35, pp. 43–51.
Jandová, Lucie. *Judikatura posledních let v oblasti pojištění a náhrady újmy.* Pojistné rozpravy. 2019, No. 36, pp. 17–23.
Jandová, Lucie. *Pojištění odpovědnosti ve světle nové judikatury.* Pojistný obzor. 2020, No. 1, pp. 10–11.
Jandová, Lucie. *Pojistná legislativa dva roky po účinnosti nového občanského zákoníku – nejasnosti přetrvávají …* Pojistné rozpravy. 2015, No. 33, pp. 70–82.
Jandová, Lucie. *Výstupy z projektu implementace NOZ v praxi pojišťoven.* Pojistný obzor. 2013, No. 3, pp. 17–18.
Karfíková, Marie. *Pojištění odpovědnosti z provozu vozidla.* Daně. 1999, No. 11.
Karfíková, Marie; Vybíral, Roman. *Povinné pojištění v moderní ekonomice.* Pojistné rozpravy. 2018, No. 35, pp. 72–75.
Kubáň, Drahomír. *Účel dohledu v pojišťovnictví.* Pojistné rozpravy. 2019, No. 36, pp. 24–30.
Kubáň, Drahomír. *Vynutitelnost dohledových opatření a sankcionování.* Pojistné rozpravy. 2018, No. 35, pp. 37–42.
Kubátová, Irena. *Nařízení o panevropském osobním penzijním produktu.* Pojistný obzor. 2019, No. 2, pp. 18–21.
Kult, Alexandr; Škrabka, Jan. *Regulace flotilového pojištění po novele v reflexi názorů ČNB.* Pojistné rozpravy. 2020, No. 37, pp. 58–64.
Kult, Alexander, Škrabka, Jan. *Zásahy orgánu dohledu do autonomie vůle v oblasti pojištění.* Daně a finance. 2020, roč. 1, s. 33-37. ISSN 1801-6006.
Kunertová, Tereza. *PEPP: Jaké změny přinese nový panevropský penzijní produkt?* Pojistný obzor. 2019, No. 2, pp. 10–11.
Kunertová, Tereza. *Povolené činnosti pojišťoven v hledáčku bruselského regulátora.* Pojistný obzor. 2016, No. 2, pp. 47–50.
Mesršmíd, Jaroslav. *K přípravě pojišťovnictví na členství ČR v Evropské unii. Pojistný obzor.* 1998, No. 4.
Mesršmíd, Jaroslav. *PEPP a důchodový systém.* Pojistné rozpravy. 2019, No. 36, pp. 3–4.
Přikryl, Vladimír; Čechová, Jana. *Revize motorové směrnice.* Pojistný obzor. 2018, No. 4, pp. 9–15.
Růžička, Hynek. *PEICL – počátek cesty k jednotnému evropskému právu?* Pojistné rozpravy. 2012, No. 29, pp. 55–63.
Šenovský, Michail; Šenovský, Pavel. *Metody hodnocení rizika průmyslových zón.* In: Červený kohout: sborník příspěvků, 13th year of the conference, Hluboká nad Vltavou, 2010.
Silberová, Zuzana. *Dohled ČNB nad povinným ručením.* Pojistný obzor. 2017, No. 1, pp. 32–34.
Silberová, Zuzana. *Směrnice IDD a její transpozice z hlediska dohledu pojišťoven.* Pojistné rozpravy. 2018, No. 35, pp. 5–10.
Šimek, Robert. *Pojistný zájem a možnosti jeho přenositelnosti.* Pojistné rozpravy. 2019, No. 36, pp. 53–64.
Šimek, Robert. *Zpráva EIOPA o vývoji struktury trhu pojišťovacích zprostředkovatelů v EU.* Pojistný obzor. 2018, No. 4, pp. 23–27.
Šmotková, Michaela. *Změny ve flotilovém pojištění a výklad souvislosti s prodejem zboží a poskytováním služby.* Pojistný obzor. 2020, No. 4, pp. 20–23.

Vostatek, Jaroslav. *Odpovědnostní pojištění motorových vozidel: quo vadis?* Finance a úvěr. 1996, Nos 4 and 5.
Vyskočil, Michal. *Operační riziko v pojišťovnách.* Pojistné rozpravy. 2019, No. 36, pp. 31–34.
Žulavská, Lucie. *Revize motorové směrnice ve světle zprávy Výboru pro vnitřní trh a ochranu spotřebitele.* Pojistný obzor. 2018, No. 4, pp. 16–17.

Case Law

Resolution of the Supreme Court of the Czech Republic of 5 February 2008, file No. 25 Cdo 1957/2006.
Resolution of the Supreme Court of the Czech Republic of 4 September 2007, file No. 25 Cdo 271/2007.
Resolution of the Supreme Court of the Czech Republic of 30 August 2006, file No. 25 Cdo 638/2005; resolution of the Supreme Court of the Czech Republic of 29 March 2011, file No. 25 Cdo 948/2010.
Resolution of the Supreme Court of the Czech Republic of 28 November 2006, file No. 30 Cdo 427/2006.
Resolution of the Supreme Court of the Czech Republic of 28 August 2012, file No. 23 Cdo 500/2012.
Resolution of the Supreme Court of the Czech Republic of 26 November 2014, file No. 25 Cdo 2904/2014.
Resolution of the Supreme Court of the Czech Republic of 22 November 2011, file No. 32 Cdo 3266/2010.
Resolution of the Supreme Court of the Czech Republic of 20 September 2010, file No. 23 Cdo 3349/2009.
Resolution of the Supreme Court of the Czech Republic of 18 May 2011, file No. 23 Cdo 1583/2010.
Resolution of the Supreme Court of the Czech Republic of 18 August 2015, file No. 25 Cdo 2773/2015.
Resolution of the Supreme Court of the Czech Republic of 14 April 2011, file No. 25 Cdo 194/2009.
Resolution of the Supreme Court of the Czech Republic of 13 June 2016, file No. 25 Cdo 1119/2016.
Resolution of the Supreme Court of the Czech Republic of 23 April 2014, file No. 25 Cdo 644/2014, published in the Collection of Judicial Decisions and Opinions under No. 94/2014.
Resolution of the Municipal Court in Prague of 24 October 2008, file No. 29 Co 436/2008, published in the Collection of Judicial Decisions and Opinions under No. 93/2009.
Resolution of the Municipal Court in Prague of 24 April 2009, file No. 21 Co 139/2009, published in the Collection of Judicial Decisions and Opinions under No. 81/2011.
Resolution of the Municipal Court in Prague of 2 November 2016, file No. 19 Co 356/2016, published in the Collection of Judicial Decisions and Opinions under No. 49/2018.
Resolution of the Financial Arbitrator of 30 August 2016, file No. FA/ZP/141/2016.

Resolution of the Financial Arbitrator of 29 December 2016, file No. FA/ ZP/1897/ 2016.
Resolution of the Financial Arbitrator of 10 January 2017, file No. FA/ZP/1922/ 2016.
Resolution of the Constitutional Court of the Czech Republic of 5 June 2008, file No. II. ÚS 409/08.
Opinion of the Supreme Court of the Czech Socialist Republic, file No. Cpj 10/83, published in the Collection of Judicial Decisions and Opinions under No. 3/1984.
Opinion of the Civil Law and Commercial Division of the Supreme Court of the Czechoslovak Socialist Republic of 15 November 1972, file No. Cpjf 93/71, published in the Collection of Judicial Decisions and Opinions under No. 64/1972.
Judgement of the Supreme Court of the Slovak Socialist Republic of 27 October 1971, file No. 1 Cz 42/71, published in the Collection of Judicial Decisions and Opinions under No. 9/1972.
Judgement of the Supreme Court of the Slovak Socialist Republic of 23 April 1975, file No. 2 Cz 20/75.
Judgement of the Supreme Court of the Czechoslovak Republic of 21 November 1974, file No. 3 Cz 66/74, published in the Collection of Judicial Decisions and Opinions under No. 24/1976.
Judgement of the Supreme Court of the Czechoslovak Republic of 19 October 1938, file No. Rv I 513/38, (Vážný No. 17076/1938).
Judgement of the Supreme Court of the Czech Republic of 7 November 2017, file No. 28 Cdo 5970/2016.
Judgement of the Supreme Court of the Czech Republic of 7 June 2000, file No. 25 Cdo 1094/98.
Judgement of the Supreme Court of the Czech Republic of 7 February 2012, file No. 32 Cdo 4034/2010.
Judgement of the Supreme Court of the Czech Republic of 6 April 2016, file No. 25 Cdo 222/2015.
Judgement of the Supreme Court of the Czech Republic of 4 January 2010, file No. 28 Cdo 3784/2009.
Judgement of the Supreme Court of the Czech Republic of 31 July 2019, file No. 29 Cdo 3580/2017.
Judgement of the Supreme Court of the Czech Republic of 31 January 2017, file No. 23 Cdo 4297/2015, published in the Collection of Judicial Decisions and Opinions under No. 73/2018.
Judgement of the Supreme Court of the Czech Republic of 31 August 2017, file No. 25 Cdo 3485/2016, published in the Collection of Judicial Decisions and Opinions under No. 10/2018.
Judgement of the Supreme Court of the Czech Republic of 31 August 2011, file No. 30 Cdo 4173/2009.
Judgement of the Supreme Court of the Czech Republic of 30 September 2009, file No. 25 Cdo 800/2008.
Judgement of the Supreme Court of the Czech Republic of 30 November 2000, file No. 29 Cdo 2941/99.
Judgement of the Supreme Court of the Czech Republic of 29 March 2011, file No. 25 Cdo 4321/2008.

Judgement of the Supreme Court of the Czech Republic of 29 April 2008, file No. 32 Cdo 1000/2007.
Judgement of the Supreme Court of the Czech Republic of 28 November 2019, file No. 25 Cdo 1976/2019.
Judgement of the Supreme Court of the Czech Republic of 28 November 2012, file No. 32 Cdo 4765/2010.
Judgement of the Supreme Court of the Czech Republic of 28 March 2007, file No. 32 Odo 1397/2005.
Judgement of the Supreme Court of the Czech Republic of 28 June 2010, file No. 23 Cdo 28/2010, published in the Collection of Judicial Decisions and Opinions under No. 43/2011.
Judgement of the Supreme Court of the Czech Republic of 27 September 2016, file No. 25 Cdo 1896/2016, published in the Collection of Judicial Decisions and Opinions under No. 26/2018.
Judgement of the Supreme Court of the Czech Republic of 27 February 2018, file No. 23 Cdo 2865/2016.
Judgement of the Supreme Court of the Czech Republic of 26 September 2007, file No. 32 Odo 1254/2005, published in the Collection of Judicial Decisions and Opinions under No. 74/2008.
Judgement of the Supreme Court of the Czech Republic of 26 November 2009, file No. 25 Cdo 968/2008, published in the Collection of Judicial Decisions and Opinions under No. 8/2011.
Judgement of the Supreme Court of the Czech Republic of 25 July 2012, file No. 23 Cdo 676/2012.
Judgement of the Supreme Court of the Czech Republic of 24 September 2015, file No. 25 Cdo 1463/2014.
Judgement of the Supreme Court of the Czech Republic of 24 July 2002, file No. 25 Cdo 499/2002.
Judgement of the Supreme Court of the Czech Republic of 23 August 2016, file No. 23 Cdo 4058/2015.
Judgement of the Supreme Court of the Czech Republic of 22 April 2008, file No. 25 Cdo 799/2006.
Judgement of the Supreme Court of the Czech Republic of 21 March 2014, file No. 25 Cdo 1002/2012.
Judgement of the Supreme Court of the Czech Republic of 19 April 2011, file No. 25 Cdo 4261/2008.
Judgement of the Supreme Court of the Czech Republic of 18 October 2017, file No. 31 Cdo 1704/2016, published in the Collection of Judicial Decisions and Opinions under No. 6/2019.
Judgement of the Supreme Court of the Czech Republic of 18 March 2015, file No. 25 Cdo 3925/2013, published in the Collection of Judicial Decisions and Opinions under No. 71/2015.
Judgement of the Supreme Court of the Czech Republic of 18 December 2018, file No. 23 Cdo 276/2018.
Judgement of the Supreme Court of the Czech Republic of 17 June 2009, file No. 25 Cdo 5175/2008.

Judgement of the Supreme Court of the Czech Republic of 17 January 2008, file No. 32 Cdo 2837/2007
Judgement of the Supreme Court of the Czech Republic of 15 May 2020, file No. 23 Cdo 2593/2018.
Judgement of the Supreme Court of the Czech Republic of 15 December 2015, file No. 23 Cdo 4210/2013, published in the Collection of Judicial Decisions and Opinions under No. 47/2017.
Judgement of the Supreme Court of the Czech Republic of 12 December 2018, file No. 23 Cdo 5969/2017, published in the Collection of Judicial Decisions and Opinions under No. 9/2019.
Judgement of the Supreme Court of the Czech Republic of 12 December 2007, file No. 25 Cdo 113/2006, published in the Collection of Judicial Decisions and Opinions under No. 93/2008.
Judgement of the Supreme Court of the Czech Republic of 11 April 2017, file No. 25 Cdo 4112/2017, published in the Collection of Judicial Decisions and Opinions under No. 64/2019.
Judgement of the Supreme Administrative Court of the Czech Republic of 28 November 2008, file No. 4 Ans 5/2007, published in the Collection of decisions of the Supreme Administrative Court under No. 1791/2009.
Judgement of the of the Supreme Court of the Czechoslovak Socialist Republic of 16 June 1979, file No. 3 Cz 32/79, published in the Collection of Judicial Decisions and Opinions under No. 36/1982.
Judgement of the Constitutional Court of the Czech Republic of 9 August 2016, file No. I. ÚS 3456/15.
Judgement of the CJEU C-80/17 of 4 September 2018, *Fundo de Garantia Automóvel v. Alina Antónia Destapado Pão Mole Juliana a Cristiana Micaela Caetano Juliana*, ECLI:EU:C:2018:661.
Judgement of the CJEU C-77/04 of 26 May 2005, *Groupement d'intérêt économique (GIE) Réunion européenne and Other v. Zurich España, Société pyrénéenne de transit d'automobiles (Soptrans)*, ECLI:EU:C:2005:327.
Judgement of the CJEU C-558/15 of 15 December 2016, *Alberto José Vieira de Azevedo and Others v. CED Portugal Unipessoal, Lda and Instituto de Seguros de Portugal – Fundo de Garantia Automóvel,* ECLI:EU:C:2016:957.
Judgement of the CJEU C-514/16 of 28 November 2017, *Isabel Maria Pinheiro Vieira Rodrigues de Andrade and Fausto da Silva Rodrigues de Andrade v. José Manuel Proença Salvador and Others*, ECLI:EU:C:2017:908.
Judgement of the CJEU C-463/06 of 13 December 2007, *FBTO Schadeverzekeringen NV v. Jack Odenbreit*, ECLI:EU:C:2007:792.
Judgement of the CJEU C-412/98 of 13 July 2000, *Group Josi Reinsurance Company SA v. Universal General Insurance Company (UGIC)*, ECLI-:EU:C:2000:399.
Judgement of the CJEU C-347/08 of 17 September 2009, *Vorarlberger Gebietskrankenkasse v. WGV-Schwäbische Allgemeine Versicherungs AG,* ECLI-:EU:C:2009:561.
Judgement of the CJEU C-343/08 of 14 January 2009, *European Commission v. Czech Republic*, ECLI: EU:C:2010:14.

Judgement of the CJEU C-334/16 of 20 December 2017, *José Luís Núñez Torreiro v. AIG Europe Limited, Sucursal en España a Unión Española de Entidades Aseguradoras y Reaseguradoras (UNESPA)*, ECLI:EU:C:2017:1007.
Judgement of the CJEU C-241/97 of 20. April 1999, Försäkringsaktiebolaget Skandia, ECLI:EU:C:1999:179.
Judgement of the CJEU C-236/09 of 1 March 2011, *Association belge des Consommateurs Test-Achats ASBL and Others v. Conseil des ministres,* ECLI-:EU:C:2011:100.
Judgement of the CJEU C-199/08 of 10 September 2009, *Erhard Eschig v. UNIQA Sachversicherung AG*, ECLI:EU:C:2009:538.
Judgement of the CJEU C-162/13 of 4 September 2014, *Damijan Vnuk v. Zavarovalnica Triglav d. d.,* ECLI:EU:C:2014:2146.
Judgement of the CJEU C-112/03 of 12 May 2005, *Société financière et industrielle du Peloux v. Axa Belgium and Others*, ECLI:EU:C:2005:280.
Judgement of the CJEU C-111/09 of 20 May 2010, *Česká podnikatelská pojišťovna, a.s., Vienna Insurance Group v. Michal Bilas*, ECLI:EU:C:2010:290.
Judgement of the CJEU C-109/99 of 21 September 2000, *Association basco-béarnaise des opticiens indépendants v. Préfet des Pyrénées-Atlantiques,* ECLI-:EU:C:2000:483.
Judgement of the CJEU C-100/18 of 20 June 2019, *Línea Directa Aseguradora SA v. Segurcaixa Sociedad Anónima de Seguros y Reaseguros,* ECLI-:EU:C:2019:517.
Judgement of the Civil Law and Commercial Division of the Supreme Court of the Czech Republic of 13 February 2019, file No. 31 Cdo 1566/2017, published in the Collection of Judicial Decisions and Opinions under No. 113/2019.
Decision of the Supreme Court of the Czechoslovak Socialist Republic of 23 September 1969, file No. 3 Cz 21/69, published in the Collection of Judicial Decisions and Opinions under No. 24/1970.
Decision of the Municipal Court in Prague of 10 January 1968, file No. 6 Co 675/67, published in the Collection of Judicial Decisions and Opinions under No. 16/1969.
Decision of the Financial Arbitrator on the objections of 30 January 2017, file No. FA/ZP/1897/2016.
Decision of the Financial Arbitrator on the objections of 11 October 2016, file No. FA/ZP/141/2016.

Selected Bibliography

Index

The numbers here refer to paragraph numbers.

Index

Index

www.ingramcontent.com/pod-product-compliance
Lightning Source LLC
Chambersburg PA
CBHW071430230926
51846CB00001B/174
9789403539720